'This is an excellent overview of the troubled existence of the Warsaw Pact. Highly recommended for everyone who wants to understand Cold War alliance systems.'

Arne Westad, *Professor of International History, London School of Economics*

The Warsaw Pact Reconsidered

The Warsaw Pact is generally regarded as a mere instrument of Soviet power. In the 1960s the alliance nevertheless evolved into a multilateral alliance, in which the non-Soviet Warsaw Pact members gained considerable scope for manoeuvre. This book examines to what extent the Warsaw Pact inadvertently provided its members with an opportunity to assert their own interests, emancipate themselves from the Soviet grip, and influence Soviet bloc policy. Laurien Crump traces this development through six thematic case studies, which deal with such well known events as the building of the Berlin Wall, the Sino–Soviet split, the Vietnam War, the nuclear question and the Prague Spring. By interpreting hitherto neglected archival evidence from archives in Berlin, Bucharest and Rome, and approaching the Soviet alliance from a radically novel perspective, the book offers unexpected insights into international relations in Eastern Europe, while shedding new light on a pivotal period in the Cold War.

Laurien Crump is Assistant Professor in the History of International Relations at the University of Utrecht, The Netherlands.

Routledge Studies in the History of Russia and Eastern Europe

1 **Modernizing Muscovy**
   Reform and social change in seventeenth-century Russia
   Edited by Jarmo Kotilaine and Marshall Poe

2 **The USA in the Making of the USSR**
   The Washington conference, 1921–1922, and 'uninvited Russia'
   Paul Dukes

3 **Tiny Revolutions in Russia**
   Twentieth century Soviet and Russian history in anecdotes
   Bruce Adams

4 **The Russian General Staff and Asia, 1800–1917**
   Alex Marshall

5 **Soviet Eastern Policy and Turkey, 1920–1991**
   Soviet foreign policy, Turkey and communism
   Bülent Gökay

6 **The History of Siberia**
   Igor V. Naumov (Edited by David N. Collins)

7 **Russian Military Intelligence in the War with Japan, 1904–05**
   Secret operations on land and at sea
   Evgeny Sergeev

8 **Cossacks and the Russian Empire, 1598–1725**
   Manipulation, rebellion and expansion into Siberia
   Christoph Witzenrath

9 **The Many Deaths of Tsar Nicholas II**
   Relics, remains and the Romanovs
   Wendy Slater

10 **Popular Religion in Russia**
   'Double belief' and the making of an academic myth
   Stella Rock

11 **Eastern Christianity and the Cold War, 1945–91**
   Edited by Lucian N. Leustean

12 **The Caucasus under Soviet Rule**
   Alex Marshall

13 **Rural Women in the Soviet Union and Post-Soviet Russia**
Liubov Denisova (Edited and translated by Irina Mukhina)

14 **Reassessing Cold War Europe**
Edited by Sari Autio-Sarasmo and Katalin Miklóssy

15 **The Baltic States from the Soviet Union to the European Union**
Identity, discourse and power in the post-communist transition of Estonia, Latvia and Lithuania
Richard Mole

16 **Life Stories of Soviet Women**
The interwar generation
Melanie Ilic

17 **Brezhnev and the Decline of the Soviet Union**
Thomas Crump

18 **Women and Transformation in Russia**
Edited by Aino Saarinen, Kirsti Ekonen and Valentina Uspenskaia

19 **Competition in Socialist Society**
Edited by Katalin Miklóssy and Melanie Ilic

20 **Young Jewish Poets Who Fell as Soviet Soldiers in the Second World War**
Rina Lapidus

21 **The Vernaculars of Communism**
Language, ideology and power in the Soviet Union
Edited by Petre Petrov and Lara Ryazanova-Clarke

22 **The Warsaw Pact Reconsidered**
International relations in Eastern Europe, 1955–1969
Laurien Crump

23 **Reassessing Orientalism**
Interlocking orientologies during the Cold War
Edited by Michael Kemper and Artemy M. Kalinovsky

The Warsaw Pact Reconsidered
International relations in Eastern Europe, 1955–69

Laurien Crump

Taylor & Francis Group

LONDON AND NEW YORK

First published 2015
by Routledge

2 Park Square, Milton Park, Abingdon, Oxon OX14 4RN
711 Third Avenue, New York, NY 10017, USA

Routledge is an imprint of the Taylor & Francis Group, an informa business

First issued in paperback 2017

Copyright © 2015 Laurien Crump

The right of Laurien Crump to be identified as author of this work has been asserted by her in accordance with the Copyright, Designs and Patent Act 1988.

All rights reserved. No part of this book may be reprinted or reproduced or utilised in any form or by any electronic, mechanical, or other means, now known or hereafter invented, including photocopying and recording, or in any information storage or retrieval system, without permission in writing from the publishers.

Notice:
Product or corporate names may be trademarks or registered trademarks, and are used only for identification and explanation without intent to infringe.

British Library Cataloguing in Publication Data
A catalogue record for this book is available from the British Library

Library of Congress Cataloging in Publication Data
Crump, Laurien.
 The Warsaw Pact reconsidered : international relations in Eastern Europe, 1955-1969 / Laurien Crump.
   pages cm. – (Routledge studies in the history of Russia and Eastern Europe ; 22)
 Includes bibliographical references and index.
 1. Europe, Eastern–Foreign relations–1945-1989. 2. Europe, Eastern–Foreign relations–Soviet Union. 3. Soviet Union–Foreign relations–Europe, Eastern. 4. Warsaw Treaty Organization. 5. Warsaw Treaty (1955) I. Title.
 DJK50.C78 2015
 327.47009'045–dc23
         2014029457

ISBN: 978-0-415-69071-3 (hbk)
ISBN: 978-1-138-10213-2 (pbk)

Typeset in Times New Roman
by Taylor & Francis Books

**To my husband
Kenneth Gabreëls
my most beloved ally**

Contents

List of illustrations	xiii
Foreword	xv
Acknowledgements	xvii
List of abbreviations	xx
Chronology of events	xxii
Note on translations	xxv

Introduction: reconsidering the Warsaw Pact	1

PART I
Embryonic emancipation, 1955–64   15

1	The Warsaw Pact in its infancy	17
2	The Warsaw Pact in the shadow of the Sino–Soviet split	57
3	The Warsaw Pact compromised by the German question	98

PART II
The dynamics of dissent, 1965–68   131

4	Warsaw Pact reforms and Westpolitik	133
5	Gaullism in the Warsaw Pact: Ceausescu's challenge	170

PART III
Crisis and consolidation, 1968–69   213

6	The limits of emancipation: the Prague Spring	215

7 Closing ranks, while clashing with China 258

Conclusion: international relations in Eastern Europe reconsidered 288

Note on the sources 302
Bibliography 305
Index 318

List of illustrations

Figures

I.1	Map of Europe showing NATO and the Warsaw Pact, ca. 1973	xiv
1.1	Nikita Khrushchev at dinner with, *inter alia*, Mao Zedong, 1959	46
2.1	Gheorghe Gheorghiu-Dej and Nikita Khrushchev at the Bucharest Conference, 28 June 1960	59
5.1	Nicolae Ceausescu and his wife on a state visit to the PRC with Zhou Enlai, June 1971	187
6.1	Nicolae Ceausescu on his visit to Alexander Dubcek (left), 15–16 August 1968	239

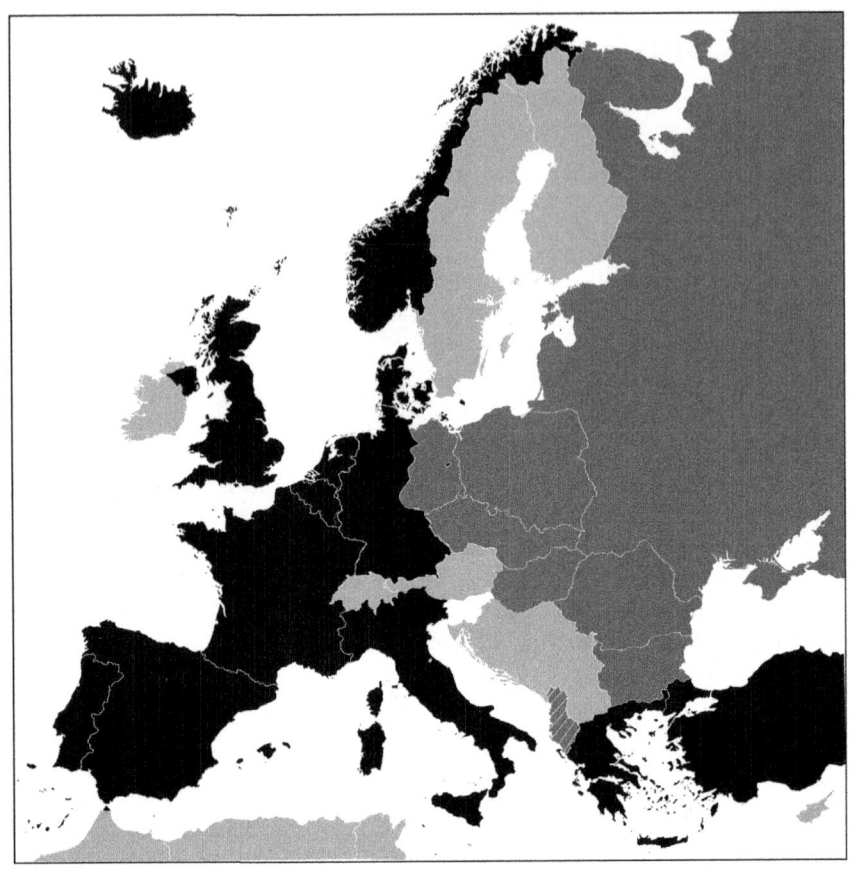

Figure I.1 Map of Europe showing NATO (black) and the Warsaw Pact (dark grey), ca. 1973
Source: commons.wikimedia.org/wiki/File:NATO_and_the_Warsaw_Pact_1973.svg

Foreword

The Warsaw Pact, overestimated during the Cold War because of its formidable military appearance, has since been largely neglected as another Soviet relic swept into the dustbin of history. Laurien Crump's innovative and meticulously researched study challenges this simplistic view by arguing convincingly that the defunct alliance was far more important for political than for military reasons. Most surprisingly, she also finds that it served better its junior members than it did its Soviet hegemon.

The book is an exemplary product of 'new Cold War history' – a history informed by multi-archival research and written from a multilateral perspective, free from the distorting lens of the bilateral relationship between the two superpowers. From that perspective, the Soviet Union's ability and even willingness to control its allies appears more limited than might be expected from the dichotomy of the Warsaw Pact as a coercive and the North Atlantic Treaty Organization (NATO) as a voluntary alliance. As the exercise of power in Moscow became progressively diluted since its Stalinist peak, the alliance originally devised by Khrushchev with the goal of outcompeting NATO offered to the Soviet dependents in Eastern Europe growing room for pursuing their own interests, jointly or separately, with or sometimes against their master – to those among them, to be sure, who cared and dared to avail themselves of the opportunity.

Spanning the Warsaw Pact's formative period from 1955 to 1969, the study sheds new light on its significance within the wider Cold War. The period extended from the proclamation of the alliance at the onset of the 'first détente', by which time the avoidance of a military clash and acceptance of the ideological division between East and West had become commonplace, to the watershed year that followed the Warsaw Pact's sole foreign military venture – the invasion in its name of its own Czechoslovak ally. The alliance's subsequent consolidation at the very moment the Soviet Union and China came closest to a war with each other because of their ideological division – a division not shared by Moscow's Eastern European allies – marked the time when the threat of a Sino–Soviet military confrontation superseded that between the two military groupings in Europe.

Crump relates the progress of emancipation, dissent and multilateralisation within the Warsaw Pact to the larger issues that divided its members. The issues ranged from the German question as the main unresolved legacy of the past, to nuclear proliferation as the most pressing challenge of the present, to the relationship with China as the defining relationship of the future. Ironically, Eastern Europe's communist regimes' lack of democratic accountability gave them more room to pursue what they perceived as their nations' security interests than was available to their NATO counterparts. The East German regime shaped the Soviet policy on Germany best to assure its own survival, Romania sought to manipulate the negotiation of the Non-Proliferation Treaty to constrain both superpowers but especially the neighbouring one, Poland designed the project for a European security conference to help increase the clout of Europe's medium-sized and small powers, such as itself.

In her account of the development of the Warsaw Pact leading to its consolidation in 1969, Crump has laid a solid foundation for a better understanding of the consequences during the second half of the Cold War. Rather than focusing on the alliance's eventual demise, it is now possible better to grasp its significance beyond the Cold War. There is ample reason to look forward to a sequel to the present book which would analyse with equal rigour the alliance's remaining years, and to hope that it will soon be written by the same author.

Vojtech Mastny
Washington
June 2014

Acknowledgements

There are so many people and institutions I have to thank for contributing to the process of writing this book that it almost seems as though I have hardly contributed anything myself. My debts start at Christ's College, Cambridge, where I was a student in Classics in a distant past. The Classics degree in Cambridge greatly sharpened my intellect, and the supervisions in Ancient Philosophy with David Sedley inspired me in particular with an intellectual rigour from which I still benefit on a daily basis. My idiosyncratic transformation from an ancient philosopher into a contemporary historian was made possible by the headmistress and deputy heads at the Utrechts Stedelijk Gymnasium, Hanneke Taat, Erik Kamerbeek and Aad van Diemen, who allowed me to combine my job as a Classics teacher with a History degree, which they even funded. I am deeply moved by the way they selflessly supported me, even when I left the school to embark on a job at Utrecht University.

I also owe a great debt to the History Department at Utrecht University, and especially the section of the History of International Relations, for stimulating my research. Maarten Prak, the department's research director, has supported me from the start, and has sparked my interest in historical research with the MA programme in Comparative History. I am most grateful to my PhD supervisors, Duco Hellema and Jan Hoffenaar, for their unflinching support, and for the fact that they were satisfied with the role of sparring partner instead of supervisor, since I often moved too fast.

I have been greatly inspired by many other colleagues and friends, with whom I have discussed my research, to name but a few: Anne-Isabelle Richard, Floris van den Eijnde, Susanna Erlandsson, Mathieu Segers, Joes Segal, Isabelle Duyvesteyn, Jacco Pekelder, Peter Malcontent, Hanneke Takken, Rolf Strootman, Kim van der Wijngaart, Elmar Hellendoorn, Luuk Slooter, René Koekkoek, José van Aelst, Lars Behrisch, Beatrice de Graaf, Anne Marieke van der Wal, Liesbeth van de Grift and, last but not least, Jef Klazen. The Research Institute of History and Culture in Utrecht has generally funded all my archival research, and has supported me in many other ways, too. The same applies to the department's subsequent directors, Ido de Haan, Josine Blok and Joris van Eijnatten, all of whom have enabled me to spread my wings. My students have also proven a continuous source of inspiration.

Moving beyond Utrecht, there are several institutions that have allowed me to broaden my horizon still further, by inviting me to seminars, conferences and visiting scholarships: the London School of Economics and Political Science, St Antony's College, Oxford, the George Washington University, the University of Padua, the ministries of foreign affairs and of defence in Prague, the University of Iași in Romania, the University of Bern, and the University of Amsterdam.

I would like to single out two of these institutes, namely the London School of Economics and St Antony's College, Oxford. Although I am an anomaly in Utrecht with my research into Eastern Europe during the Cold War, these two institutions enabled me to remain up to date with the latest research on Eastern Europe and the Cold War, engage in lively debates on the state of the art in recent scholarship, and sharpen my mind. I am particularly grateful to the London School of Economics for inviting me to several conferences, and commenting on my research on numerous occasions. I have greatly benefited from talks with Arne Westad, Piers Ludlow, Svetozar Rajak, Eirini Karamouzi and Angela Romano, in particular. I also had the fortune of being appointed as a Senior Associate Member at St Antony's College, Oxford, in the Hilary Term of 2012. There I was greatly inspired by my talks with Alex Pravda, Robert Service, Archie Brown, Richard Davy, Norman Davies and Eliza Gheorghe, all from St Antony's, and with Anne Deighton from Wolfson College.

Moreover, I have extensively travelled in Eastern Europe, covering the former Warsaw Pact countries, in order to gain a sense of the scope of the Pact, and to talk to experts able to answer any remaining questions. On these travels and on other occasions I have learnt a great deal from talks with Wanda Jarzabek, Douglas Selvage, Lorenz Lüthi, Ana Lalaj, Bernd Schäfer, Federico Romero, Jonas Flury, Christian Gerlach, André Gerrits, Silvio Pons and James Mark. I also highly appreciated the challenging observations of the members of the review committee of my doctoral dissertation: Arne Westad, Robert Service, André Gerrits, Maarten Prak and Ido de Haan. I owe a particular debt to Vojtech Mastny, who has supported my research from the outset, and whose intellect and acuity are exemplary. His research on the Warsaw Pact has been a hard act to follow, and makes me feel like a dwarf in the footsteps of a giant.

Archival research has been crucial to this book, and I have been enormously helped by various archivists. I am particularly grateful to Sylvia Gräfe from the Stiftung Archiv der Parteien und Massenorganisationen der DDR im Bundesarchiv in Berlin, Veronica Vasilov from the Arhivele Naționale Istorice Centrale ale României in Bucharest, Birgit Kmezik from the Politisches Archiv des Auswärtigen Amtes der DDR of the Ministerium für Auswärtige Angelegenheiten der DDR in Berlin, and Giovanna Bosman from the Archivio del Partito Comunista Italiano in the Fondazione Istituto Gramsci in Rome. I would also like to thank the British Council in Bucharest for funding a Romanian language course, and the Royal Netherlands Institute in Rome for facilitating my research in the archives of the Italian Communist Party. Moreover, I am most grateful to my aunt, Camilla Crump, for generously funding my travels and language course in Russia, and to various other relatives for contributing to a trip to Albania and supporting my research.

Last, but not least, I am heavily indebted to my mother for supporting me in countless ways, and to my father for proofreading the manuscript and for helping with the index. My rabbits have kept me unwavering company throughout the process, and rigorously tore apart the pages that they either did not like or liked too much. Writing this book would have been an altogether different experience if I had not met my husband, Kenneth Gabreëls, halfway through the process. He has been a huge support, not least by helping me with the footnotes! The alliance with him is an incredible source of love and joy, which has even resulted in the birth of our dearly beloved Tommy, our junior ally.

List of abbreviations

ANIC	Arhivele Naţionale Istorice Centrale ale României
AWP	Albanian Workers Party
CC	Central Committee
CCP	Chinese Communist Party
CCUAF	Commander in Chief of the United Armed Forces (WP)
CDU	Christlich Demokratische Union Deutschlands (West German)
CMFA	Committee of the Ministers of Foreign Affairs
COMECON	Council for Mutual Economic Assistance
COMINFORM	Communist Information Bureau
CPCz	Communist Party of Czechoslovakia
CPSU	Communist Party of the Soviet Union
CSCE	Conference on Security and Co-operation in Europe
CSSR	Czechoslovak Socialist Republic
CWIHP	Cold War International History Project
DRV	Democratic Republic of Vietnam (North Vietnam)
EEC	European Economic Community
ENDC	Eighteen Nations Disarmament Committee
FDP	Freie Demokratische Partei (West German liberal party)
FIG APC	Fondazione Istituto Gramsci, Archivio del Partito Comunista Italiano
FRG	Federal Republic of Germany (West Germany)
GDR	German Democratic Republic (East Germany)
HSWP	Hungarian Socialist Workers Party (from October 1956)
HWP	Hungarian Workers Party (up to October 1956)
Interkit	'China International': Eastern European institution against China
MfAA	Ministerium für Auswärtige Angelegenheiten der DDR
MLF	Multilateral Nuclear Forces
NATO	North Atlantic Treaty Organization
NLF	National Liberation Front for South Vietnam
NSWP	non-Soviet Warsaw Pact (member)
NTBT	Limited Nuclear Test-Ban Treaty

PA AA	Politisches Archiv des Auswärtigen Amtes der DDR
PCC	Political Consultative Committee
PCI	Partito Comunista Italiano
PHP	Parallel History Project on Cooperative Security
PRC	People's Republic of China
PRP	People's Republic of Poland
PUWP	Polish United Workers Party
RCP	Romanian Communist Party (from August 1965)
RWP	Romanian Workers Party (up to August 1965)
SACEUR	Supreme Allied Commander Europe (NATO)
SAPMO-BArch	Stiftung Archiv der Parteien und Massenorganisationen der DDR im Bundesarchiv
SED	Sozialistische Einheitspartei Deutschlands (East German)
SPD	Sozialdemokratische Partei Deutschlands (West German)
SU	Soviet Union
UAF	United Armed Forces (WP)
UN	United Nations
USA	United States of America
USSR	Union of Soviet Socialist Republics
WP	Warsaw Pact

Chronology of events

5 March 1953	Death of Stalin
16–17 June 1953	Uprisings in East Germany
9 May 1955	Admission of Federal Republic of Germany (FRG) to the North Atlantic Treaty Organization (NATO)
10 May 1955	Soviet disarmament proposal
14 May 1955	Foundation of the Warsaw Pact (WP)
15 May 1955	Austrian State Treaty
26 May 1955	Khrushchev's reconciliation with Tito
18–23 July 1955	Geneva summit
September 1955	Establishment of diplomatic relations between the Soviet Union and FRG
27–28 January 1956	First meeting of the WP's Political Consultative Committee (PCC) in Prague
25 February 1956	Khrushchev's Secret Speech at the 20th party congress of the Communist Party of the Soviet Union (CPSU)
June 1956	Official normalisation of Soviet-Yugoslav (diplomatic) relations
June 1956	Dissolution of the Communist Information Bureau (COMINFORM)
19 October 1956	Wladyslaw Gomulka elected first secretary in Poland
23 October 1956	Beginning of the Hungarian Revolution
24 October 1956	Intervention of Soviet troops in Hungary
30 October 1956	Soviet declaration on friendship and cooperation in Eastern Europe
4 November 1956	Second intervention of Soviet troops in Hungary
June 1957	Khrushchev survives the anti-party coup in Moscow
24 May 1958	Meeting of the PCC in Moscow
27 November 1958	Khrushchev issues a six-month ultimatum on the status of West Berlin
27–28 April 1959	Meeting of the foreign ministers of the WP countries and China
September 1959	Khrushchev's trip to the USA, meeting Eisenhower at Camp David

Chronology of events xxiii

4 February 1960	PCC meeting in Moscow on peaceful coexistence and the German question
20–22 June 1960	Third Romanian Party Congress in Bucharest
November 1960	Moscow meeting of international communist parties
13 February 1961	Albanian fourth Party Conference in Tirana
28–29 March 1961	PCC meeting in Moscow on Albania and the German question
3–5 August 1961	Meeting of WP first secretaries in Moscow on intra-Berlin border closure
13 August 1961	Beginning of the building of the Berlin Wall
17–31 October 1961	22nd Congress of the CPSU
22–28 October 1961	Checkpoint Charlie crisis between the Soviet Union and the USA in Berlin
7 June 1962	PCC meeting in Moscow on the German question
16–28 October 1962	Cuban Missile Crisis
26–27 July 1963	PCC meeting in Moscow on accession of Mongolia to the WP
3–10 March 1964	Romanian delegation visits China to mediate in Sino–Soviet split
15–22 April 1964	Extraordinary plenum of the Romanian Workers' Party Central Committee in which the 'Romanian Declaration of Independence' is made public
14 October 1964	Ouster of Nikita Khrushchev; Leonid Brezhnev becomes the party leader
16 October 1964	First successful detonation of a Chinese nuclear device
20 December 1964	First meeting of the WP deputy foreign ministers in Warsaw
19–20 January 1965	PCC meeting in Warsaw on reforms, European security, and nuclear issues
1 March 1965	Preparatory meeting of international communist conference in Moscow
4–9 February 1966	Meeting of the WP deputy ministers of defence in Moscow
10–12 February 1966	Meeting of the WP deputy foreign ministers in East Berlin
7 March 1966	France announces its withdrawal from NATO's military structures
24 March 1966	'Peace note' of FRG government to all WP states except German Democratic Republic (GDR)
7 April 1966	Meeting of WP first secretaries in Moscow
May 1966	Informal meeting of WP ministers of defence in Moscow
6–17 June 1966	Meeting of WP foreign ministers in Moscow
4–6 July 1966	PCC meeting in Bucharest on European security and Vietnam

xxiv *Chronology of events*

August 1966	Mao launches the Great Proletarian Cultural Revolution in China
31 January 1967	Romania establishes diplomatic relations with West Germany
8–10 February 1967	Meeting of WP deputy foreign ministers in Warsaw
5–10 June 1967	Six-Day War between Israel, Egypt, Jordan and Syria
14–21 December 1967	Foundation of the Interkit in Moscow
December 1967	Conclusion of the Harmel Report within NATO
3–5 January 1968	Election of Alexander Dubcek as the first secretary of the Communist Party of Czechoslovakia (CPCz)
26–27 February 1968	Meeting of WP deputy foreign ministers in Berlin
February–March 1968	Consultative meeting on international communist conference in Budapest
6–7 March 1968	PCC meeting in Sofia on the Non-Proliferation Treaty
23 March 1968	Meeting of the six socialist countries (except Romania) in Dresden
1 July 1968	Sixty-three states sign the Non-Proliferation Treaty
14–15 July 1968	Meeting of 'the five' socialist countries (except Romania and Czechoslovakia) in Warsaw
3 August 1968	Meeting of the six socialist countries (except Romania) in Bratislava
20–21 August 1968	Invasion of Czechoslovakia by 'the five' socialist countries
30 October 1968	Meeting of WP ministers of defence in Moscow
2 March 1969	Beginning of Sino–Soviet border clashes on the island of Zhenbao
16 March 1969	Meeting of WP deputy foreign ministers in Budapest
17 March 1969	PCC meeting in Budapest on military reforms and European security
17 April 1969	Removal of Alexander Dubcek as party leader of the CPCz
1 August 1975	Conclusion of the Helsinki Final Act at the Conference on Security and Co-operation in Europe (CSCE) in Helsinki

Note on translations

All the translations from the sources from the Romanian, German and Italian archives are my own, unless I refer to sources that have already been published. In the transliteration of names I have chosen not to use any accents for the sake of consistency.

Introduction
Reconsidering the Warsaw Pact

> The Warsaw Pact is a 'cardboard castle, [...] carefully erected over what most observers considered an already perfectly adequate blockhouse'.[1]
> (NATO officials about the Warsaw Pact at its foundation on 14 May 1955)

The fate of the Warsaw Pact already seemed to have been sealed upon its foundation. The stigma of a 'cardboard castle', which North Atlantic Treaty Organization (NATO) officials attached to it when it was founded in 1955, has endured, and its subsequent demise in 1991 seems to vindicate such a derogatory approach to the Warsaw Pact (WP). It suggests that the WP was a pale reflection of NATO, which at best provided the Soviet 'satellites' with a *pro forma* platform to express their opinions, but in fact enabled the Soviet Union to keep them more tightly in its grip. Contrary to conventional wisdom, the Warsaw Pact nevertheless became as much an instrument for the decision making within Eastern Europe from 1960 onwards as NATO was on the other side of the Iron Curtain. Although all non-Soviet Warsaw Pact (NSWP) countries have now become members of NATO, their experience with multilateral diplomacy was shaped within its former nemesis. Moreover, questions that currently prevail within international and European politics, such as the role of Russia, the nuclear question, (Eastern) European integration, the limits of sovereignty, institutional reforms and European security, also dominated the debates within the Warsaw Pact in the 1960s. An in-depth study of this seminal period in the evolution of the WP is not only crucial to understanding the Cold War at large, but also provides a new prism for viewing contemporary politics.

In the historiography to date the Warsaw Pact is generally considered a Soviet instrument, 'used to continue the total subordination of the smaller East European governments to the Kremlin's actual aims and policy in the post-Stalin era'.[2] The opening of the Eastern European archives since the end of the Cold War has, however, facilitated research into the Warsaw Pact from the perspective of the Soviet Union's allies. The picture that emerges from a multi-archival analysis of the WP in archives ranging from Bucharest to Berlin and Rome reveals the shortcomings of its one-sided treatment in historiography.[3] This book therefore examines to what extent the Warsaw Pact inadvertently provided the NSWP members with an instrument to assert their national interests, emancipate themselves from the Soviet grip, and influence international politics in the period 1960–69. It also measures the impact of this process on the alliance itself, which acquired a dynamic of its own in the 1960s, and analyses how the smaller allies' struggle for emancipation served to multilateralise the alliance.

The 'emancipation' of the Eastern European countries from 'satellites into junior allies' has already been analysed by the American foreign policy analyst Zbigniew Brzezinski, who shrewdly observes that 'the East European margin of autonomy increased greatly' in the first half of the 1960s, in his seminal book *The Soviet Bloc: Unity and Conflict*.[4] He nevertheless fails to link this process of 'de-satellitization' to the alliance to which these 'junior allies' belonged, and even calls the Warsaw Pact 'a useful forum for the articulation of unanimity, expressing ritualistically the bloc's support of Soviet foreign policy initiatives versus the West'.[5] Although the role of a particular NSWP member within the alliance has recently been the subject of a number of Eastern European monographs and essays, these tend to address the national perspective of the country in question, without examining the dynamics within the alliance as a whole.[6]

The books, which focus on the Warsaw Pact, hardly discuss the role of the Eastern European countries at all.[7] The greatest surge of WP research took place at the height of the 'second Cold War' in the early 1980s, when Western policy makers were particularly concerned about the Warsaw Pact's military might. Historians at the time therefore mainly focused on the military aspects of the WP, while characterising the WP as the Soviet Union's 'transmission belt',[8] and as 'the most important organization for perpetuating Soviet influence in Eastern Europe'.[9] Since most of their findings were based on little, if any, archival evidence, they steadily became obsolete after the collapse of the Soviet bloc; even so, their approach to the WP as a Soviet instrument still dominates current historiography. This shows in the only recent monograph on the Warsaw Pact, by the German historian Frank Umbach, in which the military emphasis prevails.[10]

The first five years of the WP's existence may vindicate this approach, since the Warsaw Pact's Political Consultative Committee (PCC) – its only official organ – only met sporadically in order to rubberstamp Soviet policies. Events, however, took a different turn in 1960. In this year the failed Paris summit between Nikita Khrushchev and Dwight D. Eisenhower marked an exacerbation of the second Berlin Crisis. At the same time, the public divergences between the Soviet and Chinese leaders at several international communist conferences heralded the Sino–Soviet split. In the shadow of the disintegrating communist movement and the escalation of the German question, the Albanian leader Enver Hoxha and his East German 'comrade' Walter Ulbricht began to explore the scope for manoeuvre within an alliance under pressure. Their attempts to stretch the limits of the WP paved the way for their NSWP comrades – the Romanians and Poles in particular – to assert their own interests within the alliance and thus 'emancipate' themselves from the Soviet grip. Behind the scenes of the PCC meetings an increasingly multilateral process developed, in which the NSWP members gradually redefined the alliance.

This process was marked by genuine dissent among the WP members on a wide range of issues, varying from the building of the Berlin Wall, the potential nuclearisation of West Germany and European security, to non-proliferation, the Vietnam War and ways to reform the Warsaw Pact. During the 1960s the Warsaw Pact, as an institution, was continuously in crisis, since the absence of any clear delineation of its purpose left ample room for its members to disagree on the goals and scope of the alliance.[11] The Prague Spring in 1968 exposed more fundamental differences between the WP members, since Romania disagreed with five of its WP allies on the merits of offering 'fraternal assistance' to its ally Czechoslovakia. The persistent allegation that the ensuing invasion in Czechoslovakia was carried out as a Warsaw Pact operation sealed the fate of the pact as a coercive alliance. However, the Warsaw Pact as an institution actually remained aloof from the developments in Czechoslovakia, and under pressure from increasingly assertive NSWP members the reorganisation of the alliance took centre stage instead.

This process of redefinition culminated in a series of reforms, which after acrimonious debates within the alliance were approved at a PCC meeting in March 1969. At this meeting there was genuine unanimity not only about the reorganisation of the Warsaw Pact, but also about the appeal for a European Security Conference, following a Polish initiative in 1965; this in turn paved the way for the Conference on Security and Co-operation in Europe (CSCE) and the adoption of the Helsinki Final Act in 1975. The appeal for such a conference reflected both the Warsaw Pact's search for an adequate solution to the German question, and a paradigm shift from Khrushchev's brinkmanship in the second Berlin Crisis to a more constructive proposal for European cooperation. While producing a way out of the impasse on the status of both Germanys, the meeting also confirmed the irreversibility of the Sino–Soviet split, since it coincided with Sino–Soviet border clashes at the Ussuri river. The WP thus definitively turned Westward, focusing on European détente instead of restoring communist unity. The multiple crisis that had begun in 1960 was resolved.

At the same time the PCC meeting in 1969 sealed the evolution of the WP from a so-called 'empty shell' into a more mature alliance, and marked the emancipation of the individual NSWP members.[12] It is worth researching to what extent the WP's origins as an empty shell provided its non-Soviet members not only with scope for manoeuvre, but also with the unique opportunity to define the shape of the alliance and turn it into something more substantial. In the 1960s the WP matured from an alliance that seemed to resemble a 'cardboard castle' to an alliance whose appeal for European security NATO took seriously in 1969. The emancipation of the NSWP members also led to the evolution of the alliance at large. Moreover, it anticipated a relatively independent role for the NSWP members in the Helsinki process, which has been examined recently.[13] This period from crisis to consolidation was unique in the history of the Warsaw Pact, and will be central to this book.

Redressing the balance

The period 1960–69 also merits particular consideration, as it covers the evolution of the Warsaw Pact under a particularly interesting international constellation, in which not only the second Berlin Crisis and the Sino–Soviet split, but also the Cuban Missile Crisis, the debate on Multilateral Nuclear Forces (MLF), non-proliferation, and the Vietnam War affected the dynamics of the Cold War at both sides of the Iron Curtain. Although this international context has been studied in depth on the Western side of the Iron Curtain, the role of the WP has been ignored, even in histories that claim to be all-embracing, such as Marc Trachtenberg's iconic work, *A Constructed Peace*.[14] This is particularly regrettable, since the WP began to play a considerable role in formulating the Soviet bloc's foreign policy in this period, with increasing input by NSWP members.

Moreover, these international developments also contributed to the Warsaw Pact's 'gravest crisis', which coincided with the one in NATO halfway through the 1960s.[15] As in NATO, there was considerable disagreement among the allies on the scope and purpose of the alliance, while the nuclear question also gave rise to increasing dissent. Despite a growing awareness among scholars that 'NATO as a multilateral forum offered small member states the opportunity to make their influence felt in a significant way that put to test the alliance's major powers' during its crisis in the 1960s,[16] multilateralism in the WP tends to be ignored. Here rectification is long overdue, if only because of the pronounced imbalance between research into the role of the Soviet Union's Eastern European allies in the WP and the amount of recent research on the influence of America's smaller allies in NATO.[17]

NATO's crisis in the 1960s has been researched from numerous perspectives, such as Anna Locher's research into President Charles de Gaulle's dissent or Helga Haftendorn's study of the nuclear question.[18] As the renowned historian Vojtech Mastny emphasises, there is, however, no equivalent study on the crisis in the WP.[19] Mastny himself is the driving force behind archival research on the Warsaw Pact, as coordinator of the *Parallel History Project on Cooperative Security* (PHP), in Zurich, which disseminates as much archival material as possible concerning the WP and NATO, and as editor of an impressive collection of archival sources on the WP, published in 2005.[20] Although Mastny has primarily researched the WP from a military angle, he questions whether 'the alliance's military value [...] in a hypothetical European war had been superseded by its political value'.[21] This book addresses this question, by examining the Warsaw Pact from a political perspective.

The fact that the crisis within the European Community in the 1960s has recently been studied, too, underlines all the more clearly the imbalance between research on institutions in Eastern and Western Europe during the Cold War.[22] The discrepancy is, of course, also due to the fact that NATO and the European Union still exist and that both have been, or are still, plagued with crises. However, even though the Warsaw Pact no longer exists, the topics that plagued the alliance are still relevant today: concepts of sovereignty, intergovernmentalism and supranationalism, the purpose of alliances, the response to crises and the possibilities for reform. Unlike the Warsaw Pact, the Council of Mutual Economic Assistance (COMECON), which was founded in 1949, has, however, been researched in more depth recently, notably by the American historian Randall Stone, whose book *Satellites and Commissars* has yielded some ground-breaking results. Stone convincingly argues that 'the Soviet Union's control over its satellites was much weaker than was believed during the years of the Cold War', which corroborates the central findings in this book.[23] His book nevertheless concentrates on trade in the Soviet bloc, and therefore does not deal with the international issues that were so essential to the Cold War at large.

New Cold War history

The fact that the WP has not been studied in depth for so long is all the more surprising, since it fits so well with the aims of the so-called 'new Cold War history', namely to use 'newly available information to refine, or in some cases destroy, old images and interpretations'.[24] In a canonical collection of essays by prominent scholars on new Cold War history, its founding father, the American historian John Lewis Gaddis, argues that 'the "new" Cold War history [...] is showing that zones of at least relative autonomy existed on both sides during that conflict, and that smaller powers were often in a position to influence actions of their larger counterparts'.[25] This is an insightful statement, but Gaddis and many of his colleagues nevertheless still assume that Eastern Europe was an 'empire by coercion'[26] or even a 'failed empire',[27] and that as such it apparently does not merit any further study.

In his highly influential book *We Now Know: Rethinking Cold War History*, Gaddis goes even further, and argues that '[t]he Warsaw Pact never operated as NATO did: there was little sense of mutual interest, especially after the events of 1956'. By comparing the Warsaw Pact to NATO, Gaddis tumbles into a common pitfall: the fact that the WP did not operate as NATO does not necessarily imply that its members had no mutual interest either. Excelling in sweeping statements, Gaddis continues to argue – without any recourse to archival evidence – that the 'Russians [...] knew of no way to deal with independent-thinking other than to smother it', which 'surely' resulted in 'subservience'.[28] The way Gaddis treats the WP illustrates the cursory manner in which it is discussed in many books on the Cold War.[29]

6 *Introduction*

The Warsaw Pact tends only to be referred to *en passant*, and without any explanation of its significance.

A lot of research therefore remains to be done, as the way in which the WP inadvertently served to emancipate its NSWP members has so far been overlooked. The only elaborate analysis on the leverage of a Soviet satellite over the Soviet Union is Hope Harrison's *Driving the Soviets up the Wall*, which is a stimulating analysis of how the tail could wag the dog, but it is limited to the bilateral interaction between the East German leader Walter Ulbricht and the Soviet leader Nikita Khrushchev from 1953–61.[30] The focus on *bilateral* relations on the communist side of the Cold War has become a recurrent feature in new Cold War history, which needs to be complemented by a multilateral approach. Both the Swiss scholar Lorenz Lüthi and the Russian historian Sergey Radchenko have shed a new light on the bilateral relations between China and the Soviet Union, in two thought-provoking monographs, which partly overlap with this book in both timeframe and content, since the Sino–Soviet split had a huge impact on the dynamics of the WP in the 1960s.[31] Whereas Lüthi echoes a persistent trend within new Cold War history by stressing the importance of ideas and ideology,[32] Radchenko nevertheless takes issue with this approach.

Radchenko is not alone in questioning the primacy of ideas that prevails in new Cold War history. Both the Norwegian historian Geir Lundestad and his American colleague Melvyn Leffler have questioned the renewed emphasis on ideas.[33] Leffler in particular regrets 'the loss of focus on traditional questions of security, power, and interest', because it 'simplifies the complexity of the historical process and distorts what we now do know about the Cold War'.[34] The extensive archival research that forms the foundation of this book confirms the views of Radchenko and Leffler that security concerns often overrode ideological inclinations. The emphasis in this monograph will therefore be on security, although ideological motives will be analysed wherever it seems necessary. Apart from nuancing the emphasis on ideas, this monograph places itself firmly in the tradition of new Cold War history by radically reconsidering the Warsaw Pact from a multilateral, multinational and multi-archival perspective.

Conceptualisation and strategy

The Warsaw Pact has remained a blind spot in the research on alliances, too. One of the most famous theories relating to a particular alliance is that of Geir Lundestad, who argues that the Western Europeans urged the Americans to take an active 'interest in their affairs', thus facilitating the creation of an American empire in Europe.[35] Lundestad's article was very novel, when it was written in 1986, since it focused on the internal dynamics of one particular alliance, rather than traditionally concentrating on the bipolarity between alliances. Contrasting this so-called 'empire by invitation' with the 'much more rigidly controlled empire' of the Soviet Union, Lundestad's theory fails to research the dynamics within the Warsaw Pact in an equally open-minded manner.[36] The same assumption of NATO's superiority prevails in the influential monograph *Cooperation among Democracies*, by the German historian Thomas Risse-Kappen, who assumes that the influence of smaller allies on the foreign policy of the alliance leader only applies to *democratic* alliances.[37]

The Warsaw Pact is also conspicuous in its absence in the theoretical literature on alliances in general.[38] This reflects the presupposition in historiography that it was not an alliance at all, or, at best, a 'cloak for imperial domination', as the American political scientist Glenn Snyder states in passing.[39] Snyder himself, however, unprecedentedly focuses not only on alliance formation, but also on alliance management in his book *Alliance Politics*, which means that his theories may be useful for an analysis of the WP, too. In the phase of alliance management there is, according to Snyder, an 'alliance dilemma', namely 'how firmly to commit themselves to the proto-partner and how much support to give the partner in specific conflict interactions with the adversary'.[40] There are, after all, two main risks by joining an alliance, namely *entrapment* and *abandonment*. In the first case an alliance member may be dragged into a conflict by one of its allies, and in the second case an alliance member might be abandoned by an ally through realignment. This '*tension* between the risk of abandonment and the risk of entrapment' constitutes the 'alliance security dilemma',[41] which determines the rules of the 'alliance game'.[42]

According to Snyder, the abovementioned game only applies to alliances in a multipolar system, since there is no serious risk of realignment in a bipolar system. Explicitly classifying 'the present system [...] as bipolar', Snyder advances several 'theoretical statements', which he admits 'are much more relevant to NATO than to the Warsaw Pact'.[43] Snyder has, however, overlooked an important aspect: in the 1960s the system was from the Eastern European perspective no longer unequivocally *bi*polar, as the breakdown of the Sino–Soviet alliance provided some of the WP members with an alternative ally, as the Albanian realignment with China poignantly shows. The analytical tools from the 'alliance security dilemma' are, therefore, useful to bear in mind when studying the WP, and will be addressed again in the conclusion of this book.

In order to analyse the evolution of the Warsaw Pact in the 1960s, several other concepts will also be used. The first concept that will be explored is 'emancipation'. This term has already been used *en passant* in the historiography to date,[44] but it has not yet been employed as an analytical concept to examine the development of the NSWP members. This concept will be used to denote the process according to which the NSWP members turned from being mere satellites into 'junior allies', who could contribute to the decision making within the WP. Although this is similar to the concept that Brzezinski calls 'de-satellitization',[45] it can be applied to *any* smaller ally that begins to assert its own interests at the expense of the alliance leader, and which is, accordingly, transferable to other alliances. The concept of 'emancipation' is closely linked with the extent to which the NSWP members succeeded in stretching the limits of the alliance to accommodate their national interests, which they did through exploring the 'room for manoeuvre' within the WP.

In addition, the term 'dynamics of dissent' will be coined, which indicates the way in which dissent also served as a catalyst for genuine discussion between all members within the alliance, thus, in the case of the WP, challenging and undermining Soviet hegemony. The dissent that arose in the Warsaw Pact halfway through the 1960s tends to be linked to the Romanian attitude without further analysis, and it has always been associated with crisis.[46] Its connotations have, accordingly, been negative, and seemed to testify to the alliance's weakness. Since the communist concept of 'democratic centralism' did not cater for dissent, it is interesting to examine how dissent from its earliest stages created a dynamic of its own in the WP, which gave the NSWP members a greater stake in the alliance. The 'dynamics of dissent' accordingly connote the role and impact of dissent and the way in which it served to 'emancipate' the NSWP members from the Soviet grip, while turning the WP from a 'Soviet transmission belt' into a multilateral decision-making body.

Dissent within the alliance took place at various levels. In the early 1960s it mainly emerged in the bilateral relations between the Kremlin and an NSWP member, thus serving NSWP emancipation. Later in the 1960s the bilateral tensions were gradually absorbed into the structure of the Warsaw Pact. With the absorption of dissent within the WP itself, the influence of the Soviet Union diminished, and that of the NSWP members grew. This book serves to assess the extent to which decision making within the WP thus became more multilateral, as well as the extent to which the alliance transcended the already existing bilateral ties between the Soviet Union and its so-called 'satellites'. This process will be called 'multilateralisation', and will be used to explain the evolution of the WP as a whole from a Soviet transmission belt into an alliance in its own right.

The term 'multilateralisation' has been borrowed from an article by the Swiss NATO expert Andreas Wenger, in which he argues that '[t]he successful transformation of NATO' from 'the previously hierarchical military alliance [...] to a more political and participatory alliance [...] was instrumental to the multilateralization of détente'.[47] According to Wenger, the way in which 'the United States sought to strengthen multilateral (military and political) cooperation and consultation within NATO' paved the way for a shift from super power détente between the Soviet Union and the USA to a broader concept of détente in which all the European countries had a stake, which in turn facilitated the CSCE in the early 1970s.[48]

Wenger exclusively links the multilateralisation of détente to the way in which NATO overcame its internal crisis, but this book will gauge whether the multilateralisation of the Warsaw Pact not only meant that the alliance itself became multilateral, but also preceded and formed a necessary condition for the 'multilateralisation of détente'. Although it has often been suggested that the Helsinki Process in the 1970s had a positive effect on the Warsaw Pact, since its multilateral decision making provided the NSWP members with more scope for manoeuvre,[49] this book will question whether this analysis can be turned on its head. In this case the multilateralisation of the WP would increase the stake of the smaller allies within the CSCE and thus facilitate the Helsinki Process. The concept of 'multilateralisation' is therefore essential in an analysis of the way in which the Warsaw Pact turned from a mere Soviet instrument into an instrument that the smaller allies could use to further their national interests.

The structure of the book

The abovementioned concepts will also be the guiding principles in the structure of this book, which is divided into three parts, in which *emancipation*, the *dynamics of dissent* and the WP's *multilateralisation* are the leitmotifs. Part I, 'Embryonic Emancipation', will treat the period 1955–64, in which several NSWP members began to emancipate themselves from the Soviet grip by using the alliance as an instrument to assert their national interests. The first chapter of this part will constitute an historical overview, which covers the period from Stalin's death in 1953 until Khrushchev's estrangement from Mao Zedong in late 1959. In this chapter the seminal developments within the Soviet bloc and their impact on the WP members will be treated in turn, such as Khrushchev's secret speech in February 1956, the Hungarian Revolution in the autumn of 1956, and the beginning of the second Berlin Crisis in 1958.

The Sino–Soviet split and its repercussions on the dynamics within the WP will be central to Chapter 2, which serves to assess how it both caused the first cracks within the WP and created more room for manoeuvre within the alliance in the period from 1960 to 1964. Particular attention will be paid to the way in which the Albanian and Romanian leaders explored the Sino–Soviet split to challenge Soviet hegemony.

Chapter 3 will evaluate the impact of the German question on the Warsaw Pact in the first half of the 1960s, while treating issues such as the second Berlin Crisis and the WP's stance on Multilateral Nuclear Forces within NATO, and their impact on the East German and Polish strategies within the alliance in particular. Chapters 2 and 3 will both start with the WP's PCC meeting in February 1960, which was the first meeting in which Soviet choreography was frustrated, and culminate in the first meeting ever of the WP's deputy foreign ministers in December 1964, two months after Khrushchev's downfall and the first detonation of a nuclear device in China.

Part II will deal with the 'Dynamics of Dissent' in the period from January 1965 to March 1968, during which the emancipation of the NSWP members already caused a situation in which the NSWP members disagreed more with one another than with the Kremlin on the purpose of the alliance and its foreign policy course. Chapter 4 will once again deal with the impact of dissent on the evolution of the alliance from the perspective of the German question. Both the East German and Soviet push for reforms and the Polish proposal for a conference on European security will be discussed in depth.

Chapter 5 will focus on Ceausescu's 'Gaullist' stance within the WP, by assessing the way in which Ceausescu challenged the role of the 'alliance leader', by sailing an independent course on issues such as the Vietnam War and the Non-Proliferation Treaty, which were both issues on which Chinese and Soviet leaders held diametrically opposed views. The Sino–Soviet split will accordingly again play a central role in this chapter.

The greatest shift from 'Crisis to Consolidation' took place in the period from March 1968, which marked the beginning of the Prague Spring, to March 1969, when the PCC meeting in Budapest was overshadowed by severe Sino–Soviet clashes at the Ussuri river. This period, which ultimately seals the evolution of the WP into a truly *multilateral* alliance, will be covered by Part III, the final part of the book. Chapter 6 is a slight anomaly, as it deals with a development that formally took place outside the official framework of the WP, namely the Prague Spring. This chapter will nevertheless serve to challenge persistent conventional wisdom about the WP's involvement in suppressing liberalisations in Czechoslovakia.

Chapter 7 will concentrate again on developments *within* the WP itself from the PCC meeting in March 1968 until the one in March 1969. Both the German question and the Sino–Soviet split will be central to this chapter, as it deals with reforms and European security on the one hand, and with the question of whether or not to take a stance about the Sino–Soviet border clashes at the Ussuri river, which coincided with the PCC meeting in March 1969.

The PCC meeting in 1969 marked the emancipation of the individual NSWP allies and the evolution of the alliance as a multilateral institution, leading to unprecedented unanimity on the reorganisation of the Warsaw Pact and the WP appeal for a European security conference. For the first time in its history, a proposal by the Warsaw Pact was taken seriously by NATO, which paved the way for a dialogue between East and West that culminated in the Helsinki Process. The non-Soviet Warsaw Pact members made a much larger contribution to this dialogue than they are usually credited for. The Cold War cannot be understood by looking at the superpowers alone, nor can it be comprehended by concentrating on the influence of the smaller allies within NATO, as has often been done, at the expense of the junior allies in the Warsaw Pact. This book will not only be the first monograph on the Warsaw Pact based on newly available primary sources from Eastern Europe, but it will also be unprecedented in its challenge of the unfounded but persistent assumption in historiography of the WP as a mere instrument of Soviet influence. It aims to shed a new light on key events in the Cold War through a thorough examination of the Warsaw Pact in the 1960s that does more justice to developments on both sides of the Iron Curtain, and rescues the Eastern European allies from oblivion.

Notes

1. V. Mastny and M. Byrne (eds.), *A Cardboard Castle? An Inside History of the Warsaw Pact 1955–1991* (Budapest and New York, 2005), 1.
2. Cf. J. Baev, 'The Warsaw Pact', in R. van Dijk (ed.), *Encyclopaedia of the Cold War* (London and New York, 2008), 960.
3. See 'Note on the sources' for a detailed explanation of the archives used for this book.
4. Z.K. Brzezinski, *The Soviet Bloc: Unity and Conflict. Revised and Enlarged Edition* (Harvard, 1967), 433–55.
5. Ibid., 458.
6. Cf. Wanda Jarzabek's book in Poland, *PRL w politycznych strukturach Układu Warszawskiego w latach 1955–1980* [The Polish People's Republic in the political structures of the Warsaw Pact, 1955–1980] (Warsaw, 2008), and Petre Opriş's monograph in Romania, *România în Organizaţia Tratatului de la Varsovia (1955–1991)* (Bucharest, 2008). See also the essays in M.A. Heiss and S.V. Papacosma (eds), *NATO and the Warsaw Pact: Intrabloc Conflicts* (Ohio, 2008); and T. Diedrich et al. (eds), *Der Warschauer Pakt: Von der Gründung bis zum Zusammenbruch 1955 bis 1991* (Berlin, 2009).
7. A welcome exception is Robin Remington's *The Warsaw Pact. Case Studies in Communist Conflict Resolution* (Massachusetts, 1971), but since it was written in 1971 it has largely become outdated.
8. R.W. Clawson and L.S. Kaplan (eds), *The Warsaw Pact. Political Purpose and Military Means* (Ohio, 1982), x.
9. C.D. Jones, *Soviet Influence in Eastern Europe. Political Autonomy and the Warsaw Pact* (New York, 1981), ix.
10. F. Umbach, *Das rote Bündnis. Entwicklung und Zerfall des Warschauer Paktes 1955–1991* (Berlin, 2005).
11. Cf. V. Mastny, 'The Warsaw Pact. An Alliance in Search of a Purpose', in M.A. Heiss and S.V. Papacosma (eds), *NATO and the Warsaw Pact: Intrabloc Conflicts* (Ohio, 2008), 141–60.
12. A. Korbonski, 'The Warsaw Treaty After Twenty-five Years: An Entangling Alliance or an Empty Shell?' in R.W. Clawson and L.S. Kaplan (eds), *The Warsaw Pact. Political Purpose and Military Means* (Ohio, 1982), 3.
13. For example, D. Selvage, 'The Warsaw Pact and the European Security Conference, 1964–69: Sovereignty, Hegemony, and the German Question', in A. Wenger et al. (eds), *Origins of the European Security System: The Helsinki Process Revisited* (London and New York, 2008), 85–106.
14. M. Trachtenberg, *A Constructed Peace. The Making of the European Settlement, 1945–1963* (Princeton, 1999).
15. Mastny, 'The Warsaw Pact', 148.
16. A. Locher, 'A Crisis Foretold. NATO and France, 1963–66', in A. Wenger et al. (eds), *Transforming NATO in the Cold War. Challenges beyond Deterrence in the 1960s* (Oxford and New York, 2007), 107–27, quotation at 120–21.
17. For example, L.S. Kaplan, *NATO Divided, NATO United. The Evolution of an Alliance* (Westport, 2004), for an influential analysis of the differences between various allies within NATO throughout its existence.
18. A. Locher, *Crisis? What Crisis? NATO, de Gaulle, and the Future of the Alliance, 1963–1966* (Berlin, 2010), and H. Haftendorn, *NATO and the Nuclear Revolution. A Crisis of Credibility, 1966–1967* (Oxford, 1996), respectively. See also Wenger et al. (eds), *Transforming NATO*.
19. V. Mastny, 'The New History of Cold War Alliances', *Journal of Cold War Studies* 4:2 (2002), 76. Although this article was written in 2002, its claims are still valid.

20 Mastny and Byrne (eds), *Cardboard Castle*.
21 Mastny, 'The New History', 76.
22 N.P. Ludlow, *The European Community and the Crisis of the 1960s. Negotiating the Gaullist Challenge* (London and New York, 2006).
23 R.W. Stone, *Satellites and Commissars. Strategy and Conflict in the Politics of Soviet-Bloc Trade* (Princeton, 2002), 3.
24 Cf. the 'aims and scope' of the renowned journal, *Cold War History*: www.tandfonline.com/action/aboutThisJournal?show=aimsScope&journalCode=f cwh20#.UdsKlY4jDFso (accessed 22 September 2013).
25 J.L. Gaddis, 'On Starting All Over Again: A Naïve Approach to the Study of the Cold War', in O.A. Westad (ed.), *Reviewing the Cold War. Approaches, Interpretation, Theory* (London, 2000), 31. In the same volume the Cold War historian James Hershberg calls for a 'retroactive debipolarization' of the Cold War. Cf. J. G. Hershberg, 'The Crisis Years, 1958–63', in ibid., 304.
26 L. Bohri, 'Empire by Coercion: The Soviet Union and Hungary in the 1950s', *Cold War History* 1:2 (2001), 47–72.
27 V.M. Zubok, *A Failed Empire: The Soviet Union in the Cold War from Stalin to Gorbachev* (Chapel Hill, 2007, 2009).
28 J.L. Gaddis, *We Now Know. Rethinking Cold War History* (Oxford, 1997), 289.
29 For example, Zubok, *A Failed Empire*; A. Brown, *The Rise and Fall of Communism* (London 2009); and J.L. Harper, *The Cold War* (Oxford, 2011). This also applies to books in other languages: cf. G. Soutou, *La Guerre de Cinquante Ans* (Paris, 2001); and F. Romero, *Storia della guerra fredda. L'ultimo conflitto per l'Europa* (Turin, 2009).
30 H.M. Harrison, *Driving the Soviets up the Wall. Soviet-East German Relations, 1953–1961* (Princeton, 2003).
31 L.M. Lüthi, *The Sino-Soviet Split: Cold War in the Communist World* (Princeton, 2008); and S. Radchenko, *Two Suns in the Heavens: The Sino-Soviet Struggle for Supremacy, 1962–1967* (Stanford, 2009).
32 Cf. Gaddis, *We Now Know*, 283; and Westad (ed.), *Reviewing the Cold War*, 3.
33 G. Lundestad, 'How (Not) to Study the Origins of the Cold War', in Westad (ed.), *Reviewing the Cold War*, 73; and M. Leffler, 'Bringing it Together: The Parts and the Whole', ibid., 47.
34 Leffler, 'Bringing it Together', 47.
35 G. Lundestad, 'Empire by Invitation? The United States and Western Europe, 1942–52', *Journal of Peace Research* 23 (1986), 268.
36 Ibid., 275.
37 T. Risse-Kappen, *Cooperation among Democracies. The European Influence on U.S. Foreign Policy* (Princeton, 1995), 3.
38 For example, G. Liska, *Nations in Alliance. The Limits of Interdependence* (Baltimore, 1962); S.M. Walt, *The Origins of Alliances* (Ithaca, 1987); and G.H. Snyder, *Alliance Politics* (Ithaca, 1997). See G.H. Snyder, 'Alliance Theory: A Neorealist First Cut', *Journal of International Affairs* 44:1 (1990), 103, for an assessment of the 'ancillary' treatment of alliance theories in IR theories, such as those of the realist H.J. Morgenthau, *Politics among Nations. The Struggle for Power and Peace* (New York, 1948, 1963), and the neorealists Kenneth Waltz, *Theory of International Politics* (Boston, 1979), and J.J. Mearsheimer, *The Tragedy of Great Power Politics* (New York, 2001).
39 Snyder, *Alliance Politics*, 13.
40 G.H. Snyder, 'The Security Dilemma in Alliance Politics', *World Politics* 36:4 (1984), 466.
41 Ibid., 484.
42 Ibid., 461.
43 Ibid., 484.

44 C. Békés, 'Der Warschauer Pakt und der KSZE-Prozess 1965 bis 1970', in Diedrich et al. (eds), *Der Warschauer Pakt*, 229; and Z.K. Brzezinski, *The Soviet Bloc: Unity and Conflict. Revised and Enlarged Edition* (Harvard, 1967), 442.
45 Brzezinski, *The Soviet Bloc*, 434.
46 Cf. Mastny and Byrne (eds), *Cardboard Castle*, 28–34.
47 A. Wenger, 'Crisis and Opportunity. NATO's Transformation and the Multilateralization of Détente, 1966–68', *Journal of Cold War Studies* 6:1 (2004), 24–25.
48 Wenger, 'Crisis and Opportunity', 72–73.
49 Ibid.

Part I
Embryonic emancipation, 1955–64

1 The Warsaw Pact in its infancy

'What do you imagine, that we will make some kind of NATO here?'[1]
(Soviet Supreme Commander Ivan Konev to Polish politicians in 1957)

The foundation of the Warsaw Pact on 14 May 1955 at first sight seems an anomaly. The absence of a preceding bargaining process defies most theories on the formation of alliances,[2] and the foundation of a military alliance seems out of sync with Khrushchev's zeal for détente and disarmament. The WP was, after all, founded by a Soviet leadership, which preferred 'peaceful coexistence' to further confrontation. After the death of the Soviet despot Joseph Stalin in the spring of 1953, his successors had embarked on a much more conciliatory course towards the West. Four days before the Warsaw Pact's foundation Stalin's eventual successor, Nikita Khrushchev, had even put forward the Kremlin's 'most credible disarmament proposal to date', and one day after its foundation Khrushchev signed the Austrian State Treaty, which entailed the withdrawal of all foreign troops from Austria, including Soviet ones, and declared Austria neutral.[3] In the wake of the WP's foundation, Khrushchev chose to demilitarise the Cold War still further, and withdrew Soviet troops from, *inter alia*, Romania and Finland. Moreover, there were already perfectly functioning bilateral treaties between the Soviet Union and its satellites in place, which explains why the WP has often been considered 'superfluous'.[4]

It is, therefore, imperative to examine the original objectives of the Warsaw Pact and its functioning in the first years of its existence. Only by closely considering the WP in its infancy is it possible to compare and contrast the way in which the alliance originally functioned with its evolution in the 1960s. The alliance was, however, not founded in a vacuum, and the first five years of its existence witnessed an extremely turbulent period in the history of Eastern Europe. Stalin's death on 5 March 1953 marked 'a turning point in the Cold War', as his successors embarked on an altogether 'New Course' in Soviet foreign policy, which had serious ramifications for the Eastern European satellites.[5] The Soviet change of direction already led to uprisings in Bulgaria, Czechoslovakia and Eastern Germany in 1953, and the situation spun out of control in Poland and Hungary in the autumn of 1956 after

Khrushchev had publicly distanced himself from Stalin during his 'secret speech' in February 1956. Although Khrushchev's programme of 'de-Stalinisation' facilitated the rapprochement with Josip Tito's Yugoslavia, it also estranged the Albanian and Chinese leaderships from the Soviet cause.

In this chapter the first five years of the WP's existence will accordingly be examined in the context of developments in Eastern Europe from the death of Stalin until Khrushchev's visit to the US President Dwight D. Eisenhower in the autumn of 1959. This visit sealed Khrushchev's zeal for peaceful coexistence, and illustrates the U-turn in Soviet foreign policy between 1953 and 1960. This period is also known as the Soviet 'thaw', during which Khrushchev relaxed his grip on both Soviet society and Eastern Europe as a whole.[6] Both the foundation of the WP and the more centrifugal consequences of Khrushchev's liberalisations, such as the Hungarian Revolution, should be considered in this context. Since the Kremlin's new foreign policy outlook affected the relations between the Soviet Union and all its satellites, the developments of each Eastern European country in this period will be discussed. The position of each individual WP country, as well as the character of its party leadership and the interests of the political elites, will be of paramount importance for the rest of the book. Moreover, a treatment of the wider context should serve to introduce two themes that dominated the WP's dynamics throughout the 1960s: namely, Sino-Soviet relations and the German question.

The New Course

The death of Stalin on 5 March 1953 heralded the end of an era. Already on the evening of Stalin's death his closest collaborators assumed a 'collective leadership', since none of them was powerful enough to succeed Stalin on his own, and all of them wanted to curb the power of their potential rivals.[7] Moreover, in this way Stalin's successors clearly distanced themselves from Stalin's autocratic rule. Former secret police chief Lavrentii Beria proposed Georgii Malenkov as chairman of the Council of Ministers, in return for which Malenkov appointed Beria as one of his first vice-chairmen. Beria was additionally appointed minister of internal affairs, which meant he was also in charge of state security, and Vyacheslav Molotov, another first vice-chairman, was reinstated as minister of foreign affairs.[8] The meeting in which all of this was decided lasted only 40 minutes, which gives the impression that Beria and Malenkov, who formed a close alliance, had decided in advance the course of events after Stalin's death, and had 'presented their colleagues with a *fait accompli*', as Khrushchev claimed later.[9] Khrushchev, meanwhile, became the senior secretary of the Party Central Committee, which meant he set the agenda for the Presidium meetings together with Malenkov. Although Beria, Malenkov and Molotov were generally considered 'the three most prominent leaders', it was Khrushchev who would ultimately assume the party leadership.[10]

Grappling with Stalin's controversial legacy, his successors strove to convince the West of their peaceful intentions, and even decided to conclude an armistice in the Korean War.[11] It was, ironically, the former secret police chief Beria who most vehemently supported introducing a programme of controlled reforms, the so called 'New Course', in Eastern Europe, as well as arguing in favour of a unified but neutral Germany. These reforms had become overdue anyhow, since Stalin's programme of forced agricultural collectivisation and accelerated industrialisation had wreaked havoc upon the economies within Eastern Europe.[12]

This caused a series of serious protests in the wake of Stalin's death, which began with a major riot in the Bulgarian town Plovdiv on 4 May 1953 by hundreds of tobacco workers, who protested against an increase in the work norms and who had to be appeased by a former popular deputy prime minister, Anton Iugov.[13] Compelled to adopt the Soviet 'New Course' in order to prevent further upheavals, the Bulgarian Prime Minister and party leader Vulko Chervenkov relinquished his position as party leader in March 1954 to the 'young, efficient, but self-effacing apparatchik named Todor Zhivkov', thus establishing a kind of collective leadership.[14] As a believer 'both in obedience to Moscow and in strict internal control' the Stalinist Chervenkov attempted to sail a 'New Course' mainly in economic terms, whereas Zhivkov soon developed into one of Khrushchev's most loyal disciples.[15]

Social unrest also plagued Czechoslovakia, whose president and party leader, Klement Gottwald, had died on 14 March 1953, just a few days after attending Stalin's funeral. Gottwald almost emulated Chervenkov's subservience to the Soviet Union, and with the slogan 'The Soviet Union, Our Model', he had embarked on 'an almost suicidal drive to extirpate not only national traditions but also those of the party itself'.[16] Like Stalin, Gottwald was replaced by a collective leadership too, in which the veteran trade union leader Antonin Zapotocky assumed the role of president, with the relatively inexperienced Antonin Novotny as the party leader. Novotny resembled his Bulgarian comrade Zhivkov in that their lack of prominence, personal appeal and intelligence had made them seemingly suitable candidates for the position of party leader in a duumvirate: without either powerful friends or enemies they were unlikely to cause Chervenkov and Zapotocky any trouble.[17]

The fact that industrialisation and collectivisation had exhausted the Czechoslovak economy caused at this stage more problems. On 1 June 1953 thousands of workers in the Czechoslovak town of Pilsen protested against a currency reform that was imposed from above, while turning the economic demands political by demanding the government's resignation and free elections.[18] As in Bulgaria, the party leadership embarked on a 'New Course' in primarily economic terms in order to modify the excesses of industrialisation and collectivisation. The Czechoslovak New Course nevertheless 'simply petered out during 1955 and early 1956', and the Czechoslovak leadership took its recourse again to a hard line, which culminated in 'the unveiling of a gigantic statue of Stalin on the bank of the Vltava' in the course of 1955.[19]

German economy was also in desperate need of a New Course. However, not at all in the interests of the East German party leader, Ulbricht, who had been one of Stalin's most loyal disciples, and was [determined] to cling to his power. Ulbricht had spent the whole of World War II as a committed communist in the Soviet Union, before he became the leader in the Sozialistische Einheitspartei Deutschlands (SED) in the summer of 1945, and appointed many 'Muscovite' Germans to the highest positions.[20] Having pushed Stalin into supporting the creation of the German Democratic Republic (GDR) in 1949 and the 'building of socialism',[21] Ulbricht was forced by Stalin's successors to backtrack on his economically disastrous policies in order to stem the increasing number of refugees from East to West Berlin. The new Soviet leadership regarded a moderation of Ulbricht's policies as the solution to the refugee exodus, and compelled Ulbricht to introduce the 'New Course' on 2 June.[22] Reluctant to undermine his own power by supporting liberalisation, Ulbricht did not rescind the 10 percent increase in work norms, and thus indirectly facilitated a popular uprising in the GDR on 16–17 June, which had to be quenched by Soviet tanks.[23]

Although the uprisings at first sight seem to indicate a weakening of Ulbricht's power, in fact they strengthened his position. It is therefore not farfetched to assume that Ulbricht had a vested interest in these uprisings to safeguard his own power. The greatest casualty of the uprisings, apart from the East German people, was Beria himself, the main architect of the New Course, who was sentenced to death on the charge of *inter alia* 'adopt[ing] a course for the conversion of the GDR into a bourgeois government'.[24] He was, in fact, not so much a victim of the East German uprisings as of a plot orchestrated by Khrushchev during the post-Stalin succession struggle, but his death penalty served Ulbricht well, since it enabled him to oust the much more liberal opposition, consisting of Wilhelm Zaisser and Rudolf Herrnstadt, on the same charge, and facilitated the consolidation of his own power.

Ulbricht clearly signalled to the Kremlin that his iron grip was essential in preventing any more unrest in the GDR and as such quenched any liberalising tendencies and silenced the more liberal opposition. Going against the Soviet Union's 'New Course' had accordingly paid off for Ulbricht, as it had left the Soviet leaders without any alternative to the consolidation of Ulbricht's power. Moreover, it had raised the stakes of a stable East Germany in the eyes of the Soviet leadership, which invited an official East German government delegation to Moscow for the first time since the GDR's foundation in 1949 in order 'to upgrade relations' and promise economic aid.[25] This episode clearly indicates Ulbricht's capacity to bend Soviet aims to his own advantage and to sacrifice the greater good for his own power, but Ulbricht's ability to exercise leverage over the divided Soviet leadership strongly diminished when Khrushchev ousted his rival Malenkov and appointed his friend and ally Nikolai Bulganin as prime minister in February 1955. Although Ulbricht had already succeeded in firmly consolidating his

Stalinist rule over the GDR, the consolidation of Khrushchev's power heralded a new phase in Soviet-Eastern European relations.

The foundation of a multilateral alliance

The consolidation of Khrushchev's position reinforced his novel foreign policy orientation, and culminated in a vast array of Soviet foreign policy initiatives in 1955. Khrushchev, however, needed to come to terms with the legacy of Soviet Foreign Minister Molotov, who had conducted foreign policy in a Stalinist fashion, and had convened a 'European' security conference in Moscow on 29 November 1954 in order to prevent West German rearmament through its accession to NATO, which had been agreed in the so-called 'Paris Agreements' a month earlier. Molotov's attempt to sow discord within NATO by excluding the USA and Canada from the 'European' security conference was a miserable failure: in the end only Soviet allies attended. Khrushchev, meanwhile, rallied Molotov behind a far more constructive approach, and negotiated for a state treaty with Austria, which would entail the withdrawal of all foreign troops, including Soviet ones, and declare Austria neutral. Sincerely believing in the benefits of the *de*militarisation of the Cold War, Khrushchev responded to the Western proposals to remilitarise West Germany by putting forward a genuine proposal on disarmament on 10 May 1955, one day after the Federal Republic of Germany (FRG) was admitted to NATO.[26]

The Soviet leadership nevertheless rose to the challenge of finding a response to the FRG's admission to NATO by founding its own alliance five days later during a conference with its Eastern European allies in Warsaw on 14 May 1955. The concept of a separate communist alliance had already been conceived at the 'European' security conference in November 1954. Although the foundation of the Warsaw Pact was 'thoroughly orchestrated' by the Soviet Union, the idea of a 'collective defence treaty', which would tie the Soviet allies to the Soviet Union in a multilateral alliance, was, in fact, a Polish one, which is why the alliance was founded in Warsaw.[27] Moreover, Khrushchev had sent all potential member states a letter in early March 1955 in which he argued that 'common measures were needed for [their] security [...] in case of the ratification of the Paris agreements', and he therefore proposed concluding a treaty between all the countries that had attended the 'European' security conference in 1954.[28] He enclosed a draft of the Warsaw treaty, and asked its prospective members for their opinion and potential amendments and additions. Although it is generally assumed that the treaty was '[d]rafted by the Soviets without consultation with their allies and accepted without meaningful discussion',[29] the allies had the scope to comment on both the idea and the contents of the treaty.

Moreover, the treaty carried considerable advantages to its proposed members, consisting of Albania, Bulgaria, Czechoslovakia, the GDR, Hungary, Poland, Romania and, of course, the Soviet Union itself. The East German leadership had a particular stake in the alliance, since it was the only international institution that recognised the existence of the GDR. Especially after West Germany's accession to NATO, the WP provided the GDR with a necessary boost to its legitimacy, and Ulbricht accordingly welcomed the treaty with great enthusiasm while enclosing one or two amendments in his reply to Khrushchev on the status of the GDR.[30] The same applied to the Polish and Czechoslovak party leaders, although to a lesser extent, as they, too, sought a way to secure the unrecognised borders with Germany. The Czechoslovak leadership had even supported a recent East German proposal for a 'tripartite military arrangement' together with Poland for exactly this reason.[31] Khrushchev's proposal for the Warsaw Treaty was considered a welcome means to consolidate Eastern Europe's security at a time when Western Europe tried to seize the initiative on the German question in the wake of the Paris agreements.

Even the party leaders without a direct stake in the German question were enthusiastic about the treaty. The Romanian leader Gheorghe Gheorghiu-Dej considered it 'a necessary defence measure, which needed to be taken because of the new situation created in Europe through the ratification of the Paris agreements and the revival of German militarism'.[32] The Bulgarian leadership also applauded the foundation of an Eastern European equivalent to NATO, since Bulgaria bordered Greece and Turkey, both of which had joined NATO in October 1952.[33] Meanwhile, the Albanian leadership welcomed the foundation of the alliance as a security bulwark against Yugoslav irredentism.[34] Tito had already developed plans in 1948 to unite Albania with Yugoslavia, which had caused severe resistance in the neighbouring and much smaller Albania.[35] For the party leaders of the participating countries, the Warsaw Treaty at the very least served to consolidate their own position. The Paris agreements and the enlargement of NATO had created a strong mutual Eastern European interest in closing ranks for the sake of security.

Moreover, the WP served as the institutional framework to integrate the GDR and its military forces. Complementing the existing bilateral ties between the Soviet Union and its satellites with a multilateral institution could thus facilitate a certain amount of Eastern European integration. Although the fact that the treaty was signed one day before the conclusion of the Austrian State Treaty on 15 May could be interpreted as a clear signal to the other Soviet satellites that the option of neutrality and the withdrawal of Soviet forces was not open to them,[36] it also indicates that Khrushchev was serious about relaxing the Soviet grip on international relations. This was indeed how it was interpreted by the Eastern European party leaders, who considered both the Warsaw Treaty and the Austrian State Treaty as Soviet endeavours to safeguard the 'independence and sovereignty' of individual states, while also contributing to 'international détente'.[37]

Both 'the principles of respect for the independence and sovereignty of states and of non-interference in their internal affairs', and European security were enshrined in the 'Treaty of Friendship, Cooperation and Mutual Assistance' between the abovementioned Eastern European countries, which accordingly seemed to safeguard its members' integrity both individually and collectively.[38] The Warsaw Treaty thus upgraded its Eastern European members from Soviet satellites to sovereign states, at least on paper.[39] The treaty closely mirrored the North Atlantic Treaty of 1949,[40] but the slight differences are telling: where the North Atlantic Treaty underlined the 'principles of democracy' and 'individual liberty',[41] the Warsaw Treaty cautiously referred to the 'friendship, cooperation and mutual assistance' between all contracting parties.[42] Although this reflects the different *internal* political structures of the members of the respective alliances, the treaties were identical concerning the way in which they were supposed to function as a multilateral alliance *between* states. The Warsaw Treaty's article 4 was almost identical to NATO's article 5, with its emphasis on the mutual assistance 'in the case of an armed attack in Europe on one or more of the Parties to the Treaty by any state or group of states', which would be carried out 'with all such means as [each individual state] deems necessary, including armed force'.[43] In contrast to the North Atlantic Treaty, the Warsaw Treaty nevertheless underlined the *European* nature of the treaty, the main purpose of which was evidently to deal with *European* security.

The preoccupation with European security also transpired in a striking article without equivalent in the North Atlantic Treaty, which emphasised that 'the present treaty shall cease to be operative' if 'a system of collective security be established in Europe'.[44] Emboldened by European détente, which had reached its peak halfway through the 1950s, and a number of successful Soviet initiatives, the Kremlin was so optimistic about the correlation of forces favouring the Soviet bloc, that it thought that the proposal to replace NATO and the embryonic WP with a European security system might be taken seriously. This would carry considerable advantages for the Soviet Union, since the USA would not enter the equation within this new security system, making the Soviet Union the unequivocal superpower on the European continent.[45]

The Warsaw Treaty was, accordingly, also intended as a diplomatic instrument to safeguard European security through political means. The architects of the treaty were all employed by the Soviet Ministry of Foreign Affairs, which indicates the initially political orientation of the Warsaw Pact.[46] Moreover, the Warsaw Treaty's article 3 stressed the need for consultations 'on all important international issues affecting their common interests', whereas the North Atlantic Treaty limited consultations to the threat to 'the territorial integrity, political independence or security of any of the Parties'.[47] According to the Warsaw Treaty, the main organ of the Warsaw Pact would therefore be a *'Political* Consultative Committee' (PCC), analogous to NATO's North Atlantic Council, which would consist of a number of representatives from every WP country. In actual fact the PCC almost exclusively consisted of the party leader, the prime minister, the minister of foreign affairs and the minister of defence from each member state. Unlike the North Atlantic Treaty's article 9, the Warsaw Treaty did not cater for the immediate establishment of a defence committee, which again shows that it primarily aimed to safeguard European security through political means, while reserving the military aspects as a Soviet prerogative for the time being.

According to the Romanian delegation, the 'military measures were not communicated apart from making us aware that a unified command would be created, and a Supreme Commander would be appointed, so the protocol is separate from the treaty, it has not been published, it is a secret document'.[48] The Romanians nevertheless stressed their active participation in one committee on the 'text of the treaty' and another one on 'problems concerning a unified command of the armed forces', which contradicts Mastny's claim that the treaty was 'adopted at the gathering without even the semblance of a discussion'.[49] The Romanian delegation even praised 'the comradely atmosphere, the warm friendship, and the mutual understanding' upon its return in Bucharest. Although the 'bargaining process' was short and shallow, the foundation of the WP had already created more room for individual observations and active participation than the WP members had ever enjoyed. The Romanian delegation therefore concluded that it should 'draw lessons for the future' from its 'active participation', since there 'would probably be more conferences'.[50] The mere foundation of the WP had, accordingly, already provided its members with a window of opportunity to make their voices heard in a multilateral platform, which they had hitherto lacked.

The foundation of a new kind of foreign policy

Yugoslavia was the only Eastern European country that was not a member of the Warsaw Pact, since the Yugoslav leader Tito had already been forced to break with the Soviet Union in June 1948, after Stalin had expelled Yugoslavia from the Communist Information Bureau (COMINFORM), which was an organisation 'created by Stalin [in 1947] to secure the unquestioning obedience of European Communists'.[51] According to the ground-breaking archival research of the British historian Svetozar Rajak, Yugoslavia was excommunicated in order to legitimise 'witch-hunts throughout Eastern Europe, [...] mobilise popular support behind satellite regimes', and thus 'create a monolithic Communist "camp"'. Tito's 'independent foreign policy', for which he is so well known, thus occurred 'only *after* the break with Stalin', instead of causing it, as has usually been considered the case. However, Stalin had never succeeded in creating the monolithic communist bloc he had envisaged, and the break with Tito had merely undermined Soviet authority, since Tito's 'own road to socialism' proved that the definition of socialism was not Moscow's prerogative. Meanwhile, Yugoslavia closely cooperated with NATO in the period 1950–55, which further weakened the Soviet position in the COMINFORM.[52]

Khrushchev's Warsaw Pact was, however, fundamentally different from Stalin's COMINFORM. The WP was an organisation between communist *states*, represented by their *governments*, unlike the COMINFORM, which was an organisation of communist *parties*, intended 'as a coordinating centre to ensure that [the communist parties] would fight the capitalist enemy together rather than separately'.[53] The WP was, hypothetically, even 'open to the accession of other states, irrespective of their social and political systems', and was, as such, not an intrinsically *communist* organisation.[54] Moreover, the inclusion of Albania and the GDR – both of which were not members of the COMINFORM – within the WP testified to Khrushchev's concern for the security of *all* Eastern European states instead of prioritising the spreading of communist propaganda. In contrast to the foundation of the WP, the Eastern European party leaders had not been warned at all beforehand about the Soviet intention to found the COMINFORM, but had been presented with a fait accompli at a meeting of Europe's most important communist parties in Poland in September 1947.[55]

Khrushchev even announced at the conference in Warsaw, which had served to seal the foundation of the WP, that he was planning to visit Yugoslavia several days later.[56] This was a sensational proposal, since ties with Yugoslavia had been non-existent since 1948, which implies that Khrushchev's intention to embark on a new course of foreign policy was genuine. Khrushchev's envisaged reconciliation with Tito was a fundamental reversal of Stalin's foreign policy. In an unprecedented change of direction in Soviet foreign policy Khrushchev travelled from Warsaw to Vienna to conclude the Austrian State Treaty one day later, and after nine days in Vienna Khrushchev and his entourage continued to Belgrade for reconciliation with Tito.[57] In less than two weeks Khrushchev had upgraded the Soviet satellites to WP allies, withdrawn Soviet troops from Austria, and retrospectively sanctioned Yugoslavia's independent course.

After a year of secret diplomacy Khrushchev and his comrades arrived on 26 May 1955 in Belgrade, where they signed a declaration with Tito in which they acknowledged 'that relations with Yugoslavia – and with other socialist countries – should be guided by the principle of equality'.[58] Although the Yugoslav side still did not agree to the reestablishment of party relations, the 'Belgrade Declaration' illustrated Khrushchev's tolerance for an independent kind of socialism, and his willingness to establish Eastern European relations on a more equal footing. The foundation of the WP should also be viewed in this light: the substitution of bilateral ties by multilateral ones provided the non-Soviet Warsaw Pact (NSWP) members with a stake in Soviet decision making, which they had previously lacked.

Khrushchev's zeal to establish foreign affairs on a novel footing also extended to the Soviet relations with Western Europe and the USA. In July 1955 Khrushchev again submitted the Soviet disarmament proposal 'at the first summit conference since the beginning of the Cold War', in Geneva, which Eisenhower rejected 'on the well-founded suspicion that it might be meant seriously'.[59] At the same summit the Kremlin capitalised on the foundation of the Warsaw Pact by proposing a collective security treaty, which would replace both NATO and the embryonic WP. Since the Soviet draft of a

'General European Treaty on Collective Security in Europe' was almost identical to the Warsaw Treaty, which the American Secretary of State John Foster Dulles considered a mere 'device whereby the Soviet Union projected its frontiers into the center of Europe', Khrushchev's proposal was categorically rejected.[60] The clause on a collective security system, which distinguished the Warsaw Treaty from its North Atlantic counterpart, had accordingly lost its validity. Western diplomats in Moscow were nevertheless impressed by the 'indefatigable dynamism' and 'patent self-confidence of the Soviet leaders', and Khrushchev himself was pleased with the summit, which had contributed to a relaxation of international tensions.[61] The WP, meanwhile, was there to stay.

Some of Khrushchev's initiatives across the Iron Curtain were more successful. In September 1955 he succeeded in luring the West German Chancellor Konrad Adenauer into establishing diplomatic relations with the Soviet Union without affecting the status of East Germany.[62] Khrushchev, accordingly, had again boosted the legitimacy of the GDR, since he had undermined West Germany's 'claim to sole representation' of all Germans ('*Alleinvertretungsanspruch*'). The West Germans in turn formulated the Hallstein Doctrine in December 1955, according to which the FRG would sever diplomatic relations with countries that established diplomatic ties with the GDR. The German question thus remained a delicate one, but Khrushchev's desire to improve relations with almost everyone had even affected the relations between the Soviet Union and the FRG. The so-called 'spirit of Geneva' had proven to be strong.

Khrushchev's foreign policy initiatives in 1955 testify to a genuine desire to reduce international tensions, whether within Eastern Europe at large through his rapprochement with Tito, or even across the iron curtain by reaching out to the FRG, the Soviet Union's nemesis. The Austrian State Treaty proves Khrushchev's willingness to demilitarise the Cold War, even though the foundation of the Warsaw Pact one day earlier seemed to contradict that aim. It is, however, important to bear in mind that the alliance was originally founded for political purposes, and that the military provisions were added later. The way in which the Warsaw Pact came into being accordingly does not justify the stigma of a 'cardboard castle' by NATO officials, since its foundation was part of a genuine campaign to establish relations within and outside Eastern Europe on a more equal footing. Moreover, Khrushchev's rapprochement with Tito emphasised that he, too, had broken with Stalin. The year 1955 was a watershed in Soviet international relations, and the foundation of the Warsaw Pact was symptomatic of Khrushchev's quest for a new way of conducting foreign policy.

The Warsaw Pact in practice

The Soviet leadership had also considered the international events in 1955 to be remarkable, which culminated in a reflection 'on Current Issues in Soviet

Global Policy' by the Soviet Foreign Ministry on 4 January 1956, in which the commitment to 'peaceful coexistence' anticipated Khrushchev's secret speech during the Twentieth Congress of the Communist Party of the Soviet Union (CPSU) in February 1956, which will be discussed below.[63] The report's emphasis on a further relaxation of 'international tensions', improved relations 'with certain capitalist powers', and the 'normalization' of 'relations with the United States' corresponds with the Western perception of a 'thaw' in the Soviet bloc.[64] The report was put into practice on the day of its publication, since the Kremlin had invited the leaders of the European communist parties to a summit in Moscow on 4 January to discuss international relations. During this summit Khrushchev formulated the new doctrine of 'active foreign policy', according to which 'the Soviet Union would not always have to be the first to take action', but other communist countries could take the initiative with Soviet support.[65] Thus Khrushchev unilaterally denounced Soviet unilateralism.

Two days later Khrushchev showed that he was serious about this, by convening the Warsaw Pact's party leaders to launch the alliance's first PCC meeting in a multilateral context.[66] The agenda of the meeting was, nevertheless, determined by the Soviet leadership, and the meeting was fully choreographed by the Kremlin. The actual meeting took place on 27–28 January 1956 in Prague, when the Soviet bloc still seemed to reap the benefits of European détente. There was little scope for non-Soviet initiative, since the meeting mainly consisted of prepared speeches, in which each NSWP representative applauded Khrushchev's numerous foreign policy initiatives in 1955, all of which had successfully served to tilt the 'correlation of forces' in the Soviet direction, as well as contributing to 'the cause of international détente'.[67]

Despite Khrushchev's desire for an active foreign policy, the other WP members still acquiesced in the role of passive bystanders. It has to be taken into account that the Soviet leadership was, indeed, riding on a wave of successful foreign policy initiatives, which contributed to Soviet authority. Although the absence of discussion seemed to vindicate the view of the WP as a 'cardboard castle', three important Soviet decisions were approved, which again served to liken the Warsaw Pact more to NATO. It was unanimously decided that a 'Standing Commission to develop recommendations on foreign policy issues' and a 'Joint Secretariat' would be created within the PCC, which would meet 'at least twice a year'.[68]

Moreover, the 'Statute of the Warsaw Treaty Unified Command' was presented by Soviet Marshall and Commander-in-Chief of the WP's unified armed forces Ivan Konev, and approved by all members.[69] As in NATO, the military contents had been added as an afterthought in September 1955, in a statute drawn up by the Soviet Union with no input by its allies, who were simply expected to sanction it during the PCC meeting.[70] The Statute of the Unified Command, which was kept secret throughout the WP's existence, was considerably more vague than the Warsaw Treaty, and 'left the military dimensions of the alliance entirely at Moscow's discretion'.[71] It catered for a 'Chief of Staff' and a 'Supreme Commander', to whom the 'Unified Armed Forces', consisting *inter alia* of the 'permanent representatives of the General Staff from the Warsaw Treaty states', would be 'subordinated'.[72] Since the WP ministers of defence would serve as the supreme commander's deputies, the national defence ministers would be subordinated to the Supreme Command,[73] which accordingly functioned as a supranational organ. With Soviet Marshall Konev as the supreme commander, Soviet General A.I. Antonov as the chief of staff, and Moscow as the seat of the Staff of the Unified Command, the WP had gained a military dimension under Soviet tutelage.[74] The military dimension was, meanwhile, not institutionalised within any multilateral structure, but led a kind of parallel existence in relation to the rest of the WP.

Moreover, in the wake of the integration of the West German army into NATO 'it was decided that the German Democratic Republic [would] be included in the Unified Armed Forces of the Warsaw Treaty Member-States'.[75] This East German military integration into the alliance would facilitate the remilitarisation of the GDR, while giving the East German leadership a particular stake in the Warsaw Pact. The East German leader Walter Ulbricht was especially relieved about this development, as he regarded the FRG's rearmament as a 'significant threat'.[76] The Polish participants strongly agreed with Ulbricht's assessment, since West German rearmament also posed a threat to Polish security. Thus the German question immediately occupied a central position in the first PCC meeting, which the Polish and East German leaderships gladly used to emphasise the West German threat.

Each PCC meeting would be concluded by a declaration and a communiqué, which initially served to emphasise the Warsaw Pact's strength and unanimity to the Western world. At this stage the declarations and communiqués were largely drafted beforehand by the Soviet leadership and accepted by its allies without question. They therefore served to uphold the facade of complete unity in the Soviet bloc. The declaration, which concluded this meeting, neatly summed up all the achievements in Soviet foreign policy, thus turning the WP into a propaganda platform for the Soviet Union, and corroborating the Western view of the WP as a 'useful forum for the articulation of [...] the bloc's support of Soviet foreign policy initiatives versus the West'.[77]

The signing of the declaration became particularly festive because the Chinese observer, Chen Yun, underlined the 'firm solidarity and full consensus of opinions', which tied China and the Soviet Union together, and which formed 'the main guarantee for the preservation of peace in Europe and throughout the world'.[78] With support from both its Warsaw Pact allies and the Chinese leadership, the correlation of forces did indeed seem to be in the Kremlin's favour. Albanian Prime Minister Mehmet Shehu, who had chaired the meeting, also considered the meeting a 'complete success', and stressed the 'sincere friendship' between all participants.[79] Although the praises of Soviet foreign policy seemed to confirm the traditional view of the Soviet Union as undisputed hegemon, with the Warsaw Pact as a transmission belt for its foreign policy initiatives, it is important to bear in mind that this was the second time since the foundation of the alliance that the WP members convened in this context. The mere convention of a multilateral meeting would have been unthinkable under Stalin.

The echoes of Khrushchev's secret speech

The glorious role of the Soviet Union as international peacemaker outlasted the PCC meeting only briefly. Khrushchev was still riding on a wave of successful foreign policy initiatives when he reinforced the New Course the post-Stalinist leadership was sailing during a four hour-long speech at the twentieth party congress of the CPSU on 25 February 1956, a month after the PCC meeting.[80] In this so-called 'secret speech' Khrushchev officially distanced himself from Stalin by denouncing Stalin's crimes and preaching peaceful coexistence. Although Khrushchev's appeal for a European security system thus gained credibility, he had pushed his luck too far with his formal break with Stalin. Most WP leaders still owed their power to Stalin, and had also copied his methods, and the Chinese party leader Mao Zedong in particular regarded Stalin as 'a great Marxist, a good and honest revolutionary'.[81] The speech, which was sent in full to all Eastern European party leaders, had thus undermined the legitimacy of their rule, too, while questioning the foundations of the entire world communist movement. Khrushchev had, accordingly, taken an enormous gamble: by denouncing Stalin, he had indirectly denounced many of the WP leaders, as well as antagonising Mao, the leader of the world's largest communist country.

Mao, a Stalinist himself, was enraged.[82] The Chinese leader had officially allied himself to Stalin with a friendship treaty in 1950, a year after the foundation of the People's Republic of China (PRC) in 1949. Although relations with Stalin had been troublesome during the Chinese Revolution, the Soviet leadership had provided the PRC with substantial loans for Soviet technology and equipment and hundreds of Soviet advisers. Khrushchev had initially striven to improve relations with China still further, and China was the first foreign country he visited in 1954. In April 1955 Khrushchev even agreed to provide China with the technology to develop a nuclear research programme, and in May 1955 a number of Chinese observers witnessed and approved the foundation of the Warsaw Pact.[83] The fact that Khrushchev had failed to consult Mao and other communist leaders before delivering the secret speech therefore infuriated the Chinese leadership. Deng Xiaoping, the Chinese delegate at the CPSU's twentieth party congress, accordingly accused Khrushchev of 'big state chauvinism', and the Chinese leadership was quick to identify other Soviet examples of this.[84] This marked the birth of the antagonism between the two communist great powers, as Mao himself emphasised retrospectively.[85]

During a session of the Politburo of the Chinese Communist Party (CCP) shortly after the Soviet congress Mao also identified some positive aspects of Khrushchev's secret speech. He was particularly pleased that the speech implied that the Soviet leadership had made mistakes in the past, and that it allowed other communist parties more scope for manoeuvre.[86] Khrushchev's denunciation of Stalin's personality cult nevertheless posed a particular threat to him, since his power was built on the cult around his persona. The Chinese leadership was also vexed by Khrushchev's doctrine of peaceful coexistence, as it still considered a war with the capitalist countries inevitable, and also justified the power of the CCP on this basis.[87] Mao was therefore left with two alternatives: either to denounce Stalin, or to denounce Khrushchev's de-Stalinisation, and lay a claim to the leadership of the world communist movement. The fact that Mao chose to do the latter would considerably complicate Khrushchev's foreign policy.

In the wake of his secret speech Khrushchev also 'roused [the Council for Mutual Economic Assistance] from dormancy in the spring of 1956'.[88] The COMECON, founded by Stalin in January 1949 in reaction to the Marshall Plan in order to coordinate the economy of the Soviet bloc countries, had been largely inactive as a multilateral organisation during Stalin's reign. Consisting of exactly the same countries as the WP, the COMECON provided Khrushchev with an instrument also to integrate Eastern Europe in economic terms. Khrushchev's foundation of ten permanent standing committees to facilitate economic coordination within Eastern Europe testifies to his zeal to use multilateral and intergovernmental organisations for Eastern European integration, instead of using coercion to suppress the Soviet bloc countries. As the Hungarian historian Csaba Békés puts it, 'Nikita S. Khrushchev wanted to remake the basic foundations of intra-bloc relations essentially by modifying the terms of those relations from those of *colony* to *dominium*'.[89] Khrushchev's secret speech was accordingly symptomatic for his new foreign policy offensive, which had already started in 1955.

The secret speech nevertheless caused considerable unrest in Eastern Europe, since the speech had undermined the legitimacy of Eastern Europe's 'little Stalins', too. The first country where this affected the leadership was Bulgaria, where the Stalinist Prime Minister Chervenkov was replaced by the more moderate Anton Iugov in April 1956. This consolidated the power of the party leader Todor Zhivkov, who used his loyalty to Khrushchev to boost his status within Bulgarian politics.[90] While ostensibly treading in the footsteps of Khrushchev's de-Stalinisation, the Bulgarian party kept the people under tight control in order to prevent any unrest reminiscent of the Plovdiv protests in May 1953. The Czechoslovak leadership also took a firm stance in the wake of Khrushchev's secret speech, without allowing any liberalisation, so as to prevent a repetition of the riots in Pilsen in June 1953. When Czechoslovak President Zapotocky died in November 1957, the party leader Novotny consolidated his power by also assuming the presidency. Reducing de-Stalinisation to a minimum and continuing his hard line, Novotny, too,

Soviet bloc, by 'swear[ing] that Poland needs Russian friendship more than Russians need Polish friendship', since 'without you we won't be able to exist as an independent state'.[107] The fact that he convinced his Soviet comrades of complete loyalty to the Soviet Union and his capacity to control the rapidly escalating situation consolidated his position, too.[108] It was indeed the case that the Soviet security guarantee was essential to Poland, since the Polish-German Oder–Neisse border had never been recognised by the FRG. It is, however, interesting to note that Gomulka also 'emphasised that Polish-Soviet relations "ought to be based on mutual trust and equality" and that each country ought "to possess complete autonomy and independence"'.[109] He thus managed to negotiate with the Soviet leadership from a position of strength, which would stand him in good stead within later consultations in the WP. Moreover, Gomulka also enjoyed great popular support, which bestowed on his power a legitimacy that Ulbricht lacked.

Meanwhile, the Soviet reliance on Chinese advice remains remarkable. On 21 October, after Khrushchev had left Warsaw empty handed, he asked his Chinese comrades to send a delegation to Moscow in order to mediate in the negotiations between the Polish and the Soviet leadership.[110] The Chinese delegates Liu Shaoqi and Deng Xiaoping, who had been so critical of Khrushchev's secret speech, visited Moscow from 23 to 31 October, by which time the situation in Hungary had begun to escalate too. Although Sino-Soviet relations had suffered from Khrushchev's secret speech, the Kremlin was still interested in the Chinese assessment, allegedly because 'they were further away from events in Poland and Hungary, and were not directly involved'.[111] Khrushchev, who preferred a political solution, might also have needed Chinese support in withstanding East German and Czechoslovak pressure to intervene in Poland in order to 'restore order'.[112] A potential collapse of Poland would leave the GDR and Czechoslovakia exposed to West German revanchism.

Khrushchev's reluctance to resolve the situation unilaterally also led to the convention of a meeting with party leaders from Czechoslovakia, the GDR and Bulgaria in Moscow on 24 October. The leaders of the countries, which had already experienced riots in the wake of Stalin's death in 1953, were interestingly the most eager to be consulted in the control of unrest in the Soviet bloc. Although their invitation illustrates Khrushchev's departure from an authoritarian style of leadership, it also underscores the fact that he had not considered using the Warsaw Pact as an instrument to resolve the crisis in Eastern Europe. The Romanian and Hungarian allies had been invited, too, but did not attend, but the Albanian leaders, who were also members of the WP, had not been invited at all. The alliance accordingly remained dormant. During this meeting Khrushchev explained that Gomulka had managed to 'assure the Soviet delegation that the measures being taken would not have an adverse effect on Poland's relations with the Soviet Union and the CPSU', and 'emphasised that the presence of Soviet troops on Polish territory was necessary because of the existence of NATO', which 'was greeted with loud and long applause'.[113] Although Khrushchev was reassured by the situation in Poland, he soon turned his allies' attention to Hungary, where matters were rapidly spinning out of control.

Equality on Moscow's terms

The stability of the Hungarian leadership had suffered greatly from changes in Soviet policy in the wake of Stalin's death. By the time Stalin died, Hungary was plagued by a social, political and economic crisis, which the new Soviet leadership tried to forestall by replacing the Stalinist Prime Minister Matyas Rakosi with the reform-minded Imre Nagy on 16 June 1953. Hungarian leadership struggles nevertheless complicated the implementation of the New Course, since the rivalry and conflicting interests between Rakosi, as party leader, and Nagy, as prime minister, held the Hungarian Workers Party (HWP) in a deadly embrace. When the New Course had failed to remedy the tensions in Hungary, Khrushchev finally disassociated himself from Hungary's New Course in a report on 8 January 1955.

Khrushchev's criticism of the New Course facilitated Nagy's replacement by the former Stalinist Andras Hegedus in April 1955. The new Hungarian Stalinist leadership was, however, totally incongruous with the de-Stalinisation advocated in Khrushchev's secret speech in February 1956. This ultimately made its position untenable, and forced Rakosi to resign in July 1956.[114] The Hungarian people nevertheless became particularly disgruntled about the fact that Rakosi's removal had not led to any significant concessions by the Hungarian leadership, and Hungarian discontent culminated in a series of demonstrations in October 1956. On 22 October university students in Budapest published a list of 16 demands of the Hungarian leadership, such as freedom of speech and the withdrawal of Soviet troops, and one day later the same students organised a demonstration in solidarity with the reform movement in Poland. When this demonstration escalated into an armed uprising by the evening, the Hungarian leadership asked the Soviet leaders to put down the revolt by intervening with the Soviet troops stationed in Hungary.[115] The Kremlin very reluctantly agreed to intervene after vehement discussions in the politburo that proved counterproductive.[116] The intervention of Soviet troops on 24 October only exacerbated anti-Soviet sentiments, and the uprisings turned into a fully fledged anti-Soviet liberation struggle.

Upon the arrival of Soviet troops Imre Nagy was reappointed as prime minister in order to assuage the Hungarian people and gain control over the situation. Nagy was compelled to do so by placing the party at the head of the revolutionary developments, and by enticing the Kremlin to agree to a new government programme, which entailed the dissolution of the security forces and the withdrawal of Soviet troops from Hungary altogether. Although the Soviet leadership sanctioned Nagy's measures on 28 October in exchange for his promise to stabilise the situation, the Hungarian party leadership was divided on his policies.[117] Already on 26 October, politburo member Janos Kadar was reported to have shaken 'his head as a sign of disagreement', after Nagy had suggested dissolving the security forces.[118]

However, Khrushchev was prepared to go still further, and on 30 October the Kremlin formulated a declaration in which it unprecedentedly claimed to be 'prepared to review with the other socialist countries which are members of the Warsaw Treaty the question of Soviet troops stationed on the territory of [the Hungarian, Romanian and Polish republics]'.[119] This 'Declaration by the Government of the USSR on the Principles of Development and Further Strengthening of Friendship and Cooperation between the Soviet Union and Other Socialist States' had already been drafted for several weeks, and its revision happened to coincide with the Hungarian Revolution. The declaration sealed the Soviet decision to withdraw its troops from Hungary. Its proclaimed commitment to 'the principles of non-interference',[120] although exercised in Poland, hardly seems to ring true in the case of Hungary, considering the fact that Soviet troops intervened in Hungary for a second time on 4 November 1956. This nevertheless does not mean that the declaration was purely a cynical attempt to cover up the real Soviet intentions, as some historians argue.[121] It was rather an attempt to keep all options open.

Reform-socialism, such as in Poland, had not compromised the newly formulated Soviet principle of non-interference, but the disintegration of communism altogether, which seemed imminent in Hungary, warranted intervention as a last recourse.[122] As Békés, Byrne and Rainer argue, 'in Soviet eyes, cracking the East European buffer zone would create an intolerable security threat'.[123] Despite appearances to the contrary, the Soviet leaders had therefore not ruled out intervention in their declaration by emphasising that it was everyone's 'chief and sacred duty' to 'guard the communist achievements of people's democratic Hungary'.[124] This almost seems a Brezhnev doctrine *avant la lettre*: upon closer reading of the document, it appears that the principle of non-interference only applied to states that were both communist and members of the Warsaw Pact. When Nagy decided to establish a multi-party system on 31 October 1956, thus relinquishing the communist monopoly on power, the Soviet leaders could embark on the second intervention without violating their own principles.

The decision for a second Soviet intervention on 4 November was, however, not a unilateral Soviet one. After the Chinese delegates in Moscow had informed Mao of the Soviet decision to withdraw its troops from Hungary on 30 October, the Chinese leadership decided strongly to advise the Kremlin *against* the troop withdrawal, since the Kremlin should 'prevent the imperialist attack on the big socialist family'.[125] The so-called 'counterrevolutionary Putsch in Hungary' was, accordingly, *not* an internal affair, unlike the situation in Poland, where the survival of socialism did not seem to be at stake.[126] The Chinese delegate Liu Shaoqi even accused the Soviet leaders of becoming 'historical criminals' if they did not defend socialism in Hungary,[127] while his comrades retrospectively accused the Soviets of 'capitulation'.[128] Even within the Hungarian leadership some politburo members began to view the events in Hungary in a more negative light, most notably Janos Kadar, who was invited to Moscow on 1 November. Despite Kadar's attempt upon arrival in Moscow on 2 November to convince the Kremlin not to intervene, Kadar ultimately changed sides by promising Khrushchev the next day to provide his assistance 'in order to stabilize the situation' and by agreeing to form a new Hungarian government.[129] Kadar's assessment of the situation in Hungary as a 'counterrevolution' contributed to tipping the balance in favour of intervention.[130] Subsequently ruling Hungary as a party leader from November 1956 till his retirement in 1988, Kadar continued to attempt a delicate balancing act between moderate internal reforms and loyalty to the Soviet bloc.

The Kremlin had already reached a similar conclusion after Nagy's proclamation of a multi-party system. Since Khrushchev's desire for a further demilitarisation of the Cold War had been genuine, he embarked on a very quick tour of Eastern Europe on 2 November in order to legitimise the intervention. Within one day the Chinese, Czechoslovakians, Romanians, Poles and even the Yugoslavs rallied behind Khrushchev. The communist leaders fully realised that the loss of Hungary would weaken the communist bloc, which would threaten their own security too. Khrushchev's travels prove that he sought a justification for what could otherwise have been regarded as Soviet imperialism; with Eastern European consent it turned into the salvation of communism instead. Moreover, Tito managed to convince Khrushchev against the wishes of some of his Soviet comrades to allow Kadar to form the new Hungarian government, and accordingly had some stake in Hungarian affairs after all.[131] Moscow did indeed call the shots, but the Eastern European assistance in pulling the trigger strengthened its cause.

However, it is important to note that the reason for the intervention on 4 November was *not* Nagy's declaration of neutrality and Hungary's withdrawal from the Warsaw Pact on 1 November, as is often assumed.[132] Recently disclosed archival evidence has shown that Nagy's withdrawal from the Eastern European alliance was a *reaction* to the realisation that Soviet troops were still entering Hungary, in an attempt to gain support from the United Nations (UN).[133] Hungary's lack of commitment to the Warsaw Pact was accordingly *not* the determining factor in the second Soviet intervention. The Warsaw Pact was not even used as an instrument to sanction the Soviet intervention, since the WP did not cater for one member invading the other. Although Khrushchev had consulted many of his WP allies, he had not done so within the institutional framework of the alliance, and he had forgotten about Albania altogether. Khrushchev could have used the WP for multilateral consultations, but it could not have served to justify the invasion in either political or military terms: it was, after all, intended to provide mutual assistance in case of 'an armed attack', instead of facilitating such an attack. The alliance was not founded as an instrument of coercion within Eastern Europe. Khrushchev had abolished the COMINFORM exactly because he considered the time ripe for a more equal, interstate relationship with his allies.

The 30 October declaration illustrates the extent of this new kind of 'equality'. On the one hand its contents suggest that Khrushchev genuinely strove to take the Eastern European leaders more seriously, but on the other hand the NSWP members had not been involved in drafting the declaration, which still separated the Soviet Union from 'other socialist states'. The fact that the Soviet leadership unilaterally decided about matters that affected the security of the Soviet bloc, through a Soviet declaration, indicates that its allies were still at the receiving end of Soviet directives, which confirms the traditional assumptions. There was, however, a new kind of equality, but it was one on Moscow's terms. Khrushchev's reference to the Warsaw Treaty's 'obligation to take "concerted measures necessary [...] to guarantee the inviolability of their borders and territory"' therefore seems a vain attempt to uphold the provisions of the treaty in theory, while being unable to do so in practice, since the tension between the security of the pact on the one hand and that of its individual members on the other was unresolvable.[134] If anything, the Hungarian Revolution had highlighted what the WP was *not*.

The Albanian reaction to the thaw

Khrushchev's failure to involve all WP members in the decision making about the Hungarian Revolution was particularly painful to the Albanian leadership, since it had been the only WP member that had not been consulted at all in the autumn of 1956. Although Albania was both geographically and culturally an anomaly within the alliance, since the tiny country was geographically isolated from the Soviet bloc and predominantly inhabited by Muslims instead of Slavs, the Albanian leadership had generally been on good terms with its Soviet comrades. The authoritarian party leader, Enver Hoxha, had greatly applauded Stalin's break with Tito in 1948, since he was afraid to be swallowed up by his neighbouring country Yugoslavia. Moreover, Tito's excommunication from the socialist camp enabled Hoxha to prevent being unseated by more 'right-wing' colleagues, by purging them in the wake of the anti-Titoist witch hunts. Hoxha was, therefore, particularly enthusiastic about joining the Warsaw Pact in May 1955 as a bulwark against the Yugoslav menace.

Albanian accession to the alliance was, however, controversial from the start, since Soviet Foreign Minister Molotov had 'proposed that in the composition of the Warsaw Pact Albania and the German Democratic Republic should not be included. He said: "Why should we wage war on behalf of Albania and the GDR?"'[135] With a slight tinge of irony, these geopolitically insecure countries would determine the dynamics of the Warsaw Pact at the beginning of the 1960s. Khrushchev had, however, insisted on admitting Albania to the alliance for exactly this reason, as 'it would be swallowed whole' if it were not included.[136] Initially Albania was one of its most loyal members, and Hoxha even managed to convince Khrushchev of the necessity to build an international military support base at Vlorë on the island of

Sazan, which Stalin had not approved. In this way the Albanian leadership both wanted to show its loyalty to the Soviet Union, and safeguard its own security interests, situated between the non-aligned Yugoslavia and the NATO member Greece.

Khrushchev's de-Stalinisation and his rapprochement with Yugoslavia were, therefore, viewed with increasing anxiety, since de-Stalinisation not only 'threaten[ed] Hoxha's own position at home, but Khrushchev's review of Stalin's Yugoslavia policy undermined the Albanian raison d'être for improved relations with the Soviet Union'.[137] The Albanian leadership became so displeased with the Kremlin's revision of Stalin's policies that the Albanian Prime Minister Mehmet Shehu told Soviet politburo member Anastas Mikoyan that 'Stalin made two mistakes. First, he died too early, and second, he failed to liquidate the entire present Soviet leadership'.[138] Two months after Khrushchev's secret speech the Albanian leaders even invented a plot at the third Municipal Party Conference in Tirana which enabled them to purge the party of pro-Soviet members, consolidate their power and thwart de-Stalinisation.[139]

The Hungarian Revolution in the autumn of 1956 made the Albanian leadership painfully aware of the undermining consequences of de-Stalinisation for its own position, and Hoxha still blamed Khrushchev for failing to consult Albania in a speech at the conference of communist parties in Moscow four years later, on 16 November 1960. Hoxha pointed out the 'injustice' in the fact that Khrushchev had consulted the 'renegade' Tito, 'the traitor of Marxism Leninism', about whether or not to intervene in Hungary during the Hungarian Revolution in 1956, while failing to convene the WP countries. According to Hoxha, Albania should have been consulted, as it was a member of the Warsaw Pact, common security was at stake, and 'from the moment we created the Warsaw Pact, we should have decided together, otherwise it makes no sense to talk about an alliance, about comradeship, about collaboration between parties'.[140] The Hungarian Revolution had thus painfully underlined the dormancy of the WP, and Hoxha reminded the Kremlin of the implications of its own creation.

Despite their predicament, the Albanian leaders continued to tread their ground carefully vis-à-vis the Kremlin. They decided to be 'careful', because 'without the Soviet Union our country is unable to build socialism; we cannot defend the freedom of our country by ourselves'.[141] Moreover, the Albanian leadership had calculated that 'Albania can stand on its own feet in economic terms around 1970'.[142] In the latter half of the 1950s the Albanian leadership was ideologically, geopolitically and economically dependent on the Soviet Union, without an alternative communist protector of their interests. Albanian extremism in internal politics and scepticism about Khrushchev's peaceful coexistence, which facilitated his rapprochement with Tito, drove the Albanian leaders gradually into the arms of their Chinese comrades, whose financial support of Albania rose substantially after 1956.[143] The Hungarian Revolution slowly set a trend of Sino-Albanian opposition to Soviet positions.[144] According to Li Fenglin, the Chinese ambassador to Moscow at the time, Albania even took the initiative in 'inciting Beijing's opinions'.[145] The Hungarian Revolution had thus inadvertently forged a bond between Moscow's largest and smallest allies. Although neither Mao nor Hoxha had irreversibly turned against Khrushchev at this stage, both had become increasingly critical of his policies, and Hoxha had linked his criticism to Khrushchev's mismanagement of the WP.

The Polish push for reforms

Enver Hoxha was not the only Eastern European leader to question the provisions of the Warsaw Pact in the wake of the Hungarian Revolution. Possibly emboldened by the fact that Khrushchev had solicited his advice in relation to the Hungarian Revolution, Gomulka sent a Polish delegation to Moscow in January 1957 to voice Polish criticism of the Warsaw Treaty and the 'Statute of the Unified Command'. The criticism followed an internal Polish memorandum, which was drafted on 3 November 1956 – one day before the second Soviet intervention in Hungary – and which stated that 'the document in its present form grants the Supreme Commander of the United Armed Forces certain rights and obligations, which contradict the idea of the independence and sovereignty of member-states of the Warsaw Treaty'.[146] The Polish leadership had problems with the statute's 'military provisions, as well as different bilateral agreements', which 'require a thorough analysis and revision',[147] but it did not question the existence of the alliance itself, which also served Polish security. The Polish leadership, however, criticised the 'supranational character of the Supreme Commander and his Staff, which does not correspond to the idea of independence and sovereignty of the Warsaw Treaty participating countries', and questioned '[t]he authority of the Supreme Commander', and thus the authority of the Soviet leadership itself.[148]

There was, accordingly, a tension between the Warsaw Treaty's rhetoric of sovereignty, which was modelled after the North Atlantic Treaty, and the statute of the Unified Command, which in practice served to consolidate Soviet hegemony, while reinforcing the bilateral treaties already in place. The Polish proposals were based on a detailed study of NATO's structures, and aimed to clarify the structure within the Joint Command, while curtailing Soviet power. The reaction of Soviet Supreme Commander Marshal Konev to the Polish proposals clearly indicates that the Warsaw Pact was not *really* supposed to function like NATO, as far as he was concerned: 'What do you imagine, that we will make some kind of NATO here?'[149] Its likeness to NATO was in military terms still a mere facade, and the Polish proposals temporarily vanished into oblivion. They would not enter the WP platform until almost ten years later, when they would return with a vengeance. Although the Kremlin still managed to cover up the Warsaw Treaty's discrepancy between rhetoric and reality, it would not succeed in doing so in the long run.

The Polish proposals testify to the fact that Gomulka did not envisage the Polish role in the WP as a subservient one.[150] The Polish leadership continued developing diplomatic initiatives, the most famous of which was the so-called 'Rapacki plan' in 1957, which was a plan by Polish Minister of Foreign Affairs Adam Rapacki to create a nuclear-free zone in the centre of Europe, according to which both Germanys, Czechoslovakia and Poland would agree not to store nuclear weapons.[151] Although the Polish leadership might in the first place have had its own security at heart, and especially the recognition of the much contested Oder–Neisse border, the 'Rapacki plan' was indicative of the Polish propensity to develop initiatives that were both in their own interests *and* in the interests of the Soviet bloc at large: West Germany's abstention from nuclear weapons would, after all, also ensure the security of East Germany and Czechoslovakia. The Polish historian Wanda Jarzabek has coined the phrase 'Gomulka Doctrine' for Gomulka's foreign policy strategy, which was aimed at influencing Soviet bloc policy on the German question in order to ensure the recognition of the Oder–Neisse line.[152] Gomulka would prove particularly adept at doing so within the framework of the WP by linking Poland's foreign policy interests to those of the other WP members.

In the following years Gomulka trod a fine line between appeasing the Polish people on the one hand and the Soviet leadership on the other.[153] Fully aware of the need for the Soviet security guarantee to safeguard the Oder–Neisse border, Gomulka also managed to continue emphasising Polish sovereignty.[154] In order to underscore the Polish independence from Moscow, most of the Soviet officers in the Polish Army were sent with a one-way ticket to Moscow and the number of Soviet advisers was substantially reduced. Meanwhile, the fact that Gomulka had insisted on the continued presence of Soviet troops, and had prevented the situation from spinning out of control as in Hungary, while safeguarding the monopoly of the communist party, also inspired confidence on the Soviet part.[155] Gomulka thus skilfully explored his room for manoeuvre between Soviet and popular demands. The divisions in the leadership diminished, the economy improved and de-Stalinisation took place gradually, but peacefully. Gomulka's successful balancing act and his purges of 16 percent of the party members enabled him to gain complete control of the party and the state by 1958. By the time the Polish United Workers Party held its third congress on 10–19 March 1959, Gomulka's power had been firmly consolidated.[156]

Demilitarising Romania

Meanwhile, the Romanian leaders negotiated with their Soviet comrades on altogether different terms. They expressed no interest in reforming the Warsaw Pact, but wanted instead to use the treaty as an instrument for the withdrawal of Soviet troops from Romanian territory. Although the Romanian party leader Gheorghe Gheorghiu-Dej had been a great admirer of Stalin, and had successfully purged his party of any opponents in Stalinist fashion, he had managed to remain on good terms with Moscow. Khrushchev's secret speech in February 1956 was nevertheless a particularly unpleasant surprise for Gheorghiu-Dej, who first tried to keep it secret and then convened a secret meeting for the party elite in March in order to 'fix the Party line for the next few years' by denouncing not Stalin, but de-Stalinisation.[157] Gheorghiu-Dej accordingly made a virtue out of necessity, since this move enabled him 'to reinforce his own control of the Party and to bind it more closely to his person'.[158] Gheorghiu-Dej's recourse to a paradoxically Stalinist brand of 'national communism' served as an attractive alternative, since it would both appeal to the broader public and enable him to secure his power.[159]

Meanwhile, the Hungarian revolution in 1956 enabled Gheorghiu-Dej to prove his loyalty towards Moscow. Motivated by self-interest instead of subservience, he went out of his way to provide the Kremlin with any military and strategic support it desired, considering it 'a necessary international duty'.[160] The Hungarian Revolution posed a particular threat to both his internal and external security: Gheorghiu-Dej not only feared contagion from the Hungarian liberalisation, which would undermine his own power, but he was also concerned about any claims to parts of Transylvania by a non-communist Hungary. The Romanian leadership had therefore regarded the Soviet intervention in Hungary as a great 'source of satisfaction', since the escalation of the Hungarian Revolution confirmed the Romanian Stalinist course, while discrediting de-Stalinisation.[161]

The Romanian loyalty was amply rewarded when Khrushchev agreed to withdraw Soviet troops from Romania in 1958. It had been an explicit request by defence minister Emil Bodnaras, who had already attempted to convince Khrushchev of this policy in 1955, arguing that it entailed no security risks.[162] It also followed logically from the Soviet declaration, which was formulated on 30 October 1956, according to which the Soviet Union was prepared to 'review' the stationing of Soviet troops on Romanian territory. It was in line with Khrushchev's policy of unilateral troop reductions in order to foster peaceful coexistence, and it seemed to entail no risk for either internal or external security, since Gheorghiu-Dej's power was firmly established and the country was surrounded by other Warsaw Pact states and Yugoslavia, which was, by now, on friendly terms with the Soviet Union. Moreover, Khrushchev could afford to do so, since he had definitively consolidated his power after surviving an attempted coup in June 1957. The former foreign minister, Molotov, had participated in the so called 'anti-party coup', and was expelled as ambassador to Ulan Bator, the capital of Mongolia. Molotov was replaced by his former deputy, Andrei Gromyko, and Khrushchev had assumed the office of premier as well as party leader.[163] Khrushchev thus had his hands free to execute foreign policy according to his own insights.

Possibly mistaking Romanian self-interest for subservience during the Hungarian Revolution, Khrushchev seemed to overlook that the withdrawal of the Red Army would be considered a Soviet concession to Romanian autonomy, and would accordingly increase the Romanian scope for manoeuvre. National communism could now be raised to a higher level. The withdrawal of the Soviet forces also necessitated a tighter grip by the Romanian security forces on the population, since the external threat of Soviet intervention had been removed. The ensuing terror did little to increase the support of Gheorghiu-Dej's regime, so he needed to look elsewhere in order to prop up his popularity and reduce the number of opponents. Openly professing a more autonomous course vis-à-vis Moscow was the ideal solution, since it enabled him to kill two birds with one stone: as the expert on Romania Dennis Deletant puts it, '[d]rawing on the inherent anti-Russian sentiment offered Gheorghiu-Dej a simple way of increasing the regime's popularity whilst at the same time putting a distance between himself and his Soviet master'.[164] The withdrawal of the Soviet Army from Romanian territory thus enabled the Romanian leadership to follow the Soviet model without following the Soviet Union.[165] Khrushchev had characteristically underestimated the repercussions of his own policy measures.

Further demilitarisation

On 24 May 1958 the second PCC meeting was convened in Moscow to rubberstamp the withdrawal of Soviet troops from Romania as well as other Soviet troop reductions. The Polish criticism, however striking, still remained outside the confines of the Warsaw Pact as a matter for bilateral consideration. The Kremlin was at liberty to ignore the Polish criticism, which accordingly gained no force, but it also used the WP as an instrument to approve Poland's 'Rapacki plan' as a 'valuable initiative for the elimination of the danger of the rise of a nuclear war in Europe'. The unanimous support for the Polish contribution to 'détente', and the general praise of the 'realism of the proposal' inadvertently invested the Polish leadership with power.[166] Although dissent was carefully contained and shelved beyond the alliance's confines, the alliance had already provided its Polish member with an instrument to increase its influence over Soviet bloc policy.

The fact that the PCC was convened almost two and a half years after the PCC meeting in January 1956 was, however, particularly embarrassing, since it had been decided to meet at least every six months at that meeting. In this respect the decision making in the WP thus seemed a mere formality, which bore no relation to reality. The secretariat, which was supposed to be established, had not materialised either, nor had the standing committee of foreign affairs experts. The absence of a secretariat or a standing committee seemed convenient for the Soviet leaders, who could turn something into a Warsaw Pact matter, or keep it out of its framework, according to their own wishes. The alliance thus remained a rather empty shell, which was temporarily filled on a biennial basis with Soviet-directed decision making, and then dissolved again. It was, as such, an institution that only existed when the PCC meeting convened; a kind of Sleeping Beauty, waiting to be kissed, but failing to attract any suitors on a regular basis.

With the military intervention in Hungary disappearing into the background, Khrushchev now hoped to curry favour with his allies by *de*militarising the Cold War and by finally carrying out some of the promises of the Soviet resolution on 'Friendship and Cooperation', which was drawn up in the heat of the Hungarian Revolution. Thus Khrushchev aimed also to signal to the NATO countries, which were involved in a military build-up, that he was serious in his quest for a de-escalation of international tensions. Aware of the fact that the dissolution of both NATO and the WP was beyond his reach, Khrushchev now used the Warsaw Pact as a diplomatic ploy to make a statement to the West, by proposing a non-aggression treaty between NATO and the WP.[167] Although the Hungarian Revolution had eroded Soviet power to the extent that some discussion took place within the PCC meeting, the abovementioned Soviet foreign policy initiatives were unanimously approved and eloquently explained in the ensuing communiqué, which underlined the 'complete unity, unbreakable fraternal friendship and cooperation of the socialist countries'.[168]

In the 1958 PCC meeting Khrushchev accordingly seemed to have picked up the thread he was forced to drop during all the upheavals in 1956. Posing once again as Europe's peacemaker, the Soviet leader rallied his allies behind him in another Soviet initiative for a de-escalation of the Cold War. The other allies had little scope for initiative, and unquestioningly agreed with a new, but controversial, move on the German question, according to which 'a summit conference should discuss that part of the German problem which is the responsibility of the four powers, namely, the question of a German peace treaty'.[169] After Khrushchev had once again transmitted his foreign policy directives through the platform provided by the Warsaw Pact, the alliance remained largely dormant till February 1960. The German question, which was, after all, the alliance's *raison d'être*, nevertheless remained on the Kremlin's agenda throughout the 1950s.

Ulbricht and the second Berlin Crisis

The prominence of the German question on the Warsaw Pact's agenda had provided Ulbricht with enormous leverage over Khrushchev, since Khrushchev needed Ulbricht's cooperation to execute his own foreign policy initiatives. According to the influential account of the American historian Hope Harrison, this even facilitated the birth of the GDR as the Soviet Union's 'super ally'.[170] Although the declaration of the end of the state of war with Germany on 25 January 1955, East Germany's role as co-founder of the Warsaw Pact on 15 May 1955, the Soviet-East German 'Treaty on Friendship and Cooperation' in December 1955, the creation of an East German National People's Army and its integration into the WP in January 1956 seemed to bode well for relations between the Soviet Union and the GDR, Khrushchev's secret speech in February 1956 underlined the fundamentally different outlooks of Khrushchev and Ulbricht. The criticism of Stalin's personality cult and the heralding of peaceful coexistence did not serve Ulbricht's aims at all, as he cultivated his personality with relish and preferred the largest possible distance to the FRG to peaceful coexistence.

The uprisings in Poland and the revolution in Hungary seemed to vindicate Ulbricht's scepticism of Khrushchev's conciliatory course, and the 'anti-party coup' in June 1957 further undermined his authority in East German eyes.[171] It had nevertheless enabled Khrushchev to sack his rivals Molotov, Malenkov and Kaganovich, which made Khrushchev the Soviet Union's 'undisputed leader'.[172] However, Ulbricht had managed to rise to the same position *without* having to survive a coup first. The escalation of Khrushchev's liberalising tendencies enabled Ulbricht to assert his own power and weaken his more liberal opposition, and on 3–6 February 1958, during the SED's thirty-fifth plenum, he managed to oust his opponents altogether. The failure of Khrushchev's de-Stalinisation had inadvertently served Ulbricht's Stalinisation, and thus seemed to provide him with extra leverage over Khrushchev. Ulbricht had, after all, been essential in ensuring the stability of the GDR in the wake of Khrushchev's secret speech, and he also used this feat to obtain more economic and political support from the Soviet leadership.[173]

The abovementioned PCC meeting was an attempt to use the German question in order to pave the way for Khrushchev's new foreign policy outlook. The conclusion of a German peace treaty had never materialised after World War II because of the division of Germany. Although the conclusion of a peace treaty with a unified Germany was merely hypothetical, a peace treaty with both Germanys would significantly boost the status of the GDR, as well as underlining Khrushchev's quest for peace. Khrushchev combined his campaign for a German peace treaty with an onslaught on the occupied status of West Berlin, which was a capitalist bulwark in the middle of communist East Germany. Khrushchev formulated this on 10 November 1958 in a speech he delivered in Moscow, in which he partly conceded to Ulbricht's repeated requests to grant the control of the whole of Berlin and its access routes to the GDR if the West failed to agree to a peace treaty. On 27 November Khrushchev even issued a six-month ultimatum according to which 'the Soviet Union would unilaterally transfer its authority in Berlin and over the access routes to the GDR', if the Western powers did not turn it into a demilitarised 'free city', by withdrawing their forces from West Berlin, and by signing a German peace treaty.[174]

By doing so, Khrushchev actually outwitted Ulbricht, since Khrushchev's idea of a 'free city' was less desirable from Ulbricht's point of view than the transfer of control to the GDR. In an act of brinkmanship characteristic of Khrushchev, he confidently declared that the Western powers' failure to recognise the Soviet transfer of power over the access to Berlin to the GDR would 'result immediately in appropriate retaliation' by members of the Warsaw Pact.[175] Thus Khrushchev's adversarial stance on the German question inadvertently raised the stakes of the recently created alliance too, since its members might have to be involved in a superpower confrontation. This marked the beginning of the so-called 'second Berlin Crisis'.

Khrushchev nevertheless told the Soviet ambassador in Washington, Anatoly Dobrynin, that 'war with the United States was inadmissible', but also complained of the potential US nuclear reach to West Germany, and said: 'It's high time that their long arms were cut shorter.'[176] Khrushchev's Berlin ultimatum was primarily a reaction to the rearmament of West Germany, and the Soviet fear of West German access to nuclear arms. As the US historian Marc Trachtenberg convincingly argues, the Kremlin 'wanted [its former allies] to keep West Germany from becoming too powerful', especially by preventing its nuclearisation, and the 'German nuclear question thus lay at the heart of Soviet policy during the Berlin Crisis'.[177] Khrushchev's interests in the Berlin Crisis accordingly did not coincide with Ulbricht's: whereas the former regarded the crisis as a means to prevent the Americans from facilitating West German nuclear ambitions, the latter considered it a way to consolidate the status of East Germany, while also boosting his own power vis-à-vis the Soviet Union. For Khrushchev, the Berlin Crisis was a way to control the power of West Germany within Europe at large, whereas Ulbricht perceived it as a way to increase East German power. For Ulbricht 'West Berlin was the prize, whereas for Khrushchev it was a lever to break the international deadlock'.[178]

Khrushchev's treatment of the Western powers in the second Berlin Crisis nevertheless provided Ulbricht with an example of how to exercise leverage in an asymmetric position of power: just as West Berlin was the 'Achilles heel of the West', so the GDR was the Achilles heel of the Soviet bloc, which in turn invested Ulbricht with power.[179] Indirectly passing messages to the US Administration that 'there is not going to be any war over Berlin', Khrushchev himself was less eager to force the issue.[180] In exchange for dropping his 27 May deadline, Khrushchev agreed to a conference of the foreign ministers of the four occupying countries, which would convene in Geneva on 11 May 1959.[181] He also convened a meeting of the foreign ministers of the WP countries and China on 27–28 April 1959 in order to prepare the conference in a multilateral setting. The Berlin Crisis thus proved a stimulus to multilateral consultations, whereas the WP facilitated a kind of Soviet bloc foreign policy. Before the meeting the Soviet ambassador Pervukhin asked the East German Foreign Ministry to agree 'not to go public with the already completed statute for a demilitarised free city of West Berlin'.[182] Khrushchev clearly wanted to prevent the East German delegation from moving too fast.

The East German delegation demurred and accepted the meeting's communiqué, which was in its favour since it expressed the unanimous support for 'the proposals of the Soviet Union for the conclusion of a peace treaty with Germany and for the elimination of the occupation regime in West Berlin', while underlining the East German participation in the conference.[183] The foreign ministers' conference in Geneva was unprecedented in that both an East and a West German delegation were allowed to participate, albeit at a separate table, which constituted *de facto* recognition of East Germany as well as 'equal status' for both Germanys, much to the resentment of West German Chancellor Konrad Adenauer.[184] Since the conference dragged on until August, Eisenhower attempted to force a breakthrough by inviting Khrushchev to visit the USA. Delighted with the invitation,[185] Khrushchev acquiesced in the status quo when the conference did not yield any concrete results either, much to Ulbricht's frustration, and dropped the ultimatum. Khrushchev's explanation for his patience must have particularly annoyed Ulbricht: 'They didn't recognise us for 16 years, and you want them to recognise you after 10 years. You need to wait at least 17 years.'[186]

Just as Khrushchev kept Ulbricht at bay with the prospect of a resolution of the German question that was favourable to the GDR, so the Western powers kept Khrushchev on a leash by pacifying his quest for reputation by continuing negotiations at superpower level and an invitation to the USA. While occasionally threatening the West with nuclear annihilation, Khrushchev's trip to the USA in September 1959 inspired him with such confidence that he added insult to injury by questioning the Chinese leadership on its treatment of US prisoners during a stop-over in China on his way back.[187] The fact that Khrushchev visited his Chinese comrades *after* his visit to the capitalist superpower was a profound insult to Mao, who had considerably raised Chinese production goals and precipitated 'the socialist transformation of China' by launching the overambitious 'Great Leap Forward' in the spring of 1958.[188] This radical shortcut to communism was considered 'an erroneous policy' by the Kremlin.[189] Instead of being praised for his revolutionary zeal, Khrushchev rebuked Mao for his treatment of prisoners from the 'imperialist enemy'. Mao in turn regarded Khrushchev's enthusiasm about Eisenhower 'as a peace-loving man' as totally misplaced.[190] In Mao's eyes, Khrushchev's

Figure 1.1 Nikita Khrushchev (left) at dinner with, inter alia, Mao Zedong (next to him), 1959
Source: upload.wikimedia.org/wikipedia/commons/2/28/Nikita_Khrushchev%2C_Mao_Zedong%2C_Ho_Chi_Minh_and_Soong_Ching-ling.jpg

behaviour indicated that he had abandoned Marxism-Leninism altogether.[191] It is thus no coincidence that there was, according to the US State Department, 'considerable evidence that in 1959 and early 1960 the Chinese encouraged the East Germans in their desire for a stronger line on the Berlin question than the Soviets were willing to take'.[192] If Khrushchev's Berlin ultimatum was meant to prove to his friends and foes that he was not growing soft on the West, then his behaviour after his trip to the USA did much to undermine that intention.

Ulbricht was able to exercise some leverage while the Soviet leadership was still divided after Stalin's death and when Khrushchev was in a weak position after the unrest in the Soviet bloc created by his secret speech. However, even though this helped Ulbricht in altogether ousting his opposition in 1958 and compelled Khrushchev to take a tougher stance on the German question, Ulbricht's capacity to influence Khrushchev in the period from 1958–60 seemed to have decreased significantly, *pace* Harrison. Khrushchev's procrastination resulted in several summit conferences and an invitation to be the first Soviet leader to visit the USA, but it left Ulbricht empty handed. While Khrushchev was travelling the world, the East Germans kept fleeing from the GDR. The 'super ally' had overplayed its hand, and the German question in nuclear terms still remained unsolved.

Conclusion: an alliance by default?

In the first five years of its existence the Warsaw Pact did, indeed, seem more akin to a 'cardboard castle' than a genuine alliance, particularly considering the way in which the decisions made in 1956, such as the establishment of a secretariat and a standing committee for foreign affairs, never materialised. This cardboard castle seemed to disappear from the scene altogether in between PCC meetings, to enter the stage only when it suited the Soviet leadership. Considering the functioning of the alliance in the 1950s, the views prevailing in Western diplomatic circles at the time and in current historiography seem vindicated. It was, indeed, an instrument of the Soviet leadership, which used it as a 'transmission belt' for its foreign policy directives, such as unilateral force reductions and the proposal of a non-aggression treaty, which served as Soviet propaganda. 'Unanimity' and 'unity' were fanciful phrases to adorn a Soviet facade that no one dared to demolish.

Everything that could undermine Soviet authority was carefully kept outside the scope of the alliance, and only addressed on unilateral or bilateral terms. Neither the Hungarian Revolution nor the Polish criticism on the contradiction between the rhetoric of the Warsaw Treaty and the statute of the Unified Command were allowed to spill over into WP procedures. Despite Khrushchev's new foreign policy, with more input by the Soviet allies, multilateralism seemed conspicuous by its absence. When it became clear that the alliance would not be replaced by a European security system, 'the Warsaw Pact came to stay by default', as Vojtech Mastny puts it.[193]

The WP's replacement by a European security system was, however, not its primary *raison d'être*. It was, after all, founded in reaction to the integration of West Germany into NATO, and its existence was therefore of vital importance to the GDR and other countries with a stake in the German question, such as Poland and Czechoslovakia. The German question accordingly featured not only during its foundation but also in PCC meetings, and both Khrushchev and Ulbricht began to use the alliance as an instrument to define a policy on the German question. Through the foundation of the Warsaw Pact the German question thus became an important topic for all Soviet allies. This also induced a critical analysis of the Polish leaders on the military provisions of the treaty, since the geographical proximity of West Germany raised the Polish stake in a potentially military confrontation. Although the Polish proposals for reforms were shelved, the mere existence of the WP did, at the very least, provide them with a platform to critically examine Soviet foreign policy. Moreover, the Polish Rapacki plan was approved within the WP's framework, which boosted the status of the Polish leadership. The alliance thus began to gain a dynamic of its own.

Moreover, the Warsaw Pact was a product of a genuine change in Soviet foreign policy. The fact that its foundation in 1955 coincided with the Austrian State Treaty, Khrushchev's rapprochement with Tito, and a disarmament proposal illustrates that Khrushchev was serious about establishing international relations on a new footing. The year 1955 represented, in fact, a fundamental paradigm shift in the evolution of the Soviet bloc, which is often ignored in historiography – even more so than Stalin's death in 1953 or the repercussions of de-Stalinisation in 1956. The WP, too, was part of Khrushchev's de-Stalinisation programme, since the foundation of a multilateral alliance that was more than a mere instrument of coercion would have been inconceivable under Stalin. Although the WP was largely dormant in the first five years of its existence, the mere fact that the Eastern European allies could gather in a multilateral setting and were involved, however passively, in Soviet foreign policy, was already a remarkable departure from Stalin's authoritarianism, and the NSWP members also regarded it as such.

Khrushchev's decision to abolish the COMINFORM in 1956 indicates that he intended to treat his Eastern European comrades in a different manner. The mere existence of an Eastern European alliance at least facilitated the promotion from Soviet satellites to 'junior allies'.[194] The simple fact that multilateral meetings were convened, 'constituted a qualitative change with respect to former conditions', as the Hungarian historian Csaba Békés puts it, which would allow the WP to become 'the catalyst for a new era in Soviet-East Central European relations'.[195] This was exactly why the NSWP members genuinely welcomed the foundation of the Warsaw Pact.

The issue has, however, become somewhat clouded since Soviet-East Central European relations spun out of control after Khrushchev's secret speech in February 1956. The image of Soviet tanks in Hungary is difficult to understand in relation to Khrushchev's attempts to establish a more equal kind of international relations. The Soviet declaration on 30 October 1956 was, however, more than a mere propaganda stunt, and led *inter alia* to the withdrawal of Soviet troops from Romania in 1958. Moreover, Khrushchev's consultations with most of his allies during the crisis also indicate a farewell to Soviet unilateralism. His failure to do so within a multilateral framework illustrates both that he still had to grow accustomed to the use of a multilateral institution, and that the WP was simply not intended for *internal* control.

Khrushchev's departure from a Stalinist type of foreign policy turned matters upside down within the communist movement. The rapprochement with Tito went hand in hand with estrangement from Mao, and raised considerable doubts in the eyes of the Albanian leadership. Since the communist movement gradually began to grow apart, the seeds were sown for a more important role for the Warsaw Pact in the next decade. Although the stigmas traditionally imposed upon the Warsaw Pact were to some extent valid up to 1960, the Sleeping Beauty would suddenly gain a life of her own in the early 1960s and Khrushchev's brainchild would become a recalcitrant adolescent. The conventional view of the Warsaw Pact only applies in part to its infancy, and does little to explain what happened in the next three decades. In fact, it has prevented a convincing explanation from materialising in the historiography to date. The following chapters serve to address this hiatus by closely analysing the Warsaw Pact's growth into adulthood from 1960 onwards. Despite its conception as a cardboard castle, the Warsaw Pact was there to stay. This makes an inquiry into its transformation into a genuine alliance all the more imperative.

Notes

1 V. Mastny, '"We Are in a Bind": Polish and Czechoslovak Attempts at Reforming the Warsaw Pact, 1956–69', in C.F. Ostermann (ed.), *Cold War Flashpoints*, Cold War International History Project (CWIHP) Bulletin No. 11 (Washington, 1998), 232.
2 G.H. Snyder, 'The Security Dilemma in Alliance Politics', *World Politics* 36:4 (1984), 463.
3 V. Mastny, 'Soviet Foreign Policy, 1953–62', in M. Leffler and O.A. Westad (eds), *The Cambridge History of the Cold War. Volume I: Origins* (Cambridge, 2010), 317.
4 V. Mastny, 'The Soviet Union and the Origins of the Warsaw Pact in 1955', Parallel History Project on Cooperative Security (PHP), 2003, www.php.isn.ethz.ch/collections/coll_pcc/into_VM.cfm (accessed 18 August 2013).
5 M. Kramer, 'Introduction: International Politics in the Early Post-Stalin Era: A Lost Opportunity, a Turning Point, or More of the Same?' in K. Larres and K. Osgood (eds), *The Cold War after Stalin's Death. A Missed Opportunity for Peace?* (Lanham, 2006), xiii.
6 P. Kenez, *A History of the Soviet Union from the Beginning to the End* (Cambridge, 1999, 2006), 191.
7 See Kenez, *A History of the Soviet Union*, 184–90; and W.J. Tompson, *Khrushchev. A Political Life* (New York, 1995, 1997), 114–43.
8 Cf. A. Knight, *Beria. Stalin's First Lieutenant* (Princeton, 1993), 176–201.

9 Tompson, *Khrushchev*, 115.
10 Kenez, *A History of the Soviet Union*, 187.
11 Mastny, 'Soviet Foreign Policy', 313. They finally did so in July 1953.
12 C. Békés, 'East Central Europe, 1953–56', in Leffler and Westad, *The Cambridge History*, 335.
13 See 'Report on 4 May Disturbances at the Tobacco Depot in Plovdiv, Bulgaria, 7 May 1953', in C.F. Ostermann (ed.), *Uprising in East Germany 1953. The Cold War, the German Question, and the First Major Upheaval behind the Iron Curtain* (Budapest and New York, 2001), 86–89.
14 R.J. Crampton, *A Concise History of Bulgaria* (Cambridge, 1997), 195–96.
15 R.J. Crampton, *A Short History of Modern Bulgaria* (Cambridge, 1987), 181.
16 H.G. Skilling, *Czechoslovakia's Interrupted Revolution* (Princeton, 1976), 26.
17 See for Novotny's and Zhivkov's remarkably similar background and characteristics, Skilling, *Czechoslovakia's Interrupted Revolution*, 29; and Crampton, *Short History*, 177, respectively.
18 See 'Materials for a Meeting of the Organizational Secretariat of the CPCz CC, with Attached Report on Party Activities in Plzen in Connection with the Events of 1 June 1953, 31 July 1953', in Ostermann (ed.), *Uprising in East Germany*, 113–32.
19 Skilling, *Czechoslovakia's Interrupted Revolution*, 31–32.
20 H. Harrison, *Driving the Soviets up the Wall. Soviet-East German Relations, 1953–1961* (Princeton, 2005), 17.
21 W. Loth, *Stalin's Ungeliebtes Kind. Warum Moskau die DDR nicht Wollte* (Berlin, 1994).
22 See 'USSR Council of Ministers Order "On Measures to Improve the Health of the Political Situation in the GDR", 2 June 1953', in Ostermann (ed.), *Uprising in East Germany*, 133–36.
23 Cf. H. Harrison, 'The New Course: Soviet Policy toward Germany and the Uprising in the GDR', in Larres and Osgood (eds), *The Cold War after Stalin's Death*, 193–299.
24 Harrison, *Driving the Soviets up the Wall*, 41.
25 Ibid., 44.
26 Cf. Mastny, 'Soviet Foreign Policy', 317.
27 Cf. Mastny, 'The Soviet Union and the Origins of the Warsaw Pact'.
28 Letter from Khrushchev to Ulbricht, Stiftung Archiv der Parteien und Massenorganisationen der DDR im Bundesarchiv (SAPMO-BArch), DY 30/3385, 16.
29 V. Mastny and M. Byrne (eds), *A Cardboard Castle? An Inside History of the Warsaw Pact, 1955–1991* (Budapest and New York, 2005), 77.
30 Letter from Ulbricht to Khrushchev, SAPMO-BArch, DY 30/3385, 1–2.
31 Mastny, 'The Soviet Union and the Origins of the Warsaw Pact'.
32 Minutes of the Politburo Session of 18 May 1955, Arhivele Naționale Istorice Centrale ale României (ANIC), Romanian Workers' Party Central Committee (RWP CC), Chancellery (C), 37/1955, 6.
33 Conversation between Zhivkov, Maurer, and Ceausescu, 14 February 1966, ANIC, RWP CC, International Relations (IR), 14/1966, 12.
34 A. Lalaj, 'Albanien und der Warschauer Pakt', in T. Diedrich et al. (eds), *Der Warschauer Pakt: Von der Gründung bis zum Zusammenbruch 1955 bis 1991* (Berlin, 2009), 27–42.
35 E. Biberaj, *Albania: A Socialist Maverick* (Boulder, 1990), 20.
36 Cf. V. Mastny, 'The Warsaw Pact: an Alliance in Search of a Purpose', in M.A. Heiss and S.V. Papacosma (eds), *NATO and the Warsaw Pact: Intrabloc Conflicts* (Ohio, 2008), 143.
37 Minutes of the Politburo Session of 18 May 1955, ANIC, RWP CC, C, 37/1955, 12.
38 'The Warsaw Treaty', 14 May 1955, in Mastny and Byrne (eds), *Cardboard Castle*, 77–79.

39 Cf. Békés, 'East Central Europe', 341.
40 'North Atlantic Treaty', www.nato.int/cps/en/natolive/official_texts_17120.htm (accessed 19 August 2013).
41 These principles became questionable after the accession of Greece and Turkey to NATO on 22 October 1951.
42 See V. Mastny, *Learning from the Enemy. NATO as a Model of the Warsaw Pact*, Zürcher Beiträge zur Sicherheitspolitik und Konfliktforschung Nr. 58 (Zurich, 2001), 9–10, for a more detailed comparison of NATO and the WP.
43 'The Warsaw Treaty'.
44 Ibid.
45 Mastny, '"We Are in a Bind"', 230.
46 Mastny, 'The Warsaw Pact', 143.
47 'North Atlantic Treaty'.
48 Minutes of the Politburo Session of 18 May 1955, ANIC, RWP CC, C, 37/1955, 6.
49 Mastny, 'The Soviet Union and the Origins of the Warsaw Pact'.
50 Minutes of the Politburo Session of 18 May 1955, ANIC, RWP CC, C, 37/1955, 6–7.
51 Mastny, 'Soviet Foreign Policy', 319.
52 S. Rajak, 'The Cold War in the Balkans, 1945–56', in Leffler and Westad, *The Cambridge History*, 213. For all quotes, see also the whole article: 198–220. See also S. Rajak, *Yugoslavia and the Soviet Union in the Early Cold War. Reconciliation, Comradeship, Confrontation, 1953–1957* (London and New York, 2010).
53 V. Mastny, *The Cold War and Soviet Insecurity. The Stalin Years* (Oxford, 1996), 32.
54 'The Warsaw Treaty'.
55 Mastny, *The Cold War and Soviet Insecurity*, 32.
56 Mastny, 'The Soviet Union and the Origins of the Warsaw Pact'.
57 See for this connection: 'Report of the RWP CC on the discussion of the decisions of the Warsaw conference of European States on peace and security in Europe', 21 May 1955, ANIC, RWP CC, C, 37/1955, 27.
58 Rajak, 'Cold War in the Balkans', 213.
59 Mastny, 'Soviet Foreign Policy', 318.
60 Mastny, 'The Soviet Union and the Origins of the Warsaw Pact'.
61 Mastny, 'Soviet Foreign Policy', 319.
62 Ibid.
63 'Soviet Foreign Ministry Notes on Current Issues in Soviet Global Policy', 4 January 1956, in C. Békés, M. Byrne and J.M. Rainer (eds), *The 1956 Hungarian Revolution: A History in Documents* (Budapest and New York, 2002), 106–10.
64 This was formulated in 'North Atlantic Council Document C-M(56)110: "The Thaw in Eastern Europe"', 24 September 1965, ibid., 168–77.
65 Békés, 'East Central Europe', 342.
66 V. Mastny, 'Editorial note', PHP, www.php.isn.ethz.ch/collections/colltopic.cfm?lng=en&id=17484&navinfo=14465 (accessed 25 August 2013).
67 'Declaration by the Chairman of the Council of Ministers of the Hungarian People's Republic (András Hegedüs) at the Meeting of the Political Consultative Committee', 27 January 1956, PHP, www.php.isn.ethz.ch/collections/colltopic.cfm?lng=en&id=17507&navinfo=14465 (accessed 25 August 2013).
68 'Communiqué on the Session of the Political Consultative Committee of the Warsaw Treaty Powers', 28 January 1956, PHP, www.php.isn.ethz.ch/collections/colltopic.cfm?lng=en&id=17533&navinfo=14465 (accessed 25 August 2013).
69 Ibid.
70 Mastny, '"We Are in a Bind"', 230.
71 Mastny, 'The Soviet Union and the Origins of the Warsaw Pact'.

72 'Statute of the Warsaw Treaty Unified Command', 7 September 1955, in Mastny and Byrne (eds), *Cardboard Castle*, 80–82.
73 'Text for publication about the creation of a Unified Command, strictly confidential', SAPMO-BArch, DY 30/3385, 25–26.
74 'Protocol about the creation of a Unified Command, strictly confidential', SAPMO-BArch, DY 30/3385, 19–21.
75 'Draft of the Decision to Hold a Meeting of the Political Consultative Committee', 11 January 1956, PHP, www.php.isn.ethz.ch/collections/colltopic.cfm?lng=en&navinfo=14465 (accessed 25 August 2013).
76 'Declaration by the First Deputy Prime Minister of the German Democratic Republic (Walter Ulbricht) at the Meeting of the Political Consultative Committee', 27 January 1956, PHP, www.php.isn.ethz.ch/collections/colltopic.cfm?lng=en&id=17508&navinfo=14465 (accessed 25 August 2013).
77 Z.K. Brzezinski, *The Soviet Bloc: Unity and Conflict. Revised and Enlarged Edition* (Harvard, 1967), 458–59.
78 'Statement by Chen Yun at the Signing of the Declaration of the Participating States of the Warsaw Treaty', 28 January 1956, PHP, www.php.isn.ethz.ch/collections/colltopic.cfm?lng=en&id=17523&navinfo=14465 (accessed 25 August 2013).
79 'Closing Words of the Presiding Chairman of the Albanian Council of Ministers (Mehmet Shehu)', 28 January 1956, PHP, www.php.isn.ethz.ch/collections/colltopic.cfm?lng=en&id=17522&navinfo=14465 (accessed 25 August 2013).
80 Cf. Kenez, *A History of the Soviet Union*, 192.
81 Quoted in S. Radchenko, *Two Suns in the Heavens: The Sino-Soviet Struggle for Supremacy, 1962–1967* (Stanford, 2009), 10.
82 Mastny, 'Soviet Foreign Policy', 320.
83 Q. Zhai, 'Coexistence and Confrontation: Sino-Soviet Relations after Stalin', in Larres and Osgood (eds.), *The Cold War after Stalin's Death*, 178–79.
84 Zhai, 'Coexistence and Confrontation', 180.
85 'Reply of the CC of the CCP to information of the CPSU CC on 21 June 1960 (top secret)', 10 September 1960, SAPMO-BArch, DY 30/3604, 22.
86 Zhai, 'Coexistence and Confrontation', 179.
87 'Reply of the CC of the CCP to information of the CPSU CC on 21 June 1960 (top secret)', 10 September 1960, SAPMO-BArch, DY 30/3604, 53–54.
88 Békés, 'East Central Europe', 342.
89 Ibid.
90 Crampton, *Short History*, 180.
91 Skilling, *Czechoslovakia's Interrupted Revolution*, 36.
92 Rajak, 'Cold War in the Balkans', 218.
93 A. Paczkowski, *The Spring Will Be Ours. Poland and the Poles from Occupation to Freedom* (Pennsylvania, 2003), 266.
94 Ibid., 267.
95 Ibid., 267; and J. Granville, *The First Domino. International Decision-making during the Hungarian Crisis of 1956* (Texas, 2004), 48.
96 Granville, *The First Domino*, 48.
97 Paczkowski, *The Spring Will Be Ours*, 271.
98 Ibid., 272.
99 Granville, *The First Domino*, 60.
100 A. Kemp-Welch, *Poland under Communism. A Cold War History* (Cambridge, 2008), 96.
101 Quoted in Kemp-Welch, *Poland under Communism*, 97.
102 Zhai, 'Coexistence and Confrontation', 181.
103 'Reply of the CC of the CCP to information of the CPSU CC on 21 June 1960 (top secret)', 10 September 1960, SAPMO-BArch, DY 30/3604, 25.

104 Cf. Paczkowski, *The Spring Will Be Ours*, 275; and Granville, *The First Domino*, 52–53.
105 For example, 'Meeting of a delegation of the CPSU and the CCP', July 1963, SAPMO-BArch, DY 30/3608, 71.
106 Letter from CPSU CC to CCP CC, 5 November 1960, SAPMO-BArch, DY 30/3605, 190.
107 Kemp-Welch, *Poland under Communism*, 98.
108 Letter from CPSU CC to CCP CC, 5 November 1960, SAPMO-BArch, DY 30/3605, 189.
109 Paczkowski, *The Spring Will Be Ours*, 275.
110 'Reply of the CC of the CCP to information of the CPSU CC on 21 June 1960 (top secret)', 10 September 1960, SAPMO-BArch, DY 30/3604, 25. Cf. Zhai, 'Coexistence and Confrontation', 182.
111 Kemp-Welch, *Poland under Communism*, 102.
112 Ibid.
113 'Jan Svoboda's Notes on the CPSU CC Presidium Meeting with Satellite Leaders', 24 October 1956, in Békés *et al.* (eds), *Hungarian Revolution*, 223–24.
114 See P. Kenez, 'Khrushchev and Hungary in 1956', in C. Fink *et al.* (eds), *1956: European and Global Perspectives* (Leipzig, 2006), 108.
115 Békés, 'East Central Europe', 348.
116 'Working Notes from the Session of the CPSU CC Presidium', 23 October 1956, in Békés *et al.* (eds), *Hungarian Revolution*, 217–18.
117 Békés, 'East Central Europe', 349.
118 'Report from Anastas Mikoyan and Mikhaik Suslov to the CPSU CC Presidium on Talks with HWP Leaders', 26 October 1956, in Békés *et al.* (eds), *Hungarian Revolution*, 239.
119 'Declaration by the Government of the USSR on the Principles of Development and Further Strengthening of Friendship and Cooperation between the Soviet Union and Other Socialist States', 30 October 1956, in Békés *et al.* (eds), *Hungarian Revolution*, 301.
120 'Working Notes from the Session of the CPSU CC Presidium', 30 October 1956, in Békés *et al.* (eds), *Hungarian Revolution*, 296.
121 Cf. A. Kyrow and B. Zselicky, 'Ungarnkrise 1956. Lagebeurteilung und Vorgehen der sowjetischen Führung und Armee', in W. Heinemann and N. Wiggershaus (eds), *Das internationale Krisenjahr 1956: Polen, Ungarn, Suez* (München, 1999), 112–13.
122 C. Békés, 'Cold War, Détente, and the 1956 Hungarian Revolution', in Larres and Osgood (eds), *The Cold War after Stalin's Death*, 223.
123 Békés *et al.* (eds), *Hungarian Revolution*, 210.
124 'Declaration by the Government of the USSR on the Principles of Development and Further Strengthening of Friendship and Cooperation between the Soviet Union and Other Socialist States', 30 October 1956, in Békés *et al.* (eds), *Hungarian Revolution*, 302.
125 'Reply of the CC of the CCP to information of the CPSU CC on 21 June 1960 (top secret)', 10 September 1960, SAPMO-BArch, DY 30/3604, 25–26.
126 Ibid., 25.
127 Zhai, 'Coexistence and Confrontation', 182.
128 'Meeting of a delegation of the CPSU and the CCP', July 1963, SAPMO-BArch, DY 30/3608, 72.
129 'Nikita Khrushchev's Recollections of Discussions between the CPSU CC Presidium and Hungarian Leaders János Kádár and Ferenc Münnich in Moscow', 3 November 1953, in Békés *et al.* (eds), *Hungarian Revolution*, 355.
130 'Working Notes from the CPSU CC Presidium Session with the Participation of János Kádár and Ferenc Münnich', 2 November 1956, in Békés *et al.* (eds), *Hungarian Revolution*, 337.

131 'Notes of Yugoslav Ambassador to Moscow Veljko Micunovic on Negotiations between Yugoslav and Soviet Leaders at Brioni', 3 November 1956, in Békés *et al.* (eds), *Hungarian Revolution*, 350.
132 For example, A. Kemp-Welch, 'Eastern Europe: Stalinism to Solidarity', in M. Leffler and O.A. Westad (eds.), *The Cambridge History of the Cold War. Volume II: Crisis and Détente* (Cambridge, 2010), 219.
133 See 'Telegram from Imre Nagy to Diplomatic Missions in Budapest Declaring Hungary's Neutrality', 1 November 1956, in Békés *et al.* (eds), *Hungarian Revolution*, 332.
134 'Declaration by the Government of the USSR', 300–1.
135 Minutes of a conversation between a delegation of the CPSU CC and the AWP CC, 12 November 1960, ANIC, RWP CC, IR, 76/1960, 130.
136 A. Lalaj, '"Albania is not Cuba." Sino-Albanian Summits and the Sino-Soviet Split', in C.F. Ostermann (ed.), *Inside China's Cold War*, CWIHP Bulletin No. 16 (Washington, 2007/2008), 194.
137 L.M. Lüthi, *The Sino-Soviet Split: Cold War in the Communist World* (Princeton, 2008), 201.
138 Biberaj, *Albania*, 34.
139 Letter from Albanian CC to all party organisations, April 1956, SAPMO-BArch, DY 30/3589, 32–35.
140 'Speech of comrade Enver Hoxha, First Secretary of the CC of the Albanian Workers Party, at the conference of representatives of the communist and workers parties in Moscow', 16 November 1960, ANIC, RWP CC, IR, 76/1960, 46.
141 Lalaj, 'Albanien und der Warschauer Pakt', 32.
142 Letter from Hoxha to Ulbricht, Tirana, 7 October 1958, SAPMO-BArch, DY 30/3589, 43.
143 W.E. Griffith, *Albania and the Sino-Soviet Rift* (Massachusetts, 1963), 28.
144 'Parallels in Sino-Soviet-Albanian Ideological Positions, 1956–59', in Griffith, *Albania and the Sino-Soviet Rift*, 29–34.
145 X. Liu and V. Mastny (eds), 'China and Eastern Europe, 1960s–1980s. Proceedings of the International Symposium: Reviewing the History of Chinese-East European Relations from the 1960s to the 1980s. Beijing, 24–26 March 2004', *Beiträge zur Sicherheitspolitik und Konfliktforschung Nr. 72* (Zürich, 2004), 36.
146 'Gen. Jan Drzewiecki's Critique of the Statute of the Unified Command', 3 November 1956, in Mastny and Byrne (eds), *Cardboard Castle*, 84–86.
147 'Polish Memorandum on Reform of the Warsaw Pact', 10 January 1957, in Mastny and Byrne (eds), *Cardboard Castle*, 87–90.
148 Mastny, '"We Are in a Bind"', 231.
149 Ibid., 232.
150 W. Jarzabek, *Poland in the Warsaw Pact 1955–1991: An Appraisal of the Role of Poland in the Political Structures of the Warsaw Pact*, Parallel History Project on Cooperative Security, 2010, www.php.isn.ethz.ch/collections/coll_poland/Introduction.cfm?navinfo=111216 (accessed 20 August 2013).
151 Cf. W. Jarzabek, *Hope and Reality. Poland and the Conference on Security and Cooperation in Europe, 1964–1989*, CWIHP Working Paper No. 56 (Washington, 2008), 4.
152 Jarzabek, *Hope and Reality*, 7.
153 D. Selvage, 'Khrushchev's November 1958 Ultimatum: New Evidence from the Polish Archives', in C. Ostermann (ed.), *Cold War Flashpoints*, CWIHP Bulletin No. 11 (Washington, 1998), 201, for a description of his ambivalent relationship with Khrushchev.
154 Granville, *The First Domino*, 119.
155 Paczkowski, *The Spring Will Be Ours*, 277.
156 Ibid., 286.

157 D. Deletant and M. Ionescu, *Romania and the Warsaw Pact: 1955-* Working Paper No. 43 (Washington, 2004), 9.
158 Ibid.
159 See for an analysis of Gheorghiu-Dej's personal motives behind munism: M. Retegan, *In the Shadow of the Prague Spring: Rom Policy and the Crisis of Czechoslovakia, 1968* (Oxford, 2000), 22; a neanu, *Gheorghiu-Dej and the Romanian Workers' Party: From De- ...zation to the Emergence of National Communism*, CWIHP Working Paper No. 37 (Washington, 2002).
160 Deletant and Ionescu, *Romania and the Warsaw Pact*, 61.
161 Tismaneanu, *Gheorghiu-Dej*, 20–21.
162 Deletant and Ionescu, *Romania and the Warsaw Pact*, 13–14.
163 Kenez, *A History of the Soviet Union*, 116.
164 Deletant and Ionescu, *Romania and the Warsaw Pact*, 19.
165 Ibid., 16.
166 'Draft declaration of the member states of the Warsaw Pact', May 1958, SAPMO-BArch, DY 30/3392, 34.
167 'Draft of a non-aggression pact', 1958, SAPMO-BArch, DY 30/3392, 19–22.
168 'Record of the Decisions of the Political Consultative Committee', 24 May 1958, PHP, www.php.isn.ethz.ch/collections/colltopic.cfm?lng=en&id=17642&navinfo=14465 (accessed 25 August 2013).
169 'Declaration', 24 May 1958, PHP, www.php.isn.ethz.ch/collections/colltopic.cfm?lng=en&id=17545&navinfo=14465 (accessed 25 August 2013).
170 Harrison, *Driving the Soviets up the Wall*, 12.
171 See for the anti-party coup, W. Taubman, *Khrushchev. The Man and his Era* (London, 2003), 317–23.
172 Taubman, *Khrushchev*, 364.
173 Harrison, *Driving the Soviets up the Wall*, 92–94.
174 W.R. Smyser, *From Yalta to Berlin. The Cold War Struggle over Germany* (London, 1999), 138–39.
175 Harrison, *Driving the Soviets up the Wall*, 106.
176 A. Dobrynin, *In Confidence. Moscow's Ambassador to America's Six Cold War Presidents (1962–1986)* (New York, 1995), 51–52. Cf. Taubman, *Khrushchev*, 403: 'The prospect of West Germany's getting nuclear weapons was the last straw.'
177 M. Trachtenberg, *A Constructed Peace. The Making of the European Settlement, 1945–1963* (Princeton, 1999), 252–53.
178 Taubman, *Khrushchev*, 405.
179 Harrison, *Driving the Soviets up the Wall*, 111.
180 Taubman, *Khrushchev*, 408.
181 Ibid., 412.
182 Letter from Winzer to Ulbricht *et al.*, 23 April 1959, SAPMO-BArch, DY 30/3392, 3–4.
183 'Draft communiqué for the conference of foreign ministers', SAPMO-BArch, DY 30/3392, 7.
184 Smyser, *From Yalta to Berlin*, 144.
185 Taubman, *Khrushchev*, 416.
186 Harrison, *Driving the Soviets up the Wall*, 124.
187 V.M. Zubok and C. Pleshakov, *Inside the Kremlin's Cold War. From Stalin to Khrushchev* (Harvard, 1996).
188 S. Guang Zhang, 'The Sino-Soviet Alliance and the Cold War in Asia, 1954–62', in Leffler and Westad (eds), *The Cambridge History*, 366–67; F. Dikötter, *Mao's Great Famine. The History of China's Most Devastating Catastrophe, 1958–62* (New York, 2010), 84–87; and Zhai 'Coexistence and Confrontation', 183.

189 Minutes of a session of the leadership of the Partito Comunista Italiano (PCI), 8 July 1960, Fondazione Istituto Gramsci, Archivio del Partito Comunista Italiano (FIG APC), Leadership, 1960, mf 024, 754.
190 'Second intervention by Deng Xiaoping', 24 November 1960, FIG APC, Moscow Conference, November 1960, III, mf 0474, 2933.
191 Zhai 'Coexistence and Confrontation', 186.
192 Harrison, *Driving the Soviets up the Wall*, 134.
193 Mastny, *Learning from the Enemy*, 11.
194 Cf. Z.K. Brzezinski, *The Soviet Bloc: Unity and Conflict. Revised and Enlarged Edition* (Harvard, 1967), 433.
195 Békés, 'East Central Europe', 341.

2 The Warsaw Pact in the shadow of the Sino–Soviet split

Better be dead on your feet than alive on your knees.[1]

(Albanian proverb)

At the beginning of the 1960s the Soviet Union was confronted with a simultaneous challenge from two opposite ends of the spectrum: on the one hand the Soviet leadership was increasingly undermined by the adversarial, extremist stance of its Chinese 'comrades', who regarded themselves as Lenin's real heirs, and on the other hand it had to deal with the increasing defiance of its smallest Warsaw Pact comrade, Albania. United in their criticism of Soviet 'revisionism', the Chinese behemoth and the Albanian dwarf turned in tandem against their official ally. Caught in the middle of this unlikely partnership, the WP became an increasingly important base for support of the Soviet Union, which was further undermined by the Romanian 'Declaration of Independence' in 1964. The Soviet leadership therefore had to tread its ground carefully in order not to alienate any more allies and end up in isolation. Khrushchev also had to deal with the second Berlin Crisis in this period, but 'the German Question was not considered pressing' in relation to the potential repercussions of a schism between China and the Soviet Union.[2]

As the US foreign policy adviser Zbigniew Brzezinski states, 'it is difficult to exaggerate the historical significance of the Sino-Soviet conflict',[3] and this certainly applies to the Sino–Soviet split in relation to the Warsaw Pact, which has not yet been studied in great depth. This chapter will therefore examine the impact of the Sino–Soviet split on the dynamics within the WP in the first half of the 1960s, before returning to the German question in the next chapter.

Communist unity under pressure

At the beginning of the 1960s Khrushchev still viewed the international position of the communist bloc through somewhat rose-coloured glasses. He regarded his talks with US President Dwight D. Eisenhower at Camp David in the autumn of 1959 as a breakthrough, since 'the cold war ice was oken',[4] and he was eager to share the enthusiasm of his perceived diplomatic success with his Warsaw Pact allies at the third meeting of the Political Consultative Committee in Moscow on 4 February 1960. With the motto 'better to coexist, than not to exist',[5] Khrushchev did not seem to have many ideological qualms about his rapprochement with the US president. On the contrary, he thought that the 'correlation of forces' had so obviously turned to the Soviet Union's advantage that a peace treaty with Germany and disarmament were within reach, and that 'peaceful coexistence' with the USA would by no means undermine the 'increased unity within the framework of the united socialist camp'.[6]

Retrospectively, Khrushchev's upbeat assessment of the international situation and of communist unity seems tragic irony, since the PCC meeting in question also marks the beginning of open polemics between the Soviet and the Chinese leadership. The rapprochement with the USA went hand in hand with an estrangement from China, because the Chinese leadership regarded Khrushchev's optimism about relations with the USA as a sell-out of the communist ideology. There had already been friction between both communist parties since Khrushchev's secret speech in February 1956, as de-Stalinisation and peaceful coexistence both contradicted Mao's increasingly radical politics at home, as we saw in the previous chapter. It therefore hardly seems a coincidence that Mao had sent his most left-wing representative, Kang Sheng, as an observer to the PCC meeting, to formulate the Chinese position on world politics in a speech.

Sheng pretended to support the Soviet leadership on the surface, but his repeated emphasis on 'American imperialism' as 'the principal enemy of world peace' and his warning 'against U.S. double-dealing' profoundly undermined Khrushchev's stance towards the USA. Moreover, his conclusion 'that revisionism is the main danger in the present communist movement and that it is necessary to wage a resolute struggle against revisionism' sounded particularly ominous.[7] It is important to note that the Chinese leadership decided to criticise the Soviet position openly for the first time within the context of the Warsaw Pact. The Soviet leaders were accordingly challenged within the confines of their own alliance.

Khrushchev also used the Warsaw Pact to outwit China, and on the same evening as Sheng's speech he openly denounced China at a banquet held in honour of the participants of the PCC in front of more than 500 people, while comparing the Chinese leadership with 'a worn out rubber boot, which one can only throw in a corner'.[8] When the Chinese leadership flouted unwritten rules within the WP by publishing Sheng's speech in full in a Chinese editorial, a point of no return in Sino-Soviet relations seemed to have been reached. It was, however, not so much the publication of Sheng's speech that was 'a landmark in the evolving Sino-Soviet dispute going public',[9] but rather Khrushchev's public denunciation of China at the banquet, which seemed a rehearsal of the Soviet stance at the third Romanian Party Congress in June 1960. By using the WP as a playing field for their dispute, before it had

Figure 2.1 Gheorghe Gheorghiu-Dej and Nikita Khrushchev at the Bucharest Conference, 28 June 1960
Source: commons.wikimedia.org/wiki/File:Gheorghiu-Dej_%26_Khrushchev_at_Bucharest%27s_Baneasa_Airport_(June_1960).jpg

reached the communist movement at large, both leaderships inadvertently increased the importance of the alliance.

In April of the same year the Chinese leadership astonished its Soviet colleagues by publishing the so-called 'Lenin Polemics' in Chinese newspapers, which amounted to a 'diatribe against Soviet revisionism'.[10] Under the provocative title 'Long Live Leninism', Mao openly challenged Khrushchev's leadership of the communist camp by criticising de-Stalinisation and questioning the Soviet course towards world revolution, while claiming to be the true heir to Leninism himself.[11] Khrushchev's continued belief in peaceful coexistence, even after the discovery of an American spy plane on 1 May 1960 had nipped a scheduled superpower summit in Paris in the bud, further contributed to Chinese scepticism about the Soviet course.[12] It was in this potentially explosive setting that the third Romanian Party Congress in Bucharest, to which all communist parties were invited, took place on 20–22 June 1960. At this conference the Chinese delegation openly expressed its disagreement with the Soviet and most other delegations on peaceful coexistence and 'the non-inevitability of war'.[13] Since the Soviet leadership seized the opportunity to criticise Chinese policies openly and recover its authority, the conference turned into the first open confrontation between China and the Soviet Union.

At this stage, the Kremlin still seemed to have the upper hand, since the North Korean, North Vietnamese and Albanian leaders were the only ones not to condemn the Chinese policies. The Albanian delegates were, however, careful not to support the Chinese position either, and approached both parties critically.[14] The absence of their leader, Enver Hoxha, was, however, an unprecedented act of defiance vis-à-vis the Kremlin.[15] Despite the overwhelming support for the Soviet stance, the conference therefore did not bode well for the Kremlin: although the North Korean and North Vietnamese positions could be explained in terms of their geographical proximity to China, the Albanian lack of support for the Soviet position implied not only that the communist bloc had ceased to be monolithic, but that the Soviet bloc lacked coherence, too.

Albanian defiance

The Albanian stance at the Bucharest conference was particularly striking, as it was the only WP member that had not unequivocally rallied behind the Soviet Union in denouncing China. The Albanian leadership thus seemed to capitalise on its intensified relations with China since the Hungarian Revolution in 1956. The split within the communist movement threatened to turn into a split within the Warsaw Pact too, in which the smallest Soviet ally played the largest role. The Albanian leadership was, nevertheless, still too divided at this stage to side definitively with China.

Khrushchev nevertheless overlooked this nuance, and decided to cut economic aid for Albania and withdraw some of its specialists straight after the conference.[16] This characteristically rash decision gave Hoxha's pro-Stalinist faction the upper hand during inner-party struggles that summer, in which the pro-Khrushchevite wing was decisively defeated.[17] Moreover, the party showed 'an ever increasing inclination [...] to the politics of the People's Republic of China', and those party members who voiced criticism of the Chinese position, such as Lyri Belishova and Koço Tashko, were purged.[18] The Chinese leadership particularly welcomed this move,[19] which the Soviet leaders strongly denounced.[20] At the same time, both China and Albania turned inwards. In both countries increasing radicalisation went hand in hand with severe travel restrictions, which hardly allowed foreign communists any scope for manoeuvre.[21]

When all other Eastern European leaders also cut economic aid to Albania, the Albanian leadership was forced to turn to China for further economic aid. Thus Khrushchev had ironically undermined his own position by inadvertently weakening the pro-Khrushchevite faction and enabling the Sino-Albanian friendship. This friendship was mutually advantageous: Mao had gained a cheap and loyal ally,[22] and Albania had found such a distant protector, that it would not 'become a puppet of its protector but rather would increase its own degree of independence of maneuver in foreign and domestic affairs'.[23]

Meanwhile, Khrushchev had committed the equally 'self-defeating blunder' of unilaterally withdrawing the approximately 1,400 Soviet specialists from China on 18 July, thus undermining the potential 'institutional and human leverage over the PRC', which the Soviet Union had built up in the course of ten years.[24] According to the Kremlin, the Chinese mistrust, disrespect and hostility made it impossible for the Soviet specialists to continue their work.[25] At the same time, the Albanian leadership attempted to 'mediate' between the two in a letter written to both parties at the end of August 1960, by emphasising the 'vital importance' of reaching an agreement and advising both parties 'to do everything to mend the differences of opinion' before the international Moscow conference of communist countries in November 1960. They also used the letter to underline their independent stance, since 'the Albanian Workers Party has not joined the opinion of the majority of parties', which denoted an implicit farewell to democratic centralism.[26]

It is unlikely that the Albanians expected any concrete results, but it is remarkable that the Albanians were the first to use the incipient Sino–Soviet estrangement in order to strengthen their own position and emphasise their autonomy vis-à-vis the Soviet Union. At the same time, the Albanian leadership sent a letter to the Kremlin on 2 August in which they 'accused Soviet diplomats in Albania for "interfering in the internal affairs of the AWP [Albanian Workers Party]"', since they had talked to Albanian party members about the future of the AWP, thus underlining their autonomy yet again.[27] Professing to mediate, the Albanian leaders seemed primarily interested in precipitating the Sino–Soviet split, as it would force the Kremlin to take smaller allies more seriously.

A few days before the Moscow conference the Soviet and Albanian leaders met in a vain attempt to mend matters. The 'Yugoslav question', the ouster of Lyri Belishova, and a dispute about the naval base in the Albanian town Vlorë, which was manned with Soviet submarines, took centre stage.[28] Hoxha's complaint about a quarrel between Soviet and Albanian officers, which had started after the Bucharest conference, led Khrushchev to suggest removing the base with Albanian approval, which Hoxha considered a threat.[29] Whereas Khrushchev tried to prove that he had Albanian interests at heart, by emphasising his insistence on including Albania in the WP in 1955, Hoxha kept hammering on the Soviet 'threat' of removing the naval base, even repeating Mehmet Shehu's suggestion several times 'to convene a meeting of the Warsaw Pact'.[30] Rather than reducing the tension before the Moscow meeting, the Albanian leadership had become the first NSWP member to suggest the convention of a PCC meeting, thus using the Warsaw Pact as a new arena for Soviet–Albanian disagreements. The Albanian membership of the WP thus seemed to turn into a liability.

Some half-hearted attempts to patch up the differences during the Moscow conference in November 1960 had little effect, and the Albanian leadership unambiguously sided with the Chinese against the Soviet Union from the Moscow conference onwards. It was especially 'the attitude of the Soviet comrades [...] concerning the Yugoslav question' that was considered 'not only impossible, but also opportunistic and dangerous', while Khrushchev was branded a 'Revisionist'.[31] The Polish leader Gomulka nevertheless also introduced the Warsaw Pact into the polemics, by arguing that 'this question should be discussed in the framework of the Warsaw Pact'.[32] Hoxha in turn filed an official complaint against the Soviet leadership and other 'fraternal parties', such as the Polish one, for using 'an incorrect and uncomradely jargon vis-à-vis the Albanian Workers Party'.[33] At the same time he shouted at Khrushchev throughout the conference and rebuked him for the withdrawal of economic aid, while exclaiming that 'while the rats could eat in the Soviet Union, the Albanian people were starving to death, because the leadership of the Albanian Labour Party had not bent to the will of the Soviet leadership'.[34]

Despite the profound disagreements, the Moscow conference still resulted in a common declaration, which repeatedly stressed the fact that all communist parties were 'sovereign', and 'independent', and had 'equal rights'.[35] Although this so-called 'Moscow Declaration' primarily reflected an attempt to present a united front to the non-communist world, its contents would come to haunt the Kremlin. According to the Italian Communist Party, which strongly rebuked the Chinese stance, the document represented a severely diluted compromise after the presentation of 350 amendments, and as such 'showed the weakness of the communist movement'.[36] Meanwhile, Hoxha would explore the scope for manoeuvre, which the Sino–Soviet tensions had created, to the full.

The Albanian Fourth Party Congress

The period after the Moscow Conference marked a new course in Albanian foreign policy, which heralded a further deterioration in Soviet-Albanian relations. While Hoxha's personality cult was flourishing, Khrushchev's name had almost 'disappeared' from the Albanian press, 'the struggle against revisionism in Belgrade' had intensified, and any encounter with 'Soviet comrades' was avoided.[37] At the same time, the Albanian leaders were actively engaging in talks with the Chinese leader Zhou Enlai in order to define their position vis-à-vis the 'revisionist' Khrushchev. Zhou Enlai at this stage still emphasised that Albania was a member of the Warsaw Pact, and that it therefore would be 'inappropriate for us to interfere in this [military aid] matter', and even suggested that it 'mediate' between Albania and the Soviet Union.[38] Although the Chinese leadership still trod its ground carefully vis-à-vis the Soviet Union, the Albanians seemed quite ready to force a break with the Kremlin.

The recently reshuffled Albanian leadership used its Fourth Party Conference, which began on 13 February 1961 and to which all communist parties had been invited, to define a new course for Albania within the communist movement.[39] Emboldened by the Moscow Conference, the Albanian party leaders even claimed that the Albanians and the Chinese had 'determined and safeguarded the Marxist-Leninist contents of the declaration' at the Moscow conference, while heralding Enver Hoxha as the 'defender and courageous saviour of the purity of the Marxist-Leninist doctrine', and the Albanian Workers Party as 'vanguard of the international communist movement'.[40] By placing themselves in the vanguard, the Albanians were implicitly diminishing the importance of the Soviet Union itself, which they accused of 'threatening' the 'independence and sovereignty of Albania', while emphasising their own sovereignty.[41] Moreover, by defining themselves as the vanguard of communism, the Albanian leaders seemed to place themselves above their WP allies. Although the Albanian Party Conference in February 1961 has been ignored in historiography, it seemed a turning point in Albania's foreign policy, with far-reaching consequences for the dynamics in the WP.

The Albanian leadership also emphasised Albania's importance by stressing that 'Albania is situated in a very important strategic location vis-à-vis the imperialist camp', and 'therefore represented an important facet of the fight against imperialist threats in the Mediterranean'.[42] Hoxha immediately used this as leverage over his comrades, by announcing a foiled invasion by Yugoslavia, Greece and the American Sixth Fleet – a somewhat curious coalition of Albania's potential enemies – to justify preparations for a potential war with Yugoslavia and to take control over Soviet warships in the Warsaw Pact naval base at Vlorë,[43] where they refused to raise the Soviet flag any longer.[44] Most other delegations did not take this 'comic conspiracy' very seriously, and assumed that the Albanian leadership intended to create a 'psychosis of war' in order to consolidate its own power, as Eastern and Western European reports of the conference alike show.[45] Both the Romanian and the East German leadership denounced the Albanian attitude in equally strong terms, while underlining that 'in front of the AWP a band of provocateurs, nationalists and adventurists' has 'installed itself', which has 'nothing in common with the Moscow Declaration', and is 'contrary to the line of the immense majority of communist parties'. All Eastern European delegations were carefully kept apart, while only allowed to move under surveillance of an Albanian party member, so that they could not close ranks against Albania.[46]

Moreover, this conference testifies to the remarkable fact that the Soviet–Albanian split preceded the Sino–Soviet split: even though the foreign delegations, including – after some hesitation – the Chinese, applauded the Soviet speech with great zeal, the Chinese one was generally appreciated too, whereas the Albanian one was greeted with little enthusiasm.[47] The Soviet–Albanian split accordingly turned the Warsaw Pact inside out, as its smallest ally had become more militant than its biggest rival.

Meanwhile, the Albanian party conference offered a further opportunity for talks between the Albanian leadership and the Chinese delegates, who repeated their offer 'to mediate with the Soviets'. The Albanian leaders criticised the existence of 'the revisionist groups in the leaderships of the European socialist states', thus discrediting most WP leaders too. Moreover, Hoxha used the alleged Soviet 'secret' attempt 'to liquidate Albania' by withdrawing the fleet from Vlorë as leverage over China.[48] The message was clear: if China did not support Albania, it would lose its most loyal ally. Interestingly enough, this was exactly the way Ulbricht, whom the Albanians accused of 'ideological war' with Albania, attempted to pressurise Khrushchev into unflinchingly supporting the GDR, as we shall see in the next chapter.

The confrontation of David and Goliath

The Albanian Party Conference also heralded a further deterioration of diplomatic relations between Albania and the other WP countries. The Soviet diplomats considered the situation 'perhaps still more difficult [...] than in the hostile capitalist countries', and Albanian-Polish relations had disintegrated to such an extent that the Polish leaders decided to withdraw their ambassador from Tirana in March 1961, thus creating a precedent for other NSWP members. Moreover, the specialists and advisers from virtually all WP countries were treated so badly that they were forced to withdraw, while more Chinese specialists were expected in Albania.[49] At the same time the Albanian leadership used the alleged foiled invasion by Yugoslavia, Greece and the American Sixth Fleet to take control of dozens of Soviet warships in the Warsaw Pact naval base at Vlorë, thus placing the Soviet officers effectively under Albanian command. Having declared themselves 'the vanguard of the communist movement', the Albanian leaders felt entitled to turn Soviet-Albanian relations fully upside down.

Since the communist movement was already on the verge of collapsing through its disunity, only the Warsaw Pact remained as a platform for the debates. Although it was not primarily a communist institution, the WP was the only forum where the Kremlin could attempt to foster a united front. The WP became the arena for the Soviet–Albanian split. The Kremlin accordingly convened the Political Consultative Committee on 28–29 March 1961 in Moscow to resolve the issue, thus conceding to the suggestion of Albanian Prime Minister Mehmet Shehu in November 1960. The fact that the PCC was convened under pressure from an NSWP member, with an internal WP matter rather than the imperialist enemy dominating its agenda, was unprecedented. The Albanian leadership further attempted to determine the dynamics of the meeting by sending a 16-page invective to all WP members, in which Shehu emphasised 'that the Albanian side is not at fault', but blamed the Soviet officers in turn for the 'condescending and scornful attitude toward the Albanian officers and all the Albanian personnel'. He even quoted a Soviet naval officer, who said that '[y]our Albanian heads should be quashed with a hammer since you don't have any material or technical resources: we give you everything – from work clothes to submarines, and still you don't obey us'.[50]

According to Shehu it was, however, the Soviet withdrawal of material and technical support that was the 'real cause' of '[t]he grave situation at Vlorë naval base', combined with the fact that 'some Soviet officers – and this is especially important – maintain contacts with people who were discharged from service or expelled from the Albanian Labour [i.e. Workers] Party'.[51] The crux of the issue was, accordingly, not only the Soviet withdrawal of aid to Albania in the wake of the Bucharest conference, but also the Soviet contacts with the pro-Khrushchevite communists who had been purged by Hoxha. Despite its defiance on the surface, the Albanian leadership felt profoundly undermined by the Soviet behaviour. In fact, the Sino–Soviet estrangement seems to lie at the heart of the matter, as it is the Albanian stance at the Bucharest party conference that triggered both Khrushchev's withdrawal of Soviet aid from Albania, and Hoxha's purges.

At the same time the memorandum reveals a tension between Albania's security interests on the one hand, and its leaders' zeal for autonomy on the other. By arguing that the Soviet 'dangerous and arduous path' contradicted the spirit of the Warsaw Treaty itself, the WP was used to blackmail the Soviet leadership into compliance. On the other hand, the importance of Vlorë naval base as 'the only military base of the socialist camp in the Mediterranean', and of Albania's membership of the WP as 'the only socialist country on the Mediterranean' was continuously underlined, while emphasising Albania's allegiance to the Warsaw Pact. The depiction of Albania as a loyal ally seemed to serve two purposes: in the first place it preventively shifted the blame for the Soviet–Albanian split onto the Soviet Union, thus turning the Soviet Union's 'arduous path' into a self-fulfilling prophecy;[52] and in the second place it indicated that Albania wanted to explore its room for manoeuvre *within* the confines of the alliance. Its allegiance to China was not yet irreversible.

The Soviet report on the incidents at Vlorë nevertheless sheds a different light on the Albanian 'loyalty'. It cited numerous examples of the 'refusal of members of the Albanian staff to follow Soviet orders', as well as listing a long sequence of defiant acts, including Albanian exhortations to 'go back to the Soviet Union' and Albanian threats to buy, sell and hang their Soviet comrades.[53] The insolence of the Albanian sailors mirrored the defiance of their leaders, who had invited 'the entire Diplomatic Corps and the foreign correspondents' at the Albanian delegates' 'departure to Moscow' to attend the PCC meeting.[54] The Albanian leadership obviously trusted that the PCC meeting would turn into an Albanian triumph.

The Albanian attitude could, however, count on little support at the PCC meeting. The other NSWP members rallied behind the position of the Soviet leadership, which emphasised the Albanian 'separatist line in foreign policy' and 'hostile propaganda' since the Moscow conference in a letter to their allies on the first day of the PCC meeting. The alleged invasion at the third Albanian party conference was considered a 'clumsy statement' in order 'to create the impression among the Albanian nation that Albania has been allegedly threatened with a direct military attack', so that the ensuing 'war panic' would serve to consolidate the power of the Albanian leadership.[55] This analysis fully corresponds with the Romanian and East German reports after the Albanian party conference, which indicates that most NSWP members and the Kremlin were genuinely on the same line concerning the Albanian question.

Meanwhile, the fact that none of the Warsaw Pact allies was officially informed of the allegedly imminent invasion entailed a violation of article 3 of the Warsaw Treaty, according to which the allies should notify one another of potential threats to their security. This was particularly painful as the WP was the most stable 'guarantee of the territorial integrity and the safe-guarding of national interests' that Albania had ever had.[56] The Albanian use of the Warsaw Treaty as leverage thus backfired. The Bulgarian leader Todor Zhivkov accordingly considered the 'acts of the Albanian leadership [...] incompatible with [...] the Warsaw Treaty',[57] and spontaneously issued a separate statement in which he argued that 'given the current situation in Albania, it might be more reasonable to move this Warsaw Treaty naval base'.[58] The Soviet loss of control over the WP naval base at Vlorë formed a particular threat to Zhivkov, as Albania and Bulgaria were the only WP countries that shared a border with Greece, which was a member of NATO. Any more unpredictable plots or actions from the Albanian leadership could accordingly also put Bulgarian security at risk.

The Soviet stake in Albania was, therefore, of particular importance to Zhivkov, who strongly denounced the recent anti-Khrushchevite purges within the AWP, and the creation of 'an unbearable environment of persecution against the honest Albanian communists and friends of the Soviet Union'.[59] According to Zhivkov, this lay at the heart of the Soviet–Albanian dispute. The other WP members shared Zhivkov's concern about the Albanian party, which consisted of a rare blend of Westernised intellectuals educated in America, and extreme nationalists with rather doubtful proletarian credentials, despite their advocacy of *true* Marxism-Leninism, as was emphasised in a Romanian report.[60] The NSWP members were, accordingly, quick to create a united front *against* Albania, since the Albanian course of action also affected the security interests of other WP leaders.

Meanwhile, Khrushchev attempted to prevent a further deterioration of Sino-Soviet relations by emphasising the 'unity of the socialist camp' in his speech, while stressing the importance of the friendship treaty with China, as well as promising to consult with the Asian observers 'on the most important foreign policy issues'.[61] Khrushchev was, however, fighting a lost cause. In protest at the Soviet treatment of Albania, the Chinese had only sent their ambassador instead of a delegation to the PCC meeting, who refused to read out a speech.[62] The Soviet–Albanian split thus precipitated the Sino–Soviet split.

The other WP leaders denounced the Albanian course of action in a top secret resolution, by stating that 'Albania has recently taken some steps that do not correspond to the principles and provisions of the Warsaw Treaty'.[63]

According to the resolution the Soviet naval forces would be withdrawn from Albania, if the Albanian naval officers did not submit to the Supreme (i.e. Soviet) Command of the Warsaw Pact's armed forces. Although this could be seen as an attempt 'to undermine Albania's territorial sovereignty',[64] since it would leave Albania exposed to a potential Yugoslav attack, it was exactly because the other WP members regarded the Albanian course of action as a potential threat to *their* security that they so easily rallied behind the Kremlin. The WP was, accordingly, becoming more than a mere transmission belt of Soviet interests, as the NSWP interests simply coincided with the Soviet ones on the Albanian question. Some NSWP members, such as Todor Zhivkov, had moved even faster than the Soviet leadership in suggesting the removal of the naval base at Vlorë.

The unprecedented split within the Warsaw Pact was all the more remarkable as it occurred over an internal WP matter. Although the Albanian leadership had deliberately tried to assert its independence *within* the confines of the Warsaw Pact, it had become the victim of its own attempt to play the Soviet and NSWP leaders off against one another. The other NSWP leaders were not at all enchanted by the Albanian interpretation of a treaty that applied to all of them, and regarded Albanian insolence as a greater risk to their security than Soviet hegemony. The Albanian defiance was conveniently ignored in the ensuing communiqué, so that the WP still seemed a static monolith to the outside world.

The Albanian delegates did, however, prefer to forget about the denouement of the PCC meeting too, and kept their return secret, in sharp contrast to their departure.[65] The Albanian attempt to use the Warsaw Treaty as an instrument to question Soviet hegemony, however, was not without repercussions in the long term: the Albanian leadership had set a precedent in exploring the room for manoeuvre within the Warsaw Pact. Hoxha had caused a crack in the unity of the Warsaw Pact, which facilitated a new kind of relations between the Kremlin and its NSWP comrades.

Albanian emancipation and WP multilateralisation

The PCC meeting was followed by a rapid exacerbation of Soviet-Albanian relations. The Albanian leadership had not defied the Soviet leadership with complete impunity: the Kremlin withdrew all remaining Soviet specialists from Albania and cancelled the economic aid in the following April. The Soviet response once again opened a window of opportunity for the Chinese leaders, who initiated a trade agreement with Albania. The Albanians meanwhile put their defiance of the Soviet Union into practice and openly professed their de-Stalinisation in reverse by replacing all the pictures of Khrushchev on public buildings by ones of Stalin and by allegedly putting all Soviet diplomats and officials under police surveillance.[66]

Meanwhile, the Warsaw Pact had, by its mere existence, provided the Albanian leadership with a platform for its critique of Soviet hegemony. It had also raised the status of Albania in the eyes of its Chinese 'allies', and the Chinese leader Deng Xiaoping was impressed at 'how small Albania could be the perpetrator against the big Soviet Union'.[67] It seems plausible that the Albanian leadership would not have dared to call the Soviet Union's bluff without an alternative of potential protection.[68] The link to China was, indeed, 'a significant support for the small Balkan state',[69] and the Sino–Soviet tensions thus enabled the Albanian leadership to take such a gamble. Meanwhile, Khrushchev's hasty reaction inadvertently facilitated the Sino-Albanian friendship, since 'it was the Soviet withdrawal from Vlorë that opened the door to China'.[70]

Moreover, it was only *after* their failed attempt to gain support against the Soviet Union *within* the WP that the Sino-Albanian relations drastically intensified: the Albanian contacts with China tripled in the period directly *after* the PCC meeting. The financial support and the number of Chinese specialists in Albania increased in particular.[71] It seemed, indeed, as though the Albanians had forced a break with the Warsaw Pact in order to step up the Chinese support to Albania. The Soviet suspicion that the Albanian leadership was consciously trying to exacerbate 'relations with the Soviet Union and with the other socialist members of the Warsaw Pact' therefore seems to ring true.[72]

The 'Albanian problem', as it soon came to be called, sparked a voluminous correspondence that the Albanian leadership initiated by complaining about the WP decision to withdraw the Soviet fleet from Vlorë. The Albanian leaders clearly did not want to take responsibility for dispensing with the WP, and blamed their WP allies for assuming 'that Albania had practically placed itself outside the Warsaw Pact through its politics'.[73] Albanian Prime Minister Mehmet Shehu complained that 'this attitude [...] represents an impermissible interference in our internal affairs', and cleverly copied the rhetoric of the Moscow Declaration concerning 'independence, equality, and non-interference', while applying it to the relations within the Warsaw Pact.[74] The Albanian leaders had antagonised their allies by suggesting that the sanction concerning Vlorë was a 'unilateral decision of the Soviet Union', which was refuted by all NSWP leaders, and regarded as 'an insult' by the Romanian leadership, who used it to assert their 'independence'.[75] By emphasising that the sanction was *not* a Soviet decision, but a WP decision, the NSWP leaders made a clear distinction between the WP and the Soviet Union, which tends to be overlooked within historiography.[76] The Albanian attempt to sow discord was strongly rebuked by the Bulgarian leadership in particular, and had the opposite effect: the NSWP members spontaneously closed ranks in the face of Albanian dissent.[77]

It may be tempting to attribute the NSWP response to Soviet pressure instead, but the empirical evidence points in another direction. Soviet annoyance at the fact that the Hungarians were the first to reply to the Albanian letter,[78] and internal memoranda between party leaders and their ministers about whether to reply to the Albanian letters or not, suggest that the Soviet leadership had no control over the correspondence.[79] On the contrary: the correspondence inadvertently served to liberate the NSWP members from potential Soviet pressure.

The correspondence about the Albanian problem was the ideal vehicle for the NSWP members to formulate their own stance within the WP, and to assert their autonomy vis-à-vis the Soviet Union. Since it was an issue that directly concerned the alliance and the decision making within it, the NSWP leaders felt at liberty to define the scope for manoeuvre within a pact that, at least in theory, belonged to them as much as the Soviet Union. This theory now acquired a force of its own. By denying the Albanian charge of Soviet pressure, the NSWP members did not do the Kremlin an unambiguous favour, since they implicitly also denied Soviet hegemony. This correspondence inadvertently served to multilateralise the alliance, since there was no scope for Soviet unilateralism in a dynamics that the Soviet leaders failed to control. The Albanian leadership had thus contributed to the emancipation of the other NSWP leaders, instead of emancipating themselves.

Meanwhile, the Albanian leadership continued defying the Kremlin in particular, by refusing to cooperate with the Soviet withdrawal from Vlorë, and blaming the Kremlin's unilateral withdrawal of Soviet specialists for the deterioration of relations between the two countries.[80] The Albanian leadership seemed remarkably keen to limit the dispute to a bilateral one, after it had failed to gain multilateral support, while also creating a situation for which it could retrospectively blame the Kremlin: although several diplomatic reports from other communist countries testify to the fact that the Soviet specialists were treated so badly that the Soviet leadership was forced to withdraw them, the Albanian leadership now used this against the Soviet Union.[81] By using the WP as a platform for their dispute, the Albanian leaders had, however, contributed to its multilateralisation.

Albanian exclusion

Hoxha continued his outright humiliation of the Warsaw Pact by refusing to turn up at the meeting of WP first secretaries, which was convened from 3–5 August 1961 in Moscow for the endorsement of the closure of Berlin's internal borders – a euphemism for the construction of the Berlin Wall. Even the correspondence had been delegated to a junior secretary, Hysni Kapo, who explained that Hoxha could not participate 'due to health-related reasons', but that the Albanian leadership would like to have materials to prepare the meeting.[82]

This time the Albanian leadership had gone too far in exploring the scope for manoeuvre: at the actual meeting all other first secretaries supported Ulbricht's proposal to exclude the Albanian delegation, since it had only sent a junior secretary, and they were asked to leave.[83] The Albanian defiance was, however, such that the Albanian delegation displayed 'not the slightest intention to leave' and even stayed at the buffet 'in order to continue the work against the general will'.⁸⁴ The meeting accordingly had to be cancelled for the rest of the day, which still failed to deter the Albanians, who tried to enter the Kremlin the day after, but were refused entry by the security guards. The fact that the Albanian leadership had already bought a return ticket scheduled for return on 4 August – one day before the end of the meeting – indicates that the sabotage of the meeting was premeditated.⁸⁵ The Albanians had thus forced their allies to postpone decision making on the Berlin Wall for an entire day.

Meanwhile, the Warsaw Pact reaction to the Albanian behaviour further exacerbated the Sino–Soviet differences, since the Chinese observer, Liu Siao, 'insisted upon asking for the annulment of the adopted decision, using the argument that each party has the right to send as its representative whomever it considers necessary and no fraternal party has the right to remove another party'.⁸⁶ Although none of the other participants supported the Chinese proposal for a separate declaration in protest against the Albanian exclusion, both the Albanian exclusion and the Chinese protest indicate that the differences from the Moscow conference had spilled over into the Warsaw Pact, and began to challenge Soviet control over the WP's moves.

The fact that one NSWP member could successfully propose to exclude another NSWP member from a WP meeting did, indeed, imply the end of Soviet domination. The reason for the Albanian exclusion was accordingly not its previous defiance of the Soviet Union, but its deliberate scorn of the WP's unwritten rules. The Albanian delegation made a virtue out of necessity by keeping both the meeting and the WP declaration about the closing of the inner-Berlin borders secret, producing a separate declaration about the German question instead,⁸⁷ which illustrated both the Albanian '*Sonderkurs*', and its 'self-isolation'.⁸⁸

Ulbricht was particularly grieved about the Albanian obstruction during the meeting he had convened, since the Albanian dissidence seemed to overshadow the German question. His proposal to exclude the Albanian delegation nevertheless represented his first successful initiative within the alliance. Since Hoxha was well aware of the fact that he had been outwitted by an NSWP member,⁸⁹ he complained to the leaderships of *all* WP countries and the observers a month later that '[t]he organisers of this unprecedented measure' had 'split the unity of the Warsaw Treaty and of the socialist camp'.⁹⁰ The Albanian leadership had succeeded once more in stretching its room for manoeuvre so far that it had provoked new sanctions, which it could use to discredit the WP. The Albanian attempt to undermine Soviet hegemony had, nevertheless, failed, as Ulbricht had outdone Khrushchev in his zeal to denounce Albania.

The Albanian self-exclusion went so far that the Albanian leadership did not attend the 22nd Congress of the Soviet Communist Party from 17–31 October 1961 at all, thus setting a trend that the Chinese leadership would soon follow. The Albanian absence and Khrushchev's opening speech, in which he publicly denounced the Albanians, not only confirmed the Soviet–

Albanian split,⁹¹ but also the Sino–Soviet one, since Mao had felt indirectly attacked by Khrushchev's pronounced criticism of Albania. Mao, too, blamed Khrushchev for dividing the socialist camp, and ostensibly left Moscow halfway through the conference in protest. Since all Asian leaders, apart from the Mongolian leader, Yumjaagin Tsedenbal, also refused to denounce Albania, the communist movement suddenly seemed to have split in two, with the Asian leaders and Albania on one side, and the other WP leaders and Mongolia on the other.

In the face of the disintegration of the communist movement the other WP leaders united again, and on the last day of the congress they used the issue of representation to question the status of the East Asian observer states in the Warsaw Pact – China, North Korea, Mongolia and North Vietnam – by notifying them that in their case, too, only first secretaries should attend the PCC meetings. Although the North Vietnamese leader Ho Chi Minh, and Tsedenbal seemed perfectly happy with this requirement, Mao considered the issue of representation a tacit move to exclude China from WP deliberations, and decided to sever all institutional ties with the WP in response.⁹² His appeal to 'independence, equality, and non-interference', and his argument that the level of representation was not mentioned within the Warsaw Treaty echoed both the Albanian arguments and the 'Moscow Declaration'.⁹³

The Chinese refusal to participate turned the Warsaw Pact from an alliance in which members from the entire communist bloc were represented – albeit only as observers in the case of the Asian countries – into an Eastern European alliance, which is a subtle but important shift in its nature: its reach had now shrunk considerably. On the other hand, the Sino–Soviet estrangement might have increased the WP's importance as a platform for consultations and deliberations, since decision making by the NSWP allies had previously seemed somewhat overshadowed by the Chinese involvement in the resolution of, *inter alia*, the Hungarian revolution and the Polish uprisings in October and November 1956.⁹⁴

Meanwhile, Moscow had already withdrawn its ambassador from Tirana in August of the same year, and by December 1961 all Warsaw Pact countries had severed diplomatic relations with Albania of their own accord.⁹⁵ Although the Soviet withdrawal of both its specialists and its diplomats from Albania mirrored the withdrawal from China a year earlier, it was bound to have even more severe repercussions, since the fact that it had broken off (diplomatic) relations with a Warsaw Pact 'ally' made the status of WP membership somewhat ambivalent. It is extremely curious that two allies fail to maintain diplomatic relations. At the same time, the Chinese intensified their friendship with Albania, united 'in the struggle against common enemies', as the Chinese ambassador in Tirana solemnly pledged.⁹⁶

The Warsaw Pact remained effectively powerless in the face of the united Sino-Albanian front. Although the Albanians were excluded from the ensuing PCC meetings, since they continued to refuse to send representation at the highest level, the Warsaw Treaty did not cater for a formalisation of this *de facto* exclusion. In this case, too, the Albanian leadership deliberately provoked its WP colleagues into excluding them. On a military level the Albanian leaders also made the working conditions for representatives of the Unified Command so difficult, while blocking all communication, that 'further cooperation in the framework of the Warsaw Treaty' became virtually impossible.[97] The Warsaw Pact's Supreme Commander, the Soviet Marshal Konev, was forced to leave Albania to its own devices.[98] With the motto 'better be dead on your feet than alive on your knees', the Albanian self-isolation was complete.[99]

Thus the Albanian leadership succeeded in defying the Kremlin *within* the formal confines of the Warsaw Pact. Ulbricht's insistence that the Albanian government should 'turn directly to the member states of the Warsaw Treaty' with any questions nevertheless served as a reminder that the NSWP members also had a say in the Albanian question.[100] Indeed, both the Sino–Soviet estrangement and the Soviet–Albanian split had forced Khrushchev to consult with his allies.[101] Although the NSWP members capitalised on the Albanian 'problem' for their own emancipation, the Albanian leadership attempted to make the alliance responsible for its exclusion: professing their wish to stay within the alliance, the Albanians kept a kind of leverage that they would otherwise lack.[102] Meanwhile, the Albanian leaders had cleverly forced the Soviet withdrawal from Vlorë.

The Albanian behaviour accordingly challenges two common preconceptions about the Warsaw Pact: in the first place the alliance was not as involuntary as is often assumed, as Albania actually insisted on staying within it *against the will* of their WP allies; and second, it was not primarily an instrument *of* the Soviet Union, but it could also be used as an instrument *against* the Soviet Union. This strongly distinguishes the Warsaw Pact from the COMINFORM, which Stalin used to excommunicate Tito in 1948. The WP was not only an alliance between states rather than communist parties on paper; the alliance's interstate nature compelled the Soviet leadership to treat its members as the leaders of sovereign states, rather than inferior communist parties.

The defiance of Soviet power by such a seemingly insignificant member exposed the weakness of the alliance leader all the more poignantly. The alternative of Mao's support also underlines how the Sino–Soviet estrangement had facilitated a crack within the WP. The Albanian leaders had indeed 'exploited the differences of opinion between the CCP and the other fraternal parties', as well as 'transferring the ideological differences of opinions to the domain of interstate relations', as the Soviet leadership wrote to the Chinese in 1962.[103] By doing so, they had made the differences between the Chinese and Soviet leaders increasingly difficult to bridge.

Moreover, the Albanian leadership had focused on several issues that would come to haunt the Soviet leadership in the future: the emphasis on sovereignty and non-interference in internal affairs, which was also enshrined in the Moscow Declaration; the request for materials in preparation for the meetings; the invocation of the Warsaw Treaty in defence of their own stance;

and the issuing of separate declarations in case of disagreements. All of these paved the way for the more successful emancipation of the Romanian leadership a couple of years later. As Griffith prophetically put it in 1962, 'Hoxha has been the first but hardly the last to profit from Mao's challenge'.[104]

Sino-Romanian rapprochement

Not only had the incipient Sino–Soviet split enabled the Albanian leadership to call the Kremlin's bluff, but the Soviet–Albanian split had considerably strengthened the Chinese hand vis-à-vis the Kremlin, too. The fact that both the communist movement and the Warsaw Pact had become split considerably undermined Soviet hegemony. Soviet attempts to prevent 'the existing divergences on the Albanian problem' from affecting 'relations between our parties' were thus disregarded in China.[105] The Soviet–Albanian split merely confirmed the Chinese 'assumption that the [Eastern European] countries [...] had interests of their own that could be exploited by China to help isolate the Soviet Union'.[106]

There was one other WP country in particular whose interests differed from the Soviet ones, as the Chinese leadership began to notice in 1963. Although the Romanian leadership had strongly denounced the Albanian stance at both WP meetings in 1961, it had turned against the Kremlin within COMECON during the meeting in December 1961.[107] The Soviet plans to create a kind of 'common market' with an international division of labour, which would reduce Romania to the mere provider of raw materials, would negatively affect the Romanian economy.[108] The repeated Chinese references to the Moscow Declaration and its emphasis on 'sovereignty, independence, and non-interference' in the voluminous correspondence with the Soviet leadership thus gained a special importance to the Romanian leaders. Since COMECON was concerned with economic issues, the Romanian preoccupation with sovereignty only had limited repercussions if it confined itself to COMECON. If it spilled over to the WP, it would, however, also confront the Kremlin with a *political* challenge.

From 1962 onwards Gheorghiu-Dej himself closely studied and carefully annotated the Sino-Soviet correspondence, while concentrating on the Chinese attempts to assert its independence vis-à-vis the Soviet Union. In early 1963 the Romanian leadership even commissioned a study of the Marxist-Leninist documents on 'sovereignty and national independence', which culminated in the Moscow Declaration.[109] The Romanian leaders thus only began to concentrate on these principles after the Chinese had repeatedly emphasised them.

In a meeting with the Soviet politburo member Yuri Andropov in early April 1963 in Bucharest, the attitude of the Romanian leaders echoed the Chinese one. Referring to 'the extraordinary important problem of sovereignty' and to other parts of the Moscow Declaration, Gheorghiu-Dej justified the Romanian disagreement with 'the idea of a single planning organ' within COMECON.[110] It was, accordingly, no coincidence that the Romanian leadership used the same conversation to underline its willingness to take the initiative on mending the Sino–Soviet split. Emphasising that the Romanians would 'try to contribute towards strengthening unity', since they were 'all interested in the victory of the socialist camp' of which 'the Chinese represent about two thirds', Gheorghiu-Dej was in fact seeking Soviet approval for a Romanian rapprochement with the Chinese leadership. Andropov's agreement 'that we must find solutions for strengthening unity' was interpreted as the green light.[111]

The Soviet ambassador in Bucharest, Jegalin, who had also attended part of the meetings, 'had not slept all night', because of 'the existing differences between the Romanian and Soviet comrades'.[112] Meanwhile, the Chinese leadership displayed 'a more benevolent attitude' towards the Romanian diplomats in the Chinese capital at the end of April. According to the Romanian ambassador in Beijing, the Chinese had only adopted this attitude after the Romanian Workers Party (RWP) had displayed 'a critical attitude concerning some problems within the COMECON framework', which proved that the Romanian leadership 'respects the principles enshrined in the Moscow Declaration'.[113] As a consequence, Chinese foreign affairs officials explicitly stated a desire to consult the Romanian diplomats more often. The mutual interest in sovereignty had thus begun to forge a bond between the Chinese and Romanian parties.

Contrary to conventional wisdom, the diplomatic relations between the Chinese and Romanians intensified at Chinese initiative. The Chinese leaders raised the Romanian consciousness of the Soviet 'adventurism' in breaking off diplomatic relations with Albania, after Soviet adventurism by acting unilaterally during the Cuban Missile Crisis in October 1962 had already been abundantly covered in the Chinese press.[114] It was, accordingly, not the fact that the Kremlin had flouted its allied obligations during the Cuban Missile Crisis that had sparked the more independent Romanian course, as is often suggested.[115] It was, on the contrary, the Sino-Soviet correspondence that boosted the Romanian interest in sovereignty, intensified Sino-Romanian relations, and in turn drew the Romanian attention to the Soviet unilateralism during the Cuban Missile Crisis.[116] Only in April 1964, when the relations with the Chinese had further intensified, did the Romanians conclude that '[b]ecause of the fact that we are all members of the Warsaw Pact we should have been informed, we should have discussed, we should have decided together whether it would be good or not to send those missiles there'.[117] In 1963 the Romanian leadership was still primarily interested in the Chinese focus on the Moscow Declaration, according to which 'every party is independent concerning its internal problems'.[118] This confirmed 'the righteousness of [the Romanian] position', and the 'great discrepancy' between theory and practice in the Soviet attitude towards sovereignty.[119]

The Sino-Romanian rapprochement was an essential boon to the Chinese, since the negotiations between American, British and Soviet leaders about the conclusion of a limited nuclear test-ban treaty (NTBT) in July 1963 were particularly problematic to the Chinese, who were trying to develop their own nuclear device. The negotiations, which were indeed partly directed at Chinese nuclear testing, took place in Moscow on 15 July, and accordingly coincided with a visit from a Chinese delegation to Moscow on 6–20 July in a last attempt to reverse the Sino–Soviet split.[120] During these talks Mao's emissary, Deng Xiaoping, not only expressed China's outrage at the lack of consultation with 'the fraternal countries' during the Cuban Missile Crisis, but also blamed the Kremlin for 'pursuing an unseemly goal in coming to such an agreement [the NTBT], namely: to bind China hands and feet through an agreement with the USA'.[121] Despite Soviet attempts to assuage the Chinese delegates through references to the Moscow Declaration, the Soviet delegation left with 'a profound sentiment of regret and sadness'.[122] This corresponds with Mastny's observation that the 'treaty became the catalyst of the Sino-Soviet break'.[123]

The Mongolian application

Despite the further deterioration in Sino-Soviet relations things seemed to turn for the better within the Warsaw Pact, because Yumjaagin Tsedenbal, the first secretary of Mongolia, applied to join the alliance at exactly the same time as the Sino-Soviet talks. Tsedenbal had consistently sided with his Soviet comrades in the Sino–Soviet and Soviet–Albanian split, and in a 'strictly confidential' conversation with the Chinese leader Zhou Enlai in December 1962 Tsedenbal had already strongly denounced Albania, and supported the Soviet stance, while refusing to yield to Chinese blackmail concerning the dispatch of Chinese workers to Mongolia.[124] The request of the Mongolian leadership to join the Warsaw Pact was a clear expression of its allegiance to the Soviet Union, especially considering the fact that Mongolia shared a long border with China.[125] The fact that Albania's *de facto* exclusion from the COMECON in 1962 coincided with Mongolia's admission had already adumbrated this move.[126] According to the expert on Mongolia, Sergei Radchenko, Mongolia even 'pressured the Soviet leadership to take a harder line on the PRC',[127] and its application to the WP can therefore be regarded as directed against China.

In the first instance the Mongolian application did seem a boost to the WP, since Tsedenbal's emphasis on its importance underscored the concept of the Warsaw Pact as a 'voluntary alliance'[128] and made it almost seem an 'empire by invitation'.[129] Khrushchev therefore eagerly endorsed the Mongolian application, and attempted to convince the other WP members of its benefits in a letter he sent on 10 July 1963,[130] while in a second letter five days later calling for a PCC meeting on 26 and 27 July to discuss the application.[131]

The Mongolian application nevertheless exposed the Warsaw Pact's fragility, since it compelled its members to exercise some introspection regarding its functioning. Although the united front against Albania in 1961 might have deceived Khrushchev into believing that his NSWP allies would back the Soviet Union in this case, too, the application in fact revealed a further crack within the alliance. The Romanian and Polish allies were particularly critical, and the independent stance they were enabled to adopt vis-à-vis the Soviet Union would prove irreversible.

The Romanian leaders discussed the issue during a politburo meeting on 18 July 1963, in which they elaborately and self-consciously prepared their stance at the ensuing PCC meeting. They felt particularly confident, since they had just 'achieved a very big success' at a COMECON meeting, where they had 'succeeded to make [the Soviet Union] retreat' in terms of the common market, which would have 'implications concerning sovereignty, independence etc.' They criticised the Soviet leadership for omitting to send them, as a WP country, Tsedenbal's letter of application, and decided that it would be good tactics 'to show what implications Mongolia's intention of entering into the Warsaw Treaty Organisation would have'.[132]

Those implications entailed that it would create 'military blocs within the [communist] camp', and 'would mean the extension of the pact into another zone than the European one'. As such it would implicitly be targeted against China, since 'Mongolia only has borders with two countries'.[133] This would be a significant shift in the identity of the Warsaw Pact as an alliance directed against NATO. Referring to an appeal by Khrushchev not to 'disclose the divergences', Gheorghiu-Dej emphasised that 'we are in a favourable situation […], since the principal problem which gnaws at [Khrushchev] is the problem with the Chinese'. The Sino–Soviet split had thus turned into a sword of Damocles, which the NSWP members could wield to defend their case. Moreover, the Romanians predicted problems with the UN, where the Warsaw Treaty Organisation was registered, if their decision making had no legal basis in the treaty.[134] The treaty's claim to legitimacy inadvertently limited the scope for manoeuvre of the Soviet Union itself. Rather than a 'paper tiger', the treaty turned into a Trojan Horse.[135]

The Romanian concerns were mirrored in a letter written two days later by Polish Foreign Minister Adam Rapacki. Rapacki nevertheless expanded on 'the problem of Albania in the Warsaw Pact', since its potential veto would 'have a legal basis', and argued that it could 'inflame existing differences' with Romania, which would be likely to develop 'a negative stance' on this matter.[136] The allusion to Romanian obstruction within the WP was unprecedented. Mongolia's application thus turned from a potential triumph for the Warsaw Pact's popularity into a thorny issue. Its treatment does, however, also reflect the fact that the smaller allies gained increasing room for manoeuvre within the WP, since Albanian and Romanian opposition could still be conclusive. In addition, the Sino–Soviet split loomed larger than the imperialist threat, which underlines how the 'Cold War' *within* the communist world began to overshadow the one outside it.[137]

At the PCC meeting on 26–27 July 1963 the Mongolian issue nevertheless took a different turn, since the Soviet leadership itself unexpectedly questioned Mongolian admission, considering the expansion of the WP contradictory to the signing of the nuclear test-ban treaty, which was concluded on the previous day to defuse international tensions.[138] Khrushchev's initial enthusiasm for the Mongolian application nevertheless suggests that his political U-turn was caused by the unexpectedly critical Polish and Romanian stance instead, which undermines the conventional reading that he was primarily concerned about the coincidence with the nuclear test-ban treaty.[139] On the contrary, Khrushchev's courting of Tsedenbal's favour coincided with severe disputes about the NTBT between the Soviet and Chinese leaders, which might have stimulated him to find a new ally elsewhere. When that initiative caused friction within the Warsaw Pact, Khrushchev had to sacrifice the Mongolian application to WP unity. Confronted with the escalation of the Sino–Soviet split, Khrushchev could ill afford to alienate his WP allies.

Khrushchev had accordingly withdrawn his own proposal in an attempt to save face. Although he had successfully pre-empted Polish criticism, the Romanians gave 'a vague and useless reply', according to the Hungarian report.[140] The Romanians themselves, meanwhile, considered their opposition to the Mongolian question a great success within the WP, which was not altogether unjustified since it seemed as though a Soviet initiative had unprecedentedly been blocked by an NSWP member.[141] A decision on the Mongolian application was subsequently 'postponed' and the Mongolian application was also omitted from the ensuing communiqué, as was, astonishingly, the presence of Tsedenbal. As in the Albanian case, the failure to respond to dissent resulted in its denial, making the WP seem much less dynamic than it actually was.[142]

The Romanian and Polish responses underline Lüthi's interpretation of the episode as 'an unsuccessful Soviet attempt to turn the Warsaw Pact Organization against the People's Republic'.[143] The Sino–Soviet split had caused Khrushchev to overplay his hand once again and to undermine the Soviet position within the alliance. Whereas the Albanian insolence had stimulated the other WP members to close their ranks in 1961, the Mongolian application had ironically enabled them to drift apart. Although the other NSWP leaders still seemed to side with the Soviet leadership, the Mongolian application allowed the Romanian leaders, and to some extent the Poles, to use the Warsaw Treaty as an instrument to explore their own scope for manoeuvre. Although Tsedenbal, unlike Hoxha, did not profit from Mao's challenge, Gheorghiu-Dej certainly did.

Romanian mediation

The PCC meeting in July 1963 marked a reorientation in Romanian foreign policy away from the loyal WP members to communist dissidents and other Soviet enemies. This also shows in the trade agreements that it concluded with Albania, China and the FRG in the same year.[144] Not only did the Romanians choose to trade with the 'dissidents' within the communist bloc, but they also intensified relations with the West German 'revanchists'. The Warsaw Pact, meanwhile, received scant attention, and it was therefore in line with the Romanian conduct to undermine Ulbricht's attempt in January 1964 to convene a PCC meeting on 19 March, which will be discussed at greater length in the next chapter.[145] The Czechoslovak suggestion to put 'the destructive activity of the PR China' on the agenda might have antagonised the Romanians too,[146] and they told Khrushchev that April was not suitable, instead of replying to Ulbricht.[147] Greatly offended, Ulbricht refused to comply with Khrushchev's request to propose a different date,[148] and waited for a personal response from Gheorgiu-Dej, who ultimately – at the end of March – replied that April was simply impossible.[149] In April the Romanian leaders were far too busy asserting their own independence, as we shall see below.

On 14 February 1964, a month after the East German attempt to convene the PCC, the Romanian leaders wrote a letter to their Chinese and Soviet comrades in which they asked the Soviet leadership not to publicise its criticism of the Chinese, and the Chinese leadership to stop the open polemics. They also suggested measures for 'restoring communist unity', and proposed a meeting with the Chinese leadership 'concerning problems related to the unity of the socialist camp and the communist world movement'.[150] The Romanians sent the letter to the leaders of all communist parties in the world, which left the Kremlin with little alternative but to comply. As the Romanian historian Mihai Retegan puts it, '[t]he escalation of the misunderstandings between the two communist centers was naturally used by the leaders in Bucharest to make themselves heard in a choir where there was a single soloist – Moscow'.[151] However, the Romanian leaders achieved much more than that: their mediation in the Sino–Soviet split would force Moscow to play the Romanian tune with the whole communist movement as an audience. The letter had prompted enthusiastic responses from 31 leaders of communist parties worldwide, including those in Western countries, and had thus made the Romanian leadership a player on the global stage.[152]

The Romanian leadership was, meanwhile, very conscious of its own worth. Gheorgiu-Dej even underlined in a meeting in which he discussed the Romanian delegation's visit to China that 'it is no easy matter, it is a move of great importance and responsibility', for which 'we need to possess many more qualities: agility, tact, perseverance, patience, while anticipating everything that could happen'. In the same meeting it was suggested that they 'elaborate a new document' that would expand on the 1957 and 1960 Moscow Declarations, and which they could 'present at an international meeting'. Conscious 'of the fact that we are called "mediators" and that they say that we are opportunists', the Romanian leaders stressed that '[i]t is out of the question that we exercise neutrality, when we exercise Marxism-Leninism', and that '[our] action […] is very important and will remain inscribed in the history of our party, because we have intervened at a moment when we were one step away from splitting the socialist camp'.[153] The Sino-Soviet mediation thus primarily served to boost the prestige of the Romanian leadership.

The Kremlin, meanwhile, seemed to be under such pressure from the Sino–Soviet split, that it was willing to interpret the Romanian strategy charitably. Although the Soviet diplomat Iljuchin considered 'the chances of success for the Romanian move slim', he emphasised in a conversation with the East German leadership that 'the Romanian attempt to stop the dangerous development should be highly esteemed'.[154] The Romanian attempts to emphasise 'that the RWP does not adopt the role of a mediator in the resolution of the differences of opinion', seriously believed in the feasibility of its enterprise, and was not at all interested in 'the prestige of its own party', nevertheless was met with scepticism in the GDR.[155] Gomulka had already advised the Soviet leadership to take the initiative in improving relations with China, while warning it against any attempts at mediation by other parties in October 1963.[156] The NSWP leaders were, accordingly, not at all enchanted with the Romanian move.

Meanwhile, it gave the Romanian leaders the opportunity to be taken seriously by the Chinese: meeting with a top-level Chinese delegation was, as such, a success in itself, even though Gheorgiu-Dej confessed that 'I cherish no illusion whatever that we shall obtain capitulation from the Chinese', but argued that 'even a chance of a few percentages to subdue the Chinese' would suffice to justify the struggle. He considered the Romanian strategy an opportunity to tell the Soviet comrades that they, too, 'should not cherish the illusion that they are always right', while calling the Romanian attitude 'nothing else but a service, since we do not stand with our arms crossed and do nothing'.[157] However, not only political and ethical motives played an important role. The fact that China was potentially 'a big market' was particularly attractive to the Romanian leadership, since the differences within COMECON had rendered alternative trade partners all the more essential.[158]

During the talks between the Romanian and the Chinese delegations on 3–10 March, the Romanians 'completely agreed [with the Chinese] that relations between socialist countries should be based on the principles of equality and non-interference in domestic affairs', as consolidated in the 1960 Moscow Declaration. Moreover, the WP was a regular topic of conversation, and was considered a mere 'formality' by the Romanians, since there were 'more problems', such as the lack of consultation during the Cuban Missile Crisis, which the Chinese in particular considered outrageous and used to heighten the Romanian awareness of their role in the alliance.[159]

The Romanian proposal for a common appeal to cease the polemics met, however, with little enthusiasm, since the Chinese insisted that 'nothing prevent[ed] Khrushchev from doing what he wanted' anyhow. The Chinese even put the Romanians on the defensive by asking why they had changed their mind on the Chinese attitude within a year, thus forcing the Romanians to confess that they had been mistaken to side with the Soviet Union against China in the past.[160] Although the Romanian attempt to cease the polemics had failed, the Chinese did emphasise that they would like to have 'more regular contact' with the Romanians in future, which served to consolidate Sino-Romanian relations still further.[161]

At the same time the Soviet leadership was so eager to show its goodwill that it attempted to patch up the differences with China by emphasising the communist parties' 'equal rights' in its correspondence with the Chinese, while agreeing to meet with the Romanian party leaders on their way back from China in Gagra on 15 March 1964 to discuss future steps.[162] Meeting the Soviet leaders in the town of Gagra on the Black Sea instead of Moscow, *after* meeting the Chinese leadership in Beijing, already indicates the way in which the Romanians had forced the Soviets to adopt a lower profile. The high-level Soviet delegation that awaited the Romanians at Gagra, consisting of, *inter alia*, Khrushchev, Mikoyan and Andropov, illustrates how seriously the Soviets took the Romanian leaders, who proudly observed that '[w]e truly enjoyed a lot of attention'.[163] Khrushchev nevertheless also expressed his 'displeasure' at the Romanian attempt 'to condition the convention of the [PCC] meeting', to which the Romanians replied that it was 'an elementary, democratic right of each party to know in advance what would be discussed at such a meeting'.[164]

The Romanian leadership concluded from the meeting in Gagra that the Soviets 'have entered a situation from which they cannot escape', and decided to propose an appeal to 'strive after the ending of the polemics'.[165] Gheorghiu-Dej officially suggested in a letter to Khrushchev on 25 March 'that the CPSU CC [Central Committee], the CCP CC, and the RWP CC would direct a common appeal in order to cease the open polemics to all communist and worker parties'.[166] Thus the Romanian leadership indirectly placed itself on a level with the CPSU and the CCP in a letter that was also sent to all WP leaders. By enclosing the draft of the appeal, which was full of such principles as 'non-interference', 'independence and national sovereignty', the Romanian leadership used the Moscow Declaration to (re)define its own stance within the communist bloc.[167] Although Gheorghiu-Dej had presented this in the politburo as a Soviet proposal, Khrushchev referred instead to 'your new proposal' at Gagra,[168] and repeatedly stressed that he only agreed to the appeal 'if the leadership of the CCP unconditionally ceases the public polemics, and stops splitting the communist movement', as he had already mentioned during the meeting at Gagra.[169]

The Sino–Soviet split forced the Kremlin to treat the Romanians gently, but the Soviet diplomat in Bucharest, Suchanov, criticised the 'exceptional position' of the Romanians in a conversation with his East German colleague, comparing Romania to 'an extraordinarily stubborn and bad-tempered adolescent'.[170] The Romanian 'mediation' was considered Romanian obstinacy. The fact that successful mediation had always been out of the question was, however, irrelevant to the Romanians: what mattered was the fact that their mediating *pose* had underlined Romanian sovereignty in both Chinese and Soviet eyes. Meanwhile, the Romanian party leaders were convinced that '[t]he Soviets have missed a great opportunity. What lack of suppleness! What rigidity!', which is a strong contrast with their self-proclaimed 'agility'.[171]

The Romanian declaration of independence

On a superficial level the Romanian endeavour had failed: their appeal for unity had been undermined by their visit to Beijing. On a more profound level the Romanians had nevertheless been very successful indeed: their attempts at mediation in the Sino–Soviet split had placed them, as self-proclaimed mediator between the two communist great powers, on a different level from their WP comrades. This had facilitated their opposition to Ulbricht's attempts to convene his allies, and had emphasised both their sovereignty and their autonomy. Meanwhile, the Soviet leadership was forced to participate in the mediation game, since the Sino–Soviet split had placed it in a vulnerable position. The Romanians themselves considered that they had 'succeeded only partially', but that they had 'motives to continue'.[172] They obviously wanted to keep a finger in the pie.

The Romanians recycled the draft appeal to all the communist parties as a basis for the formulation of their own stance, in a manifesto that has later been called 'the Declaration of Independence', and has been considered 'the turning-point of Romania's *public deviation* in its foreign policy'.[173] According to Gheorgiu-Dej: '[w]e shall not participate in the polemics between parties through this appeal, but we shall have the opportunity to take a position against unjust methods which they use', and '[t]owards the end of the document, like a chanson, which sounds pleasantly to the ears, we shall have our appeal for the ending of the polemics'.[174] Assuming the role of the mediator within the Sino–Soviet split thus enabled the Romanians to make their independent stance within the communist movement a whole lot easier to swallow. The Romanian confidence had enjoyed such a boost that Gheorgiu-Dej even stressed in a preliminary talk about the plenum with the Chinese Ambassador Liu Fan that 'it is possible that we express points of view with which you will not agree, it is possible that our points of view will be different from those of the CPSU'.[175] The Romanians were emphatically not inclined to sing the Chinese tune either.

The Romanian leadership presented the appeal at an extraordinary plenum of the RWP CC on 15–22 April 1964, which had been convened 'to deal with questions concerning the differences of opinion in the communist world movement'.[176] It ironically coincided exactly with Ulbricht's suggested date of the PCC meeting. The appeal attracted 'numerous foreign journalists', and seemed to follow logically from the 'conversations' of the Romanian with the Chinese and Soviet leaders, which had served further to crystallise 'our position in relation to the most important current problems'. The politburo member Vasilichi Gheorghe even 'consider[ed] the most important result of this action from our party that […] we have all become cleverer at the end of this action, so to speak, we know the matters much more than we knew them before'. The mediation in the Sino–Soviet split had, indeed, increased the Romanian self-consciousness, as well as contributing to their emancipation. Moreover, it also served to underline 'that we are a mature party, that we are a party with a sense of responsibility, that we are a party capable of judging and of perceiving the matters with our own eyes'.[177]

The declaration included an appeal to 'the principles of national independence and sovereignty, equality, [...] non-interference in the domestic affairs, the respect of territorial integrity, on the principles of socialist internationalism'.[178] Since the Romanian leadership had appropriated the Moscow Declaration for its own purposes, it was indeed 'the first time a small party had something to say about the big problems of Communism, and dared to speak as equals with the great powers'.[179] Under the pretext of mediating within the Sino–Soviet split, the Romanian leaders had actually re-emphasised the equality of *all* communist parties in order to confirm their own equality.

At the same time the declaration served as an implicit protest against the WP, and as such explained the Romanian reluctance to participate in another PCC meeting. Although the declaration mentioned the alliance only once, in relation to a non-aggression treaty between the WP and NATO, the role of the Warsaw Pact was discussed time and again in the accompanying plenary session. In this meeting especially the attempts to coordinate the Political Consultative Committee in a COMECON-like fashion were criticised, as well as Ulbricht's proposal to convene the PCC, the Soviet 'introduction of a coordinating programme', which only served Soviet interests, and the fact that the Soviet leaders 'had confronted us with several *fait accomplis* within the Warsaw Pact, without prior consultations'.[180] The declaration was slightly less explicit on this front, and 'turned against any higher form of cooperation between the socialist countries', while attempting to 'reach a loosening of the cooperation', and to 'increase the scope for manoeuvre'.[181]

As such it was directly targeted against Khrushchev's and Ulbricht's attempts to increase foreign policy coordination within the WP, which will be further discussed in the next chapter. Ulbricht's zeal to convene a PCC meeting seems to have inspired the Romanians to formulate a declaration that seemed deliberately anti-Ulbricht. Two months later the East German diplomatic services even had access to 'reliable sources' which suggested that '[t]he RWP did not agree with some decisions of the Warsaw Pact. It would accordingly no longer cooperate actively, but would merely observe the development in the Warsaw Pact'.[182] Ironically, this is exactly the role his allies feared de Gaulle would adopt within NATO.[183]

In the wake of the extraordinary plenum the Romanian leadership decided to make its emancipation from the Soviet grip felt at home, too, by, *inter alia*, substituting Romanian street names for Russian ones and abolishing the compulsory study of Russian at school, thus creating 'an anti-Soviet atmosphere', according to vehement Soviet criticism.[184] A month after the RWP meeting a great number of public meetings were held, in order to divulge the new course in Romanian foreign policy to a wider audience, which successfully served to capitalise on anti-Soviet sentiments and increase the popularity of the leadership. Soviet influence was thus eradicated from Romanian society at different levels. Meanwhile, Soviet distrust vis-à-vis Romania had increased to such an extent that the house in Moscow of the Romanian military representative in the Warsaw Pact was bugged 'in the name of proletarian internationalism!'[185]

In the same year, Romania also started to cultivate links with Western states, for example by turning diplomatic offices into embassies.[186] At the beginning of August 1964 a top-level Romanian delegation even went to Paris, on 'the first such trip ever made to a Western nation by an Eastern-bloc head of government other than Nikita S. Khrushchev himself'.[187] The choice of France was of course no coincidence: visiting NATO's most recalcitrant member, the Romanian delegation implicitly emphasised its stance in the Warsaw Pact.[188]

Had Romania been a member of NATO, it would indeed have behaved like France: in stark contrast to the Albanian leadership, the Romanian leadership did not so much begin to turn against Khrushchev as a *Soviet* leader, but against 'hegemonic tendencies in general, against the idea of the superpowers' responsibility in international matters in particular', as the Romanian historian Elena Dragomir convincingly argues.[189] Romania had never considered the Albanian course of siding with China, since it was not in favour of the hegemonic tendencies of *either* of the communist great powers. This might be one of the reasons why the Kremlin had more patience with Romania. Refusing to take sides in the Sino–Soviet split, the Romanian leaders had indeed occupied 'a neutralist and centrist position', as the East Germans observed.[190] The Romanian challenge seemed subtler than the Albanian one, and it had successfully called Khrushchev's bluff. Having agreed to the Romanian appeal to communist countries, he had indirectly sanctioned their independence too.

The aftermath

At the beginning of July 1964 a high-level Romanian delegation went to Moscow to discuss Soviet-Romanian relations with its Soviet comrades. The Warsaw Pact featured prominently on the agenda, which was proposed by the Romanians, who wanted to discuss the procedures of convening the PCC meetings and determining the agenda, 'the lack of consultations in problems which concern the member states', the potential reforms of the pact, including 'the creation of a permanent organ for foreign policy', both of which the Romanians vehemently opposed, and the 'independent position of each country in problems of foreign policy' as well as its 'sovereign right'.[191] The Romanian declaration of independence was thus seamlessly applied to Romania's role in the Warsaw Pact. It was no coincidence that the Soviet leaders called the declaration 'a manifestation of anti-Sovietism'.[192]

On these issues, the Soviet leaders were mainly forced on the defence, especially when the Cuban Missile Crisis was brought up time and again as the prime example of the Soviet lack of consultation, which compelled Khrushchev to admit that '[y]ou truly have the full moral high-ground when you criticise us for not informing you about sending missiles to Cuba', even confessing that '[w]e recognise that we are at fault'.[193] Moreover, Khrushchev underlined his great esteem for the Polish leader Gomulka and the East German Ulbricht, while stressing that he had very equal discussions with these WP leaders. 'Equality' was, accordingly, not a Romanian prerogative.

Meanwhile, the Chinese leadership was well aware of the opportunities the Romanian dissidence offered in terms of further weakening the Soviet Union. Zhou Enlai himself summoned the Romanian ambassador, D. Gheorgiu, on 17 July 1964, in order to point out to what extent the Kremlin had compromised the interests of other communist countries, while comparing the Soviet Union to 'tsarist Russia' and stressing that it desired 'that all socialist countries would be subordinate to the Soviet Union'. Meanwhile, he 'admired with sympathy' the Romanian leaders for their 'resistance against the [great] pressures exercised by the USSR', and accepted an invitation to send a Chinese delegation to Romania to discuss this.[194] The Chinese added that '[i]f all [WP members] will rise against Khrushchev, then his adventure will be reined in',[195] and thus made the Romanians aware of the WP's potential in eroding Khrushchev's power. At a meeting with their Romanian comrades at the end of August, the Albanian envoy, Manush Myftiu, went still further, and predicted that Romania would soon face the same fate as Albania and would therefore have to form a bloc with China, North Korea and North Vietnam. He emphasised that the 'goal of transforming the Warsaw Pact from a defence treaty of socialist countries into a weapon of blackmail, threat and exploitation, of domination in Khrushchev's hands, is clear'.[196]

The Sino–Soviet split had again contributed to the emancipation of one of the NSWP countries, since Romania's involvement as 'mediator' had enabled the Romanian leadership to formulate an autonomous course. Moreover, it not only 'provided Romania [with] a distinct status within the communist bloc', as Rijnoveanu puts it, but it actually put the Romanian leaders *above* the Warsaw Pact, since they posed as a mediator in a conflict that transcended the confines of the Soviet alliance. Although 'the Romanian leaders were far from having the necessary power to play a significant role in settling the Sino-Soviet divergences', their attempt to do so was sufficient to increase their status.[197] The process was much more important to the Romanians than the result. Instead of giving Moscow the moral high ground in its estrangement from China, the Romanian 'mediation' further eroded Soviet power by vindicating Romanian dissent. After the Sino–Soviet split had revealed that the communist bloc was not a monolith, it provided the Romanians with the opportunity to break through the monolithic structure of the Soviet bloc. Meanwhile, Romanian sovereignty was consolidated at Soviet expense.

The impact of Romanian independence

On 14 October 1964 Khrushchev's ouster, which will be discussed at greater length in the next chapter, seemed to provide a brief window of opportunity for the improvement of Sino-Soviet relations, since the new leadership allegedly wanted to 'write a new page' in terms of their relations with the Chinese.[198] In fact, however, the Chinese leaders complained to their Romanian comrades about 'the same insults after the fall of Khrushchev'.[199]

Putting their independence into practice, the Romanian leadership vetoed another proposal by Ulbricht to convene a PCC meeting to discuss MLF on 27–28 November 1964.[200] At a cocktail party in Moscow in celebration of Khrushchev's ouster, the Romanian Foreign Minister Maurer explained to Ulbricht that he objected to the method with which the meeting had been convened, as the Romanians wanted to know the items on the agenda on time so as to be well prepared.[201] They nevertheless reluctantly agreed to an unprecedented compromise, according to which a meeting of deputy foreign ministers would be convened on 10 December 1964, followed by a PCC meeting in January 1965.[202] The East German leadership had suggested this in complete exasperation at the Romanian obstinacy.[203] In a conversation between an East German diplomat in Warsaw and the Polish PUWP member Zenon Kliszko, the latter defined Albania as 'the Achilles heel of the socialist camp', because the Albanian 'front had indeed spilled over to Romania'.[204] The Romanians used the Albanian question in order to underline their own emancipation from the Soviet grip: the Romanian deputy foreign minister, Pompiliu Macovei, suggested inviting the Albanians again to the PCC meeting in January, which was ultimately approved with little enthusiasm.[205] In addition, Macovei stressed that all observers, including the Chinese, should be invited to the PCC meeting in January, too. Macovei's suggestions were most severely criticised by the Polish deputy foreign minister, Naszkowski.[206]

Moreover, Macovei vetoed both a common communiqué about the contents of the meeting in question and the preparation of a communiqué that would be published after the PCC meeting in January 1965, because it would make the meeting itself redundant. This led to a two-hour discussion, which remained unresolved but in which Naszkowski, supported by the Soviet Sorin and the East German Winzer, again took the lead in an attempt to win Macovei over to their stance by presenting two alternative communiqués. Although Macovei vetoed this attempt too, it is interesting to note that a new dynamic was burgeoning within the Warsaw Pact, in which the Romanian dissidence was mainly countered by a Polish search for alternatives, thus leaving the Kremlin somewhat empty handed. A meeting without a communiqué was unprecedented, and testified to the way in which the WP had turned into much more than a rhetorical ploy. Soviet choreography had yielded to NSWP manoeuvrability.

The Romanian obstinacy frustrated Ulbricht's aims, since the Romanians had deliberately sought to paralyse the meeting by giving their delegate,

Macovei, 'a limited mandate', according to which he was 'not to sign any document whatsoever, nor even to accept the smallest communiqué in the press'.[207] As the Romanian vice-premier, Emil Bodnaras, explained to Chinese Ambassador Liu Fan shortly after the meeting, '[a]ccepting a communiqué in the press concerning the meeting of deputy foreign ministers, would have blocked our freedom of action'.[208] The absence of a pre-concocted communiqué for the PCC meeting in January 1965 increased the scope for manoeuvre not only for the Romanians, but also for their comrades.

Moreover, Bodnaras emphasised that 'we want to orient the discussions within the framework of the Political Consultative Committee's session in other directions than the other members of the Warsaw Treaty Organisation want'. He had specifically informed the Chinese about this, because he thought that they should join the WP again as observers, as will be explained at greater length in Chapter 5. As such, they could play a significant role in widening the scope of the Warsaw Pact as a vehicle of the international communist movement 'in order to promote another spirit than that of the whip'.[209] The Romanian leadership began to attach increasing importance to the alliance, since participation within the WP could turn in their favour, by influencing Soviet bloc policy and emphasising Romanian sovereignty through cultivating an autonomous stance. Unlike the Albanians, the Romanians were careful to explore the scope for manoeuvre *within* the Warsaw Pact.

Conclusion: emancipation and multilateralisation

The situation within the Warsaw Pact halfway through 1964 seemed a far cry from Khrushchev's optimism four years earlier. The Sino–Soviet split had escalated, and the dynamics within the Warsaw Pact had begun to spiral out of Soviet control. Instead of serving as an instrument to further Soviet interests, it inadvertently turned into an instrument that some of the NSWP members skilfully employed to undermine the Soviet hegemony and strengthen their own domestic position. Khrushchev was more often than not at the receiving end of the initiatives of other WP members. The Sino–Soviet split was bound to result in a Pyrrhic victory for the Soviet Union.

The defiance of tiny Albania was particularly humiliating, since it exposed the Soviet incapacity to prevent even its smallest ally from siding with its biggest rival. Chinese protection provided the Albanian leadership with an escape route out of the Soviet grip. Keeping up the appearances of communist unity and fearing an escalation in Sino-Soviet relations, the Kremlin was weak in the face of Albanian defiance. The Albanian leadership thus set a precedent by using the WP as an instrument to further its own national interests and undermine Soviet ones, instead of vice versa. The Albanian emancipation from Moscow's grip facilitated the WP's multilateralisation by challenging Soviet unilateralism and raising the self-consciousness of the other NSWP members.

Both the Albanian refusal to leave the alliance and the Mongolian application to join it not only refute the common assumption of the WP as an *involuntary* alliance, but also illustrate how the Warsaw Treaty could be employed to undermine the Soviet position. Using both the treaty and the Sino–Soviet split as instruments to argue against Soviet support of Mongolian admission, the Romanian and Polish leaders formulated an individual response and increased their room for manoeuvre. Although the failure of the Mongolian application prevented the WP's reorientation against China *de iure*, the Mongolian episode illustrated that the alliance threatened to become reoriented against China *de facto*.

In the deliberations about the Mongolian application in 1963, the split with China loomed large, whereas NATO did not even feature. The Warsaw Pact was not only, as Vojtech Mastny argues, perennially 'in search of a purpose', but in the early 1960s it even seemed to have lost its original purpose of uniting in the face of 'imperialism'.[210] WP unity vis-à-vis China had become more important. With the Chinese observers, the Chinese interests had been ousted too. The split with China fundamentally challenged the WP's communist credentials, which had not been enshrined in the Warsaw Treaty anyhow. The subsequent identity crisis of the alliance also contributed to the increased room for manoeuvre, since the NSWP leaders could participate in reshaping the identity of both the pact and its members.

The Romanian leaders in particular seized the opportunity provided by the Sino–Soviet split, since they continued to explore their possibilities in order also to challenge the Soviet Union in a bilateral context in the period after the Mongolian application. By presenting themselves as a mediator between China and the Soviet Union, they pulled some of the strings and actually broke through the institutional confines of the Warsaw Pact. Having successfully refashioned their own identity from Soviet pawn to Soviet 'equal', the Romanian leaders began to define the rules for a new game, which would have a huge impact on the alliance in the second half of the 1960s. By leaving the initiative to Romania and even approving Romanian mediation, Khrushchev increased the Romanian scope for manoeuvre so much that he indirectly sanctioned the Romanian declaration of independence. The Romanian 'mediation' had enabled the Romanians to emphasise their sovereignty and independence from the Soviet Union.

After the Romanian leadership had successfully prevented the WP from turning *against* China through the potential admission of Mongolia, it also attempted to draw China again into the alliance by closely consulting with the Chinese ambassador in Bucharest in the wake of its declaration of independence. Whereas the Albanian leadership challenged the Soviet authority within the WP to strengthen its domestic position and to further national interests, the Romanian leadership pursued the same goal by playing the Soviet Union and China off against each other, while pretending to mediate between the two. It had, however, carefully studied the Albanian precedent, and understood what the limits were. Although the Romanian emancipation largely developed outside the confines of the WP, it paved the way for its *Sonderkurs* within the alliance in the second half of the 1960s. Instead of siding with the Chinese and defying the Kremlin, the Romanian leaders adopted a more subtle strategy: they were emancipated from the Soviet grip, while remaining within the Soviet alliance.

At the same time, the Sino–Soviet split had increased the importance of the WP, since it remained as the only platform to close ranks with the Kremlin after the communist movement had crumbled. With the major communist powers moving in two directions, the communist movement had effectively ceased to operate from 1960 onwards. Although the break in the communist movement spilled over into the WP through the Soviet–Albanian split, the WP could never provide a viable alternative to the communist movement. Apart from the fact that it was considerably smaller, its *interstate* nature prevented it from turning into a forum of communist *parties*. Within the WP, European security, not communist ideology, was paramount, even though the WP members still had to find a way to separate the two. The WP's increasing importance over the communist movement accordingly meant a considerable shift from ideology to security within the Soviet bloc.

The Sino–Soviet split had not only exposed Sino-Soviet unity as a fairy tale, but it had also undermined the consensus within the WP. The WP monolith, too, had turned into a mosaic that was neither a paper tiger nor a cardboard castle. In the shadow of the Sino–Soviet split, the WP had developed a dynamic of its own, which turned it into an alliance that was not as rose coloured as Khrushchev hoped in 1960, but was at least multi-coloured. That in itself was a notable achievement, as the embryonic emancipation of some of the smaller allies actually began to turn the WP into a more multilateral alliance. After Albania and Romania had called the Soviet bluff, the ground rules were established for an altogether new game.

Notes

1 'Information on the Meeting with Comrade Chen Yi, 27 July 1961', in A. Lalaj, '"Albania is not Cuba." Sino-Albanian Summits and the Sino-Soviet Split', in C. F. Ostermann (ed.), *Inside China's Cold War*, CWIHP Bulletin No. 16 (Washington, 2007/2008), 228.
2 Minutes of a session of the leadership of the PCI, 8 July 1960, FIG APC, Leadership, 1960, mf 024, 757.
3 Cf. Z. Brzezinski, *The Soviet Bloc: Unity and Conflict. Revised and Enlarged Edition* (Harvard, 1967), 397.
4 'Declaration', 4 February 1960, PHP, www.php.isn.ethz.ch/collections/colltopic.cfm?lng=en&id=17643&navinfo=14465 (accessed 25 August 2013).
5 'Report on PCC Meeting by the Bulgarian Prime Minister (Anton Iugov) to Bulgarian Politburo Session', 11 February 1960, PHP, www.php.isn.ethz.ch/collections/colltopic.cfm?lng=en&id=17883&navinfo=14465 (accessed 25 August 2013).
6 'Declaration', 4 February 1960, PHP.
7 'Kang Sheng's Speech at the meeting of the Warsaw Pact Political Consultative Committee', 4 February 1960, PHP, php.isn.ethz.ch/collections/colltopic.cfm?

id=16320&lng=en.Cf. 'Speech by comrade Kang Sheng at the meeting of the Warsaw Pact Political Consultative Committee', 4 February 1960, SAPMO-BArch DY 30/3386, 87–99.
8 Letter from CPC CC to CPSU CC (top secret), 10 September 1960, SAPMO-BArch, DY 30/3604, 30.
9 V. Mastny, 'Meeting of the PCC, Moscow, 4 February 1960, Editorial Note', PHP, www.php.isn.ethz.ch/collections/colltopic.cfm?lng=en&id=17885&navinfo=14465 (accessed 25 August 2013).
10 L. Lüthi, *The Sino-Soviet Split: Cold War in the Communist World* (Princeton, 2008), 163.
11 'Vive le Leninisme, 1870–1960', Beijing, 1960, FIG APC, China, 1960, mf 0474, 1173.
12 Letter from CPC CC to CPSU CC (top secret), 10 September 1960, SAPMO-BArch, DY 30/3604, 48. This is corroborated by V.M. Zubok, *Khrushchev and the Berlin Crisis (1958–1962)*, CWIHP Working Paper No. 6 (Washington, 1993), 17: 'The Soviet embassy in Beijing reported that the Chinese "used the aggravation after the failure of the Paris summit" to oppose "for the first time directly and openly" the foreign policy of the CPSU.'
13 Intervention by the PCI, Bucharest, 25 June 1960, FIG APC, Bucharest Conference, 1960, mf 0474, 2535.
14 Lüthi, *The Sino-Soviet Split*, 172.
15 W.E. Griffith, *Albania and the Sino-Soviet Rift* (Massachusetts, 1963), 41.
16 Lüthi, *The Sino-Soviet Split*, 173; and Griffith, *Albania and the Sino-Soviet Rift*, 46–47.
17 Lüthi, *The Sino-Soviet Split*, 202; and A. Lalaj, 'Albanien und der Warschauer Pakt', in T. Diedrich *et al.* (eds), *Der Warschauer Pakt: Von der Gründung bis zum Zusammenbruch 1955 bis 1991* (Berlin, 2009), 36.
18 'Department of foreign policy and international relations. Information to com. Ulbricht', Berlin, 13 October 1960, SAPMO-BArch, DY 30/3589, 154.
19 Letter from Paul Wandel, GDR diplomat in Beijing, to Ulbricht, 11 September 1960, SAPMO-BArch, DY 30/3605, 79.
20 Cf. letter from the CPSU CC to the CCP CC, 5 November 1960, SAPMO-BArch, DY 30/3605, 200.
21 Letter from Beijing from an envoy of the PCI to Giuliano Pajetta, 25 August 1960, FIG APC, China, 1960, mf 0474, 0973; and 'Note on Albania by Franco Portone', 9 October 1961, FIG APC, Albania, 1961, 0483, 2349.
22 Griffith, *Albania and the Sino-Soviet Rift*, 175.
23 Ibid., 2.
24 Lüthi, *The Sino-Soviet Split*, 176.
25 See also 'Strictly confidential letter from Khrushchev to SED CC about withdrawal of Soviet specialists from China', 18 July 1960, SAPMO-BArch, DY 30/3605, 21–24; and 'Strictly confidential memorandum from Soviet embassy in China to Chinese Ministry of Foreign Affairs', ibid., 18 July 1960, 28–33.
26 Letter from AWP CC to CPSU CC and CCP CC, 27 August 1960, SAPMO-BArch, DY 30/3589, 129–37.
27 CPSU note to the delegations of the communist parties at the Moscow Conference, 8 December 1960, ANIC, RWP CC, IR, 76/1960, 73.
28 Minutes of a conversation between a delegation of the CPSU CC and the AWP CC, 12 November 1960, ANIC, RWP CC, IR, 76/1960, 118–34. Cf. Lalaj (ed.), '"Albania is not Cuba"', 190–95, for the strikingly similar Albanian version of the minutes.
29 Ibid., 132–33.
30 Ibid., 131–33. Cf. Lalaj (ed.), '"Albania is not Cuba"', 194.

90 *Embryonic emancipation, 1955–64*

31 GDR Embassy in Budapest, 30 November 1960, SAPMO-BArch, DY 30/3589, 156–58. Cf. Minutes of a conversation between a delegation of the CPSU CC and the AWP CC, 12 November 1960, ANIC, RWP CC, IR, 76/1960, 119: 'The divergences were in the Yugoslav question', which caused the deterioration of relations after the Bucharest conference.
32 Minutes of the PCI leadership, 9 December 1960, FIG APC, Leadership, 1960, mf 024, 876.
33 Declaration of the Albanian Workers Party at the Moscow Conference of communist and workers parties, ANIC, RWP CC, IR, 76/1960, 62.
34 Quoted in Lüthi, *The Sino-Soviet Split*, 189.
35 'Declaration of the conference of representatives of communist and workers parties', ANIC, RWP CC, IR, 81/1960, 125, 126, 135, 156.
36 Minutes of the PCI leadership, 9 December 1960, FIG APC, Leadership, 1960, mf 024, 880–81.
37 Extract from the memorandum by GDR diplomat, König, December 1960/January 1961, SAPMO-BArch, DY 30/IV/2/20/99, 179–82.
38 'Memorandum of Conversation with Comrade Zhou Enlai', Beijing 18 January 1961, in Lalaj (ed.), '"Albania is not Cuba"', 196, 199.
39 Letter from Hoxha to RWP CC, 22 December 1960, ANIC, RWP CC, C, 7/1961, 43.
40 'Report of the RWP delegation which participated in the IVth Congress of the Albanian Workers Party', February 1961, ANIC, RWP CC, C, 81/1960, 1.
41 Ibid., 2.
42 Information on the Albanian Party Conference, 26 February 1961, FIG APC, Albania, 1961, mf 0483, 2333.
43 Ibid., 3. See also the report by König, 17 April 1961, SAPMO-BArch, DY 30/IV/2/20/99, 190.
44 Letter from CPSU CC to Ulbricht, 28 March 1961, SAPMO-BArch, DY 30/3590, 29–46.
45 Cf. Report by König, 17 April 1961, SAPMO-BArch, DY 30/IV/2/20/99; 'Report of the RWP delegation which participated in the IVth Congress of the Albanian Workers Party', February 1961, ANIC, RWP CC, C, 81/1960; Information on the Albanian Party Conference, 26 February 1961, FIG APC, Albania, 1961, mf 0483, 2331–44.
46 'Report of the RWP delegation which participated in the IVth Congress of the Albanian Workers Party', February 1961, ANIC, RWP CC, C, 81/1960, 3, 14–15.
47 Ibid., 10. Cf. Information on the Albanian Party Conference, 26 February 1961, FIG APC, Albania, 1961, mf 0483, 2331–44.
48 'Talks with Chinese delegation', 25 February 1961, in Lalaj (ed.), '"Albania is not Cuba"', 205–6, 210.
49 'Further information about the attitude of the Albanian comrades after the fourth Party Conference', Tirana, 24 March 1961, SAPMO-BArch, DY30/3590, 49–53.
50 'The Soviet-Albanian Dispute: Albanian Memorandum on Incidents at Vlorë Naval Base', 22 March 1961, PHP, www.php.isn.ethz.ch/collections/colltopic.cfm?lng=en&id=17891&navinfo=14465 (accessed 25 August 2013).
51 Ibid.
52 Ibid.
53 Ibid.
54 Report by König, 17 April 1961, SAPMO-BArch, DY 30/IV/2/20/99, 190.
55 'Central Committee of the CPSU to the First Secretary of the PUWP (Władysław Gomułka)', 28 March 1961, PHP, www.php.isn.ethz.ch/collections/colltopic.cfm?lng=en&id=17893&navinfo=14465 (accessed 20 September 2013).
56 Letter from CPSU CC to Ulbricht, 28 March 1961, SAPMO-BArch, DY 30/3590, 29–46.

57 'Speech by the Bulgarian First Secretary (Todor Zhivkov)', 29 March 1961, PHP, www.php.isn.ethz.ch/collections/colltopic.cfm?lng=en&id=17894&navinfo=14465 (accessed 25 August 2013).
58 'Statement by the Bulgarian First Secretary (Todor Zhivkov) on Albania', 29 March 1961, PHP, www.php.isn.ethz.ch/collections/colltopic.cfm?lng=en&id=17889&navinfo=14465 (accessed 25 August 2013).
59 Ibid.
60 'Some problems concerning the construction of the AWP', ANIC, RWP, C, 81/1961, 16. Cf. Griffith, *Albania and the Sino-Soviet Rift*, 13.
61 Speech by First Secretary of the CC of the CPSU, Nikita Khrushchev, 29 March 1961, PHP, www.php.isn.ethz.ch/collections/colltopic.cfm?lng=en&id=17897&navinfo=14465 (accessed 4 December 2013).
62 Lalaj (ed.), '"Albania is not Cuba"', 223.
63 'Resolution of the Political Consultative Committee of the Warsaw Pact', 14 April 1961, ANIC, RWP CC, IR, 1/1961, 3–4.
64 Lalaj, 'Albanien und der Warschauer Pakt', 37.
65 Report by König, 17 April 1961, SAPMO-BArch, DY 30/IV/2/20/99, 190.
66 Griffith, *Albania and the Sino-Soviet Rift*, 81.
67 'Memorandum of Conversation, Comrade Adyl Kellezi with Comrade Zhou Enlai', 20 April 1961, in Lalaj, '"Albania is not Cuba"', 223.
68 See D.S. Zagoria, *The Sino-Soviet Conflict 1956–1961* (Princeton, 1962), 370.
69 Lalaj, 'Albanien und der Warschauer Pakt', 40.
70 Lüthi, *The Sino-Soviet Split*, 205.
71 Relations between Albania and China in 1960 and 1961, Berlin, 6 January 1962, SAPMO-BArch, DY 30/IV/2/20/99, 235–45.
72 Letter from A. Kossygin to the Albanian Government, 26 April 1961, SAPMO-BArch, DY 30/3590, 100.
73 Letter from Mehmet Shehu to WP leaders/observers, April 1961, SAPMO-BArch, DY 30/3590, 55–62.
74 Ibid.
75 Letter from Maurer to the Albanian Government, Bucharest, 21 June 1961, SAPMO-BArch, DY 30/3591, 221.
76 Cf. the more conventional claim from the Albanian historian Ana Lalaj, in 'Albanien und der Warschauer Pakt', 29: 'Die Beziehungen zwischen Albanien und dem Warschauer Pakt lassen sich im Grunde auf die Beziehungen zwischen Albanien und der Sowjetunion reduzieren.'
77 Letter from Anton Iugov to the Albanian government, Sofia, 17 May 1961, SAPMO-BArch, DY 30/3590, 176–81.
78 Letter from Neumann to König, Berlin, 23 May 1961, SAPMO-BArch, DY 30/3590, 172–73; and Ferenc Münnich to the Albanian Government, Budapest, 18 April 1961, SAPMO-BArch, DY 30/3590, 82–84.
79 For example, Letter from König to Neumann, Berlin, 5 May 961, SAPMO-BArch, DY 30/3590, 164; and Letter from Florin to Ulbricht, SAPMO-BArch, DY 30/3592, 52.
80 Letter from Hoxha/Shehu to CPSU CC and government, Tirana, 06/07/1961, SAPMO-BArch, DY 30/3591, 41.
81 For example, 'Note on Albania by Franco Portone', 9 October 1961, FIG APC, Albania, 1961, 0483, 2349–52.
82 Letter from Hysni Kapo to Walter Ulbricht, Tirana, 22 July 1961, SAPMO-BArch, DY 30/3591, 172.
83 'Statement from Ulbricht about Albanian behaviour', SAPMO-BArch, DY 30/3478, 11–14. See also ANIC, RWP CC, C, 2/1961, 220–25 for the minutes of this session, particularly 222–23 for Ulbricht's proposal.

84 Minutes of the meeting of WP party leaders, 3 August 1961, ANIC, RWP CC, C 2/1961, 223.
85 Minutes of the meeting from 3–5 August 1961, top secret, *Politisches Archiv des Auswärtigen Amtes* (PA AA), Berlin, *Ministerium für Auswärtige Angelegenheiten der DDR* (MfAA), G-A 474, 21.
86 Minutes of the meeting of WP party leaders, 3 August 1961, ANIC, RWP CC, C 2/1961, 224.
87 'Estimate of the attitude of the Albanian People's Republic on the conclusion of a German peace treaty', Berlin, 3 October 1961, SAPMO-BArch, DY30/IV/2/20/99, 227–29.
88 Letter from CPSU CC to AWP CC, 21 August 1961, SAPMO-BArch, DY 30/3592, 16.
89 Letter from the Albanian Ministry of Foreign Affairs to the East German Embassy in Tirana about the unilateral East German decision to withdraw the diplomats, Tirana, 26 December 1961, SAPMO-BArch, DY30/3592, 153.
90 Letter from Hoxha to CPSU CC, 6 September 1961, SAPMO-BArch, DY 30/3592, 82.
91 Griffith, *Albania and the Sino-Soviet Rift*, 88.
92 Letter from CCP CC to CPSU CC, 20 November 1961, DY 30/3386, 230–33. Cf. L.M. Lüthi, 'The People's Republic of China and the Warsaw Pact Organization, 1955–63', *Cold War History* 7:4 (2007), 485.
93 Lüthi, 'The People's Republic of China', 485.
94 See e.g. Letter from the CCP CC to the CPSU CC, 10 September 1960, SAPMO-BArch, DY 30/3604, 19–147; and Chapter 1 of this book.
95 Griffith, *Albania and the Sino-Soviet Rift*, 85; and Lalaj, 'Albanien und der Warschauer Pakt', 38. Cf. Letter from the Albanian Ministry of Foreign Affairs to the East German Embassy in Tirana about the unilateral East German decision to withdraw the diplomats, Tirana, 26 December 1961, SAPMO-BArch, DY 30/3592, 150–61; and 'Directive of tasks of the RWP CC', 15 December 1961, in which the Albanian ambassador in Bucharest was also declared a 'persona non grata': ANIC, RWP CC, C, 3/1962, 17; and ibid., 19, for the withdrawal of the Romanian ambassador from Albania in October 1961.
96 Quoted in Griffith, *Albania and the Sino-Soviet Rift*, 87.
97 Letter from Grechko to General Bekir Baluku, the minister of defence in Albania, January 1962, SAPMO-BArch, DY 30/3593, 4–5.
98 Letter from the CPSU CC to all Party organisations and all communists in the SU, 22 January 1962, SAPMO-BArch, DY 30/3593, 38.
99 'Information on the Meeting with Comrade Chen Yi', 27 July 1961, in Lalaj (ed.), '"Albania is not Cuba"', 228.
100 Letter from Ulbricht to Khrushchev, 16 January 1962, SAPMO-BArch, DY 30/3387, 1–2.
101 See e.g. letter from Ulbricht to Khrushchev, January 1962, SAPMO-BArch, DY 30/3606, 17–23.
102 Lüthi, *The Sino-Soviet Split*, 208.
103 Letter from CPSU CC to CCP CC, 31 May 1962, SAPMO-BArch, DY 30/3606, 123.
104 Griffith, *Albania and the Sino-Soviet Rift*, 176.
105 Letter from CPSU CC to CCP CC, 22 February 1962, ANIC, RWP CC, IR, 50/1962, 10.
106 X. Liu and V. Mastny (eds), *China and Eastern Europe, 1960s–1980s. Proceedings of the International Symposium: Reviewing the History of Chinese-East European Relations from the 1960s to the 1980s. Beijing, 24–26 March 2004*, Zürcher Beiträge zur Sicherheitspolitik und Konfliktforschung Nr. 72 (Zurich, 2004), www.isn.

ethz.ch/isn/Digital-Library/Publications/Detail/?ots591=CAB359A3-9328-19CC-A
1D2-8023E646B22C&lng=en&id=10435 (accessed 23 August 2013), 10.
107 Note of discussion between Ghizela Vass and Soviet official Scacicov, 17 February 1962, ANIC, RWP CC, IR, 14/1962, 12, 15.
108 Cf. L. Țăranu, L., România în Consiliul de Ajutor Economic Reciproc, 1949–1965 (Bucharest, 2007).
109 'Documents on sovereignty and national independence', ANIC, RWP CC, IR, 29/1963.
110 'Report on a discussion with comrade Andropov during lunch', 2 April 1963, ANIC, RWP CC, IR, 13/1963, 2.
111 Note of the talks with Andropov, 3 April 1963, ANIC, RWP CC, IR, 13/1963.
112 'Problems, which have arisen from discussions with comrades Andropov, Jegalin, and Karipscenko', ANIC, RWP CC, IR, 13/1963, 15.
113 Letter from the Romanian ambassador in Beijing, D. Gheorghiu, to the Foreign Ministry, Top Secret, 25 May 1963, ANIC, RWP CC, IR, 55/1963, 5.
114 Information from the Romanian Embassy in Beijing, ANIC, RWP CC, IR, 1/1963, 57.
115 See R.L. Garthoff, 'When and Why Romania Distanced Itself from the Warsaw Pact', in J. Hershberg (ed.), Cold War Crises, CWIHP Bulletin No. 5 (Washington, 1998), 111; and L. Watts, Romanian Security Policy and the Cuban Missile Crisis, CWIHP E-Dossier No. 38 (Washington, 2013), www.wilsoncenter.org/publication/e-dossier-no-38-romania-security-policy-and-the-cuban-missile-crisis (accessed 25 August 2013).
116 An account of the Cuban Missile Crisis falls outside the scope of this book. See for the most lucid and well documented account to date: A. Fursenko and T. Naftali, 'One Hell of a Gamble.' Khrushchev, Castro and Kennedy, 1958–1964 (London and New York, 1998).
117 Minutes of the plenary session of the RWP CC, from 15–22 April 1964, ANIC, RWP CC, C, 16/1964, 17.
118 Conversation between the Chinese ambassador in Bucharest and Leonte Rautu (RWP), 19 June 1963, ANIC, RWP CC, IR, 1/1963, 64.
119 Cf. Minutes of the meeting of the RWP CC Politburo meeting of 26 June 1963, C, 34/1963, 2–32.
120 Cf. M. Trachtenberg, A Constructed Peace. The Making of the European Settlement, 1945–1963 (Princeton, 1999), 283–84.
121 Lalaj (ed.) '"Albania is not Cuba"', 178. Cf. 'Meeting of a delegation of the CPSU and the CCP, July 1963', SAPMO-BArch, DY 30/3608, 1–287.
122 Remark by Soviet representative, B.N. Ponomarov, 13 July 1963, ANIC, RWP CC, IR, 26/1963, 170.
123 V. Mastny, China, the Warsaw Pact, and Sino-Soviet Relations under Khrushchev, PHP, www.php.isn.ethz.ch/collections/coll_china_wapa/intro_mastny.cfm?navinfo (2002), 2 (accessed 25 August 2013).
124 'Report of a conversation between Zhou Enlai and Tsedenbal in China, strictly confidential', 26 December 1962, SAPMO-BArch, DY 30/3606, 259–86.
125 The Mongolian move was also motivated by security reasons. Cf. S. Radchenko, The Soviets' Best Friend in Asia: The Mongolian Dimension of the Sino-Soviet Split, CWIHP Working Paper No. 42 (Washington, 2003), 2.
126 The Chinese leaders seemed to have anticipated this. See 'Memorandum of Conversation between Deng Xiaoping, Wang Jiaxiang, Hysni Kapo, and Ramiz Alia', 19 June 1962, in Lalaj (ed.), '"Albania is not Cuba"', 234.
127 Radchenko, The Soviets' Best Friend in Asia, 12.
128 See 'Mongolian Request for Admission to the Warsaw Pact', 15 July 1963, PHP, www.php.isn.ethz.ch/collections/colltopic.cfm?lng=en&id=20907&navinfo=14465 (accessed 25 August 2013).

129 G. Lundestad, 'Empire by Invitation? The United States and Western Europe, 1942–52', *Journal of Peace Research* 23 (1986), 263–77.
130 Letter from Khrushchev to Ulbricht (and other WP leaders), 10 July 1963, SAPMO-BArch, DY 30/3387, 47–49.
131 Confidential letter from Khrushchev to Ulbricht (and other WP leaders), about convention of PCC meeting, 15 July 1963, SAPMO-BArch, DY 30/3387, 52–53.
132 Minutes of the meeting of the RWP CC Politburo meeting of 18 July 1963, ANIC, RWP CC, C, 39/1963, 117.
133 Ibid.
134 Minutes of the meeting of the RWP CC Politburo meeting of 18 July 1963, ANIC, RWP CC, C 39/1963, 121, 124. Cf. Griffith, *Albania and the Sino-Soviet Rift*, 27.
135 Mao Zedong, 'US Imperialism is a Paper Tiger', 14 July 1956, www.marxists.org/reference/archive/mao/selected-works/volume-5/mswv5_52.htm (accessed 20 September 2013).
136 'Memorandum by the Polish Foreign Minister (Adam Rapacki)', 20 July 1963, PHP, www.php.isn.ethz.ch/collections/colltopic.cfm?lng=en&id=17905&navinfo=14465 (accessed 25 August 2013).
137 Cf. Lüthi, *The Sino Soviet Split*, for this wordplay.
138 See 'Excerpts of Report to the Hungarian Politburo on the PCC Meeting by the First Secretary of the MSzMP (János Kádár)', 31 July 1963, PHP, www.php.isn.ethz.ch/collections/colltopic.cfm?lng=en&id=17907&navinfo=14465 (accessed 25 August 2013).
139 Mastny, *China, the Warsaw Pact*, 3.
140 Ibid.
141 For example, Minutes of the plenary session of the RWP CC, which took place on 17.II.1964, ANIC, RWP CC, C, 6/1964, 23.
142 'Communiqué', 26 July 1963, PHP, www.php.isn.ethz.ch/collections/colltopic.cfm?lng=en&id=17906&navinfo=14465 (accessed 25 August 2013).
143 Lüthi, 'The People's Republic of China', 479.
144 'Information report to the Ministry of Foreign Affairs of the GDR, section Romania', 14 January 1964, SAPMO-BArch, DY 30/IVA2/20/368, 19 and 24.
145 Letter from Ulbricht to Khrushchev, Berlin, 24 January 1964, SAPMO-BArch, DY 30/3387, 61–62. Cf. Letter from Ulbricht to Gheorgiu-Dej, ANIC, RWP CC, C, 6/1964, 44–45.
146 Letter from Novotny to SED CC, 15 February 1964, SAPMO-BArch, DY 30/3877, 80.
147 Letter from Khrushchev to Ulbricht, 20 March 1964, SAPMO-BArch, DY 30/3387, 90–91.
148 Letter from Ulbricht to Gheorghiu-Dej, 26 March 1964, SAPMO-BArch, DY 30/3387, 95.
149 Letter from Gheorgiu-Dej to Ulbricht, no date, SAPMO-BArch, DY 30/3387, 98. Cf. Minutes of the RWP CC Politburo session on 30–31 March 1964, ANIC, RWP CC, C, 12/1964, 33, for the Romanian discussion on this letter.
150 Letter from the RWP CC to the CCP CC, Bucharest, 14 February 1964, ANIC, RWP CC, C, 5/1964, 16. Cf. C. Rijnoveanu, *A Perspective on Romania's Involvement in the Sino-Soviet Conflict (1960–1965)*, Cold War History Research Centre, Budapest, www.coldwar.hu/html/en/publications/Rom_Sino_Riv.pdf (May 2009), 1 (accessed 25 August 2013).
151 M. Retegan, *In the Shadow of the Prague Spring: Romanian Foreign Policy and the Crisis of Czechoslovakia, 1968* (Oxford, 2000), 37.
152 Response from several communist parties to the RWP's letter, 4 April 1964, ANIC, RWP CC, IR 12/1964, 35.

153 Minutes of the RWP CC Politburo meeting of 28 February 1964, ANIC, RWP CC, C, 9/1964, 7, 8, 11, 20.
154 'Memorandum about a conversation with comrade Iljuchin from the Soviet embassy', 20 February 1964, SAPMO-BArch, DY 30/IVA 2/20/354, 55–56.
155 'Memorandum about a conversation with comrade Lazarescu, deputy director of the department of international relations in the RWP CC', Bucharest, 11 March 64, SAPMO-Barch, DY 30/IVA2/20/354, 68–71. Letter from Ambassador Dölling to Florin, Moscow, 10 March 1964: 'The Romanian ambassador, who himself speaks Russian badly, conveyed all that in a tone to justify the move of the Romanian CC.'
156 Gomulka advised Khrushchev on the Sino–Soviet rift in the abovementioned letter, written on 8 October 1963, published in D. Selvage, *The Warsaw Pact and Nuclear Nonproliferation, 1963–1965*, CWIHP Working Paper No. 32 (Washington, 2001), 29.
157 Ibid., 22.
158 Minutes of the RWP CC Politburo session on 30–31 March 1964, ANIC, RWP CC, C, 12/1964, 24–26.
159 Minutes of the conversations between the RWP CC and the CCP CC, 3–10 March 1964, ANIC, RWP CC, IR, 31/1964, I, 174–75.
160 Ibid., 251–52. In the same vein the Romanians also regretted that they 'did not rise against the attacks directed at the Albanian Workers' Party': see Minutes of the RWP CC Politburo meeting on 24 March 1964, ANIC, RWP CC, C, 11/1964.
161 Minutes of the conversations between the RWP CC and the CCP CC, 3–10 March 1964, ANIC, RWP CC, IR, 31/1964, I, 174–75.
162 Letter from the CPSU CC to the CPC CC, 7 March 1964, ANIC, RWP CC, C, 17/1964, 249.
163 Minutes of the plenary session of the RWP CC from 15–22 April 1964, ANIC, RWP CC, C, 16/1964, 45.
164 Meeting between Bodnaras and Liu Fan, 5 September 1964, ANIC, RWP CC, IR, 5/1964, 108.
165 Minutes of the RWP Politburo Session, 18 March 1964, ANIC, RWP CC, C, 10/1964, 20; Gheorghiu-Dej, quoted in ibid., 71.
166 Letter from Gheorgiu-Dej to Khrushchev, 25 March 1964, SAPMO-BArch, DY 30/3655, 139–40.
167 Romanian draft appeal as appendix to the abovementioned letter, SAPMO-BArch, DY30/3655, 141–50.
168 Khrushchev to RWP CC, 31 March 1964, SAPMO-BArch, DY 30/3655, 167.
169 Khrushchev to RWP CC, 28 March 1964, SAPMO-BArch, DY 30/3655, 161–62.
170 'Information report to the Ministry of Foreign Affairs of the GDR, section Romania', 8 April 1964, SAPMO-BArch, DY 30/IVA2/20/368, 73.
171 Minutes of the RWP CC Politburo session on 30–31 March 1964, ANIC, RWP CC, C, 12/1964, 6.
172 Minutes of the RWP Politburo Session, 18 March 1964, ANIC, RWP CC, C, 10/1964, 19.
173 D. Deletant and M. Ionescu, *Romania and the Warsaw Pact: 1955–1989*, CWIHP Working Paper No. 43 (Washington, 2004), 72.
174 Minutes of the RWP CC Politburo meeting on 2 April 1964, ANIC, RWP CC, C, 13/1964, 9–10.
175 Meeting between Gheorgiu Dej and Liu Fan, 10 April 1964, ANIC, RWP CC, IR, 5/1964, 24.
176 'Information report to the Ministry of Foreign Affairs of the GDR, section Romania', 8 April 1964, DY30/IVA2/20/368, 73.
177 Minutes of the plenary session of the RWP CC from 15–22 April 1964, ANIC, RWP CC, C, 16/1964, 47, 113, 245.

Embryonic emancipation, 1955–64

178 'Declaration of the position of the RWP in questions of the international communist and workers' movement', Bucharest, 22 April 1964, SAPMO-BArch, DY 30/IVA2/20/354, 161–93. See ANIC, RWP CC, C, 16/1964, 47ff for the Romanian version of the appeal.
179 Retegan, *In the Shadow of the Prague Spring*, 41.
180 Minutes of the plenary session of the RWP CC from 15–22 April 1964, ANIC, RWP CC, C, 16/1964, 42–44, 164, 242–43.
181 'Information about the attitude of the RWP leadership to the politics of the CCP leadership. Strictly confidential', Berlin, 29 April 1964, SAPMO-BArch, DY 30/IVA 2/20/359, 12.
182 'Information report to the Ministry of Foreign Affairs of the GDR, section Romania', 17 June 1964, SAPMO-BArch, DY 30/IVA 2/20/368, 126.
183 Cf. A. Locher, 'A Crisis Foretold. NATO and France, 1963–66', in A. Wenger *et al.* (eds), *Transforming NATO in the Cold War. Challenges beyond Deterrence in the 1960s* (Oxford and New York, 2007), 107–27.
184 Discussions between delegations of the RWP CC and the CPSU CC, Moscow, July 1964, ANIC, RWP CC, C, 36/1964, 158.
185 Meeting between Gheorghe Apostol, Emil Bodnaras and Liu Fan, 28 July 1964, ANIC, RWP CC, IR, 5/1964, 34, 50. Cf. Retegan, *In the Shadow of the Prague Spring*, 41.
186 For example, in Sweden, Italy, Japan the USA (!) and Norway. Retegan, *In the Shadow of the Prague Spring*, 42.
187 *Newsweek*, 10 August 1964, 'The New Rumania: A Satellite Looks West', ANIC, RWP CC, IR, 125/1964, 3–8.
188 Cf. for a very positive description of de Gaulle, whom the Romanians considered 'more intelligent than Mikoyan': Minutes of a conversation between Gh. Gheorgiu-Dej with a delegation of the AWP (com. M. Myftiu), 24 August 1964, ANIC, RWP CC, IR, 18/1964, 17.
189 E. Dragomir, 'The Perceived Threat of Hegemonism in Romania during the Second Détente', *Cold War History* 12:1 (2012), 116.
190 'Summary, trade department', Bucharest, 31 July 1964, SAPMO-BArch, DY 30/IVA2/20/359, 39.
191 Romanian proposal for the agenda of the discussions between the delegations of the RWP CC and the CPSU CC, ANIC, RWP CC, C, 36/1964, 12–13.
192 Discussions between delegations of the RWP CC and the CPSU CC, Moscow, July 1964, ANIC, RWP CC, C, 36/1964, 158.
193 Ibid., 47–48, 209–10. See ibid., 134–35, 144–48 and 157–59 for further discussions on the Warsaw Pact.
194 Conversation between Zhou Enlai and D. Gheorghiu, 17 July 1964, ANIC, RWP CC, C, 93/1963, 45, 47, 49.
195 Minutes of a conversation between a Romanian delegation and Zhou Enlai, convened at Chinese initiative, 29 September 1964, ANIC, RWP CC, C, 55/1964, I, 25.
196 Minutes of a conversation between comrade Gh. Gheorgiu-Dej with a delegation of the AWP CC (com. M. Myftiu), 24 August 1964, ANIC, RWP CC, IR, 18/1964, 10–11.
197 Rijnoveanu, *Perspective on Romania's Involvement*, 5, 10.
198 Information from CPSU member E.D. Karpescenko on the way to Moscow, 5 November 1964, ANIC, RWP CC, C, 70/1964, 10.
199 Minutes of the discussions between the Romanian party and government delegation and the Chinese party and government delegation, Moscow, 8 November 1964, ANIC, RWP CC, C, 70/1964, 72.
200 Letter from Gheorgiu-Dej to Ulbricht, 19 November, 1964, SAPMO-BArch, DY 30/3387, 184–85.

201 'Reception on the evening of 7 November', ANIC, RWP CC, C, 70/1964, 31.
202 Letters from Ulbricht to individual Warsaw Pact leaders, 24/11/1964, DY30/3387, 205–16.
203 Letter from Ulbricht to Gheorgiu-Dej, 24 November 1964, SAPMO-BArch, DY 30/3387, 201–2.
204 'Memorandum of a conversation between diplomat Mewis and PUWP party member, comrade Zenon Kliszko', 24 November 1964, SAPMO-BArch, DY 30/3387, 235–36.
205 The new Soviet leadership had allegedly said that 'an atomic bomb would suffice for Albania': Meeting between Liu Fan and Bodnaras, 24 November 1964, ANIC, RWP CC, IR, 5/1964, 165.
206 Meeting between Emil Bodnaras and Liu Fan, Bucharest, 12 December 1964, ANIC, RWP CC, IR, 5/1964, 192.
207 Meeting between Emil Bodnaras and Liu Fan, 12 December 1964, ANIC, RWP CC, IR, 5/1964, 188.
208 Ibid., 191–93.
209 Ibid., 196–97.
210 V. Mastny, 'The Warsaw Pact: An Alliance in Search of a Purpose', in M.A. Heiss and S.V. Papacosma (eds), *NATO and the Warsaw Pact: Intrabloc Conflicts* (Ohio, 2008), 141–60.

3 The Warsaw Pact compromised by the German question

> Comrade Ulbricht sleeps soundly, while we struggle with his problems.[1]
> (Khrushchev to the Romanian delegation in Gagra, March 1964)

The German question was both the Warsaw Pact's *raison d'être* and its greatest bone of contention. Founded in response to West Germany's accession to NATO, the WP was an important instrument to boost the status of East Germany. The East German leader, Walter Ulbricht, became increasingly aware of this, and in the first half of the 1960s he began to use the alliance as a platform to force a speedy resolution of the second Berlin Crisis.[2] Most of the literature on the second Berlin Crisis from an Eastern European perspective, however, focuses on the *bilateral* relation between Ulbricht and Khrushchev, such as Hope Harrison's iconic work *Driving the Soviets up the Wall*.[3] After Khrushchev's six-month ultimatum on a German peace treaty and the demilitarisation of West Berlin in November 1958 had expired with impunity, Ulbricht nevertheless considered the time ripe to move the issue into the WP's multilateral arena. This implied that other WP members were involved too, such as the Polish leader Gomulka, who also had a considerable stake in the German question.

Caught in increasing tension between Polish and East German interests, the Kremlin faced the task of positioning itself on such complicated issues as the building of the Berlin Wall in August 1961, a peaceful resolution of the second Berlin Crisis, and NATO's project of nuclear sharing through Multilateral Nuclear Forces (MLF), which could also affect the nuclearisation of the FRG. In the shadow of the Sino–Soviet split, the Soviet stance on the German question was of particular significance: the Kremlin could ill afford to be checkmated on too many chessboards simultaneously. Nor could the East German and Polish leaderships afford to see their sovereignty and security compromised by Khrushchev's inclination to grow soft on the FRG and tolerate its nuclearisation, even though Ulbricht and Gomulka also had conflicting interests on this matter. The Soviet leadership could no longer go it alone on the German question, and the Warsaw Pact became the instrument for going it together. This chapter accordingly complements the previous one on the Sino–Soviet split, by examining the period from January

1960 to December 1964 from the perspective of the German question, while focusing on the members with the greatest stake in the issue – namely, the GDR and Poland. These two chapters together provide a comprehensive account of the issues that affected the dynamics of the WP in the first half of the 1960s.

Warsaw Pact (dis)harmony on the German question

In September 1959 Khrushchev thought he had achieved a breakthrough in the peaceful resolution of the second Berlin Crisis, since he judged his visit to President Eisenhower in the USA in September 1959 as his 'hour of glory'.[4] Since Khrushchev's ultimatum on a peace treaty with both Germanys and the demilitarisation of West Berlin had already expired four months earlier, it was imperative to reach an understanding with Eisenhower on the German question. Eisenhower conceded that America was 'not trying to perpetuate the situation in Berlin', and promised to attend a four-power conference, much to Khrushchev's delight, while forcing Khrushchev to withdraw his ultimatum in turn.[5] Although the meeting with Eisenhower had by no means resolved the stalemate on the Berlin question, Khrushchev returned to the Soviet Union euphoric, and promised a huge crowd that welcomed him on his arrival in Moscow a 'new era of peace'.[6]

It was in this mood that Khrushchev convened the WP members on 4 February 1960 for the first PCC meeting since he had issued his Berlin ultimatum in November 1958. Breathing 'the spirit of camp David', Khrushchev hoped to use the WP to consolidate his alleged gains concerning a peace treaty. The PCC meeting was preceded by a conference of the WP's foreign ministers, at which the Soviet-prepared agenda was supposedly approved 'without discussion'.[7] The draft declaration, which was to be published after the PCC meeting, nevertheless provoked considerable discussion, and 'the delegations, especially those of the German Democratic Republic, Czechoslovakia and Poland, presented a number of substantive and editorial comments'. It is no coincidence that these countries in particular commented on the declaration, since they had a vested interest in the matter: recognition of the GDR would also secure the inviolability of the borders they shared with East Germany. The Kremlin seemed to appreciate this fact, and therefore accepted the comments of its allies.[8]

During the actual PCC meeting the WP allies rallied behind Khrushchev's confident stance, according to which 'we are not going to make any compromise on principle',[9] and welcomed 'with great satisfaction the agreement reached by the Soviet Union, the U.S.A., Great Britain and France on the convening of a summit conference in Paris in May of this year'.[10] The four powers that occupied Berlin would attend the Paris summit in order to reach a peaceful resolution on the second Berlin Crisis, and the status of West Berlin. The NSWP members also supported Khrushchev's proposal to sign a separate treaty with the GDR '[i]f the Western powers continue to delay the negotiations of the peace treaty [...], with all the resulting consequences for West Berlin'. Gomulka in particular seized the opportunity to assert Polish interests, and added that the 'draft declaration correctly underscores the inviolability of the Western borders of Poland and Czechoslovakia'.[11] Khrushchev's brinkmanship in the German question impinged on the national interests of several NSWP members, who were accordingly stimulated to use the WP as an instrument to promote their own goals.

The ensuing declaration, too, underscored the importance of the recognition of the borders, which probably reflected the considerable Polish and Czechoslovak input. Repudiating West German 'revanchism and border revision and [...] the policy of German remilitarisation and atomic armament', the declaration clearly illustrates the extent to which a German peace treaty should serve to undermine any West German attempts to expand eastwards. The conditions of the peace treaty were intended to curb West German nuclear ambitions, which constituted a serious threat to all Eastern European countries.[12] The 'complete unanimity', which was habitually emphasised in the ensuing communiqué, was accordingly more than mere rhetoric.[13] United against a common West German enemy, the WP members were unified by the division of Germany on the surface. The German question nevertheless caused tension at a more profound level.

The East German leadership was not at all pleased with the way in which its Polish comrades appropriated the 'German problem'. Ten days after the PCC meeting the Polish leadership convened the Sejm (Polish parliament) in order to claim the German question as 'the key problem of Polish foreign policy', while also emphasising 'that Poland stands "in the centre" of the current system of international relations, and actively influences it'.[14] Polish Foreign Minister Adam Rapacki assured the Sejm that the consensus at the PCC meeting was fully in line with Polish foreign policy,[15] and stressed 'that Poland actively participates in this policy', *inter alia*, through his own proposal of 'the creation of a nuclear free zone in Middle Europe', which was a reference to the famous Rapacki plan.[16] At the same time the Poles took the initiative in creating a common stance on disarmament with their Czechoslovak and East German neighbours. This left their East German allies somewhat empty-handed, who accordingly criticised the 'exaggeration of Poland's active role in foreign policy'.[17] It also illustrates the way in which the Poles, too, could use the German question to formulate their own foreign policy goals, while employing their active participation in the WP to boost the prestige of both Poland and its leadership. The German question had thus turned into a Polish trump.

Khrushchev, meanwhile, was beginning to lose his grip on the German question. His confidence in a peaceful resolution of the Berlin Crisis was thoroughly undermined by the U2 spy incident on 1 May 1960, during which an American spy plane was shot down on Soviet territory, just before the superpower summit was about to take place in Paris. Khrushchev's procrastination had led to humiliation instead of victory. Pressure grew on

Khrushchev to show his teeth, and to avoid antagonising the hardliners in Berlin, Moscow or Beijing further. A deliberately unrealistic request for Eisenhower's apologies during the Paris conference and the fact that Khrushchev did not feel taken seriously resulted in the failure of the summit.[18] Although the increased antagonism greatly appealed to Ulbricht, it was not the East German leader but the American president who had inadvertently compelled Khrushchev's more unyielding stance.

Brinkmanship versus caution

Khrushchev's initial reaction to the failed Paris summit was not brinkmanship but caution. He did not want to create the impression that he had deliberately thwarted the summit in order to increase his antagonism towards West Germany, and he continued by procrastinating, much to Ulbricht's despair.[19] Caught between the Western refusal to give in on the one hand and Ulbricht's pressure to undertake action on the other hand, Khrushchev's reduced room for manoeuvre resulted in inaction on his part.[20] Ulbricht, meanwhile, decided to fill the vacuum that Khrushchev had created by acting unilaterally, and from August 1960 onwards he took measures to restrict travel into East Berlin, despite Soviet warnings to become more 'flexible' and attempts to prevent him from acting unilaterally.[21] As Harrison argues, '[t]he same lever Khrushchev sought to use against the West (access to Berlin) he found Ulbricht using without his approval during the final year of the Berlin Crisis'.[22]

Moreover, just as Khrushchev used the Berlin Crisis to arrange summit meetings with the US leadership, so Ulbricht used it to raise the stakes of the bilateral meetings between him and Khrushchev. Having secured such a meeting on 30 November 1960, Khrushchev promised a separate peace treaty with the GDR by the end of 1961, if a joint one did not materialise. Considering the potential failure to conclude a peace treaty in 1961 a great 'blow' to Soviet prestige,[23] Khrushchev seemed confident that he could deal with an economic embargo from the West that might result from a separate peace treaty.[24] With the motto 'the GDR's needs are also our needs', he seemed to offer Ulbricht unqualified support. Ulbricht nevertheless overplayed his hand by proposing to negotiate single-handedly with the three Western powers, while refusing to recognise the FRG as a 'sovereign state'.[25] Khrushchev gradually began to realise that he had invested Ulbricht with more power than he had bargained for by raising the stakes of a German peace treaty.

The more acute problem for the prestige and economy of the Soviet bloc was the exodus of refugees from the GDR, which had escalated by the beginning of 1961. The status of the GDR was accordingly under threat from different sides: internally, because many of its citizens attempted to flee, and externally, because its existence was not recognised. This heightened the urgency for the conclusion of a peace treaty, which would at least provide East Germany with *de facto* recognition of its sovereignty. This seemed a nonstarter considering Khrushchev's procrastination. In fact, the East German leadership was much more impressed with its Polish neighbour Gomulka, who had paid a very successful visit to New York, as well as succeeding in 'involving a wide circle of the population in the foreign policy problems'.[26] Ulbricht therefore tightened the bonds with Poland, by intensifying the diplomatic contacts and increasing the number of East German consulates in Poland,[27] while also keeping a close watch on the Polish relations with the FRG.[28] In order to make any progress on the issue of a peace treaty, Ulbricht needed Gomulka's support just as much as Khrushchev's. The Polish stake in the German question had therefore provided Gomulka with diplomatic leverage.

Still fearing further Soviet paralysis, Ulbricht wanted to involve his Warsaw Pact allies in the matter. Ulbricht not only requested another meeting with Khrushchev in a letter on 18 January 1961, but he also proposed that 'after the consultation of the party and governmental delegations of the USSR and GDR, a meeting of the Political Consultative Committee of Warsaw Pact States take place', since 'until now, the majority of the Warsaw Pact states have considered the peaceful resolution of the German question and the West Berlin question as a matter which only concerns the Soviet Union and the GDR'.[29] Not getting anywhere on a bilateral level, Ulbricht seemed to think that a discussion of a peace treaty within the WP's multilateral framework might provide him with additional leverage over Khrushchev. Meanwhile, Ulbricht organised a trip of a GDR delegation to China without Soviet approval, since he was prone to 'use the relationship with the PRC in bargaining with the Soviet Union', as a former GDR diplomat in Beijing explained.[30] Although Ulbricht by no means went as far as his Albanian and Romanian allies in exploiting the Sino–Soviet split to put the Kremlin under pressure, he occasionally played the Chinese card in the early 1960s, when the Sino–Soviet split had not yet become irreversible.

Khrushchev nevertheless moved more shrewdly than he has often been credited for. However 'boldly' the 'tail [...] wagged the dog',[31] the PCC meeting, which was about to take place in March 1961, was *not* convened at Ulbricht's request.[32] Ulbricht's manipulation of Khrushchev had its limits. Although Khrushchev supported the idea of a bilateral meeting, he put Ulbricht on hold concerning the suggested convention of a PCC meeting.[33] Meanwhile, Khrushchev had already written a letter to all WP leaders on 24 January in which he proposed a PCC meeting in Moscow at the end of March on modernisation of the WP armed forces.[34] By omitting the German question from the agenda, he seemed tacitly to have reminded Ulbricht that the Kremlin still called the shots. The bilateral meeting never materialised at all, and the PCC meeting, which was convened on 28–29 March 1961, accordingly did not take place *after* the bilateral Soviet-GDR meeting, thus depriving Ulbricht of the opportunity to coordinate his stance with the Kremlin.[35] Moreover, Khrushchev underlined in his letter to Ulbricht that '[i]f we don't succeed in coming to an understanding with Kennedy, we will, as agreed, choose together with you the time for their implementation'.³⁶ Superpower negotiations were still priority number one for Khrushchev.

The Warsaw Pact as Ulbricht's instrument

In late February 1961 Khrushchev received the much coveted invitation from US President John F. Kennedy, who had been inaugurated one month earlier, to another summit in May or June. Khrushchev's stance in the Berlin Crisis was accordingly one of the central topics of the PCC meeting in Moscow on 28–29 March, which was nevertheless overshadowed by the Albanian question, as we have seen in the previous chapter. Starting his speech with Kennedy's suggestion to meet in May in order 'to exchange opinions', Khrushchev attempted to impress his WP allies by promising that '[we] will not needle them unnecessarily', and by stressing the importance of 'a united, tight-ranked front'. Confronted with the Sino–Soviet split and Albanian defiance during this meeting, unity was all the more imperative.

Khrushchev continued to underline that a separate peace treaty with the GDR was only a last resort, if a peace treaty 'with both German states' were to fail. He explained his optimism by arguing that '[t]he issue [of a peace settlement] gave us strong leverage, allowing us to affect the position of Western powers in many areas of our relations', while forcing them 'to sit with us and discuss the most pressing international problems'. Relishing the opportunity of any more superpower discussions, Khrushchev emphasised that he would not undertake any action before the next superpower summit with Kennedy. Although Khrushchev underlined his firm commitment to a separate peace treaty with the GDR in the worst case scenario, he also emphasised that 'our governments will probably have to exchange opinions [...], before the final decision is made'.³⁷ Whereas Ulbricht might have hoped that a WP conference could serve to speed things up, Khrushchev preferred to use the alliance as an instrument to slow down Ulbricht's unilateral collision course.

Ulbricht nevertheless rebuked his allies for already 'having left the Western powers two years' time to get used to the conclusion of a peace treaty with Germany'. He accordingly emphasised 'the necessity' of coordinated action within the WP, while underlining the sovereignty of the GDR and its role as a 'bastion of peace' in the world. Although he supported Khrushchev's stance, he bypassed the Soviet Union altogether by explaining that the Central Committee of the Sozialistische Einheitspartei Deutschlands (SED) had proposed five points to the West German president 'in order to pave the way to a peaceful resolution'. These points were, however, mere propaganda, as a West German response to his proposals would constitute *de facto* recognition of the GDR, which was out of the question. While narrowly focusing on the interests of the GDR, Ulbricht tried to prod his comrades into action by using the possibility that 'the failure of a peace treaty [...] facilitates the atomic armament of the West German militarists' as leverage over his allies and using the exodus of refugees as an argument to close the sectoral border in Berlin. Arguing at the same time that he planned to control West Berlin in the near future instead of Khrushchev, he asked his allies for money in case of a West German economic blockade.[38]

In his attempt to use the Warsaw Pact as an instrument to strengthen Khrushchev's resolve regarding a peace treaty, Ulbricht had overplayed his hand: the other allies 'argued against the closing of the borders with West Berlin', with Khrushchev's support.[39] The ensuing communiqué did not echo Ulbricht's militant stance, but merely mentioned the necessity of 'concluding a peace treaty with both German states, and, in this connection, rendering harmless the seat of danger in West Berlin by converting it into a demilitarised free city'. The GDR did not even enter the equation. The communiqué did, however, focus more explicitly on the dangers of the 'equipment [of the West German army] with missile-nuclear weapons', which illustrates that the nuclearisation of West Germany began to overshadow the recognition of East Germany.[40] Ulbricht's proactive stance had forced Khrushchev to retreat: he was presumably loth to invest Ulbricht with more power. The PCC meeting had accordingly served to moderate Ulbricht's unilateral actions, rather than catalysing those of Khrushchev.

It was, however, the first time that an extraordinary meeting of the East German politburo was convened in order to discuss the PCC meeting.[41] This illustrates that the East Germans began to consider the alliance an important instrument for East German foreign policy objectives. In February 1960 they had still paid more attention to an agricultural conference than the PCC meeting.[42] Moreover, the very dynamics of the Berlin Crisis contributed to the emancipation of *all* WP allies, as Khrushchev's zeal to 'exchange opinions' and coordinate 'appropriate actions' went beyond mere rhetoric:[43] if Khrushchev's brinkmanship on the German question were to escalate into war, he would have to rely on his allies for military support, which forced him to take them seriously. The crisis would not only 'give an impetus for the transformation of the Warsaw Pact from mainly an accessory of Soviet diplomacy to something more akin to a military alliance',[44] as we shall see in the next chapter, but it would also plant the seeds for foreign policy coordination.

Raising the stakes again

A letter from the Soviet Ambassador Pervukhin in Berlin to Soviet Foreign Minister Gromyko in May 1961 shows how the Soviet and East German sides were growing apart concerning the peace treaty. Pervukhin emphasised that 'our German friends sometimes exercise impatience and a somewhat one-sided approach to this problem, not always studying the interests of the entire socialist camp or the international situation at the given moment'. He was critical of the East German idea to negotiate directly with the Western powers after the conclusion of a peace treaty, and suggested concluding 'a temporary agreement on West Berlin' to normalise the situation in West Berlin in negotiations with the three Western powers.[45] The Soviet leaders were not at all keen to yield their bargaining power to Ulbricht, and therefore moderated their stance on the peace treaty.

Khrushchev, meanwhile, was far from inclined to forego his prerogative of negotiating with the Western powers, and considered the superpower summit in Vienna on 3–4 June more decisive than Ulbricht's pressure. When the summit with the American president failed, because of 'Khrushchev's aggressive, almost threatening, tone', Khrushchev's policy options narrowed.[46] Kennedy had emphasised that the Western powers would under no circumstances leave West Berlin, but were less concerned with bilateral agreements between the Soviet Union and the GDR, which would not impinge on Western rights.[47] In order to save face, Khrushchev still emphasised his commitment to a separate peace treaty with the GDR, but considering the risks that would entail, this remained an empty threat.

Having lost faith in Khrushchev's political clout, Ulbricht again turned to Gomulka, as 'the struggle for the conclusion of a peace treaty with Germany and for the resolution of the West Berlin problem had entered a new phase' after the failed superpower summit in Vienna. Emphasising that 'West Berlin is a hole through which 1 billion Marks flees our Republic annually', Ulbricht suggested closer economic cooperation between the GDR, Poland and Czechoslovakia.[48] He also prodded Khrushchev into action by writing to him that '[i]t is also important through the joint efforts of all socialist countries to further discredit even more German revanchism and militarism, [...] and at the same time to thoroughly prepare the conclusion of a peace treaty in the countries of the Warsaw Treaty states'. Emphasising that 'West German imperialism [...] demands nuclear weapons for NATO, i.e. obviously its own army', Ulbricht yet again underscored the urgency of a peace treaty.[49]

It was clear to Khrushchev that some progress had to be made after the failed summit with Kennedy, and he finally conceded Ulbricht's initial request to convene the Warsaw Pact leaders.[50] Khrushchev allowed Ulbricht to invite his allies for a meeting from 3–5 August in Moscow, thus unprecedentedly foregoing the Soviet prerogative of convening such meetings.[51] The meeting was, however, not conducted within the framework of the PCC, as it primarily dealt with an *internal* issue, and only the party leaders were invited. In order to heighten the sense of urgency, Ulbricht told Soviet Ambassador Pervukhin at the end of June 'to tell Khrushchev that "if the present situation of open borders remains, collapse is inevitable".'[52] By shifting the problem from the recognition of the GDR to the problem of the open borders, Ulbricht had inadvertently undermined the need for a peace treaty. Closing the intra-Berlin borders now became the top priority. Contingency plans were already drawn up in order to stem the flight of refugees to the FRG, and on 4 July Pervukhin concluded in a report to Gromyko that 'closing the sectorial border in Berlin in one or another way [...] could be necessary'.[53] It seems likely that Khrushchev gave Ulbricht permission to build a wall on 6 July.[54] As

Khrushchev later related to Hans Kroll, the West German ambassador to Moscow, '[t]he wall was ordered by me due to Ulbricht's pressing wish'.[55]

The multilateral meeting, which Ulbricht had desired since January, was preceded by a bilateral meeting between Ulbricht and Khrushchev on the morning of 3 August, as Ulbricht had requested.[56] In this meeting everything went according to Ulbricht's wishes, as Khrushchev already agreed with the closure of the intra-Berlin border.[57] The ensuing meeting of WP party leaders merely served to create a united front behind Khrushchev and Ulbricht and to rubberstamp their decisions, which was initially challenged by Albanian dissent, as we have seen in the previous chapter. This set-up confirms the assumption of the Warsaw Pact as a Soviet transmission belt and supports the argument of the historian Douglas Selvage, that '[t]he GDR – even more than the Soviet Union – believed that the Warsaw Pact should serve as a transmission belt for Soviet directives', which 'was to convey foreign policy directives to the other socialist states aimed at bolstering the GDR's international position'.[58]

The East German leader, meanwhile, attempted to put his arguments about the need for a separate peace treaty with the GDR into a somewhat less narrow framework. Ulbricht emphasised that '[a] peace treaty will ensure an international-legal consolidation of the existing and established borders between the German Democratic Republic and the Polish People's Republic, between the German Democratic Republic and the Czechoslovak Socialist Republic, and also the borders between the German Democratic Republic and the Federal Republic of Germany'. Mindful of the PCC meeting in March, Ulbricht anticipated the involvement of the Polish and Czechoslovak leadership, while also casting his net wider by even arguing that such a peace treaty would 'answer [...] the interests of all peoples'. He then used this argument as leverage for his plea for economic help from the other WP leaders 'with the goal of making the GDR economically independent from the FRG'. Moreover, he stated that the refugee exodus necessitated that the Warsaw Pact states should agree to control the intra-Berlin borders in the same way as the borders with the Western European states.[59]

Despite his attempt to identify his own needs more with those of his WP allies, Ulbricht's speech still mainly dealt with the East German problems and therefore failed to convince his comrades on all fronts. Although the closure of the borders met with general approval at the meeting, the allies were more reluctant to provide Ulbricht with economic aid.[60] The Polish leader Gomulka, who had apparently already told Khrushchev time and again to shut the inner-Berlin borders, took the lead in charting a course towards resolving the Berlin Crisis.[61] Expressing his 'principled agreement' on the necessary 'measures' concerning 'the open borders in Berlin', Gomulka emphasised that 'those measures' should be executed 'now'.[62] Thus Gomulka decoupled Ulbricht's proposal to close the border from a separate peace treaty with East Germany, which could always be concluded at a later stage, and urged the former at the expense of the latter. Considering the eventual outcome, it was not Ulbricht's stance, but Gomulka's, which carried the day.

Gomulka further undermined Ulbricht's zeal to use the peace treaty to boost his own authority, by arguing that Poland should take the initiative on the peace treaty together with Czechoslovakia and the Soviet Union. Moreover, Gomulka understood the question of economic aid, but added that the GDR should cooperate economically more closely with its allies through COMECON, rather than demanding more economic assistance.[63] In this case, too, the WP leaders rallied behind Gomulka instead of Ulbricht, and those most directly involved, namely the Czechoslovak leader Antonin Novotny and the Hungarian leader Janos Kadar, supported Gomulka with particular enthusiasm.[64] Kadar even mentioned the potential 'bankruptcy' of the GDR several times – a word that the GDR leaders systematically crossed out in their documents! The convention of a WP meeting seemed to have facilitated Polish involvement in the German question, which inadvertently eclipsed Ulbricht.

Khrushchev meanwhile provided Ulbricht with unqualified support, and emphasised that a potential 'liquidation of the GDR' would imply that the 'West Germany army [would be] at our borders'.[65] Khrushchev proved very sensitive to Ulbricht's threats about losing the GDR. The reluctant attitude of most other WP leaders therefore drove Khrushchev to despair, and fully contradicted his confident reassurance during the meeting with Ulbricht in November 1960, 'that the Soviet Union and the other socialist states could and would provide the GDR with the necessary economic aid to survive an embargo'.[66] In an attempt to save face, Khrushchev vehemently 'criticized unnamed leaders of Eastern European socialist countries for "national narrow-mindedness" in their approach to the GDR's difficulties'.[67] The failure of the summit with Kennedy in June had driven him once more straight into the arms of Ulbricht. The other Warsaw Pact leaders were, however, less keen to join this deadly embrace. The Warsaw Pact had, as such, made an important contribution to resolving the Berlin Crisis, since the NSWP refusal to assist the GDR economically would play an important role in Khrushchev's ultimate decision to abstain from a peace treaty. This multilateral forum had undermined the bilateral understanding between Khrushchev and Ulbricht, as well as bringing a halt to Ulbricht's unilateralism.

To some extent the WP meeting at the beginning of August did, however, serve as the Soviet transmission belt of the GDR's national interests, as it seemed to create a united front in support of closing the borders in Berlin. Despite his apparent triumph, Ulbricht nevertheless overplayed his hand by expanding his bilateral negotiations with Khrushchev to the Warsaw Pact's multilateral platform. Although Harrison convincingly argues that 'Ulbricht's tenacious, opportunistic, self-confident personality helped him to push events in the direction he wanted',[68] this same personality worked against him within the frame of the WP. By linking the fate of the GDR with that of the Soviet bloc, Ulbricht gained support for closing the borders between East and West

Berlin, but by his repeated emphasis on the interests of the GDR he lost the good will of his Warsaw Pact comrades. Gomulka, meanwhile, had won their support.

Driving himself up the wall

The Warsaw Pact nevertheless served to enhance the legitimacy of the border closure, and during a five-hour extraordinary SED politburo meeting on 7 August 1961 the WP meeting was discussed at length. From this meeting it becomes evident that the building of the Wall was indeed sanctioned by Ulbricht's allies, as it was concluded from the meeting that 'the anticipated measures' would be carried out between 12 and 13 August.[69] On the night of Saturday 12 to Sunday 13 August, the intra-Berlin border was speedily sealed off by barbed wire, to be replaced by concrete blocks four days later. The Warsaw Pact support exonerated the East German leadership, as becomes clear from a declaration in the SED newspaper *Neues Deutschland* on 13 August, which stated that '[t]he governments of the Warsaw Pact countries' had proposed the closure of the inner-Berlin borders to 'the parliament and the government of the GDR'.[70] Other WP leaders, such as the Poles, nevertheless preferred to downplay their role in the decision making, especially when the barbed wire gradually began to be replaced by concrete blocks.[71] Meanwhile, Kennedy's pragmatic reaction that 'a wall is a hell of a lot better than a war' summed up the lack of Western protest.[72]

In a letter to Khrushchev on 15 September 1961 Ulbricht attributed the success of the entire operation (ironically codenamed 'Rose') to the fact 'that the Warsaw Pact states acted unanimously under the leadership of the Soviet Union'.[73] Ulbricht not only considered the successful construction of the Wall a prelude to the long-coveted peace treaty, but also thought it entitled the East Germans to further control over the situation in East Berlin, which was officially still under Soviet occupation.[74] Khrushchev took the opposite view and replied in a letter on 28 September that 'measures which could exacerbate the situation, especially in Berlin, should be avoided'.[75] After another characteristic U-turn, Khrushchev now seemed to think that no steps needed to be taken beyond border closure. Since the Wall had solved the pressing problem of the refugee exodus and the economic brain-drain, it had undermined the necessity for a separate peace treaty and it had allayed the Soviet fears about the GDR as a 'superdomino'.[76] Moreover, any attempts to turn West Berlin into a 'free city' seemed ludicrous after it had been sealed off by the Wall. Although Ulbricht continued to press Khrushchev for the conclusion of a separate peace treaty with the GDR, the spell was broken.

Khrushchev sealed his U-turn on the peace treaty during the 22nd CPSU Congress in Moscow from 17–31 October. In his speech on 17 October he emphasised 'peaceful coexistence' and retracted the 31 December deadline for the German peace treaty.[77] Since the Chinese delegation had already left the conference in a rage about Khrushchev's denunciation of Albania,

Khrushchev no longer 'needed to look over his shoulder' in order to appease the Chinese.[78] This congress accordingly marked the Soviet decision to prioritise peaceful coexistence over Sino-Soviet relations.[79] Because this also implied a more moderate stance on the Berlin Crisis, Ulbricht was not at all pleased, and furiously stressed in his speech three days later that the peace treaty was 'a task of the utmost urgency'.[80] The Soviet–East German disagreements were out in the open.

It accordingly seems hardly a coincidence that Ulbricht took a measure to escalate the second Berlin Crisis during the Moscow conference. On 22 October, five days after Khrushchev's speech and two days after his own, Ulbricht instructed East German guards at the crossing points between East and West Berlin not to let personnel of the three Western powers pass without identification. Since such border controls were officially the prerogative of the four occupying powers, Ulbricht had unilaterally decided to appropriate this prerogative in order to force Khrushchev into supporting him. The measure immediately escalated when the US diplomat Allan Lightner refused to show his travel documents to the East German guards on the way to the opera in East Berlin on the evening of 22 October. The American side responded by sending US soldiers to accompany Lightner into Berlin, which sparked an East German decree the next morning according to which all foreigners, except those in the military uniforms of the Western powers, would have to show travel documents to East German guards. By unilaterally issuing a new decree, Ulbricht compelled Khrushchev either to support him or the US side.

Meanwhile, the Americans forced the Kremlin to commit, too, by continuing to send American officials in civilian clothes to the crossing points, calling for US soldiers if the East German guards refused to comply. By 26 October the situation had escalated to such an extent that the American side brought up ten tanks to escort US officials into East Berlin. Khrushchev ultimately responded to the American tanks with an equal number of Soviet ones, seemingly supporting Ulbricht. At the same time the presence of Soviet tanks clearly illustrated that Khrushchev refused to allow Ulbricht to manage the crisis single-handedly, while usurping any more Soviet prerogatives. After a 24-hour standoff from 27–28 October the Soviet tanks withdrew one by one, and so did the American ones. Although Ulbricht seemed to have succeeded in raising the stakes of the second Berlin Crisis, he had inadvertently undermined the East German claim to sovereignty: the East German guards had succeeded in provoking the crisis on Ulbricht's orders, but Khrushchev had to resolve it. Any further East German claims to manage the situation in Berlin single-handedly had lost credibility.[81]

The link between the Checkpoint Charlie standoff and Ulbricht's zeal for further control over Berlin became clear in a letter that the East German leadership wrote to all participants in the CPSU congress on the last day of the conference (30 October) – two days after the Checkpoint Charlie crisis. In this letter Ulbricht used the American 'provocation' at Checkpoint Charlie to urge Khrushchev into conceding more prerogatives to the East German border guards, while emphasising that a settlement on the status of West Berlin and a peace treaty had become all the more urgent in order to prevent any further 'violation of the sovereignty of the GDR'. He also pressed for 'further tactics', since Khrushchev had withdrawn his ultimatum on the peace treaty, and even suggested convening the foreign ministers of the Warsaw Pact in order to force Khrushchev to conclude a peace treaty after all.[82] Ulbricht's attempt to use a multilateral framework once again to bypass bilateral negotiations with the Soviet Union nevertheless backfired. The suggested Warsaw Pact meeting never materialised, and Khrushchev explained to Gomulka after the CPSU congress instead that 'signing a peace treaty with the GDR might exacerbate the situation', which must have sounded like music to Gomulka's ears.[83]

Moreover, Ulbricht's intransigence had driven Khrushchev into West German arms instead. Ten days after the conference Khrushchev ordered the West German ambassador in Moscow, Hermann Kroll, to tell Chancellor Adenauer that '[t]he Soviet government, and N.S. Khrushchev personally regard the agreement that was achieved in Rapallo [...] as a great historic act, which was of no little use to both sides', and they intended 'a genuine improvement of the relations between the USSR and the Federal Republic'.[84] This was a particularly painful remark, as the treaty concluded at Rapallo in 1922 constituted a Soviet-German agreement in the wake of World War I to cooperate diplomatically, while striving for the revision of the boundaries of Poland. Khrushchev's renewed interest in something along the lines of the Rapallo agreement now seemed targeted against the GDR and in favour of the FRG. Ulbricht had pushed the limits too far during the Checkpoint Charlie crisis. After the peace treaty had receded into the background, rapprochement with the FRG became all the more imperative. Khrushchev had to find a way to control the consequences of West German rearmament, and now attempted to do so by currying the favour of the West German chancellor. If the German question could not be solved through Ulbricht, it had to be solved through Adenauer.

The Wall was Khrushchev's way to silence Ulbricht. Khrushchev had accordingly outplayed both Ulbricht and the West: threatening the West and enticing Ulbricht with a separate peace treaty, both parties had to acquiesce in a Wall without a treaty. The fact that the GDR had been recognised *de facto*, but not *de iure*, did not bother Khrushchev as much as Ulbricht. Khrushchev had solved the refugee problem and the Wall had literally cemented the GDR's place in the Soviet bloc. At the beginning of 1962, Khrushchev officially denounced altogether the need for a separate peace treaty during a CPSU presidium meeting.[85] He told Ulbricht in a private conversation that the maximum had been achieved on 13 August, and that 'you are willing to provide a signature, but we have to provide for you economically'.[86] Apart from achieving his aims with the Wall, Khrushchev realised that the Sino-Soviet split had escalated beyond repair, so that he no longer had to worry about appeasing the Chinese leadership by standing firm on the German question.

The East German leadership nevertheless refused to give up on the peace treaty,[87] and tried to force the issue at a brief PCC meeting, which was convened on 7 June 1962 after a COMECON meeting. Although the WP meeting concluded with a declaration in which a separate peace treaty was mentioned, this was merely *pro forma*. Explaining once more 'that we have already achieved what we intended to achieve with a peace treaty', Khrushchev relegated the peace treaty to the realm of mere propaganda. It had become an empty mantra that was only murmured by Ulbricht.[88] The fact that he had also prevented Ulbricht from referring to 'West German revanchists' in the declaration, because 'the negotiations were being conducted between the Soviet Union and the United States and did not involve West German revanchists', was indicative of Ulbricht's loss of leverage over Khrushchev, and of Khrushchev's attempted rapprochement with the FRG.[89] Although Ulbricht disagreed with Khrushchev that the Berlin Wall had made a separate peace treaty redundant, the other WP leaders sided with the Kremlin. The GDR no longer entered the equation, and the Wall allowed Khrushchev once again to concentrate on superpower negotiations at Ulbricht's expense.

After the building of the Berlin Wall Khrushchev's attitude towards Ulbricht accordingly reversed. Instead of supporting him, Khrushchev now used the Warsaw Pact as a platform further to undermine Ulbricht's credibility. He even confided to the first secretary of the Czechoslovak Communist Party, Antonin Novotny, that he had met Ulbricht several times on his own so as to criticise him severely in private, and added that 'his age is beginning to show; I know this all too well, having known Stalin. Combined with the huge power that Ulbricht holds in his hands, these manifestations of senility are very dangerous indeed'.[90] Having vied for a position as Khrushchev's 'super ally',[91] Ulbricht had inadvertently turned into a senile ally instead.

The German question in nuclear terms

The East German leaders seemed to realise that their strategy had failed, and were particularly well aware of the fact that their Polish neighbours had been more successful in their foreign policy than they had. They envied their 'active involvement [...] in the UN and other international organisations', and their capacity to maintain 'a greater sense of manoeuvrability'.[92] During 1962 the East Germans therefore deliberately and successfully tried to intensify and improve their relations with Poland through an active exchange of delegations and reporters, while also intensifying the political and economic bonds.[93]

Good neighbourly relations with the Poles had become particularly important considering Khrushchev's zeal to improve East-West relations. The West German foreign minister, Gerhard Schröder, had the same ambition, and between March 1963 and March 1964 he agreed trade missions with Poland, Hungary, Romania and Bulgaria, thus isolating the GDR.[94] In order to mitigate the West, the Kremlin decided to stop its opposition to NATO's plan to create MLF in its alliance, which would allow its allies, including the FRG, joint control over a few strategic nuclear weapons. This form of nuclear sharing had already been proposed during Eisenhower's last year in power, but had clearly come into shape under Kennedy. Although French President Charles de Gaulle categorically rejected MLF in January 1963, and other NATO members 'remained ambivalent', the US Administration considered it the best way to remedy 'the shortfall in medium-range ballistic missiles in Europe', as well as catering for the 'West German interest in the nuclear affairs of the alliance'.[95] Whereas Khrushchev had prioritised his fear of West German nuclearisation over East-West relations at the beginning of the Berlin Crisis, he had reversed his priorities after the crisis had ended. Potential West German control of nuclear weapons would, however, severely impinge on the national security of Poland and the GDR.

Khrushchev realised that this was a sensitive issue in the Warsaw Pact, and particularly in Poland and the GDR. On 2 October 1963 he therefore sent Gomulka a memorandum in which he attempted to justify his reversed stance by explaining that he had only dropped the prohibition of the establishment of joint nuclear forces in his negotiations about a non-proliferation treaty with the US leadership on the condition that 'the Americans take upon themselves the obligation not to permit a situation in which West Germany might obtain the possibility of being in charge of nuclear weapons'.[96] Gomulka was outraged by this 'potential shift in Soviet policy', which 'threatened the security and stability of the Polish and East German communist regimes'.[97] As soon as he had read the letter, Gomulka telephoned Khrushchev and demanded the convention of another WP meeting to discuss the issue, since he did not consider Khrushchev's stance in line with the alliance.[98] Instead of using the WP to pressurise Khrushchev, as Ulbricht had attempted, Gomulka intended to use the alliance as an instrument to moderate Khrushchev's policies.

Moreover, Gomulka strongly denounced Khrushchev's course in a long letter six days later, in which he also argued that 'the creation of multilateral nuclear forces would strengthen Bonn's [...] atomic blackmail against the Warsaw Pact states', and advised Khrushchev to consult with the Chinese Communist Party instead.[99] Shrewdly detecting the link between Khrushchev's 'Rapallo policy' and the Sino–Soviet split, Gomulka urged Khrushchev to mend the latter at the expense of the former, to the great delight of the East German leadership.[100] Again, Gomulka's ability to look at the broader picture starkly contrasted with Ulbricht's more narrow approach towards the matter. In a meeting between the Soviet Deputy Foreign Minister Vasilii Kuznetsov and the GDR politburo on 14 October 1963 Ulbricht merely asked 'for understanding [of the] somewhat different situation in [East] Germany'.[101] The GDR leaders found themselves in an increasingly vulnerable position, since the hardliner Konrad Adenauer was succeeded by the more moderate Ludwig Erhard as chancellor of the FRG on 16 October. This raised the stakes of Khrushchev's Rapallo policy, which made it more likely that Khrushchev would sacrifice East German interests to his rapprochement with West Germany.

The Polish leaders, meanwhile, attempted to involve their East German neighbours in the broader implications of MLF, and halfway through December 1963 the Polish Foreign Minister Adam Rapacki even expressed 'the urgent desire' to visit the GDR, just before he would discuss the issue with the Belgian Foreign Minister Paul-Henri Spaak in Warsaw.[102] This suggests that the Polish leadership must have been aware of the disagreements within NATO, in which Spaak – the former secretary-general – was one of the most important smaller allies. The East German leaders nevertheless concentrated so narrow-mindedly on the 'somewhat different situation in Germany' that they did not seize the opportunity to unite with the Poles on MLF and to be informed about the latest developments in NATO, but rejected Rapacki's offer under the pretext of illness and too much work.[103] Thus Polish manoeuvrability met East German inflexibility.

The Ulbricht doctrine

Ulbricht was not enthusiastic about the Polish 'Gomulka plan' either, an updated version of the 'Rapacki plan', in which the Polish leader put forward a proposal for a nuclear freeze in Poland, Czechoslovakia and the two Germanys on 28 December 1963, and Ulbricht argued that 'recognition of the GDR [was] to take priority over regional disarmament'.[104] Ulbricht stole both the Soviet and Polish thunder instead, by proposing his own pan-German arms-control initiative, which presupposed recognition of the GDR, on 2 January 1964. On the same day Khrushchev wrote a letter to all Warsaw Pact members in which he argued that there was 'a growth of the practice of consultations between socialist countries concerning problems about foreign politics'. He therefore supported 'the representatives of some fraternal parties', who 'expressed the desire [...] to establish a closer contact between socialist countries, [...] especially in the domain of a more complete coordination of their positions in international problems'. In order to do so he proposed 'more systematic consultations', which could be achieved 'through the regular convention of meetings of the ministers of foreign affairs of the Warsaw Pact member states (except Albania)'.[105]

Khrushchev optimistically proposed that a meeting of the WP's deputy foreign ministers take place in January 1964, in order to 'consult about some problems concerning the resumption of the Eighteen Nations Disarmament Committee in Geneva' (ENDC). The sudden impetus for foreign policy coordination was, accordingly, clear: several WP leaders considered it opportune to meet in order to coordinate a common stance before negotiating on nuclear issues, such as MLF and non-proliferation, with their colleagues from

NATO during the ENDC convention in February 1964. As five WP countries were members of the ENDC (Bulgaria, Romania, Czechoslovakia, Poland and the Soviet Union), a convention of the WP deputy foreign ministers seemed a logical move to prepare for the meeting. It would, however, mean involving East Germany in the negotiations, even though it was not a member of the ENDC as its sovereignty was not recognised by the NATO members.

The Romanians vehemently opposed Khrushchev's proposal, as they considered the establishment of 'an organ with a permanent character' of foreign policy consultation contrary to 'each country's indisputable sovereign right' to establish its own foreign policy, and therefore preferred the ad hoc convention of such meetings when necessary. They also shrewdly reminded Khrushchev that the problem so far had not been the absence of the right kind of organ for consultations, but the absence of consultations per se, as the Kremlin could easily have convened the PCC to consult the other WP members on disarmament or the Cuban Missile Crisis, which they failed to do.[106] Proving that they had nothing against attending a meeting when necessary, the Romanian leaders agreed to come to Moscow from 8–9 January to prepare for the ENDC. The Romanian leadership had, however, carefully kept such a meeting outside the WP framework, thus *de facto* excluding the East Germans from the negotiations. The Romanian move testified to a new Romanian concern to prevent the WP from turning into an instrument that Ulbricht could use to further East German national interests.

The East German leaders nevertheless considered mutual consultations within a WP framework advantageous, for exactly the same reason as their Romanian comrades did *not*. Khrushchev's proposal provided them with a systematic say through further WP consultations. Ulbricht accordingly wrote a letter to Khrushchev on 24 January in which he suggested convening a PCC meeting on 19 March 1964 to draft a communiqué on 'Questions about the abstention from violence and disarmament'.[107] Ulbricht had, in fact, already drafted a speech to this end, thus intending to use the alliance again as a transmission belt for *his* foreign policy interests, while compensating for East German exclusion from the ENDC negotiations.[108] Ulbricht accordingly emulated Khrushchev's proposal from early January by attempting to convene the PCC instead of merely the deputy foreign ministers, which testifies to his zeal for using the Warsaw Pact for his own purposes.

Ulbricht had not discussed the proposed date with Khrushchev beforehand, and without waiting for his reply already sent a letter to all WP leaders on 28 January in order to invite them to the suggested PCC meeting without Khrushchev's approval.[109] In this unprecedented attempt to call the shots within the WP, Ulbricht fully undermined Khrushchev's authority. Khrushchev managed to regain some control over the procedure, by forwarding Ulbricht's letter to the other WP members, together with his reply, in which he suggested convening the PCC in February or April instead.[110] Although Khrushchev embraced Ulbricht's proposal for the WP meeting, the dynamics within the alliance had changed so much that Ulbricht primarily needed the approval of his NSWP comrades. Without their support, Ulbricht would not succeed in using the WP to promote East German interests, as he had learnt at the meeting of WP party leaders from 3–5 August 1961.

Meanwhile, Ulbricht realised that he needed to mend matters with Gomulka in order also to gain his support for convening the PCC. One day after writing Khrushchev, he accordingly also tried to placate Gomulka by proposing in a letter a meeting of WP foreign ministers or deputy foreign ministers to discuss the 'Gomulka plan', to which the SED agreed in principle.[111] Ulbricht had thus tried single-handedly to take over the choreography of the WP. Gomulka was, however, not amused by Ulbricht's unilateralism, and strongly 'regretted' the fact that Ulbricht had rejected Rapacki's proposal to meet in December 1963, while secretly preparing a 'proposal about the abstention of nuclear weapons of both German states' instead. Although Gomulka agreed to convene a PCC meeting, he opposed convening the foreign ministers or deputy foreign ministers, as 'mutual consultations in the second half of December last year would have been more useful'.[112] The moment for such consultations had passed.

Moreover, Gomulka emphasised that he had already 'coordinated the foundations' of his proposal 'during consultations with fraternal countries' to prepare the disarmament in Geneva in the framework of the ENDC, thus referring to the consultations in Moscow on 8–9 January. Mentioning 'conversations with representatives of the WP members', and 'preparatory conversations with a number of Western countries', Gomulka shrewdly reduced the East German point of view to irrelevance, while adding that both sides had enthusiastically received his 'initiatives'. Stating *en passant* that he would keep 'the ambassadors of the socialist states in Warsaw informed' about the contacts with Western countries, Gomulka clearly underlined the supremacy of Polish diplomacy.[113] This remark must have been a particular blow to Ulbricht, since diplomatic contacts with the 'Western countries' were not open to him, because they had not recognised the GDR. Gomulka was, however, also more in tune with the WP's burgeoning multilateralism than Ulbricht, whose narrow concern with the status of the GDR had prevented him from achieving his goals. Bypassing Gomulka had been a faux pas that had undermined the GDR's own aims.

The East German unilateralism was also thwarted by the Romanians, who first ignored the proposal to convene the PCC and then vetoed it, as we have seen in the previous chapter.[114] Whereas the East Germans received little support from Khrushchev in this matter,[115] Khrushchev even confessed to the Romanian delegation at Gagra in March that '[c]omrade Ulbricht sleeps soundly, while we struggle with his problems'.[116] Meanwhile, the Romanian leaders used this opportunity to play off the Kremlin and the East German party top against each other by writing to Khrushchev that they would only consider a PCC meeting if they received all the relevant materials beforehand so as to prepare the meeting, thus echoing the Albanian request three years earlier.[117] Khrushchev duly replied that '[s]ince the initiative for the convention of this meeting arose not from the CC of the CPSU, it is self-evident that we have no obligation to prepare documents for this meeting'.[118] Khrushchev's willingness voluntarily to forego the Soviet prerogative of preparing such meetings is unprecedented. Both the meeting's preparation and its convention had become contingent on the consent of the NSWP members.

Failing to accept their defeat, the East German leaders attempted to entice the Soviet leadership into a meeting of foreign ministers to discuss MLF instead, by referring to Khrushchev's proposal from early January to organise such meetings.[119] At this stage, the Kremlin had lost its enthusiasm for sponsoring another meeting, which would never materialise. Ulbricht had thus been outwitted by the Romanians, who firmly opposed his transmission belt approach, but began to use the WP to assert their own independence instead. The East German struggle for recognition seems to have been more vulnerable than the Romanian striving for independence.

Ulbricht's single-minded preoccupation with the status of the GDR also manifested itself in his concern about Khrushchev's invitation of the West German Chancellor Erhard to Moscow in March 1964. Ulbricht used his fear of a Soviet-FRG rapprochement to talk Khrushchev into concluding a friendship treaty between the Soviet Union and the GDR in May 1964.[120] At the same time Ulbricht's Deputy Foreign Minister Winzer, who was the brain behind many of Ulbricht's initiatives, proposed to call the East German quest for recognition, equality and a normalisation of relations between both Germanys the 'Ulbricht doctrine', as 'our own German peace doctrine' for 'foreign propaganda'. After the 'Rapacki plan' and the 'Gomulka plan', the East Germans also felt like asserting their authority by putting forwards a 'positively formulated proposal'.[121] Ulbricht's deputy foreign minister seemed to sense more acutely that a constructive proposal to counterbalance the Hallstein doctrine might serve East German aims more than Ulbricht's antagonism.[122]

The denouement

The Ulbricht doctrine was, however, quickly undermined by the visit of Khrushchev's notorious son-in-law, Alexei Adzhubei, to West Germany in the summer of 1964. In his talks with West German journalists and politicians, Adzhubei openly praised 'the spirit of Rapallo', and stated that 'it was impossible to talk with a man like Ulbricht', who 'would not live long anyhow', since 'he suffered from cancer'.[123] The East German leadership issued a formal complaint about the lack of Soviet consultation regarding this delicate visit. The Polish move to record some of Adzhubei's compromising conversations on tape was, however, still more effective in undermining Khrushchev. The tape was passed on to Yuri Andropov, the Soviet secretary responsible for relations with the socialist states, who accordingly gained very sensitive information on Khrushchev's son-in-law.[124] This time Khrushchev had overplayed his hand in a number of ways: by compromising the interests of two of his WP allies through his intended rapprochement with the FRG he had inadvertently encouraged their assertiveness, and by sending his son-in-law to West Germany he had raised more suspicions about his Rapallo policy.

At the beginning of September 1964 Khrushchev nevertheless attempted again to gain support for his initiative on WP foreign policy coordination in an informal setting. He presented his plans at a reception in Prague to celebrate the 20th anniversary of the Slovak uprisings, where the foreign ministers of Poland, Hungary and Bulgaria 'happened' to be present, too. The Romanians nevertheless concluded that Khrushchev had deliberately organised this gathering of a select group of potentially supportive WP leaders 'to base the relations between the countries participating in the Warsaw Pact on a different foundation' and 'to exercise control'.[125] The Romanians were, unsurprisingly, excluded from this manoeuvre.

However, Khrushchev did not exercise any control for much longer. On 14 October 1964 his fellow presidium members forced him to resign, after he had been compelled to break off his holiday. According to the Soviet ambassador in Washington, Anatoly Dobrynin, it was 'a real palace revolution', whose 'principal architects', the politburo members Leonid Brezhnev, Mikhail Suslov and Nikolai Podgorny, had organised it long in advance.[126] In *Pravda*, the Communist Party's newspaper, Khrushchev's policies were condemned two days later for their 'subjectivism and drift in Communist construction, harebrained scheming, half-baked conclusions and hasty decisions and actions divorced from reality'.[127] Both the unforeseen consequences of Khrushchev's de-Stalinisation and his brinkmanship in the second Berlin Crisis and the Cuban Missile Crisis were severely criticised by his former comrades. Khrushchev, who was taken by surprise, responded in his defence that '[t]he fear is gone and we can talk as equals'.[128] Such a peaceful palace coup would, indeed, have been inconceivable under Stalin. Leonid Brezhnev, who had been in control of the defence industry since 1956, succeeded Khrushchev as general secretary; his outlook will be discussed at greater length in the next two chapters. Whereas Khrushchev retired – severely depressed – and died from old age in 1971, his successors initially 'did not suggest any changes whatsoever [in foreign policy]'.[129] Having consolidated their own power, Brezhnev and his comrades still had a lot of difficult nuts to crack in foreign policy.

Khrushchev's ouster was greatly applauded by Gomulka, who reacted by underlining in an address to the Polish Central Committee in November 1964 that in 'matters in which our party, our government, our country, are deeply and directly interested, we demand, have the right to demand, and always will demand that these matters be discussed with us and approved'.[130] Moreover, China's successful detonation of a nuclear device two days after Khrushchev's downfall changed the Soviet stance on non-proliferation, and the new leadership condemned the MLF on 15 November 1964. As the Chinese possession of a nuclear device at the height of the Sino–Soviet split posed a particular threat to the Soviet leaders, they had to take a firm stance on any forms of potential nuclear proliferation.

Meanwhile, Ulbricht seized the opportunity to try his luck with Khrushchev's successor, Leonid Brezhnev, and six days after Khrushchev's downfall he wrote to Brezhnev in order 'to renew [the East German] initiative to convene a PCC meeting' on MLF. Enclosing the draft of a letter that Ulbricht intended to send 'at short notice' to all Warsaw Pact leaders, and emphasising that the East German deputy foreign minister, Otto Winzer, was ready to go to Moscow straightaway for preliminary consultations, Ulbricht explicitly attempted to pressurise Brezhnev into approving the convention of a meeting.[131] The suggestion for bilateral preparations, reminiscent of that in January 1961, again seemed to illustrate that Ulbricht preferred to regard the WP as an East German-Soviet coproduction, while using the convention of PCC meetings as an instrument to boost his own status. In the enclosed draft letter to his allies Ulbricht suggested convening a meeting in the second half of November, as 'a unified stance of the Warsaw Pact members could serve to increase the resistance of certain NATO members against MLF' before NATO convened in December.[132] In addition, Ulbricht had enclosed an appeal on MLF that should be published after the PCC meeting.[133]

Ulbricht's attempt to choreograph the meeting beforehand was, however, thwarted by Brezhnev himself. Although Brezhnev approved the convention of a PCC meeting, he reminded Ulbricht that other WP leaders, too, could add items to the agenda.[134] The East Germans nevertheless seemed hard to restrain, and also delivered an East German draft of a non-proliferation treaty to the Kremlin in early November.[135] Moreover, the East German Foreign Ministry drafted a proposal for further foreign policy coordination within the Warsaw Pact, based on the resolution of the PCC meeting in January 1956. The East German officials at the Foreign Ministry suggested activating the standing committee for foreign policy questions and the secretariat that had been created on paper during that PCC meeting, but had never materialised.[136] What might have been a rhetorical embellishment eight years previously now came to be regarded as a means to turn the WP into a still more useful instrument for (East German) foreign policy coordination. Getting nowhere with the peace treaty, reforms turned into the new East German pet project. Khrushchev's ouster had created a window of opportunity for the East Germans: in the first three weeks of Brezhnev's reign they were remarkably active on the foreign policy front.

The Romanian leaders shrewdly observed that the actual invitation was dated '6 November', which was when Ulbricht was with Brezhnev in Moscow. Ulbricht's initiative, however, actually preceded and caused his visit to Moscow.[137] The Romanian leadership underestimated the way in which the GDR charted its own course. Ulbricht was, however, very keen to gain Soviet support for the East German quest for recognition, and Brezhnev's rise to power enabled Ulbricht to make another bid for the GDR as the Soviet Union's 'super ally'. The Romanians, meanwhile, considered the fact that

Ulbricht wrote his final letter from Moscow as proof that 'the new Soviet leadership is preoccupied to re-establish the hegemony of the CPSU over the socialist countries', while using the WP 'for [Soviet] confirmation of its political and military dominance over the other socialist countries'. In order to prevent this from happening, the Romanians vehemently opposed the creation of 'a permanent organ of the ministers of foreign affairs, which in fact should direct the entire foreign policy of the countries participating in the Warsaw Pact'.[138]

This time not only the Romanians, but also the Czechoslovaks slowed down the unilateral East German initiatives by disagreeing with the date of the meeting in a letter addressed to all WP leaders.[139] The Romanians did not agree with its convention per se, but they proposed convening the PCC meeting in January 1965, in order to await any decisions from the NATO convention on 15 December at which MLF would be discussed, as they considered the opposition of France potentially sufficient to thwart NATO.[140] This seemed a valid argument which was not primarily aimed at paralysing WP procedures. The Czechoslovaks, meanwhile, proposed the second half of January, as they considered November too soon to be well prepared.[141] Two new considerations in convening a meeting thus transpired: in the first place the developments concerning MLF raised the WP leaders' awareness of the potentially disruptive role of specific member states in NATO, such as France; and second, the request for thorough preparation indicated that the PCC meetings were beginning to be considered as more than a rhetorical accessory of the Kremlin. When the Albanian leaders first requested this in 1961 it seemed a mere ploy to obstruct the alliance's progress.

In the draft letter, written in Ulbricht's name on 24 November, Winzer stated that the SED politburo had 'taken into account the wishes' of the Czechoslovak CC and the RWP CC, and had 'agreed to the postponement of the meeting until January 1965'.[142] While stressing the East German role in granting the wishes of other NSWP members, the Kremlin's point of view was not even mentioned. The NSWP members controlled one another instead in the timing of the PCC meeting, and the East Germans proposed convening a meeting of deputy foreign ministers instead on 10 December without prior consultation with the Soviet Union. Moreover, Winzer reminded both the Romanians and the Czechoslovaks that the SED CC 'regretted' that no ordinary PCC meeting had taken place for more than three years, 'although in January 1956 the resolution was approved "that the Political Consultative Committee would convene when necessary, but no less than twice a year"'.[143] Alluding to the January 1956 meeting, Winzer paved the way for more intense forms of consultation within the PCC.

The seeds of multilateralisation

The East German role in these reforms also raised the profile of the Warsaw Pact within the East German politburo. After obtaining Ulbricht's approval to present both documents to the politburo, Winzer succeeded in putting both the Warsaw Pact and indirectly himself on the agenda of the East German party top.[144] Winzer emphasised that it was 'necessary to convene a meeting of the deputy foreign ministers of the Warsaw Pact members in early December [...] to ensure the success of the PCC meeting, and its agenda and results'. Moreover, the 'nuclear armament of West Germany' and the 'differences of opinion within the imperialist camp' necessitated 'treating the question of MLF as the central theme' of the PCC meeting. Limiting the PCC meeting to issues that directly affected the GDR seemed an attempt to choreograph the PCC meeting fully beforehand. Although Winzer suggested that there should not be 'a main speech', but that 'every delegation should be given the equal possibility to present their opinions and proposals',[145] the Romanians assumed that Ulbricht would use this opportunity 'to become the principal referent'.[146] On both a domestic and a foreign policy level the WP had thus gained importance for the GDR.

Winzer's proposal of a meeting of WP deputy foreign ministers was approved by the SED politburo, and Ulbricht immediately sent a letter to invite his allies to this meeting.[147] The differences of opinion, inherent in true multilateralism, had thus inadvertently led to the *de facto* creation of a new organ, namely the meeting of deputy foreign ministers, alongside the PCC. Moreover, they also inspired a vehement debate about the topics that would be on the agenda: should it be merely about MLF (which the East German and Hungarian leaderships preferred)[148] or should there be room for other kinds of foreign policy issues (as the Czechoslovak leadership desired)?[149] Gomulka once again took the most nuanced position, stressing on the one hand the importance of uniting against MLF, while emphasising on the other that postponing the meeting until January was not a problem.[150]

In a meeting between the East German diplomat Mewis and the Polish politburo member Zenon Kliszko, the latter explained to his East German comrade that 'the victory of the Labour Party in England' and 'the stance of de Gaulle' would make it likely 'that the MLF would no longer be created this year', so it would be advisable to await further developments in NATO.[151] Again, the Poles seemed more in touch with the developments within NATO than their East German counterparts and, in fact, used exactly the same arguments as the Romanians for postponing the PCC meeting until January. Although the GDR leaders were eager to call the shots, they did not seem to have enough know-how to do so. The East German lack of diplomatic channels with Western European countries considerably limited the capacity to be informed.

The East Germans were, nevertheless, still keen to direct the multilateral process in accordance with their own wishes, and Winzer resumed conversations with his Polish colleague Naszkowski and the Soviet Sorin shortly before the deputy foreign ministers convened 'to guarantee a common and coordinated stance'.[152] By this stage the NSWP members took the initiative in these preparatory talks: the Pole Naszkowski defined MLF and the preparation of the PCC meeting in January as the central themes on the agenda of the deputy foreign ministers meeting.[153]

The deputy foreign ministers convened on 10 December 1964 in Warsaw. After the East German Deputy Foreign Minister Winzer had begun the meeting by explaining the necessity of a 'common stance of all socialist countries' against the MLF, preferably also within the general assembly of the United Nations, the Soviet Sorin backed up Winzer's stance, as had been agreed beforehand, and also 'turned against the aim of the USA, to separate the MLF from the question of non-proliferation'. Despite Khrushchev's hesitancy at an earlier stage, the Poles, East Germans and Soviets were obviously again united in their unequivocal opposition to MLF, as were all the other Warsaw Pact deputy foreign ministers. The East Germans managed to rally enough support for defining the 'struggle against the MLF' as the 'main theme' on the agenda of the PCC meeting in January 1965.[154]

The Romanian veto of the East German proposal to issue a communiqué and to prepare another one for the PCC meeting nevertheless undermined the 'unified stance' that all other WP deputy foreign ministers intended to present to the rest of the world, as we have seen in the previous chapter. A new precedent had accordingly been set: although all WP members agreed on the substance of the meeting, namely the opposition to MLF, Romanian disagreement on procedural matters, in this case the communiqué, still served to prevent the WP members from committing themselves to one particular stance. Whereas the East Germans ensured that the German question would take centre stage, the Romanians attempted to maintain maximum flexibility. Moreover, they tried to prevent a predominantly East German stamp on the meeting in particular: the Romanian deputy foreign minister conceded that the Polish side *could* propose a draft communiqué, but this was in turn rejected by both Winzer and Sorin.

The meeting seemed to draw the Soviet and East German sides even closer to one another. On the day after the meeting the necessity for more cooperation came up in a private conversation between Winzer and his Soviet colleague Sorin, in which Winzer's suggestion to activate the standing committee for foreign policy questions, which had been created on paper in January 1956 but had never materialised, was applauded by Sorin. The Soviet deputy foreign minister even encouraged the GDR to present the proposal on WP reforms at the PCC meeting in January 1965.[155] Although Winzer had not achieved all East German aims in the multilateral setting of the deputy foreign ministers meeting, since the Romanians had vetoed both communiqués, he had been considerably more successful on a bilateral level: Sorin's enthusiasm for the East German proposal for reforms was, to some extent, a triumph.

Sorin nevertheless also used the conversation to curb East German ambitions. He informed Winzer that the Soviet side in principle agreed with Ulbricht's draft of a non-proliferation treaty, which the East German delegation had handed over to Brezhnev in early November, but added that there were still several paragraphs that needed to be rewritten. Sorin criticised the

East German rhetoric, such as the appeal for 'the fight against MLF', which according to the Soviet side should be 'less propagandistic' and more to the point. He added that the Soviet leaders considered the emphasis on the negative consequences of the MLF and of the role of West Germany 'exaggerated'. With the conclusion 'the shorter, the better', Sorin chided the East German tendency towards lengthy invectives.[156] The conversation with Sorin was, accordingly, a mixed blessing for Winzer. Although his Soviet colleague had explicitly acknowledged the East German contribution to the proceedings of the Warsaw Pact, he had also emphasised that there were limits to NSWP initiatives. In the Brezhnev era the Kremlin would again attempt to assume control over the dynamics within the Warsaw Pact.

Conclusion: manoeuvres in a multilateral arena

Brzezinski's concept of 'de-satellitisation' might be somewhat too extreme, but his observation that the 'satellites' of the Soviet Union turned into its 'junior allies' in the first half of the 1960s does seem to apply to both Poland and – in the light of the previous chapter – Romania.[157] The Polish and Romanian leaders had emerged as the strongest players in the first half of the 1960s, after emancipating themselves by asserting their individual stance on the German question and the Sino–Soviet rift, respectively. The position of the GDR, meanwhile, had become less urgent after the Wall had resolved the Berlin Crisis, and its leadership could therefore no longer count on its allies' undivided attention. Moreover, Ulbricht's failure to cast his national interests into a wider framework, as Gomulka did, undermined his credibility. The way in which the dynamics of dissent not only emancipated individual WP members, but also contributed to the evolution of the WP at large, will be examined in the next part of this book.

Ulbricht's awareness of the GDR's status as the Soviet Union's 'super ally' or 'superdomino' enabled him to defy the Kremlin only to a certain extent.[158] Although Harrison concludes that the second Berlin Crisis invested Walter Ulbricht with power, as he could use the fragile status of the GDR as leverage over Khrushchev, it transferred even more power to his Polish ally Gomulka, on whose support Ulbricht was to a large extent dependent. The WP angle therefore sheds a new light on Ulbricht's capacity to exercise pressure, which was not quite as large as is often assumed. The Polish leadership in particular had a vested interest in the German question, which paved the way to its emancipation from the Soviet grip. The multilateral perspective accordingly serves to give Gomulka the credit he is due in the second Berlin Crisis, as the traditional bilateral approach often relegates him to oblivion. Unlike Ulbricht, Gomulka convincingly identified his own interests with those of his WP colleagues, and did not isolate himself from them. Ulbricht's personality was not conducive to compromise.

Having successfully used the alliance as an instrument to legitimise the closing of the borders, Ulbricht's grip on the WP diminished significantly after the Wall was built. The Warsaw Pact, ironically, defined the limits of his emancipation. The Warsaw Pact meeting from 3–5 August 1961 might have briefly seemed Ulbricht's finest hour, as it finally compelled Khrushchev to undertake some action, but his emancipation did not even outlast the meeting. It is safe to surmise that his allies' refusal to assist the GDR economically had contributed to Khrushchev's policy change on a peace treaty, as Khrushchev's justification for doing so echoes their arguments. Narrowly concentrating on the GDR's interests, Ulbricht failed to rally personal support. Meanwhile, the Berlin Crisis provided Ulbricht's allies with an instrument to formulate their separate stance. Initially a lever of Ulbricht, he had inadvertently transferred his leverage to his NSWP comrades, some of whom were more successful than he was in emancipating themselves from the Soviet grip. Khrushchev's brinkmanship during the second Berlin Crisis ultimately paved the way for the burgeoning emancipation of Gomulka, who successfully used the Warsaw Pact as a platform to rally support against some of the designs of Khrushchev and Ulbricht.

The beginning of the German question obviously preceded the Sino–Soviet split, but the latter seemed to have strongly influenced Khrushchev's increasingly moderate stance in the second Berlin Crisis and his initially pro-Western stance on the MLF, which in turn compelled the East German and Polish leaders to emancipate themselves from the Soviet grip to safeguard their own security interests. Deeming the relationship with China beyond repair, he needed to ensure some Western support in order to avoid fighting a 'Cold War' on two fronts simultaneously. Moreover, Ulbricht's intransigence during the Checkpoint Charlie crisis encouraged the Soviet leadership to begin courting the FRG by forging a new 'Rapallo policy', as Ulbricht's ambitions to control Berlin had turned him into a liability. In the following period mounting disagreements between the Soviet Union, Poland and the GDR on the FRG's potential access to nuclear weapons gave a novel impetus to the scope for emancipation and dissent.

Gomulka manoeuvred more successfully than Ulbricht. As the Polish historian Wanda Jarzabek argues, the Rapallo policy 'motivated the Polish regime to launch a more active policy towards the FRG and other Western countries' in order to prevent 'the Warsaw Pact's German policy to be dictated exclusively by Moscow, or belong to East Germany's special privileges'.[159] Gomulka used his diplomatic clout to gain support for the 'Gomulka plan' both within the Warsaw Pact and beyond. The East German leadership nevertheless did not accept the Polish proposal to coordinate a stance on MLF in December 1963, and bypassed Gomulka with an East German proposal on German disarmament that no one took seriously. The subsequent East German attempt to convene the PCC was thwarted by the Romanians, who strove to prevent the East German transmission belt approach. In the competition for the Kremlin's most powerful ally Gomulka had unquestionably outstripped Ulbricht. The East German zeal for further foreign policy consultation had, however, led to the convention of the WP's deputy foreign ministers in December 1964, thus sealing the alliance's incipient multilateralisation.

This was no mean achievement either, and it testifies to the embryonic East German emancipation into a 'junior ally', too. The East German emancipation is all the more remarkable, as it pertains to a country that was not even recognised internationally. Although Gomulka had been much more successful in marrying Polish national interests with WP interests, Ulbricht had perceived the WP's potential in providing the East German leadership with an opportunity for boosting the status of the GDR. It was, after all, Ulbricht who asked Khrushchev in January 1961 to convene a WP meeting. Ulbricht was eager to exploit the fact that the German question was the Warsaw Pact's *raison d'être*. With the WP as the only framework for East German recognition, the East German insecurity explains Ulbricht's ambition to use the WP as an instrument to further East German national interests. Ulbricht's predicament was, after all, still more difficult than Gomulka's. Even though both countries shared some geopolitical constraints, such as the fact that their German borders were not recognised, the East German material confines were much more serious: ruling a country that was not recognised at all, Ulbricht was not in a position to cultivate diplomatic relations with Western European countries, which Gomulka and Rapacki did so successfully.

This chapter has, however, also shown that the Polish leaders proved better diplomats *within* the framework of the WP. Whereas Gomulka and his foreign minister closely worked in tandem, Ulbricht moved almost as unilaterally within the East German politburo as he did within the WP. The insecurity of East Germany's status combined with the intransigence of the East German leader meant that Ulbricht gradually began to overplay his hand. He became more prone than Khrushchev himself to use the WP as a transmission belt for his foreign policy interests, and accordingly caused more opposition, *inter alia*, from the Romanian leadership. Ulbricht's vested interest in manoeuvring within the WP in the first half of the 1960s seemed to be greater than Khrushchev's. The dynamics of the impact of the Sino–Soviet split and the German question on the WP had spiralled out of Khrushchev's control. Khrushchev's brainchild seemed to become a liability for the Soviet leadership itself. It remained to Brezhnev to regain control over the process, and to prevent the embryonic emancipation of the NSWP members from eclipsing Soviet choreography altogether, as we shall see in the next part of this book.

Notes

1 Minutes of the plenary session of the RWP CC from 15–22 April 1964, ANIC, RWP CC, C, 16/1964, 44.
2 See Chapter 1 of this book for an explanation of the second Berlin Crisis in the period 1958–60.
3 H. Harrison, *Driving the Soviets up the Wall. Soviet East German Relations, 1953–1961* (Princeton, 2005). Cf. G. Wettig, *Chruschtschows Berlin-Krise 1958 bis 1963. Drohpolitik und Mauerbau* (Berlin, 2006); M. Lemke, *Die Berlinkrise 1958*

bis 1963. Interesse und Handlungsspielräume der SED im Ost West Konflikt (Berlin, 1995); J.L. Gaddis, *We Now Know. Rethinking Cold War History* (Oxford, 1997); V.M. Zubok and C. Pleshakov, *Inside the Kremlin's Cold War. From Stalin to Khrushchev* (Harvard, 1996).
4 W. Taubman, *Khrushchev. The Man and his Era* (London, 2003), 419.
5 Ibid., 438.
6 Ibid., 440.
7 V. Mastny, 'Meeting of the PCC, Moscow, 4 February 1960, Editorial Note', PHP, www.php.isn.ethz.ch/collections/colltopic.cfm?lng=en&id=17885&navinfo= 14465 (accessed 25 August 2013).
8 'Report on the PCC Meeting for Czechoslovak Party Politburo', 20 February 1960, PHP, www.php.isn.ethz.ch/collections/colltopic.cfm?lng=en&id=17884&navinfo=14465 (accessed 25 August 2013).
9 'Report on PCC Meeting by the Bulgarian Prime Minister (Anton Iugov) to Bulgarian Politburo Session', 11 February 1960, PHP, www.php.isn.ethz.ch/collections/colltopic.cfm?lng=en&id=17883&navinfo=14465 (accessed 25 August 2013).
10 'Declaration', 4 February 1960, PHP, www.php.isn.ethz.ch/collections/colltopic.cfm?lng=en&id=17643&navinfo=14465 (accessed 25 August 2013).
11 'Report for Czechoslovak Party Politburo', 20 February 1960, PHP.
12 Cf. M. Trachtenberg, *A Constructed Peace. The Making of the European Settlement, 1945–1963* (Princeton, 1999), for the link between the second Berlin Crisis and the nuclearisation of the FRG.
13 'The exchange of views revealed complete unanimity': 'Communiqué', 4 February 1960, PHP, www.php.isn.ethz.ch/collections/colltopic.cfm?lng=en&id=17880&navinfo=14465 (accessed 25 August 2013).
14 'About several questions on foreign policy, which were discussed at the Sejm on 16 and 17 February 1960', SAPMO-BArch, DY 30/IV/2/20/284, 362, 367.
15 '"Our foreign policy – a policy of peace", speech by the Foreign Minister Adam Rapacki in the Sejm', 17 February 1960, SAPMO-BArch, DY 30/IV/2/20/184, 376.
16 'Resolution of the Sejm of the PRP, Trybuna Ludu', 17 February 1960, SAPMO-BArch, DY 30/IV/2/20/184, 389–389b. Cf. Chapter 1 of this book on the Rapacki plan.
17 'Memorandum about a conversation with the Czechoslovak diplomat Rezek on 29/02/1960 at the Ostbahnhof', SAPMO-BArch, DY 30/IV2/20/184, 358.
18 Minutes of the failed preliminary Paris summit, 15–18 May 1960, DY 30/3507, e.g. 208–9 and 233.
19 Cf. V.M. Zubok, *Khrushchev and the Berlin Crisis (1958–1962)*, CWIHP Working Paper No. 6 (Washington, 1993); Harrison, *Driving the Soviets up the Wall*; H. Harrison, *Ulbricht and the Concrete 'Rose': New Archival Evidence on the Dynamics of Soviet East German Relations and the Berlin Crisis, 1958–1961*, CWIHP Working Paper No. 5 (Washington, 1993), Appendix A, 71.
20 Cf. Zubok, *Khrushchev and the Berlin Crisis*, 20; and Harrison, *Driving the Soviets up the Wall*, 139, on Khrushchev's diminished room for manoeuvre.
21 Harrison, *Driving the Soviets up the Wall*, 147. For a more detailed discussion of Ulbricht's unilateral actions, cf. ibid., 144–47.
22 Ibid., 139.
23 Harrison, *Concrete 'Rose'*, Appendix A.
24 D. Selvage, 'The End of the Berlin Crisis. New Evidence from the Polish and East German Archives', in C. Ostermann (ed.), *Cold War Flashpoints*, CWIHP Bulletin No. 11 (Washington, 1998), 218.
25 Harrison, *Concrete 'Rose'*, Appendix A, 74.
26 'Memorandum about a conversation of comrade Moldt with comrade Stasiak, chef of the department of propaganda in the PUWP CC on 9 January 1961', Warsaw, 12 January 1961, SAPMO-BArch, DY 30/IV/2/20/185, 23–25.

27 'Re: Establishment of consulates of the German Democratic Republic in the People's Republic of Poland', 25 January 1961, SAPMO-BArch, DY 30/IV/2/20/185, 47–52.
28 'The relations between Poland and West Germany', Warsaw, 10 February 1961, SAPMO-BArch, DY 30/IV/2/20/185, 74–99.
29 Letter from Ulbricht to Khrushchev, 18 January 1961, SAPMO-Barch, DY 30/3508, 59–73.
30 Quoted in Harrison, *Driving the Soviets up the Wall*, 165. This is the explanation from Horst Brie, a former GDR diplomat at the embassy in Beijing.
31 Harrison, *Driving the Soviets up the Wall*, 139.
32 *Pace* Harrison, *Driving the Soviets up the Wall*, 163; and Zubok, *Khrushchev and the Berlin Crisis*, 24.
33 Letter from Khrushchev to Ulbricht, 30 January 1961, SAPMO-BArch, DY 30/3508, 114–16.
34 Letter from Khrushchev to SED CC, 24 January 1961, SAPMO-BArch, DY 30/3386, 116–17.
35 Letter from Khrushchev to WP leaders, 15 March 1961, SAPMO-BArch, DY 30/3386, 120–21.
36 Harrison, *Concrete 'Rose'*, 88.
37 'Speech by the First Secretary of the CC of the CPSU (Nikita S. Khrushchev)', 29 March 1961, PHP, www.php.isn.ethz.ch/collections/colltopic.cfm?lng=en&id=17897&navinfo=14465 (accessed 25 August 2013).
38 Ulbricht's speech, 29 March 1961, SAPMO-BArch, DY 30/3386, 161–80.
39 Zubok, *Khrushchev and the Berlin Crisis*, 24–25. Cf. Harrison, *Driving the Soviets up the Wall*, 169: 'According to Sejna [the Czechoslovak minister of defence], "Ulbricht put forward a proposal to make crossing the border from East to West Berlin impossible ... But none of the Warsaw Pact states agreed, [and] Romania opposed it especially vehemently".'
40 'Communiqué', 29 March 1961, PHP, www.php.isn.ethz.ch/collections/colltopic.cfm?lng=en&id=17886&navinfo=14465 (accessed 25 August 2013).
41 'Protocol No. 15/61, of the extraordinary session of the politburo on Saturday 1 April 1961', SAPMO-BArch, DY 30/JIV2/2A 813, 1.
42 'Protocol No. 6/60, of the session of the politburo on Thursday, 8 February 1960', SAPMO-BArch, DY 30/JIV2/2/687, 1.
43 'Speech by the First Secretary (Khrushchev)', 29 March 1961, PHP.
44 V. Mastny, 'Meeting of the PCC, Moscow, 28–29 March 1961, Editorial Note', PHP, www.php.isn.ethz.ch/collections/colltopic.cfm?lng=en&id=17899&navinfo=14465 (accessed 25 August 2013).
45 Harrison, *Concrete 'Rose'*, Appendix D.
46 A. Dobrynin, *In Confidence. Moscow's Ambassador to America's Six Cold War Presidents (1962–1986)* (New York, 1995), 45.
47 Cf. Harrison, *Driving the Soviets up the Wall*, 175.
48 Letter from Ulbricht to Gomulka, draft of the political part of the letter by Winzer, June 1961, SAPMO-BArch, DY 30/3655, 36.
49 Harrison, *Concrete 'Rose'*, 96.
50 Ibid.
51 Letter from Ulbricht to WP leaders, convening WP meeting (no date), SAPMO-BArch, DY 30/3386, 212–13.
52 Harrison, *Driving the Soviets up the Wall*, 185.
53 Harrison, *Concrete 'Rose'*, Appendix F, 100.
54 Harrison, *Driving the Soviets up the Wall*, 186.
55 Quoted in ibid.
56 Letter from Ulbricht to Khrushchev, July 1961, SAPMO-BArch, DY 30/3478, 4–5.
57 Harrison, *Driving the Soviets up the Wall*, 194.

58 D. Selvage, 'The Warsaw Pact and the German Question, 1955–70', in M.A. Heiss and S.V. Papacosma (eds), *NATO and the Warsaw Pact: Intrabloc Conflicts* (Ohio, 2008), 178.
59 'Speech by Walter Ulbricht on 3 August 1961', SAPMO-BArch, DY 30/3478, 43–94.
60 In order to maintain strict secrecy, the planned construction of the wall was not mentioned in any transcripts (Zubok, *Khrushchev and the Berlin Crisis*, 27), and the words 'be closed' were only spoken at the conference but omitted from the final records (Harrison, *Driving the Soviets up the Wall*, 197).
61 Selvage, 'The End of the Berlin Crisis', 222. 'Gomulka: I would have shut it far earlier. How many times I told Khrushchev about it.'
62 Gomulka's speech, PA AA, MfAA, G-A 474.
63 Ibid.
64 Cf. the speeches by Kadar and Novotny, PA AA, MfAA, G-A 474.
65 Khrushchev's speech, PA AA, MfAA, G-A 474.
66 Selvage, 'The End of the Berlin Crisis', 218.
67 Zubok, *Khrushchev and the Berlin Crisis*, 27.
68 Harrison, *Driving the Soviets up the Wall*, 142.
69 'Protocol No. 39/61 of the extraordinary session of the politburo on Monday, 7 August 1961', SAPMO-BArch, DY 30/JIV2/2A841, 1–12.
70 'Declaration of governments of the Warsaw Pact States (13 August 1961)', SAPMO-BArch, DY 30/IVA2/20/1140, 30–31.
71 'Information: Polish mood concerning Berlin', Warsaw, 22 August 1961, DY 30/IV/2/20/185, 199–205.
72 Quoted in Harrison, *Driving the Soviets up the Wall*, 207.
73 Letter from Ulbricht to Khrushchev, Berlin, 15 September 1961, SAPMO-BArch, DY 30/3509, 95.
74 W.R. Smyser, *From Yalta to Berlin. The Cold War Struggle over Germany* (London, 1999), 168; cf. Ulbricht's letter to Khrushchev on 15 September (above).
75 Letter from Khrushchev to Ulbricht, 28 September 1961, SAPMO-BArch, DY 30/3509, 105–7.
76 Harrison, *Driving the Soviets up the Wall*, 143.
77 Lemke, *Die Berlinkrise*, 175.
78 Zubok also argues this (*Khrushchev and the Berlin Crisis*, 29), but does not mention the coincidence with the 22nd party congress. This was also the interpretation in the FRG: 'Material about some aspects about the journey of Adzhubei to West Germany', Berlin, 3 November 1964, SAPMO-BArch, DY 30/3497, 266–67.
79 See Chapter 2 for the role of the 22nd CPSU party congress in the Sino–Soviet split.
80 Smyser, *From Yalta to Berlin*, 171.
81 Cf. Smyser, *From Yalta to Berlin*, 172–78, for a lucid account of the Checkpoint Charlie crisis; cf. Harrison, *Driving the Soviets up the Wall*, 213–14.
82 Letter from Ulbricht to Khrushchev, SAPMO-BArch, DY 30/3509, 190–202.
83 Cf. Selvage, 'The End of the Berlin Crisis', 223, for the primary evidence of this meeting.
84 Conversation between the West German ambassador in Moscow, H. Kroll, and Khrushchev, 9 November 1961, SAPMO-BArch, DY 30/3509, 236.
85 Ibid., 215.
86 Summit between Soviet and East German leadership, 26 February 1962, PA AA, MfAA, G-A 476.
87 'Plan of foreign policy measures in the first half year of 1962', SAPMO-BArch, DY 30/3381, 28–57.
88 Ibid.
89 'Czechoslovak Summary of the PCC meeting', 7 June 1962, PHP, www.php.isn.ethz.ch/collections/colltopic.cfm?lng=en&id=17903&navinfo=14465 (accessed 25 August 2013).

128 *Embryonic emancipation, 1955–64*

90 'Extract of Memorandum of Conversation between the First Secretary of the CC of the CPSU (Nikita S. Khrushchev) and the First Secretary of the KSC (Antonín Novotný)', 8 June 1962, PHP, www.php.isn.ethz.ch/collections/colltopic.cfm?lng=en&id=17902&navinfo=14465 (accessed 25 August 2013).
91 Harrison, *Driving the Soviets up the Wall*, 143.
92 'Annual report of 1961 of the GDR Embassy in the People's Republic of Poland', Warsaw, 22 December 1961, DY30/IV/2/20/185, 260–63.
93 Report on exchange of delegations and reporters, SAPMO-BArch, DY 30/IV/2/20/171, 29–46.
94 Smyser, *From Yalta to Berlin*, 205.
95 A. Priest, 'From Hardware to Software: The End of the MLF and the Rise of the Nuclear Planning Group', in A. Wenger *et al.* (eds), *Transforming NATO in the Cold War. Challenges beyond Deterrence in the 1960s* (Oxford and New York, 2007), 149–50. See also Trachtenberg, *A Constructed Peace*, chapters 7 and 8, for an extremely elaborate account of the West German interest in NATO's nuclear affairs.
96 'Memorandum, 2 October 1963', in D. Selvage, *The Warsaw Pact and Nuclear Nonproliferation, 1963–1965*, CWIHP Working Paper No. 32 (Washington, 2001), 20.
97 Ibid., 2.
98 Ibid., 4.
99 Letter, Gomulka to Khrushchev, 8 October 1963, in ibid., 22–26. Cf. D. Selvage, *Poland and the Sino-Soviet Split, 1963–1965*, CWIHP E-Dossier No. 10, www.wilsoncenter.org/publication/e-dossier-no-10-poland-and-the-sino-soviet-rift-1963-1965 (accessed 25 August 2013).
100 'Annual report 1963, embassy of the GDR in the PR Poland, Warsaw', 3 February 1964, SAPMO-BArch, DY30/IVA2/20/331, 84.
101 Selvage, *The Warsaw Pact and Nuclear Nonproliferation*, 33.
102 Conversation between Deputy Minister König and the Polish diplomat Dr Tomala, 16 December 1963, SAPMO-BArch, DY 30/IV A 2/20/329, 12.
103 Conversation between Deputy Minister König and the Polish diplomat Dr Tomala, 17 December 1963, SAPMO-BArch, DY 30/IVA2/20/329, 13.
104 See Selvage, *The Warsaw Pact and Nuclear Nonproliferation*, 8.
105 Letter from Khrushchev to Gheorgiu-Dej, Moscow, 2 January 1964, ANIC, RWP CC, C, 6/1964, 31–32.
106 Letter from Gheorgiu-Dej to Khrushchev, Bucharest, January 1964, ANIC, RWP CC, C, 6/1964, 36.
107 Letter from Ulbricht to Khrushchev, Berlin, 24 January 1964, SAPMO-BArch, DY 30/3387, 61–62.
108 Speech by Ulbricht, draft, 1964, no date, SAPMO-BArch, DY 30/3382, 18–52.
109 Minutes of the plenary session of the Central Committee of the Romanian Workers' Party, 17 February 1964, ANIC, RWP CC, C, 6/1964, 41–42.
110 Letter from Ulbricht to Gheorgiu-Dej, 28 January, ANIC, RWP CC, C, 6/1964, 44–45, and letter from Khrushchev to Ulbricht, 11 February, ibid., 45–46.
111 Letter from Ulbricht to Gomulka, 25 January 1964, SAPMO-BArch, DY 30/3387, 65–66.
112 Letter from Gomulka to Ulbricht, Warsaw, 13 February 1964, SAPMO-BArch, DY3 0/3387, 72–75.
113 Ibid., 72–75.
114 Letter from Gheorghiu-Dej to Ulbricht, no date, SAPMO-BArch, DY 30/3387, 98.
115 Letter from Khrushchev to Ulbricht, 20 March 1964, SAPMO-BArch, DY 30/3387, 90–91.
116 Minutes of the plenary session of the RWP CC from 15–22 April 1964, ANIC, RWP CC, C, 16/1964, 44.

Compromised by the German question 129

117 Letter from Gheorgiu-Dej to Khrushchev, 19 February 1964, ANIC, RWP CC, C, 17/1964, 300–1.
118 Letter from Khrushchev to Gheorghiu-Dej, 10 March 1964, SAPMO-BArch, DY 30/3387, 85–87. Cf. Letter from Gheorgiu-Dej to Khrushchev, 19 February 1964, ANIC, RWP CC, C, 17/1964, 304–5.
119 Winzer's draft of Ulbricht's letter to Gromyko, 13 April 1964, SAPMO-BArch, DY 30/3393, 11.
120 Selvage, *The Warsaw Pact and Nuclear Nonproliferation*, 9.
121 Letter from Winzer to Ulbricht, 23 May 1964, SAPMO-BArch, DY 30/3382, 16–17.
122 See the Hallstein Doctrine, Chapter 1 of this book.
123 'Material about some aspects about the journey of Adzhubei to West Germany', Berlin, 3 November 1964, SAPMO-BArch, DY 30/3497, 264–66.
124 Selvage, *The Warsaw Pact and Nuclear Nonproliferation*, 12–13.
125 Meeting between Bodnaras and Liu Fan, 5 September 1964, ANIC, RWP CC, IR, 5/1964, 108.
126 Dobrynin, *In Confidence*, 128.
127 Quoted in Taubman, *Khrushchev*, 620.
128 Quoted in G.S. Barrass, *The Great Cold War. A Journey through the Hall of Mirrors* (Stanford, 2009), 146.
129 Dobrynin, *In Confidence*, 128.
130 Selvage, *The Warsaw Pact and Nuclear Nonproliferation*, 12.
131 Letter from Ulbricht to Brezhnev, 20 October 1964, SAPMO-BArch, DY 30/3387, 100–1.
132 Letter from Ulbricht to WP leaders, 21 October 1964, SAPMO-BArch, DY 30/3387, 104–7.
133 Draft appeal of the PCC, SAPMO-BArch, DY 30/3387, 113–23.
134 Confidential letter from Brezhnev to Ulbricht, 4 November 1964, SAPMO-BArch, DY 30/3387, 136–37.
135 Draft appeal of a non-proliferation treaty, 6 November 1964, SAPMO-BArch, DY 30/3387, 138–41.
136 'Information about the organs of the WP', Berlin, 19 November 1964, SAPMO-BArch, DY 30/3387, 192–93.
137 Meeting between Bodnaras and Liu Fan, 24 November 1964, ANIC, RWP CC, IR, 5/1964, 159–61.
138 Ibid., 165.
139 Ibid., 166.
140 Letter from Gheorgiu-Dej to Ulbricht, 19 November 1964, SAPMO-BArch, DY 30/3387, 184–85; cf. Meeting between Bodnaras and Liu Fan, 24 November 1964, ANIC, RWP CC, IR, 5/1964, 164.
141 Letter from Novotny to Ulbricht, 18 November 1964, SAPMO-BArch, DY30/3387, 175–76; cf. Meeting between Bodnaras and Liu Fan, 24 November 1964, ANIC, RWP CC, IR, 5/1964, 166.
142 Letter from Ulbricht to Novotny, drafted by Winzer, 24 November 1964, SAPMO-BArch, DY 30/3387, 197–98.
143 Ibid.; Identical letter from Ulbricht to Gheorgiu-Dej, SAPMO-BArch, DY 30/2287, 201–2.
144 Protocol No. 49/64, of the session of the politburo on Tuesday 24 November 1964, DY 30/ J IV 2/2/964, 1–3.
145 'Appendix No. 1 to protocol No. 49/64 from 24.11.1964', SAPMO-BArch, DY 30/ J IV 2/2/964, 10–16.
146 Meeting between Bodnaras and Liu Fan, 12 December 1964, ANIC, RWP CC, IR, 5/1964, 187.
147 Letters from Ulbricht to Kadar, Gomulka, and Zhivkov, 24 November 1964, SAPMO-BArch, DY 30/3387, 205–16.

148 Memorandum, Kundermann to Herpold, Berlin, 30 November 1964, SAPMO-BArch, DY 30/3387, 237.
149 Letter from Novotny to Ulbricht, 3 December 1964, SAPMO-BArch, DY 30/3387, 247–48.
150 Letter from Gomulka to Ulbricht, 1 December 1964, SAPMO-BArch, DY 30/3387, 238–40.
151 'Memorandum about conversation between diplomat Mewis und PUWP politburo member, comrade Zenon Kliszko', 24 November 1964, Warsaw, SAPMO-BArch, DY 30/3387, 235–36.
152 GDR report of the deputy foreign ministers meeting, December 1964, SAPMO-BArch, DY 30/3393, 13.
153 This might be a consequence of the fact that Gomulka was allegedly particularly close to the new leadership. Cf. Minutes of the discussions with a government and party delegation from the R.P.R. with a party and government delegation from the R.P. China, Moscow, 8 November 1964, ANIC, RWP CC, C, 70/1964, 69.
154 GDR report of the deputy foreign ministers meeting, December 1964, SAPMO-BArch, DY 30/3393, 13–25.
155 Conversation between Winzer and Sorin, 11 December 1964, PA AA, MfAA, A 1805.
156 Ibid.
157 Z.K. Brzezinski, *The Soviet Bloc: Unity and Conflict. Revised and Enlarged Edition* (Harvard, 1967), 433; cf. Selvage, *The Warsaw Pact and Nuclear Nonproliferation*, 2, for a similar observation.
158 Harrison, *Driving the Soviets up the Wall*, 143.
159 See W. Jarzabek, *Hope and Reality. Poland and the Conference on Security and Cooperation in Europe, 1964–1989*, CWIHP Working Paper No. 56 (Washington, 2008), 4.

Part II
The dynamics of dissent, 1965–68

4 Warsaw Pact reforms and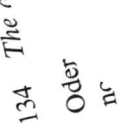

> We are not against the Warsaw Treaty, but against transgressing it.[1]
> (Nicolae Ceausescu in a conversation with Leonid Brezhnev, July 1966)

On 18 January 1965 the Polish leader Wladyslaw Gomulka was casually flicking through East German proposals for the impending PCC meeting, 'while waiting for the arrival of the delegations [of the other WP members]' at Warsaw's railway station.[2] The Romanian leader Gheorghiu-Dej was, however, furious that the East German leaders had only disseminated their proposals on reforms, non-proliferation, and a draft communiqué a few days before the PCC meeting was to start on 19 January, and he arranged a bilateral meeting with Gomulka to share his frustration. He also organised to meet the East German leader Walter Ulbricht bilaterally to rebuke him strongly 'about the method that you have adopted', since '[o]ur politburo has not had the possibility' to study the documents, and therefore 'has no mandate to discuss this'.[3]

This kind of dynamics between the non-Soviet Warsaw Pact members is illustrative for the development of the Warsaw Pact halfway through the 1960s. By 1965 the alliance was no longer the 'instrument of Soviet diplomacy' it is often considered to be within historiography.[4] Under the influence of the Sino–Soviet split and the second Berlin Crisis, it had inadvertently developed into a *multi*lateral platform, which the abovementioned Romanian, Polish and East German party leaders in particular began to use to further their own interests. Nor was the 'sense of mutual interest' so 'little' as tends to be suggested, but most of its members did, *pace* John Lewis Gaddis, share a vested interest in, *inter alia*, consolidating the structure of the alliance and using it as a vehicle to formulate their view on European security.[5]

This chapter will therefore examine the way in which the NSWP members used the discussion on reforms and European security as an instrument to further their own interests, with particular emphasis on the Romanian members on the one hand, and the East German and Polish ones on the other, who represented both extremes in the ensuing debate. Both topics are manifestations of the German question, in which the East German and Polish side had a particular stake, striving for recognition of the GDR and the

...sse line, respectively, whereas the Romanian leadership sought to ...lise relations with West Germany instead. Tracing the developments from ... PCC meeting in January 1965 to the meeting of deputy foreign ministers in February 1967, just after the Romanians had succeeded in establishing diplomatic contacts with the FRG, this chapter serves to analyse the conflicting interests within the WP on the German question, and its impact on the alliance at large. The next chapter will complement this one by analysing the way in which the conflicting interests on both non-proliferation and the Vietnam War provided an impetus to further emancipation of the NSWP members in the period from January 1965 to March 1968. Together, these two chapters analyse how 'the dynamics of dissent' between all WP members contributed to the Warsaw Pact's evolution into a multilateral institution.

The crisis in context

Khrushchev's downfall on 14 October 1964 sealed the end of a period in which his theory of 'peaceful coexistence' had been severely damaged by his practice of brinkmanship during, *inter alia*, the second Berlin Crisis and the Cuban Missile Crisis. The CPSU politburo had charged Khrushchev both for his failures in domestic policy and the decline of the Soviet economy, and for his inclination to take risks in foreign policy. His successor, Leonid Brezhnev, who had been instrumental in organising Khrushchev's downfall, was averse to brinkmanship, and strove after the prevention of war, the preservation of the European borders established after World War II, and peace and stability in Europe. Although he had no experience in international relations, he was not inhibited by ideological qualms either, and established himself as 'the driving force for détente'.[6]

Détente could, according to Brezhnev, only be cultivated from a position of strength, and between 1965 and 1970 the Soviet expenditure on defence increased by 40 percent in order to reach nuclear parity with the USA, which finally happened by the early 1970s. The military build-up was also a reaction to the American strategy of flexible response, which in Eastern Europe was interpreted as an American attempt to enable conventional warfare in the nuclear age for the sake of 'gaining time and reinforcing positions', before NATO would embark on a nuclear strike anyhow.[7] This military build-up earned Brezhnev the support of the Soviet military-industrial complex, which he had already served since 1956, when he had been promoted to 'candidate member of the Politburo in charge of the defence industry'.[8] It also served to consolidate his power vis-à-vis his more conservative rivals, Mikhail Suslov, Nikolai Podgorny and Aleksander Shelepin. Meanwhile, Prime Minister Aleksei Kosygin, who initially represented the Soviet Union abroad, and Foreign Minister Andrei Gromyko helped Brezhnev to build détente with the USA, such as with the non-proliferation treaty, which was signed on 1 July 1968.

The military build-up under Brezhnev also had its impact on the WP. Reversing Khrushchev's policy of cutting conventional forces, Brezhnev expanded both conventional and nuclear forces, and concluded several agreements with WP allies on installing Soviet nuclear warheads on the territories of other WP members.[9] Both the second Berlin Crisis and the Cuban Missile Crisis had already prompted Khrushchev to arm other WP members 'for the first time [...] with operational and tactical nuclear-weapon delivery missiles' from 1961 onwards.[10] Moreover, Khrushchev had conducted joint military manoeuvres with the NSWP armies from October 1962 – i.e. from the Cuban Missile Crisis – onwards,[11] but these manoeuvres had never been discussed within the PCC. Under Khrushchev the WP's military structures had led a virtually parallel existence to the rest of the WP, with the 'Statute of the Unified Command' almost relegated to oblivion. This was, however, no longer possible under Brezhnev's expansion of nuclear and conventional forces within the WP.

Where Khrushchev had only facilitated the *potential* deployment of nuclear missiles in WP countries, Brezhnev concluded several bilateral agreements that provided for the *actual* stationing of Soviet tactical nuclear warheads on East German, Polish, Czechoslovak and Hungarian territory between 1965 and 1967.[12] The deployment of nuclear warheads was obviously directed against a potential attack from Western Europe, which explains the fact that the Balkans were exempted from such agreements, which also enabled Brezhnev to get round the almost certain Romanian refusal. The above-mentioned agreements were nominally concluded 'within the framework of the Warsaw Pact',[13] but there is no evidence of any PCC meetings where these agreements have actually been discussed. Since the WP had no equivalent to NATO's dual-track system, leaving the nuclear warheads in WP countries under direct Soviet command, the exact prerogatives of the Soviet Supreme Commander, and the bearing of the WP's 'Statute of the Unified Command' became an increasingly urgent question for discussion within the WP in the second half of the 1960s, as we shall see in this chapter.

Moreover, the NSWP challenge to Soviet hegemony also continued to manifest itself in political terms. Brezhnev's zeal for superpower détente became clouded by the fact that the smaller European countries on both sides of the Iron Curtain began to chart their own course towards détente halfway through the 1960s.[14] Both the second Berlin Crisis and the Cuban Missile Crisis had clearly illustrated the dangers of bipolarity to the junior allies within NATO and the WP alike, who had become increasingly suspicious of the way in which the Soviet and American leaderships had determined the course of international relations over their heads. Several allies in both alliances took initiatives to improve intra-European relations of their own accord, and a new kind of détente began to take shape that was not bipolar but multilateral. 'The multilateralisation of détente' accordingly challenged superpower détente, and invested the smaller countries in both NATO and the WP with more power.[15]

France and Romania had openly begun to rebel against their respective alliance leaders, while reaching out to potential partners on the other side of the Iron Curtain. The Romanian declaration of independence in April 1964, in particular, marked a Romanian attempt to look Westwards, while intensifying its contacts with many Western European countries, including the FRG, also to boost the Romanian economy. According to an East German report, which considered the April declaration the foundation of Romanian politics for a long time, the Romanians were striving for a normalisation of relations with the FRG, and would establish diplomatic relations as soon as West Germany consented.[16] Apart from enhancing Romania's prestige internationally, such relations would give an enormous boost to Romania economically: as one of the most backward countries within the WP, Romania desperately needed a shortcut to economic growth. Moreover, Romania's trade within Eastern Europe had declined from 70 to 45 percent, because of the Romanian refusal to integrate into COMECON.[17] Romania therefore increasingly needed to turn to Western Europe in economic terms.

Meanwhile, West German Chancellor Ludwig Erhard, the successor to Konrad Adenauer, had become sceptical about Adenauer's attempts to unify Germany, and began to muse on ways to improve relations with Eastern Europe instead. The German question thus gained a new dimension. Increased contacts between West Germany and Eastern Europe nevertheless posed a particular threat to the leader of the GDR, Walter Ulbricht, as such relations did not apply to the GDR. On the contrary, the FRG still claimed to represent the whole of Germany according to its *Alleinvertretungsanspruch*, and thus denied the existence of the GDR. Ulbricht's fears that a rapprochement between the FRG and Eastern Europe would come at the expense of East Germany were not without grounds, as we have seen in the last chapter: Khrushchev's Rapallo policy, which even consisted of a Soviet approval for West German participation in Multilateral Nuclear Forces (MLF), did indeed undermine the status of the GDR. The East German leadership thought that 'West Germany [...] had had too much scope for manoeuvre within the socialist countries in the last couple of years' under Khrushchev, and it accordingly intended to use the WP to increase the East German scope for manoeuvre at West German expense.[18] Although Brezhnev had denounced MLF shortly after his rise to power, Ulbricht was thus still desperate to get the German question on the agenda of the WP.

Finding a more understanding ally in Brezhnev, Ulbricht had already convened the WP's deputy foreign ministers on 10 December 1964, as we have seen in the previous chapter. Although the meeting was meant to put the German question in the limelight by discussing the alliance's position vis-à-vis NATO's plans on MLF, the Romanian dissent had undermined Ulbricht's attempts to use the WP as a transmission belt for East German interests.[19] Behind the scenes Brezhnev had nevertheless approved several East German proposals to institutionalise the WP, such as a standing committee on foreign policy, regular PCC meetings, and a secretariat.[20] These reforms thus appeared on the agenda of the PCC meeting in Warsaw in January 1965.

Ulbricht's attempts to take the lead on the German question were, however, outwitted by the Polish leadership, since the Polish foreign minister, Adam Rapacki, had seized the initiative on the German question by proposing a conference on European security during the General Assembly of the UN in December 1964.[21] Choosing *not* to consult the Kremlin, unlike Ulbricht, the Polish leadership proposed a conference without unrealistic preconditions, and with the potential participation of both Canada and the USA.[22] This proposal was far more sophisticated than Khrushchev's idea in 1955 for a European security system under Soviet supervision.[23] Rapacki's proposal accordingly illustrates a keen awareness of the burgeoning multilateralisation of détente, since a junior ally had made a major proposal for the relaxation of international tensions.

At the same time Rapacki's proposal was also intended to boost Polish sovereignty, by linking the proposal to 'the recognition of the existing borders in Europe, including the Oder–Neisse Line; recognition of the GDR; and the FRG's renunciation of access to nuclear weapons in any form'.[24] Thus Rapacki cleverly wedded European détente to the three main goals of Polish foreign policy.[25] Under the guise of relaxing international tensions, Rapacki's proposal was, accordingly, a more subtle denunciation of Khrushchev's Rapallo policy. Using the multilateral forum of the General Assembly of the UN, the Polish leadership attempted to prevent the Kremlin from sacrificing Polish or East German interests to a rapprochement with West Germany. It had also found a more ingenious way to thwart the project of MLF, by making European security dependent on its absence. Apart from multilateralising détente in the process, Gomulka also sought 'to multilateralise the foreign policy of the Warsaw Pact' by discussing the proposal of the European security conference during the PCC meeting in January 1965.[26]

The PCC's paralysis

The stakes for the meeting were high. It was the second PCC meeting since 1956 that did not take place in Moscow, and the first one ever that was not convened by the Kremlin, but by Ulbricht, whose attempts to do so had been thwarted for a year by his Romanian comrades. Although the meeting's original agenda, which focused on MLF, had become obsolete by the fact that NATO had already shelved MLF halfway through December 1964, it followed from a Polish and East German attempt to put the German question on the agenda in two very different ways, and consolidate their own sovereignty. It was, at the same time, the first PCC meeting after the Romanian declaration of independence, which had signalled a rapprochement with, *inter alia*, West Germany. The German question had, accordingly, become a particularly sensitive issue.

At the actual PCC meeting Ulbricht indeed seemed most tireless in his defence of WP reforms, and he emphasised in his speech that 'the dangers, which are linked to the atomic armament of West Germany [make] it necessary that the Warsaw Pact member states consult more regularly and cooperate more closely'.[27] For the East German leaders the WP reforms were connected with the survival of East Germany. Brezhnev wholeheartedly agreed, and added a military angle to Ulbricht's proposals by saying that the structure of the organs of the supreme commander should be revised too, as well as creating a staff of the Unified Command.[28] In a marked contrast to Khrushchev, Brezhnev intended to use the WP not primarily as 'a platform for launching his assorted diplomatic initiatives',[29] but as an instrument to facilitate his military build-up. He accordingly utilised the East German push for reforms on foreign policy as a vehicle for his own proposals on military reforms.

The Polish leader Gomulka moved, however, more independently from Soviet consent, and gave a new twist to the meeting's dynamics. Agreeing that the German question was the central issue in European security, he reiterated the Polish proposal for a European security conference, while emphasising that European security should stretch further than disarmament, and also include recognition of the GDR.[30] Turning both the GDR and Ulbricht's proposals into an object of the much larger Polish plan for a European security conference, Gomulka had once more succeeded in appropriating the German question.

Meanwhile, the Romanian leadership had already pre-empted any East German moves on WP reforms by writing to Brezhnev that 'within every communist party [the] prevailing principle, according to which the minority has to yield to the majority, cannot be applied to the relations between communist and workers parties'.[31] Thus justifying the right of veto within the WP, Gheorghiu-Dej emphasised that the WP was not a mega-politburo in which democratic centralism could be used to stifle the view of the minority. The Romanians viewed the proposals on reforms as a way 'to strengthen the Soviet Union in the role of the hegemon', as they told their Chinese comrades,[32] and ignored them altogether during the meeting. Gheorghiu-Dej argued instead for a European security system that liquidated all military blocs (e.g. both NATO and the WP) and promoted the unity of all socialist countries. This was a clever move, as it referred back to article 11 of the Warsaw Treaty, and showed at the same time that the Romanians, too, took European security to heart. Moreover, the call for socialist instead of Warsaw Pact unity sounded politically correct, but was hardly realistic as it would include China.[33]

In the ensuing discussions Gheorghiu-Dej even justified omitting WP reforms and the European security conference from his speech, as MLF was the actual topic on the agenda. When Gomulka pushed the issue of reforms, Gheorghiu-Dej riposted that he did 'not understand why these new organs are necessary', as the deputy foreign ministers 'cannot act except under instructions from superior party and government bodies in our countries'. The Romanian attempt to prevent the WP from becoming a supranational body under Soviet hegemony by stressing the role of the national governments in decision making could, however, count on little support. Brezhnev backed Ulbricht's proposals and Ulbricht complained that '[s]uch consultations have been extremely sporadic in the last two or three years', clearly referring to the fact that the Romanians had time and again vetoed the convention of the PCC. Gheorghiu-Dej nevertheless outwitted Ulbricht by emphasising that 'the real issue' was that '[t]he materials should be sent out on time, not twenty-four hours before our departure to Warsaw, as happened now'.[34] Ulbricht's surprise strategy was used against him: blamed for lack of professionalism, he lost the moral high ground.

Gomulka cleverly used the fact that 'Rapacki came forward at the UN with a proposal related to the question of European security' without consulting anyone in advance to stress the fact that more consultations would have been useful. Meanwhile, he inadvertently drew his allies' attention to the fact that the Poles had moved independently of the Soviet leadership, and he blackmailed the Romanians by stressing that '[i]f you do not want to participate, we will consult with those countries that want to'.[35] Conceding that such a meeting might be necessary, Gheorghiu-Dej nevertheless opposed the East German concept of a statute to *regulate* the foreign minister meetings. Gomulka's observation that there had hardly been any consultations because 'there was no statute' paradoxically confirmed the Romanian success: without a statute they could safeguard their room for manoeuvre. Although the East Germans wanted to commit everything to paper in order to invest the WP, and indirectly themselves, with more power, the Romanians wanted to retain the utmost flexibility by avoiding exactly that. The Romanian dissent drove their comrades to despair, as the Hungarian leader Janos Kadar eloquently voiced:[36]

> The foreign ministers of the NATO countries get together and consult; so do the foreign ministers of the Arab, African, and Latin American countries. We are the only ones who cannot get together. Why? What is happening at this session is a crying shame. Why on earth can't we get together more often and discuss issues of interest to us?[37]

The editorial committee, which discussed the final communiqué, also ended in a stalemate.[38] Denying any right to decide anything within the confines of the PCC, the Romanian delegates rendered the alliance powerless as an institution, let alone a supranational one. The Romanian treatment of the WP as an intergovernmental assembly of representatives of sovereign states had turned into a self-fulfilling prophecy. Ulbricht's attempts to institutionalise the alliance had achieved nothing: despite the overwhelming support for more regular meetings, the Romanian obstruction had sufficed to undermine the East German initiative on reforms. The East German attempt to boost its own status at the long-awaited PCC meeting thus came to nothing; even the German question was appropriated by the Polish proposal for a European security conference, which was hardly discussed, but approved nevertheless.[39]

Meanwhile, Brezhnev had made a modest, but important start at paving the way for military reforms in the alliance under the disguise of supporting the East German initiative on reforms. At the same time, he had begun stealthily to reassert Soviet authority, while also respecting the interests of the other WP members. Although the meeting ended in a stalemate, it testified to the fact that the WP had become a platform to discuss such important issues.

The Romanian change of direction

The Romanians regarded the PCC meeting as their victory, and proudly stated in a conversation with their Chinese comrades that their allies 'were forced to eliminate the problems from the communiqué with which we did not agree'.[40] Regarding the Soviet proposal to reform the statute of the Unified Command as a way 'to keep a tighter rein over the countries of the WP', Romanian Prime Minister Maurer explained that 'the principle of unanimity' and the 'logical position' of the Romanians had ensured that the assumed Soviet attempt to increase control was frustrated.[41] The absence of democratic centralism accordingly challenged any attempt to use the WP as a transmission belt for the party leaders' national interests. At the same time, the East German leadership also regarded the PCC meeting as an East German triumph, as it had consolidated its position domestically.[42]

The East Germans therefore suggested a meeting of WP foreign ministers in June.[43] This had quite the opposite effect on the Romanians: fully aware of the unremitting East German drive for reforms, the Romanian Ministry of Foreign Affairs prepared a long report on 'The Position of Romania vis-à-vis the Warsaw Pact' in August 1965.[44] This was the first extensive analysis of the alliance, written five months after Nicolae Ceausescu had succeeded Gheorghiu-Dej, who had died in March 1965. Ceausescu had, *inter alia*, been appointed as Gheorghiu-Dej's successor, because of 'his attitude against the control of the Kremlin'.[45] Moreover, the report coincided with the adoption of a new Romanian constitution in August 1965, in which the country was renamed the 'Socialist Republic of Romania', and the party was no longer called the 'Romanian Workers Party', but the 'Romanian Communist Party' (RCP). This meant a break with the Romanian past as well as with the Soviet Union. The analysis of Romania's position vis-à-vis – rather than *within* – the Warsaw Pact thus heralded further emancipation from the Soviet grip through the WP.

The report also served as preparation for bilateral talks with the Kremlin, scheduled for September. It contained a detailed analysis of all the PCC meetings, with particular emphasis on the success of Romanian opposition in the WP, such as to the accession of Mongolia to the alliance and to WP reforms. Meanwhile, it underlined that 'some member states have tried to use the Warsaw Pact for goals contrary to its provisions'. In order to prevent this, the Romanian delegation to the Soviet Union should discuss items such as the convention of the PCC, the East German proposal for a permanent foreign policy organ, the necessity for preliminary consultations, the signing of documents by government representatives, and the timely dissemination of documents.[46] The professionalisation of the alliance had become a distinct Romanian priority.

According to the Romanian report all WP members 'had to agree with the date and place of the PCC meeting, as well as the agenda', which 'corresponds to the principle of equality of states'. Moreover, it was underlined that according to article 3 of the Warsaw Treaty, the WP was only meant for 'important problems, which affect the common interests of its member states', whose decisions 'belong exclusively to the competence of the party and government leaders of each country'. For the first time it was explicitly stated that the 'Warsaw Treaty was an international *intergovernmental* concept', which was a term that was not used within the treaty. Moreover, the report emphasised that Soviet unilateralism during the Cuban Missile Crisis was illegal, as it fell within the jurisdiction of the WP.[47] The Warsaw Treaty thus became an important instrument to prevent both unilateralism and supranationalism.

Armed with such arguments, the Romanian delegation, led by Ceausescu himself, discussed both bilateral and multilateral relations in great detail during its visit to the Kremlin in September 1965. Ceausescu emphasised that the WP should have 'a more democratic base for its activities', and suggested that the meetings would take place by rotation in all participating countries, that the subjects at stake 'would be known in time by every party and government', and that a 'technical secretariat, in which every country would be represented, would be commissioned to prepare the materials, and not some country or other'.[48] Ceausescu's proposals clearly served to bypass East German unilateralism.

Moreover, Ceausescu suggested improving the unified command by creating an intergovernmental council of all WP defence ministers, each with the right of veto. The armed forces would accordingly be maintained on a national level, instead of being subordinated to the Soviet supreme commander, who would be reduced to the role of 'coordinator'. Pretending to comply with the Soviet desire for reforms, Ceausescu accordingly suggested 'improvements' that would considerably tie the hands of the Soviet leaders.[49] The Romanians seemed to have slightly modified their strategy: instead of opposing any reforms, they chose the apparently positive route of suggesting them. Thus their proposals seemed to have a legal basis in the Warsaw Treaty, however detrimental to Soviet hegemony.

The Romanian change of direction greatly pleased Brezhnev, who did, however, emphasise that the 'principle of unanimity' did not suit the PCC, 'because that would mean the right of veto, which cannot function between socialist countries'. Ceausescu's reply left Brezhnev nonplussed: stating that 'we shall never feel bound to any kind of decision with which we do not agree', especially if it concerns 'our problems', he asked whether Brezhnev would agree if the majority decided about problems concerning the Soviet Union. Forced to deny this, Brezhnev implicitly agreed with Ceausescu's assumption that all WP countries were equal.⁵⁰ Brezhnev had thus unwittingly conceded the *de facto* right of veto to the Romanians, which would enable them to prevent the WP from developing in any direction that did not appeal to them. It would also force the Kremlin to consult with the Romanians in order to ensure their minimal support. Brezhnev nevertheless emphasised that he had never had 'such [constructive] discussions', and promised that 'a phone call would suffice for me to come to Bucharest'.⁵¹ Both Brezhnev and Ceausescu had set a precedent: their predecessors Khrushchev and Gheorghiu-Dej had never held bilateral consultations in order to discuss proceedings within the multilateral alliance; they had used the Sino–Soviet split as a pretext for consultations instead.

Allied arguments

The need for official consultations and a better preparation of WP meetings was something Brezhnev took to heart. Treading his ground more carefully, Brezhnev had also consulted delegations from many other WP countries in the autumn of 1965, which had led to a quest for reforms 'of the structure and functioning of the pact, especially of its military organs', as Brezhnev wrote in a letter to his comrades on 7 January 1966. All delegations, apart from the Romanian one, had voiced explicit support for a statute of the PCC, a secretariat that was not only technical, and a standing committee for foreign policy. The latter had in fact already been agreed upon during the PCC meeting in Prague in January 1956, but had never been implemented. Brezhnev thus practised what Khrushchev had preached. Underlining that 'the representatives of the fraternal countries […] had requested that the CC of the CPSU would take the initiative', Brezhnev took the initiative away from the East German leaders, while emphasising that his proposals were supported by the majority of the WP leaders.⁵²

Meanwhile, the suggestion to reform the WP militarily had surreptitiously gained priority over foreign policy reforms. Brezhnev intended to create a unified military staff, as well as clarifying the powers of the supreme commander in order to turn the alliance into a 'genuine, rather than merely formal, counterpart of NATO', while facilitating its use for military purposes.⁵³ He thus addressed the Polish criticism from 1956–57 on the vague description of the supreme commander's prerogatives in the Statute of the Unified Command.⁵⁴ According to 'unofficial talks with Soviet comrades', the Soviet leaders also planned to establish a 'Military Advisory Council' as advisory body to the PCC, which 'would be composed of defence ministers and the Supreme Commander of the Unified Armed Forces, on equal footing'. Although it seemed likely that '[k]ey positions, such as supreme commander, chief of staff […] would be staffed by representatives of the Soviet Army', the Kremlin kept its allies in the dark as to the exact nature of its intentions.⁵⁵

This was, however, a deliberate strategy. Brezhnev carefully avoided acting in an authoritarian manner, by inviting the input and proposals of the other allies. He also unprecedentedly suggested convening *two* meetings, one of the deputy ministers or ministers of defence, and another one of the deputy foreign ministers or the foreign ministers, to discuss the reforms on military matters and foreign policy, respectively. Brezhnev thus curbed the East German transmission belt approach by stimulating other allies to contribute proposals too, and by convening the meetings himself. The initiative was accordingly firmly in Brezhnev's hands, however much he involved his allies, and Brezhnev even trusted that the foreign policy committee and the secretariat would 'already be formed in 1966'.[56]

The Polish, East German, Czechoslovak and Hungarian leaders had a particular interest in the coordination of foreign policy and military issues, as they had recently consented to the stationing of Soviet nuclear warheads on their territory. The Czechoslovak leadership therefore suggested that the 'military council [should] function as a subcommittee of the PCC that would ensure common strategy and appropriate military planning'.[57] Meanwhile, the Polish Ministry of Defence proposed that the supreme commander and the chief of staff 'should be appointed by the Pact's [military] Council', and should be 'subordinated to the Council', and thus clearly intended to diminish the supreme commander's authority, while decreasing the Soviet hold on military matters.[58] The Soviet ability to pull the nuclear trigger thus stimulated the NSWP allies to shape the contents of the reforms as far as they could. The WP had not only become an instrument to curb West German nuclear ambitions, but it could serve to regulate Soviet ones too.

Polish Foreign Minister Rapacki nevertheless wholeheartedly agreed with Brezhnev's initiative to increase the 'elasticity and efficiency' of the WP, and severely criticised the PCC for having 'been transformed into summit meetings, called up sporadically, generally not properly prepared, which adopt spectacular resolutions'. He suggested creating a Council of the Warsaw Pact for summit meetings instead, which would 'decide on key issues, with the rule of unanimity', while restoring the PCC 'to its original character', namely 'an elastic forum for consultations of foreign ministers'.[59] The Council would thus become a supranational and deliberative organ, which the Romanians wanted to avoid at all costs, whereas the further institutionalisation of the WP would also require a general secretary and a secretariat, which, together with the other Polish proposals, would make the WP a more similar counterpart of NATO.

A coordinated stance on foreign policy had become particularly important at a time when the government in Bonn had begun to activate its policy towards Eastern Europe. Ulbricht was, however, not at all pleased that Brezhnev had seized the East German initiative on reforms, and claimed that Brezhnev's proposals were in fact his own.[60] After Khrushchev's passivity, Ulbricht now had to deal with a Soviet leader who undermined his monopoly on the German question altogether. The East German foreign minister, Otto

Winzer, was, therefore, determined to ensure that the initially East German proposals on political reforms would carry the day. He suggested in a letter to the SED leadership to 'immediately start with the elaboration of our own conceptions regarding the proposals enclosed with the letter'. He added that '[a]lthough our representatives should not in any case attend the proposed meetings with their own readymade proposals, they should, however, have a clear conception and argumentation about the important issues', since 'there are various opinions on the proposals for the structure and functioning of the organisation of the Warsaw Pact, which we can partly not agree with'.[61] Winzer also seemed to have learned from the fiasco in January 1965 that the East Germans should not present their allies with a fait accompli. The East German strategy had grown more subtle.

Ulbricht sent a letter to Brezhnev in early February in which he underlined that the need for more narrow and systematic cooperation was founded on the Warsaw Treaty. Arguing again for more frequent PCC meetings at the highest level of representation and a secretariat in Moscow, Ulbricht also dealt with the issue of unanimity: conceding the principle of unanimity, he nevertheless stressed that one member's disagreement on the implementation of decisions could not prevent its implementation in all other countries.[62] This proposal was clearly meant to bypass the Romanian veto; the Romanian dissent had thus sparked new proposals. However, not only Brezhnev was briefed in advance. The GDR delegates received a detailed briefing from their East German superiors full of 'political directives [...] for the meeting of deputy foreign ministers of the Warsaw Pact'.[63] The East German delegation was better prepared than ever; the East Germans were determined to rise to the Romanian challenge.

The Romanian rebuttal

The Romanians, meanwhile, were at least as well prepared. The Romanian politburo had agreed to the convention of the meetings, since Ceausescu, too, thought that 'some improvements are necessary, in the sense that this organisation should not become supranational, as it tends to do'.[64] The Romanian leadership accordingly welcomed convening the WP members in order to *prevent* further institutionalisation of the WP. Maurer had therefore written a detailed memorandum in which he outlined the arguments for the Romanian stance during the meeting for the deputy foreign ministers, which was to take place in Moscow from 10–12 February 1966. He emphasised that the Romanian delegation had always striven for ample preparation of PCC meetings. Clearly referring to the East German surprise proposals in January 1965, Maurer stressed that there was nothing wrong with the WP per se, and that a *technical* secretariat would suffice to ensure that every delegation would be well prepared.[65]

The other Soviet/East German proposals were also rejected on legal grounds. The statute for the Political Consultative Committee would entail '*a change of the legal status* of the Political Consultative Committee and, therefore, its *transformation* from a *consultative* organ [...], into a *deliberative* organ'. Taking into account that Brezhnev and Kosygin had 'implicitly left the option to decide by majority [instead of unanimity] open' in their conversations in September 1965, this would in fact mean 'the creation of a supranational organism, [...] thus contradicting the provisions of the Warsaw Treaty'. The same applied to a permanent committee on foreign policy, which was deemed 'unacceptable', as the '[f]oreign policy of each state is established by the party and the government in question'.[66] The Warsaw Treaty was accordingly used in order to prevent the Warsaw Pact from becoming a deliberative and supranational alliance. The Romanian leaders wanted to remain firmly in charge of their own foreign policy, including potential diplomatic relations with Western European countries, such as the FRG.

In addition, Maurer had instructed the Romanian delegation 'to oppose every proposal tending towards the establishment of any kind of subordination of the Political Consultative Committee to the Command of the United Armed forces or the General Staff', since 'according to the provisions of the Treaty any problems regarding [its] organisation or functioning [...] belong *exclusively to the competence of the WP member states*, and not to the jurisdiction of the Political Consultative Committee'. The Romanian delegation accordingly only had a 'mandate [...] for an *exchange of opinions with a preliminary character*', and should stress time and again that the proposed reforms contradicted 'the Warsaw Treaty and the principles on which the relations between sovereign and independent states are based (which are included in the Treaty's preamble and in article 8)'. Not only were the East German and Soviet arguments thus rebutted one by one, but a sophisticated *'working method*' was also devised, according to which the Romanians could hijack the entire meeting.[67] Although the East Germans were well prepared, they had failed to devise an overall strategy. The Romanians were one step ahead.

Ceausescu reinforced these arguments during a lengthy speech, in which he argued that 'various studies on armies in capitalist countries, especially of the NATO bloc', indicated that the WP countries distinguished themselves in their intergovernmental approach, respecting 'the principles of independence, sovereignty and non-interference in internal affairs', which were firmly enshrined in the Warsaw Treaty. Cleverly insinuating that intergovernmentalism was intrinsic to communism, the proposed reforms inadvertently provided the Romanians with ammunition to limit the PCC's scope still further. Moreover, Ceausescu undermined the drive to model the WP after NATO by reminding his comrades of the fact that NATO, which was at that time in crisis, represented the capitalist world.[68] Selectively using contested concepts from the debates within NATO, the Romanian challenge to the WP was graver than ever.

Romania's 'triple no!'

At the meeting of the deputy ministers of defence in Moscow from 4–9 February 1966 the Romanian delegation did indeed succeed in blocking any reforms. According to a Hungarian report, the Romanian delegation disagreed with the rest that 'the establishment of a Military Consultative Council under the PCC would be desirable, [but] proposed that the Military Council should be subordinated to the Commander in Chief of the United Armed Forces [CCUAF], and that, on the principle of parity it should make collective decisions in every question within the authority of the CCUAF'. This meant that any measure 'should only take effect after the approval of the government of the member states'.[69] Moreover, only the Romanian delegates insisted that the supreme commander and the chief of staff not be an army officer from the Soviet Union. Arguing that the supreme commander should not be a Soviet officer, the Romanian delegates went even further than the existing practice within NATO, where the Supreme Allied Commander Europe (SACEUR) was – and still is – always an American officer. This was a fundamental challenge to Soviet authority.

The Romanian delegation nevertheless did 'make concrete proposals to resolve the problems on the agenda', but 'they seemed to be steps in the wrong direction in relation to the existing practices' in the eyes of its allies.[70] By stressing that the armies that participated in the United Armed Forces should only be subordinate to their national leadership and not to the Unified Command, the Romanian proposals blocked further military integration within the alliance.[71] In an attempt to ensure both an intergovernmental aspect and the right of veto, the Romanians had once again succeeded in undermining Soviet proposals. The Hungarian participants therefore concluded that '[w]e should anticipate the existing differences of opinion between the political bodies also to pose difficulties in the resolution of the fundamental military issues'.[72] The WP's military could well be affected by Romanian dissent too.

The 'existing differences of opinion' also dominated the meeting of the deputy ministers of foreign affairs in Berlin from 10–12 February, during which everything went according to the Romanian plan. The other WP allies reluctantly accepted the Romanian 'formula' that the 'purpose of the meeting is an exchange of opinions', which prevented the 'creation of organs' – the main item on the agenda.[73] Polish Deputy Foreign Minister Marian Naszkowski concluded that the Romanian leaders were 'aiming at nothing less than "to paralyse the alliance and transform its organs into noncommittal discussion clubs"'.[74] Exasperated by the Romanian dissent during the meeting of deputy ministers of defence, the Polish and Czechoslovak delegations withdrew their proposals on reforms altogether in an attempt to avoid further paralysis.[75] The other allies were forced to sacrifice their own proposals to WP unity, and rallied behind the Soviet ones instead. The Romanian dissent, primarily meant to increase their scope for manoeuvre, thus eclipsed the proposals of the other NSWP members, and considerably curbed *their* input. The meeting thus seemed to follow the same pattern as the PCC meeting in January 1965, during which all WP members apart from Romania agreed to the political reforms.

Meanwhile, those members with a vested interest in the German question attempted to convince Romanian Deputy Foreign Minister Malita in private interviews of the need to make the WP more similar to NATO. Both Ulbricht and Naszkowski ardently argued for the establishment of a secretary-general and a headquarters, and told Malita that 'a place where we can meet' would enable everyone to 'listen to one another and our actions would be the result of common deliberations'. Soviet Deputy Foreign Minister Ilichev emphasised in another private interview that 'the Romanian intervention deviated from everyone else's point of view', and that they had 'said no three times over: no to the secretariat, no to the permanent committee, no to the statute'. Ilichev even suggested establishing the secretariat in Bucharest. According to Winzer, 'the proceedings of the meeting of deputy ministers of defence had given the Soviet comrades ground to employ such exceptionally careful tactics'.[76] The Soviets, too, seemed to change their method in light of earlier experience, but to no avail. The Soviet aim 'to activate the efficacy of the Warsaw Pact and to make it more flexible' was overruled by Romania's 'triple non'.[77] The Romanians were not interested in a more flexible WP, but in maintaining their flexibility *within* the alliance. The drive for institutionalising the WP in the same way as NATO seemed irreversible, but the Romanians stuck to their guns.

In the face of Romanian dissent the other allies decided to support the Soviet proposals by default. Whereas the other delegations 'feared that the Romanian delegation would not continue these discussions', the Romanians were afraid 'that our position would be treated as obstructionist, isolated'.[78] They accordingly objected to the first draft of the protocol in which the other delegations 'wanted to say that they came with positive proposals and we introduced polemics'.[79] The Romanians practised a delicate balancing act: while fundamentally disagreeing with all other delegations, they refused to be isolated. At least on paper, they succeeded. The final protocol contained only one paragraph, and was limited to the 'strictly factual' remark that the WP deputy foreign ministers 'had met in Berlin for an exchange of opinions on the improvement of the activities of the WP', as the Romanians had requested.[80] So much for a meeting that was intended to turn the WP into an institution that could compete with NATO.

This was another defeat for the East Germans, who had underlined in conversations with Ilichev 'how useful a declaration would be for the GDR', as it could serve to boost the status of East Germany and create a common stance against the FRG.[81] The Romanian delegates did indeed feel victorious, and remarked in the politburo meeting afterwards that 'the more uncertainty we sow regarding what is going to happen in the future, the more the idea grows in the other delegations that there should be a new foundation for discussions, which takes our point of view into account'. Although Ceausescu concluded that the other delegations would go home with extra food for thought,[82] the other delegations were not so optimistic. Emphasising that everyone 'voiced similar views [...] with the exception of the Romanian delegate', the Hungarian delegates considered the fact 'that the Romanian side had no intention to engage in a discussion about the issues raised by the Soviet comrades [...] unacceptable', and mused on a way 'to persuade the Romanian side to give up their position'.[83] The meeting of deputy foreign ministers had certainly given them food for thought, albeit very different from that of Ceausescu.

A West German move

The Romanian strategy had frustrated the Soviet push for reforms, too, and the East German leadership felt it could reclaim the initiative on political reforms. Several weeks after the deputy foreign ministers' meeting, Ulbricht sent a letter to all WP leaders in which he emphasised the necessity of reforms and further cooperation, and argued again in favour of making decisions at PCC meetings, which should take place at the highest level of representation. Refuting Romania's objections one by one, he even turned the Romanian arguments on sovereignty and independence on their head:

> The experiences of the German Democratic Republic prove that there are no contradictions between the national interests and sovereignty of the Warsaw Pact states and a closer, and institutionally broadened cooperation in the community of the Warsaw Pact. On the contrary: the sovereignty and independence of every member state is consolidated to the extent that all members strengthen their unity in the organisation of the Warsaw Treaty.[84]

For the GDR, and to a lesser extent for Poland and Czechoslovakia, the WP was, indeed, essential for their sovereignty, as the division of Germany had prevented their German borders from being officially sanctioned. The WP was the only international institution that recognised the GDR at all. Other countries, too, considered the alliance essential for collective security. Thus the Bulgarian leader Todor Zhivkov explained to Maurer and Ceausescu that Bulgaria was located on NATO's frontline (Greece and Turkey) and needed the alliance to survive.[85] The East Germans accordingly felt sufficiently confident to enclose revised proposals for a statute of the PCC, a standing committee on foreign policy issues and a unified secretariat. These drafts were 'based on the Soviet proposals', but also contained East German, Czechoslovak and Polish suggestions – all of them WP members with a vested interest in the German question.[86] The Romanians seemed alone in considering the WP and sovereignty mutually exclusive; for their allies the reforms would strengthen both the WP and their own status.

The East German proposals were, however, ironically eclipsed by a West German initiative: the West German government in Bonn had sent a 'peace note' to all WP countries except the GDR on 24 March 1966, which 'proposed to conclude bilateral treaties on a mutual renunciation of force', while declaring its willingness to participate in a disarmament conference.[87] This 'peace note' is often regarded as a 'turning point' in Bonn's treatment of Eastern Europe, as it was the first major concession of a West German government to Eastern Europe.[88] Although some Eastern European countries perceived this as a chance to improve bilateral relations with the FRG and to collaborate more closely economically, the note soon became a bone of contention, because the West German government still refused to recognise the GDR and the Oder–Neisse border, thus failing to sanction the status quo.

The East German and Polish leaders were accordingly not so enchanted by the West German overtures. The Polish leadership feared it would stimulate another Rapallo policy in the Kremlin – i.e. rapprochement with the FRG at Polish expense – and the East German leadership was furious about not being addressed at all, because the West German government still stuck to its *Alleinvertretungsanspruch*. The Poles accordingly replied that they would not consider any negotiations unless Bonn recognised the Oder–Neisse border and the GDR, while renouncing the use of nuclear weapons, and thus repeated the same conditions as those for a European security conference. The Czechoslovak leadership nevertheless reneged on these Polish conditions, which it had usually supported. Prague was, in fact, already negotiating with Bonn about further economic ties, and even considered establishing diplomatic relations.[89] The Czechoslovak response caused particular concern in the GDR, as it seemed as though an ally was compromising on the German question. A peace note that failed to recognise the post-war reality seemed nothing but a Trojan Horse to the Polish and East German leaders.

The Romanian leadership embraced the Eastern policy (*Ostpolitik*) by the FRG still more enthusiastically, as it was a real boost for any attempts at establishing diplomatic relations, and after the peace note both cultural and economic ties between Romania and the FRG flourished more than ever.[90] The Kremlin, meanwhile, was also interested in a new beginning in the relations with West Germany, which was in line with Brezhnev's quest for détente, and could serve to boost the Soviet Union economically. Although the Soviet Union was the only Eastern European country that already had diplomatic relations with the FRG since 1955, Brezhnev was eager to normalise relations with the FRG *de facto*. On this topic Brezhnev unwittingly shared a vested interest with his Romanian comrades.

In order not to bypass his Polish allies, Brezhnev sent a draft reply to the Polish government, in which he showed his willingness to enter into a dialogue with the FRG. Brezhnev added that the Oder–Neisse border had 'nothing to do' with the FRG, since it was the border between the GDR and Poland, and thus fully undermined Polish aims for consolidating the borders.[91] Instead of defending the interests of his Polish and East German comrades,

Brezhnev even echoed the Romanian point of view by proposing to dissolve the military blocs and replace it with a European security system. The Soviet perspective on the German question thus seemed to have shifted in a new direction. The Polish reaction was predictably furious, and Rapacki told a Soviet foreign policy official that the draft was unacceptable.[92] The final Soviet reply to the FRG on 17 May was much more amenable to the Polish goals, and stressed the importance of recognising both the post-war borders and the GDR, while condemning West German foreign policy. The Kremlin had apparently decided to sacrifice a rapprochement with the FRG for Polish and East German interests. Thus Warsaw had undermined a rebirth of the Rapallo policy.

The Romanian method revisited

Meanwhile, Ulbricht had once more lost control over the German question. When Brezhnev finally convened the WP's first secretaries, as Ulbricht had initially suggested, he claimed that he had decided to do so after meeting with Ceausescu, Gomulka and Novotny. The meeting took place on 7 April 1966 in Moscow, two weeks after the West German peace note, and therefore prioritised 'the problem of European security' over Ulbricht's proposals for reforms. The alliance's initial division in the wake of the peace note had made a united stance on European security and the German question all the more imperative, and Brezhnev had accordingly appropriated the Polish emphasis on European security, which had been discussed during the PCC meeting in January 1965. The next PCC meeting was scheduled for July 1966, and Brezhnev suggested putting '[t]he problem of European Security' on the agenda, as well as the 'improvements of the activities of the Warsaw Pact'. Brezhnev proposed 'adopting a political document' at that meeting, 'which would be directed against aggression, against militarism, against [West] Germany', and 'in favour of security in Europe'.[93] Since East Germany was not in a position to reply to the West German peace note, the WP would reply instead with a fully fledged declaration on European security. The ball would again be in West Germany's court.

Brezhnev thus seemed to close ranks with the hard-liners on the German question, but Ceausescu was delighted that 'for the first time since the Warsaw Pact exists we discuss the problems on time, as well as the agenda of the following session'. Moreover, his proposal to host the meeting in Bucharest was unanimously accepted. Emphasising that 'we should make the maximum effort to ensure that the materials are prepared as well as possible', Brezhnev clearly showed that he took the Romanian criticism on preparation seriously. Brezhnev thus prioritised ensuring Romanian good will over pleasing Ulbricht, whose revised proposals had to wait until July. In a meeting of WP defence ministers in May 1966 the Soviet delegation even conceded that the Unified Command of the armed forces would coordinate, rather than command, the armed forces of the Warsaw Pact, and that the armed forces from each country would be subordinate to their national leadership instead of the Unified Command.[94] In the wake of the West German peace note Brezhnev seemed to side with the ally who had responded as constructively as he would have liked to do, even though his rhetoric on the German question seemed designed to please Gomulka and Ulbricht instead of Ceausescu.

Brezhnev lived up to his promise, and convened a meeting of the ministers of foreign affairs a month before the PCC meeting.[95] The Romanian leaders eagerly seized the opportunity to be as well prepared as possible, and carefully studied the Soviet proposal for a 'Declaration on the Improvement of Peace and Security in Europe'.[96] The Kremlin had obviously succumbed to Polish and East German pressure in the wake of the West German peace note, and stressed the 'rebirth of revanchism and militarism in West Germany' after the Potsdam agreement in 1945, while contrasting the aggression from the NATO countries with the Warsaw Pact's peaceful stance. Strongly denouncing the Washington-Bonn axis, and West Germany's 'aggressive' stance vis-à-vis the GDR, the Soviet declaration seemed a rather incongruous reply to the West German 'peace note'.[97]

Some of the proposals were, however, more directed towards the relaxation of international tensions, such as 'the convention of a *pan-European conference*' on European security and the proposal that all WP members should participate actively in the conference, which would considerably increase their room for manoeuvre in the international arena. The Romanian leaders nevertheless considered the Soviet draft in the first instance 'an attack against the FRG', in which the 'constructive proposals' played only a 'secondary' role, and 'the danger of the European situation' was exaggerated.[98] The Romanians proposed to emphasise the 'favourable conditions for détente', as well as the necessity for a normalisation of bilateral and multilateral relations between NATO and WP countries instead. Calling the resolution of the German question crucial to European security, the Romanians exhorted both German states to contribute to the development of inter-European relations. They thus implicitly justified the way in which the West German government had reached out to Eastern Europe, while condemning the rigid stance of their East German and Polish allies.[99]

The Romanian leaders argued instead that the declaration should result from a broader initiative – i.e. one that went beyond the WP – and only favoured participating in a European security conference as long as it would 'not become a rigid platform that would hinder the initiatives and actions of every socialist state in European questions'.[100] The Romanian message was clear: they would, for once, go along with their WP allies, if the declaration served to *increase* their scope for manoeuvre. In an ironic reversal of roles, the Romanian leaders even composed their own communiqué in advance. Emphasising that 'the existence of military blocs [...] represents an anachronism that is incompatible with the independence and national sovereignty of the people', the Romanians considered the European conference an opportunity 'for the multilateral development of normal relations between all

European states'.[101] Implicitly facilitating their burgeoning relations with the FRG, while undermining the Polish attempt to use the conference to pressurise West Germany to recognise the borders of Poland and the GDR, the Romanians had appropriated the Polish proposal for a European security conference for their own purposes.

'Some' against 'others'

The Romanian draft was, in fact, very close to the initial Soviet response to the West German peace note, which had been denounced by Rapacki, and therefore provided the Kremlin with a convenient pretext to present the rest of the WP with an alternative. The Soviet leadership accordingly forwarded the complete Romanian draft to the other WP members one day before the start of the conference of the WP foreign ministers, who were not amused.[102] The other six allies decided to meet informally in order to agree on a common declaration, and outwit the Romanians just before the conference began.[103] This sealed the division between the one (Romania) and the remaining six. This deliberate strategy against the Romanians was both unprecedented and futile: the official meeting on 6–17 June 1966 in Moscow – the longest such meeting in the WP's history – followed the usual pattern.[104] The Romanian delegates rejected all proposals on reforms and stood their ground on European security.

East German Foreign Minister Otto Winzer accused the Romanians of *under*estimating the international situation and downplaying West German 'revanchism and imperialism', and emphasised his full agreement 'with all the other proposals of the Soviet and Polish comrades', since 'the Bonn-Washington axis should not be overlooked'.[105] Winzer clearly formed a united front with the Polish and Soviet delegations, with which he had regular discussions behind the scenes.[106] Meanwhile, Romanian Foreign Minister Manescu eloquently defended the Romanian draft, including the principles of sovereignty and independence, and greatly exhausted the patience of the other WP members when they had still not come to an agreement two days later.[107] The East German allies were particularly exasperated by the Romanian 'deliberate delaying tactics', which threatened to undermine their drive for recognition.[108]

The Romanian delegation thus took a fundamentally different view of the purpose of a European security conference, which should not primarily be directed *against* West Germany, but *in favour* of more diplomatic contact between all European countries, including the FRG. The Romanian delegates clearly envisaged the declaration as a positive response to the West German peace note, rather than an attack against West Germany. The new *Ostpolitik* should be complemented by a new 'Westpolitik' within the Warsaw Pact: in the Romanian view the time was ripe to reach out to West Germany, too. The Romanians were *ob*structive *inside* the Warsaw Pact, but *con*structive *outside*, as opposed to their WP allies, who were more interested in strengthening the ties *within* the alliance. This time the Romanian delegation nevertheless had a vested interest in being 'determined to cooperate with the other representatives to reach a common declaration', as it very much supported the *concept of a European security conference*.[109]

The result of the fundamental disagreement was nevertheless the same: Polish Deputy Prime Minister Naszkowski argued that the 'six delegations had shown a maximum of good will regarding the Romanian stance', and that it was impossible 'to take seven texts as a starting point', as Manescu had suggested. In a message to Warsaw, Naszkowski shrewdly observed that 'the [Romanian] mild assessment of West German policy has a clear motive', as the Romanian leaders 'strove to draw closer to the FRG, especially where it concerns the economic advantages'.[110] Agreeing with Manescu that the 'document should have a constructive character', Naszkowski nevertheless underlined that it 'should unmask and reject the aggressive forces'.[111] Meanwhile, Gromyko attempted to compromise, by arguing that West Germany could participate too, while also defending 'the specific interests of our countries', such as the recognition of the GDR.[112] Manescu accordingly argued that the Romanian opinion was not 'in principle different from the other opinions', whereas a distinction between six delegations and one would make it impossible for the meeting to proceed.[113] Testing the fine line between independence and isolation, he made the other delegates responsible for a potential impasse, while trying to prevent a break on the issue of a European security conference.

Brezhnev, for whom European security was a priority, was determined to prevent a break too, and used his position as a host to have a long conversation halfway through the conference with Manescu, who complained about the attitude of '"some" against "others"'. Brezhnev, who seemed 'nervous and agitated', emphasised that 'the Soviet leadership would be delighted if at the Bucharest conference *a good declaration* would be adopted'. He even argued that 'the fact that the meeting would take place in Bucharest *gives it the right to say that the success or the failure of the meeting would be attributed in the first place to its hosts, and to comrade Ceausescu personally*'.[114]

Both sides attempted to resolve the issue in a secret meeting between Manescu and Gromyko later that day. Rewriting the Soviet draft together, the Soviet side agreed to greater emphasis on principles, foreign relations, and a more constructive tone, and the Romanian side conceded to quoting the Potsdam agreement and criticising the politicians from the militarist circles in the FRG.[115] The Romanian insistence on rewriting the document inadvertently served a Soviet purpose: although the Kremlin was loth to antagonise its Polish and East German allies, it actually shared the Romanian view on the need for a normalisation of relations with the FRG. Meanwhile, the Romanians clearly had the political will to agree on a declaration on European security, and managed to put a decisive stamp on a declaration that had deliberately been drafted in their absence. The stakes of the other WP

The success of the Romanian strategy

The Romanian leaders were determined to cultivate the impasse on reforms during the PCC meeting that they hosted in Bucharest on 4–6 July 1966, while gaining approval for the Soviet-Romanian proposal on European security. The East German leaders, meanwhile, had become increasingly insistent in their zeal for foreign policy coordination, since the West German *Ostpolitik* had made a united Eastern European stance all the more urgent, and they had, accordingly, presented another 'draft decision' on reforms.[116] In order to prevent this, the Romanian hosts arranged daily meetings with the Soviet delegation, which they used to sow confusion and to gain concessions behind closed doors. In their first meeting with Brezhnev and Soviet Premier Kosygin, Ceausescu and Maurer claimed that the East Germans had retracted their proposals on foreign policy coordination, and suggested taking it off the agenda. Brezhnev agreed with apparent relief, ironically stating that it was 'a problem that had not been sufficiently prepared'.[117] In the wake of the West German peace note he seemed displeased that Ulbricht had once again taken the initiative, and was amenable to the Romanian wishes instead. In a conversation with the East German delegation later that day, Ceausescu insisted that the Soviets had taken the reforms off the agenda and that the meeting had been prepared accordingly.[118] Pretending it was an unfortunate misunderstanding, the Romanians had brilliantly used their position as hosts to manipulate the agenda.

The Romanians intended to prevent discussing military reforms at all costs, too, despite recent concessions from the Kremlin, such as the hypothetical agreement to appoint a supreme commander from any WP country instead of the Soviet Union.[119] Ceausescu and Maurer entered into a dense discussion with Brezhnev and Kosygin on the legal implications of WP reforms. Explaining the difference between deliberative and consultative, supranational and intergovernmental, and majority rule versus unanimity, the Romanian delegation insisted that they were 'not against the Warsaw Treaty, but against transgressing it'.[120] Brezhnev and Kosygin failed to understand 'who would take decisions if the PCC could not decide', and were shocked to hear that 'when six countries want something, but the seventh does not want it [...], no decision can be taken'. Brezhnev feared that 'nothing would remain of his alliance', and that the Romanian proposals 'would enchain the activity of the whole organism', to which Ceausescu replied that 'everything must be viewed through another prism'.[121]

With their claim that '[w]e want to introduce order and legality in all this', the Romanians completely checkmated the Soviet leadership. They compelled Brezhnev to concede that the most recent East German proposals, which insisted that the PCC could 'take decisions', conflicted with 'the principles of the Warsaw Treaty', where its consultative nature is underlined. Brezhnev exclaimed, 'we are not prepared. Give us time to prepare!' After Maurer emphasised that it was time that the Soviets, too, got into action, Brezhnev answered that he 'needed at least a year', even though the reforms had already been discussed for 18 months.[122] In sharp contrast to the Romanian leaders, their Soviet comrades had failed to devise a strategy to further their own interests. It only seemed to dawn on Brezhnev during this meeting that Soviet authority was contested and that Romanian dissent was a serious challenge, not only to other NSWP members, but also to the Soviet Union itself.

The Soviet drive for military reforms was thus thwarted, too, and Brezhnev succeeded in persuading his allies at the PCC meeting to postpone the discussion on reforms altogether for the sake of 'our real unity', while referring to his 'exchange of opinions with comrade Ceausescu'.[123] Since the Romanian leadership strove to improve its relations with the FRG without having to worry about Soviet nuclear warheads on Romanian soil, any further coordination on military or political issues was not in Romanian interests. The fact that all proposals on reforms were removed from the agenda was clearly a defeat for Ulbricht, who, according to the Romanians, 'had no clue'.[124] What remained was the declaration on European security, which Ceausescu had used as an example of good practice, as every government had had plenty of time to comment on it beforehand.[125] The Romanian-Soviet cooperation on European security seemed far more fruitful than the East German-Soviet collaboration on reforms:[126] the declaration was unanimously accepted with only a few minor concessions to accommodate East German interests, such as adding the word 'sovereign' to German Democratic Republic.[127] With the Romanians agreeing on their own proposal, there was no one left to disagree.

Meanwhile, the declaration served Polish and Czechoslovak interests, too, as it made 'the inviolability of the borders a foundation of a lasting peace in Europe', while conditioning 'the normalisation of the situation in Europe' on 'the recognition of the actually existing borders', including the Oder–Neisse border.[128] The Romanian appeal for the simultaneous dissolution of both military blocs had, nevertheless, been approved, as well as the emphasis on a normalisation of intra-European relations. The Romanian delegation had successfully managed to prevent a condemnation of West Germany, and had kept the road to diplomatic relations with the FRG open by casting the WP response to the peace note in a more positive mould.

The Romanian strategy proved most effective. The reforms were not discussed for the first time in 18 months and the declaration on European security was unanimously approved.[129] Even though the proposal was originally Polish, the Romanians could claim credit, as it was approved at the meeting they hosted, and based on a Soviet-Romanian draft. It soon came to be known as the 'Bucharest declaration'. Ironically, the only positive measure the Warsaw Pact had achieved in several years was thus associated with Romania. The Bucharest conference is, indeed, considered 'the first serious initiative of Eastern Europe in institutionalising the East-West relations', as well as 'the first important step on the road to signing the Helsinki Final Act in 1975'.[130] The way to Helsinki had been paved in Romania.

The aftermath

In the period after the Bucharest declaration, the Romanian leadership became even more active on the diplomatic front outside Eastern Europe, as was noted with some apprehension by diplomats from other WP countries.[131] Having insisted on the emphasis on the 'normalisation' of relations with other European countries including the FRG, the Romanian leadership could now use this part of the declaration to justify potential diplomatic relations with the FRG. Ignoring the insistence on the recognition of the Oder–Neisse border and the GDR, the Romanian politicians attempted to lure their West German colleagues into diplomatic relations by not posing any preconditions. The East German and Polish diplomats in Bucharest duly reported to their superiors in Berlin and Warsaw about the intensified contacts between Romania and West Germany, though adding with relief that Foreign Minister Manescu had postponed a visit to the FRG, while awaiting more 'favourable conditions', after Ludwig Erhard's CDU-FDP (Christlich Demokratische Union Deutschlands–Freie Demokratische Partei) coalition had collapsed in October 1966.[132]

In December 1966 a new West German government was formed, led by the Grand Coalition of Chancellor Kurt Kiesinger (CDU) and the social democrat Willy Brandt as vice-chancellor and foreign minister. Willy Brandt had personally witnessed the adverse effects of the division of Germany as mayor of West Berlin, and therefore strove to improve relations with Eastern Europe. The new government emphasised in a declaration on 13 December that 'it was very much interested in putting its relations with the Warsaw Pact states on a new footing', but it still refused to recognise the GDR or the Oder–Neisse border.[133] Ulbricht accordingly wrote a letter to the Soviet ambassador in Berlin, Abrassimov, to request the convention of a conference of WP foreign ministers as the 'next step [...] in the German Question', while attempting to forestall any Romanian 'initiatives'.[134]

In a number of East German declarations the passages of the Bucharest declaration were therefore emphasised in which the West German recognition of the GDR and the Oder–Neisse border was demanded, which should be a precondition for 'normal diplomatic relations between West Germany and the socialist countries'.[135] The linkage of the normalisation of intra-European relations to the demands for recognition thus created a different interpretation from the Romanian one. The Romanian response to the establishment of a new West German government was, therefore, quite the opposite: they immediately organised Manescu's visit to the FRG.

In the meantime, the Polish leader, Gomulka, had also pressurised the Kremlin to convene the WP countries, so as to unite on the German question and prevent Romania from developing any further initiatives with the FRG.

Although Brezhnev told a Polish delegation during a meeting in Lansk (Poland) on 18 January that he was intending 'to give the bloc countries [a] green light for talks with West Germany', he added that he was 'worried' that the situation would spin out of control, as 'the Romanians were already establishing diplomatic relations with the FRG'.[136] Brezhnev was no longer in a position to sanction the foreign policy of other WP members. Gomulka cultivated Brezhnev's concerns, and warned him that 'the Warsaw Pact is dissolving', while pressurising him to backtrack on his German policy.[137] Gomulka even attempted to convince Brezhnev to make any diplomatic relations with the FRG conditional upon Poland's traditional demands: the recognition of the Oder–Neisse line, recognition of the GDR, and renunciation of nuclear weapons.[138] It was nevertheless not only Polish pressure, but also the fact that the Romanians moved too fast that impelled Brezhnev to change his course again, and convene the WP foreign ministers. Although he favoured a normalisation of relations with the FRG, the establishment of diplomatic relations was still one step too far.

The Soviet ambassador in Bucharest, A.V. Basov, could, however, count on little sympathy when he attempted to convince Ceausescu to approve a meeting of WP foreign ministers in Berlin on 6–10 February, while emphasising that it would concern 'a mere exchange of opinions'.[139] Ceausescu insisted that the meeting seemed premature, since the West German government had only just been established, and that Manescu was busy. Manescu was in fact 'busy' travelling to the FRG. The Romanian politburo nevertheless reluctantly decided to approve the meeting in question on the condition that it would *not* take place in Berlin, while attempting to postpone it until 20 February, when Manescu would return from his travels abroad.[140] The Romanian leadership kept the Kremlin in the dark, until Manescu had succeeded in officially establishing diplomatic relations with the FRG on 31 January 1967. As this move 'represented the first major breach in East European solidarity with respect to the German problem', the East German leadership publicly condemned it, which infuriated the Romanians.[141]

Soviet Prime Minister Kosygin even had to call Ceausescu personally on 4 February, two days before the meeting was scheduled, in order to persuade him to participate. Ceausescu replied again that he would only consider it if the meeting did not take place in Berlin, and indeed constituted 'an exchange of opinions', in which 'the actions of Romanian foreign policy would not be the subject of discussion'.[142] After one more phone call they agreed that the meeting would take place under Romanian conditions: two days later than planned, from 8–10 February, in Warsaw, as an exchange of opinions. The Romanian leadership had thus undermined all the East German aims: the diplomatic relations between Romania and the FRG were irreversible, and neither could the meeting be used to condemn the Romanian move, nor did it take place in Berlin. Thus the Kremlin, too, was prevented from condemning Romania's '*Alleingang*' in its foreign policy.

The Polish leadership was furious at the Romanian interference in the meeting. Polish Ambassador Baramowski told East German Deputy Foreign Minister Oskar Fischer that the Polish leadership was planning to take a stance against Romania anyhow during the conference, and that it supported the East German condemnation of the Romanian move. The Romanians had, after all, failed to consult any of their allies by stealthily establishing diplomatic relations with the FRG in full awareness of the fact that a conference of the ministers of foreign affairs was about to take place.[143] The Polish and East German indignation stemmed in particular from the fear that other WP countries would follow the Romanian example, and leave Poland and the GDR isolated.

According to an East German report, both Hungary and Czechoslovakia showed a 'weakening attitude' and a 'willingness to compromise' where it concerned relations with the FRG. The Hungarian comrades even seemed to 'approve the Romanian actions to a certain extent'.[144] They did, indeed, want to keep all options for diplomatic contacts with the FRG open, and were, in fact, already engaging in conversations with their West German colleagues,[145] interested in potential 'economic benefits'.[146] Although all other WP members publically condemned the Romanian '*Alleingang*', Gomulka and Ulbricht now needed to rally their allies behind them in also condemning the concept of diplomatic relations with the FRG, which was a much trickier issue. The normalisation of relations with West Germany did not only serve the national interests of Romania.

In their past zeal for condemning Soviet unilateralism, the Romanians had ironically become the champion of unilateralism when it suited their purpose. Their East German and Polish allies meanwhile found themselves in a considerably weakened position: the West German government had gained an Eastern European ally without recognising the GDR and the Oder–Neisse border. Using the Bucharest declaration to justify their move, the Romanian leaders had thus ignored the part that was most crucial to some of its allies. They had employed the declaration on European security for exactly the opposite goals to the Polish intentions: instead of boosting the status of the GDR and Poland, the diplomatic relations with the FRG served Romanian prestige and the Romanian economy at Polish and East German expense.

Division on the German question

During the actual conference the Romanian conditions seemed to be fulfilled: the diplomatic relations between Romania and the FRG were not mentioned *explicitly*, and the conference dealt primarily with the resonance of the Bucharest declaration instead of the new West German government. The concern over the diplomatic relations with West Germany nevertheless carried the day. All WP foreign ministers apart from the Romanian one closed ranks in condemning the current West German foreign policy moves, and underlining that diplomatic relations with the FRG should only be considered if the

FRG recognised East Germany and the Oder–Neisse border. The six also emphasised the need for a united front against the FRG, thus implicitly condemning the Romanian breach of this unity. Romanian Deputy Prime Minister Malita, meanwhile, justified the Romanian move by explaining that the diplomatic relations with the FRG were in line with the Bucharest declaration and formed a boost to the recognition of the GDR, since it had inadvertently forced the West German government to break with the Hallstein Doctrine: by establishing diplomatic relations with a country that recognised the GDR, the West German government had *de facto* recognised the existence of two Germanys and sanctioned the status quo.[147]

Although no one sided with Malita, there was, however, a difference of nuance between the speeches: the Hungarian foreign minister focused on the need for a normalisation of bilateral relations with Western European countries, and the Czechoslovak delegate was also more moderate. Thus a different interpretation of the Bucharest declaration again seemed to lie at the core of these speeches: using the declaration either to emphasise the necessity for the normalisation of diplomatic relations or for the demands of the FRG to recognise the status quo, the WP six, too, were less united than they appeared to be.

The six nevertheless did issue a protocol on Polish, East German and Soviet initiative and under Polish pressure in which they stated that diplomatic contacts with the FRG could only be considered if West Germany 'recognised the existing borders', ceased its claim to sole representation of Germany, and stopped any attempt to attain access to nuclear weapons.[148] Although the Romanian conditions seemed fulfilled on the surface, the eventual fulfilment of the Polish conditions had a profound impact, too. The acceptance of Gomulka's preconditions, which would come to be known as the 'Warsaw Package', both served 'to defend the sovereignty of Poland and the GDR by taking a hard-line stance towards Bonn', and prevented Gomulka's allies from establishing diplomatic relations with the FRG unless Bonn recognised Polish and East German borders.[149] During a conference of European communist leaders in Karlovy Vary in April 1967, which Romania boycotted, the delegates even approved a 'declaration for peace and security in Europe', which conditioned a collective European security system on recognition of the existing borders in Europe.[150]

Since the document was not signed by Malita, it both sealed the Romanian *Alleingang* and, unprecedentedly, the lack of unity within the WP. Whereas the other WP allies had concluded a whole range of new friendship treaties with the GDR to prevent it from becoming isolated in Europe, it underlined Romania's isolation within the Warsaw Pact. Romania was, however, not the declaration's greatest victim: the Romanian scope for manoeuvre had already been safeguarded by Romania itself, but the other WP members were severely constrained by the Polish demands. Romania had moved too fast for the other allies, as the Kremlin was not in a position to prevent diplomatic relations with the FRG altogether. Gomulka had now attempted to outstrip the

Kremlin by doing so. The Romanian move had enabled the Polish and East German allies to compel their Soviet comrades to condemn something that they did not oppose in principle, and had thus done them an inadvertent favour. However, the declaration considerably limited the scope for manoeuvre of the other allies.

The Hungarian leadership was particularly displeased with the strong stance against the FRG, and strongly disapproved of the fact 'that in Warsaw a text was actually accepted without a fundamental discussion, which was not even known within our CC'. The text itself was considered to 'eliminate the possibility of the necessary tactical moves in politics', as the Hungarian Secretary Zoltan Komoczin stated in a letter afterwards.[151] The declaration of the 'six' had clearly been drafted in a hurry and without consent from various WP leaders. The German question thus began to divide the Warsaw Pact in a more complicated manner, since other WP leaders started to assert their room for manoeuvre against Polish and East German interests. The 'Warsaw Package' was initially a Polish triumph, but it would alienate some of Warsaw's allies in the long run. The Romanian *Alleingang* would not be *allein* for much longer.

Conclusion: the Warsaw Pact's transformation

During the second half of the 1960s the WP members began to develop a more self-conscious attitude towards the alliance, which seemed to transform the so-called 'cardboard castle' into a platform for serious discussion. Instead of being convened on an *ad hoc* basis to discuss isolated issues without any preparation, the WP grew into a multifaceted organism in which different organs, whether officially sanctioned or not, began to take shape. Although the PCC had only met sporadically in the first half of the 1960s, in the years 1965–67 there were meetings at the level of military representatives, deputy ministers of defence, deputy foreign ministers, foreign ministers, first secretaries and, last but not least, the PCC meetings themselves. Whereas most members backed the East German and Soviet proposals to streamline the WP still further, the Romanian leadership prevented its allies from turning the WP into an institution in which decisions were made supranationally. Claiming that the proposed reforms lacked any legitimacy in the Warsaw Treaty and refusing to commit any suggestions on reforms to paper, the Romanians succeeded in maintaining their scope for manoeuvre.

Brezhnev's leadership of the Soviet Union also contributed to a new kind of dynamics within the WP. In contrast to Khrushchev, Brezhnev attempted to regain some control over the alliance, especially in military terms, by proposing military reforms. Brezhnev's willingness to consult his allies was an important step towards the alliance's multilateralisation. Moreover, Brezhnev's stationing of nuclear warheads in several WP countries raised the stakes for consultations: these bilateral agreements had made it all the more necessary to constrain potential Soviet unilateralism on nuclear matters in a multilateral arena. In this sense the Romanian opposition to the military reforms did their allies a service, however much it might have paralysed the discussions in the WP. The Soviet preponderance in military might did, accordingly, not translate into an equal amount of political clout within the WP, where the Kremlin had to struggle to withstand the Romanian challenge.

The Romanian dissent entailed more than merely exercising the right of veto; it was founded on a sophisticated analysis of the Warsaw Treaty, which served as a yardstick to gauge the legitimacy of the proposals. The Romanians were the first to develop an explicit 'method' in furthering their national interests at WP meetings. Wielding the Warsaw Treaty, the principle of unanimity and the lack of mandate as their weapons, the Romanians succeeded in determining the WP meetings to a great extent. Moreover, in their examination of supranationalism versus intergovernmentalism the Romanians were far ahead within Eastern Europe. Brezhnev's failure to grasp these concepts during the PCC meeting in July 1966 was even a reason to shelve the reforms for another year after optimistically claiming earlier that year that the reforms could be completed in several months.[152]

The Romanian critical attitude heightened the consciousness of the other WP members too: the East Germans began to prepare for the meetings with much greater care, and the Kremlin started consulting with the delegations in advance and developed a willingness to compromise. Several NSWP reports show an increasingly critical reflection of the WP meetings, and the realisation that they, too, needed to develop a strategy to counter the Romanian dissent. At the heart of the disagreements between Romania and the other WP members lay a different interpretation of the concept of 'flexibility': whereas the Romanians wanted a loosely structured WP to maintain their flexibility *inside* the alliance, most other members wanted a clearly structured alliance so as to make the WP more flexible in dealing with the *outside* world as an alliance. The institutionalisation of the WP, especially in terms of its foreign policy, would serve the interests of those members who had a vested interest in the German question; it would, however, limit the WP members' scope for manoeuvre in the international arena as individuals. The Romanians therefore favoured professionalising the procedures within the alliance to institutionalising it.

Thus the German question lay at the core of the proposed reforms in two ways: it was the Romanian zeal to establish diplomatic relations with the FRG that drove the Romanian leaders to reject categorically any attempt to restructure the WP, whereas the fear of a potentially nuclearised West Germany drove the East Germans, the Poles and almost all other WP members to turn the WP into a more serious counterpart to NATO that could withstand the West German threat. The Romanians wanted a weak Warsaw Pact so as to strengthen their independent stance towards Western Europe, whereas other NSWP members, notably the GDR and Poland, wanted to gain strength vis-à-vis West Germany by strengthening the Warsaw Pact.

The German question was also the great catalyst for the WP drive for a declaration on European security. Here the difference between the WP members came to a climax: Romania had an interest in promoting the emphasis on 'normalisation' in the Bucharest declaration, and in preventing reforms in order to be free in its politics towards the FRG. The WP members with a vested interest in the German question, such as the GDR and Poland, preferred to interpret the Bucharest declaration as an appeal to cement the status quo, which could be further safeguarded by transforming the WP into a supranational institution that could meet the West German challenge. The condemnation of the Romanian unilateralism in its policy vis-à-vis the FRG followed the usual pattern of 'six' against 'one', but the distinction between Romania and some other WP countries began to blur underneath the seemingly united surface where it concerned the actual opening towards West Germany.

The Bucharest declaration in fact allowed the Romanian leadership to use the WP as a cover for a serious and unprecedented breach in coordinated WP foreign policy by going it alone on the German question.[153] The Soviet attitude in the wake of the peace note in March 1966 was a delicate matter: forced to defend Polish and East German interests, the Kremlin was in fact more amenable to the Romanian emphasis on a normalisation of relations with the FRG. The Polish leader, Gomulka, therefore had to promote his own national interests by officially making diplomatic relations with the FRG conditional upon the recognition of the GDR and the Oder–Neisse line through the 'Warsaw Package', which considerably limited the scope for manoeuvre of his allies.

The Romanian emphasis on a normalisation of intra-European relations in the Bucharest declaration not only did the Kremlin an inadvertent service, but also proved a boost for the bilateral relations of most WP members with Western European countries, which enabled them to develop their own foreign policy. Through the increased number of *bi*lateral relations, the WP inadvertently *multi*lateralised: each WP member began to define its own interests more explicitly, while regarding the WP as an instrument to further these. The Bucharest declaration thus served as a catalyst of NSWP 'emancipation'.[154] The fact that some allies only reluctantly rallied behind the Polish and East German delegates during the meeting in February 1967 shows that the traditional division of Romania versus the rest no longer applied. Some WP members began to respond to West German *Ostpolitik* with their own 'Westpolitik'. Bilateral relations beyond the Iron Curtain gained importance over WP unity.

It is, therefore, too simplistic merely to blame the Romanians for paralysing the alliance.[155] Nor was it primarily the 'contradiction between the Romanian and the Soviet perspective about reforms' that 'determined the [...] development of the communist alliance', as is often assumed.[156] The Romanian strategy was not primarily directed against the Soviet Union, but against any ally whose proposals would limit the Romanian scope for manoeuvre. It was the Romanian resistance to the East German transmission belt approach *and* to the Soviet tendency to coordinate the alliance that stimulated a surprising extent of critical reflection on the actual purpose of the Warsaw Pact and the intention of the Warsaw Treaty. Although the Romanians frustrated the aims of their allies time and again, they also prevented the alliance from turning into an instrument of one single member.

The Romanians could prevent the actual reforms, but not the transformation of the alliance itself. Almost in spite of themselves, the Romanians contributed to the WP's transformation. The dynamics of dissent thus proved more constructive than is generally assumed. Far from paralysing the alliance, it contributed to its multilateralisation, since its members became increasingly aware of the interests that either united or divided them. The quest for European security remained in the mutual interest of all WP members. The existence of the WP facilitated conducting this quest in a multilateral context, and *that* in itself was in the interests of all WP members, however much they disagreed on its actual definition. At the same time, the Romanians increased their own room for manoeuvre at the expense of that of their allies: by blocking the reforms, the Romanians also curbed the policy options of many of their allies. Gomulka seemed to have taken this strategy to heart when he considerably narrowed his allies' scope for manoeuvre with the Warsaw Package. The WP thus increasingly became the arena in which NSWP members competed for more scope for manoeuvre, not with the Soviet Union, but with each other. This mutual competition sparked the emancipation of the NSWP members, both from the Soviet Union, and from one another.

Notes

1 Minutes of discussions with the Soviet delegation, 4 July, 19.30–22.30, ANIC, RCP CC, IR, 94/1966, II, 160.
2 'Meeting between Gheorghiu-Dej, Maurer, and Gomulka', 18 January 1965, ANIC, RWP CC, IR, 15/1965, 94.
3 Ibid., 108.
4 For example, A. Korbonski, 'The Warsaw Treaty After Twenty-five Years: An Entangling Alliance or an Empty Shell?' in R.W. Clawson and L. Kaplan (eds), *The Warsaw Pact: Political Purpose and Military Means* (Delaware, 1982), 17.
5 J.L. Gaddis, *We Now Know: Rethinking Cold War History* (Oxford, 1997), 289.
6 S. Savranskaya and W. Taubman, 'Soviet Foreign Policy, 1962–75', in M. Leffler and O.A. Westad (eds), *The Cambridge History of the Cold War. Volume II: Crisis and Détente* (Cambridge, 2010), 140.
7 Cf. J. Hoffenaar, 'East German Military Intelligence for the Warsaw Pact in the Central Sector', in J. Hoffenaar and D. Krüger (eds), *Blueprints for Battle. Planning for War in Central Europe, 1948–1968* (Lexington, 2012), 86.
8 Savranskaya and Taubman, 'Soviet Foreign Policy', 142.
9 M. Kramer, 'The Kremlin, the Prague Spring, and the Brezhnev Doctrine', in V. Tismaneanu, *Promises of 1968: Crisis, Illusion, and Utopia* (Budapest and New York, 2010), 279–80.
10 M. Uhl, 'Soviet and Warsaw Pact Military Strategy from Stalin to Brezhnev: The Transformation from "Strategic Defense" to "Unlimited Nuclear War", 1945–68', in Hoffenaar and Krüger (eds), *Blueprints for Battle*, 46.

11 Kramer, 'The Kremlin', 279.
12 M. Kramer, '"Lessons" of the Cuban Missile Crisis for Warsaw Pact Nuclear Operations', in J.G. Hershberg (ed.), *The Cold War in the Third World and the Collapse of Détente in the 1970s*, CWIHP Bulletin No. 8/9 (Washington, 1996), 350.
13 Kramer, 'The Kremlin', 280.
14 See J. Hanhimäki, 'Détente in Europe, 1962–75', in Leffler and Westad (eds), *Cambridge History of the Cold War II*, 198–218.
15 See A. Wenger, 'Crisis and Opportunity. NATO's Transformation and the Multi-lateralization of Détente, 1966–68', *Journal of Cold War Studies* 6:1 (2004), 22–74 for this term.
16 'Information File, Romanian People's Republic. Strictly Confidential', Berlin, July 1965, SAPMO-BArch, DY 30/IVA2/20/364, 360, 389–90.
17 Kramer, 'The Kremlin', 285.
18 'Information about the meetings in Berlin, esp. with Axen', 3–6 February 1965, FIG ACP, GDR, mf 0527, 2595.
19 Cf. Selvage on the Soviet 'transmission belt' approach in: 'The Warsaw Pact and the German Question, 1955–70: Conflict and Consensus', in M.A. Heiss and S.V. Papacosma (eds), *NATO and the Warsaw Pact: Intrabloc Conflicts* (Ohio, 2008), 179.
20 Letter from Brezhnev to Ulbricht, 13 January1965, SAPMO-BArch, DY 30/3388, 52.
21 W. Jarzabek, *Hope and Reality: Poland and the Conference on Security and Cooperation in Europe, 1964–1989*, CWIHP Working Paper No. 56 (Washington, 2008), 6.
22 Jarzabek, *Hope and Reality*, 6.
23 W. Jarzabek, 'Poland in the Warsaw Pact 1955–91: An Appraisal of the Role of Poland in the Political Structures of the Warsaw Pact', Parallel History Project on Cooperative Security (PHP), www.php.isn.ethz.ch/collections/coll_poland/Introduction.cfm?navinfo=111216 (accessed 26 August 2013).
24 D. Selvage, 'The Warsaw Pact and the European Security Conference, 1964–69: Sovereignty, Hegemony, and the German Question', in A. Wenger, V. Mastny and C. Nuenlist (eds), *Origins of the European Security System: The Helsinki Process Revisited* (London and New York, 2008), 86.
25 Cf. W. Jarzabek, '"Ulbricht Doktrin" oder "Gomulka Doktrin"? Das Bemühen der Volksrepublik Polen um eine geschlossene Politik des kommunistischen Blocks gegenüber der westdeutschen Ostpolitik 1966/1967', *Zeitschrift für Ostmitteleuropa Forschung* 1:55 (2006), 87.
26 Selvage, 'The Warsaw Pact and the European Security Conference', 86.
27 Ulbricht's speech at the PCC meeting in January 1965, PA AA, MfAA, G-A 541.
28 Brezhnev's speech at the PCC meeting in January 1965, ANIC, RWP CC, IR, 15/1965, 37.
29 V. Mastny, '"We Are in a Bind": Polish and Czechoslovak Attempts at Reforming the Warsaw Pact, 1956–69', in C.F. Ostermann (ed.), *Cold War Flashpoints*, CWIHP Bulletin No. 11 (Washington, 1998), 232.
30 Gomulka's speech at the PCC meeting in January 1965, ANIC, RWP CC, IR, 15/1965, 40–49.
31 Letter from RUWP CC to CPSU CC, 4 January 1965, SAPMO-BArch, DY 30/3655, 185.
32 Meeting between Bodnaras and Liu Fan, 1 January 1965, ANIC, RWP CC, IR, 4/1965, 9.
33 Gheorghiu-Dej's speech at the PCC meeting in January 1965, ANIC, RWP CC, IR, 15/1965, 66–77.
34 Minutes of the meeting of first secretaries, 20 January 1965, ANIC, RWP CC, IR, 15/1965, 124–25.

Warsaw Pact reforms and Westpolitik 165

35 'Polish Minutes of the Discussion at the PCC Meeting in Warsaw', 20 January 1965, PHP, www.php.isn.ethz.ch/collections/colltopic.cfm?lng=en&id=17921&navinfo=14465, 14 (accessed 26 August 2013).
36 Kádár's speech, ANIC, RWP CC, IR, 15/1965, 50–55.
37 'Polish Minutes', 20 January 1965, PHP.
38 Minutes of the editorial committee, 28 January 1965, ANIC, RWP CC, IR, 4/1965, 48.
39 'Communiqué', 20 January 1965, PHP, www.php.isn.ethz.ch/collections/colltopic.cfm?lng=en&id=17910&navinfo=14465 (accessed 26 August 2013).
40 Meeting between Bodnaras and Liu Fan, 27 January 1965, ANIC, RWP CC, IR, 4/1965, 39.
41 Conversation between Maurer, Bodnaras and Liu Fan, 28 January 1965, ANIC, RWP CC, IR, 4/1965, 56.
42 'Information about some developments of the SED politics', 7 April 1965, FIG ACP, GDR, mf 0527, 2614.
43 Letter from Ulbricht to Gomulka, 22 April 1965, SAPMO-BArch, DY 30/3388, 455.
44 'The Position of Romania vis-à-vis the Warsaw Pact', ANIC, RCP CC, IR, 38/1965 I, 32–47.
45 D. Preda et al. (eds), *România – Republica Federală Germania. Începutul relațiilor diplomatice 1966–1967. Vol. I* (Bucharest, 2009), xxiv.
46 'The Position of Romania vis-à-vis the Warsaw Pact', ANIC, RCP CC, IR, 38/1965 I, 32–47.
47 Ibid.
48 Meeting between Ceausescu and Liu Fan, 21 September 1965, ANIC, RCP CC, IR, 4/1965, 201.
49 Ibid., 203–4.
50 Ibid., 204–6.
51 Conversation between Bodnaras and Liu Fan, 28 October 1965, ANIC, RCP CC, IR, 4/1965, 215.
52 Letter from Brezhnev to Ulbricht, 7 January 1966, SAPMO-BArch, DY 30/3388, 43–44.
53 Mastny, '"We Are in a Bind"', 232.
54 See Chapter 1 of this book.
55 'Document no. 4, Memorandum by the Polish Ministry of National Defence, 26 January 1966', in Mastny, '"We Are in a Bind"', 240.
56 Letter from Brezhnev to Ulbricht, 7 January 1966, SAPMO-BArch, DY 30/3388, 43–44.
57 V. Mastny, 'Learning from the Enemy: NATO as Model to the Warsaw Pact', *Zürcher Beiträge zur Sicherheitspolitik und Konfliktforschung* no. 58 (2001), 22.
58 'Memorandum of the Polish Ministry of National Defence, 26 January 1966', in Mastny, '"We Are in a Bind"', 241.
59 'Memorandum by Polish Foreign Minister Adam Rapacki', 21 January 1966, in ibid., 238–40.
60 Letter from Ulbricht to Brezhnev, 15 January 1966, SAPMO-BArch, DY30/3389, 8–9.
61 Letter from Winzer to Ulbricht, Stoph and Honecker, Berlin, 13 January 1966, SAPMO-BArch, DY30/3388, 92.
62 Letter from Ulbricht to Brezhnev, 3 February 1966, SAPMO-BArch, DY 30/3389, 38.
63 'Political directives for the delegation of the GDR for the meeting of deputy foreign ministers of the Warsaw Pact', Berlin, 3 February 1966, SAPMO-BArch, DY 30/3389, 56–62.
64 Meeting of the Romanian Politburo, 20 January 1966, ANIC, RCP CC, C, 6/1966, 5.

65 Memorandum on the Romanian stance, ANIC, RCP CC, C, 11/1966, 15–19.
66 Ibid., emphasis in original.
67 Directives for the Romanian delegation, ANIC, RCP CC, C, 11/1966, 20–23, emphasis in original.
68 'Protocol no. 4 of the meeting of the RCP CC Permanent Presidium', 2 February 1966, ANIC, RCP CC, C, 11/1966, 10. See for NATO's crisis due to De Gaulle's obstruction: A. Locher, *Crisis? What Crisis? NATO, de Gaulle, and the Future of the Alliance, 1963–1966* (Baden-Baden, 2010), 60–92.
69 'Report to the Hungarian Socialist Workers' Party Political Committee on the Meeting of the Deputy Foreign Ministers [and on the Meeting of the Deputy Ministers of Defence in Moscow]', 10 February 1966, PHP, www.php.isn.ethz.ch/collections/colltopic.cfm?lng=en&id=17226&navinfo=15700 (accessed 26 August 2013).
70 Ibid.
71 C. Rijnoveanu, 'Rumänien und die Militärreformen des Warschauer Paktes 1960 bis 1970', in T. Diedrich, W. Heinemann and C.F. Ostermann (eds), *Der Warschauer Pakt. Von der Gründung bis zum Zusammenbruch 1955 bis 1991* (Berlin, 2009), 213.
72 'Report to the Hungarian Socialist Workers' Party', 10 February 1966, PHP, 3.
73 Minutes of the permanent presidium of the RCP CC, 16 February 1966, ANIC, RCP CC, C, 17/1966, 13.
74 Polish Deputy Foreign Minister Naszkowski cited in V. Mastny, 'Learning from the Enemy. NATO as a Model of the Warsaw Pact', *Zürcher Beiträge zur Sicherheitspolitik und Konfliktforschung* No. 58 (Zurich, 2001), 22.
75 Mastny, 'Learning from the Enemy', 25.
76 Minutes of the permanent presidium of the RCP CC, 16 February 1966, ANIC, RCP CC, C, 17/1966, 15, 20.
77 Speech by Ilichev, SAPMO-BArch, DY 30/3394, 19; cf. De Gaulle's 'Triple Non', in A. Locher, 'A Crisis Foretold: NATO and France, 1963–66', in A. Wenger, C. Nuenlist and A. Locher (eds), *Transforming NATO in the Cold War. Challenges beyond Deterrence in the 1960s* (Oxford and New York, 2007), 108.
78 Minutes of the permanent presidium of the RCP CC, 16 February 1966, ANIC, RCP CC, C, 17/1966, 19.
79 Ibid., 19; see SAPMO-BArch, DY 30/3394, 63–74 for the suggested protocol.
80 Ibid., 19; see SAPMO-BArch, DY 30/3394, 75–76 for the actual protocol.
81 'Memorandum about a conversation between the deputy prime minister, comrade O. Fischer, with the deputy prime minister, comrade L.F. Ilichev', 7 February 1966, SAPMO-BArch, DY 30/3382, 76.
82 Minutes of the permanent presidium of the RCP CC, 16 February 1966, ANIC, RCP CC, C, 17/1966, 19, 21.
83 'Report to the Hungarian Socialist Workers' Party', 10 February 1966, PHP.
84 Letter from Ulbricht to all WP first secretaries, Berlin, top secret, 22 February 1966, SAPMO-BArch, DY 30/3389, 72.
85 Conversation between Zhivkov, Maurer and Ceausescu, ANIC, RCP, IR, 14/1966, 12.
86 Letter from Winzer to Ulbricht, 23 February 1966, SAPMO-BArch, DY 30/3389, 67–68.
87 W. Jarzabek, 'Preserving the Status Quo or Promoting Change. The Role of the CSCE in the Perception of Polish Authorities, 1964–89', in O. Bange and G. Niedhart (eds), *Helsinki 1975 and the Transformation of Europe* (London and New York, 2008), 145.
88 Jarzabek, '"Ulbricht Doktrin" oder "Gomulka Doktrin"?' 88.
89 Ibid., 93–94.
90 Preda et al., *România – Republica Federală Germania*, 23–31.

91 Jarzabek, '"Ulbricht Doktrin" oder "Gomulka Doktrin"?' 90.
92 Ibid., 91.
93 Minutes of the meeting of first secretaries in Moscow, April 1966, ANIC, RCP CC, IR, 48/1966, 3–9.
94 Rijnoveanu, 'Rumänien und die Militärreformen', 215.
95 Minutes of Meeting, 6 June 1966, PHP, www.php.isn.ethz.ch/collections/colltopic. cfm?lng=en&id=19335&navinfo=15699 (accessed 26 August 2013).
96 Soviet proposal for a Declaration on the Improvement of Peace and Security in Europe, ANIC, RCP CC, C, 65/1966, 59 ff.
97 Internal Soviet draft, 9 June 1966, PA AA, MfAA, G-A 546, 28–41.
98 'Observations about the Soviet draft of the "Declaration Concerning the Improvement of Peace and Security in Europe"', ANIC, RCP CC, C, 65/1966, 59–68.
99 Declaration about the foundation of peace and security in Europe, Proposal of the Romanian delegation, 5 June 1966, 7–27, PA AA, MfAA, G-A 546.
100 'Observations about the Soviet draft of the "Declaration Concerning the Improvement of Peace and Security in Europe"', ANIC, RCP CC, C, 65/1966, 59–68.
101 Communiqué of the Political Consultative Committee meeting of the member states of the Warsaw Pact, Romanian draft, ANIC, RCP CC, C, 65/1966, 86–97.
102 Draft of the Romanian declaration, Moscow, 5 June 1966, SAPMO-BArch, DY 30/3395, 27–47.
103 See Minutes of the Bulgarian Communist Party CC Plenum – Report on the PCC Meeting by the Deputy Head of State (Stanko Todorov), 12 July 1966, PHP, www.php.isn.ethz.ch/collections/colltopic.cfm?lng=en&id=17948&navinfo=14465 (accessed 26 August 2013).
104 C. Békés, 'Der Warschauer Pakt und der KSZE-Prozess 1965 bis 1970', in Diedrich et al. (eds), Der Warschauer Pakt, 227.
105 Speech by the foreign minister of the GDR, Otto Winzer, 6 June 1966, SAPMO-BArch, DY 30/3395, 55–66.
106 Letter from Hegen to Ulbricht, Stoph, Honecker and Axen, 16 June 1966, ibid., 99–100.
107 Speech by the Romanian Minister of Foreign Affairs, Manescu, 6 June 1966, ibid., 67 72.
108 Letter from Hegen to Ulbricht et al., 16 June 1966, SAPMO-BArch, DY 30/3395, 99–100.
109 Ibid.
110 Naszkowski cited in W. Jarzabek, 'Die Volksrepublik Polen in den politischen Strukturen des Warschauer Vertrags zu Zeiten der Entspannung und der "Ostpolitik"', in Diedrich et al. (eds), Der Warschauer Pakt, 136.
111 Speech by Polish deputy foreign minister Naszkowski, 8 June 1966, SAPMO-BArch, DY 30/3395, 77.
112 Speech by Soviet Foreign Minister Gromyko, 8 June 1966, SAPMO-BArch, DY 30/3395, 83–89.
113 Speech by Romanian Foreign Minister Manescu, 8 June 1966, SAPMO-BArch, DY 30/3395, 90.
114 'Conversation between Brezhnev and Manescu, Top Secret, Extremely Important', ANIC, RCP CC, C, 73/1966, 26–39.
115 'Conversation between C. Manescu and A. Gromyko, Top Secret, of Utmost Importance', ANIC, RCP CC, C, 73/1966, 40–45.
116 Draft decision on reforms, 1 June 1966, PA AA, MfAA, G-A 546, 107–12.
117 Minutes of discussions with the Soviet delegation, 3 July 1966, 10.30–12.30, ANIC, RCP CC, IR, 94/1966, II, 130.

118 Discussions with the East German delegation, 3 July 1966, ANIC, RCP CC, IR, 5/1966, 15–16.
119 See 'Soviet Draft Statute on the Unified Command of the Warsaw Pact', 2 July 1966, PHP, www.php.isn.ethz.ch/collections/colltopic.cfm?lng=en&id=17990&navinfo=14465 (accessed 26 August 2013).
120 Minutes of discussions with the Soviet delegation, 4 July, 19.30–22.30, ANIC, RCP CC, IR, 94/1966, II, 160.
121 Minutes of discussions with the Soviet delegation, 4 July, 19.30–22.30, ANIC, RCP CC, IR, 94/1966, II, 153–76.
122 Ibid.
123 Minutes of the meeting of first secretaries and prime ministers, afternoon session, 6 July 1967, ANIC, RCP CC, IR, 94/1966, I, 197.
124 Minutes of the Romanian Party Politburo Meeting, Report on the PCC Meeting by the General Secretary of the RCP (Nicolae Ceausescu), 12 July 1966, PHP, www.php.isn.ethz.ch/collections/colltopic.cfm?lng=en&id=17947&navinfo=14465 (accessed 26 August 2013).
125 Minutes of discussions with the Soviet delegation, 4 July, 19.30–22.30, ANIC, RCP CC, IR, 94/1966, II, 159.
126 'Common Romanian-Soviet draft declaration on Peace and Security in Europe', ANIC, RCP CC, IR, 95/1966, 181–99.
127 Minutes of the meeting of Ministers of Foreign Affairs, 5 July 1966, ANIC, RCP CC, IR, 94/1966, II, 39.
128 Jarzabek, '"Ulbricht Doktrin" oder "Gomulka Doktrin"?' 92.
129 See for the actual declaration 'Public Declaration on Security in Europe', 8 July 1966, PHP, www.php.isn.ethz.ch/collections/colltopic.cfm?lng=en&id=17953&navinfo=14465 (accessed 26 August 2013). A lot of Romanian requests seem to be implemented.
130 Békés, 'Der Warschauer Pakt und der KSZE-Prozess', 227.
131 'Information report, 14.–26.10.1966', Bucharest, 26 October 1966, SAPMO BArch, DY 30/IVA2/20/372, 209.
132 'Information report, 30.9.–13.10.1966', Bucharest, 13 October 1966, ibid., 192; cf. Jarzabek, '"Ulbricht Doktrin" oder "Gomulka Doktrin"?' 94, for the Polish stance.
133 E. Moreton, *East Germany and the Warsaw Alliance. The Politics of Détente* (Boulder, 1978), 52.
134 Letter from Ulbricht to Abrassimov, 17 January 1967, SAPMO-BArch, DY 30/3396, 192–93.
135 'Document on diplomatic relations of socialist countries with the FRG', 24 January 1967, SAPMO-BArch, DY 30/3396, 196–99; and 'Evaluation about diplomatic relations with the FRG', 25 January 1967, ibid., 200–8.
136 Jarzabek, '"Ulbricht Doktrin" oder "Gomulka Doktrin"?' 96.
137 Selvage, 'The Warsaw Pact and the European Security Conference', 87.
138 Ibid.
139 Meeting between Basov and Ceausescu, 25 January 1967, ANIC, RCP CC, IR, 3/1967, 6.
140 Romanian politburo meeting about convention of meeting, 26 January 1967, ANIC, RCP CC, C, 7/1967, 2–3.
141 Moreton, *East Germany and the Warsaw Alliance*, 51.
142 'Phone conversation between Ceausescu and Kosygin', 4 February 1967, ANIC, RCP CC, C, 14/1967, 4–9.
143 'Memorandum about a conversation between Oskar Fischer und Baramowksi', 5 February 1967, SAPMO-BArch, DY 30/3396, 215–17.
144 'Attitude from Bulgarian Comrades and diplomats from other embassies on the establishment of diplomatic relations between Romania and the FRG', February 1967, 244–48, PA AA, MfAA, A 5394.

145 Cf. Ceausescu's remark in his conversation with Basov, 25 January 1967, ANIC, RCP CC, IR, 3/1967, 6.
146 Mastny, 'The Warsaw Pact', 148.
147 Speech by Malita, 8 February 1967, SAPMO-BArch, DY 30/3396, 48–49.
148 Minutes of an agreement, Warsaw, January 1967, SAPMO-BArch, DY 30/3396, 153–54.
149 Selvage, 'The Warsaw Pact and the European Security Conference', 87.
150 Ibid., 87–88.
151 Letter from Komoczin to Axen and all other WP secretaries, 17 February 1967, SAPMO-BArch, DY 30/3396, 234–35.
152 Minutes of discussions with the Soviet delegation, 4 July, 19.30–22.30, ANIC, RCP CC, IR, 94/1966, II, 153–76.
153 Cf. Moreton, *East Germany and the Warsaw Alliance*, 51.
154 Békés, 'Der Warschauer Pakt und der KSZE-Prozess', 229.
155 Polish Deputy Foreign Minister Naszkowski, cited in Mastny, 'Learning from the Enemy', 22.
156 For example, Rijnoveanu, 'Rumänien und die Militärreformen', 222.

5 Gaullism in the Warsaw Pact
Ceausescu's challenge

> It used to be very easy: the SU [Soviet Union] proposed something, and the other socialist countries adopted it without discussions. Now it is no longer that simple. Every [country] has its own opinions.[1]
> (Gromyko's personal secretary at the PCC meeting in July 1966)

The Romanian leaders not only successfully blocked any initiative to limit their scope for manoeuvre by resisting reforms within the WP. Apart from preventing the alliance from superseding national interests by turning into a supranational institution, they also strove to stretch the limits of the alliance in another way: after they had used their mediation within the Sino–Soviet Split in 1964 to emancipate themselves *outside* WP confines, they then intended to exploit their *special relationship* with the Chinese leadership *inside* the alliance. Since its declaration of independence in April 1964, the Romanian leadership had begun to cultivate relations with China, the rest of Asia and Albania, whereas relations with other Eastern European countries had deteriorated.[2] Romania began to adopt an increasingly idiosyncratic stance within the communist movement, while also attempting to include Albania and China again in the WP. This chapter will therefore continue the theme of the second chapter, and examine how the Romanian leadership attempted to use several global issues that were affected by the Sino–Soviet split, such as the Vietnam War and non-proliferation, to maintain its scope for manoeuvre within the WP, while playing the Chinese card to call the Soviet bluff.

After focusing on various WP countries in the previous chapter, the actual facts vindicate an almost exclusive focus on Romania within the alliance in this one. Whereas the views on European security and reforms differed among several WP leaderships, the Romanian leadership was the only one not to side unequivocally with the Kremlin during the Sino–Soviet split. This particularly affected the Romanian stance on the Vietnam War and a non-proliferation treaty, and sealed a division between 'the six' other WP members and Romania. At least until the Chinese Cultural Revolution in the summer of 1966, the Romanian leaders regularly consulted their Chinese comrades on issues that were discussed within the alliance, and cultivated a more militant stance on the Vietnam War, and they were the only WP member to oppose a non-proliferation treaty almost until its conclusion in July 1968. Covering the period from the first acrimonious debate on the non-proliferation treaty during the PCC meeting in January 1965 till the meeting convened by the Romanians in March 1968 in an attempt to reach a coordinated stance on – or against – non-proliferation, this chapter serves to investigate the motives behind the Romanian *Alleingang* within the WP on issues related to the Sino-Soviet Split, such as non-proliferation and the Vietnam War.

The Vietnam War

At the beginning of 1965 there was an interplay of several factors that offered the Romanian leadership a window of opportunity to reap further benefits from the Sino–Soviet split. In the first place, Khrushchev's ouster on 14 October 1964 brought a new collective leadership into power, whose first secretary, Leonid Brezhnev, considered 'the strengthening of [socialist] unity' of great importance, and was therefore eager to repair the Sino–Soviet split.[3] Brezhnev's quest for European security went hand in hand with an attempt also to relax tensions within the communist world. Together with Prime Minister Alexei Kosygin, Brezhnev defied the scepticism of Soviet foreign policy experts on Sino-Soviet relations in an attempt to 'mend fences with China', by ceasing the polemics.[4] Although talks with a Chinese delegation headed by Zhou Enlai in November 1964 ended in a failure, Kosygin convinced Brezhnev that rapprochement with China was particularly imperative, as the Chinese and Soviet leaderships needed to form a united front against American imperialism in the Vietnam War. As Marxists they should, after all, stand on the same side of the barricades.[5] Brezhnev therefore joined Kosygin in attempting to rally the Chinese behind them in the Vietnam War, even though the Chinese did not seem responsive at all.[6]

From the American perspective, however, the Vietnam War simply represented a battleground between communism and anti-communism.[7] The US Administration had supported the 'Republic of South Vietnam', led by the anti-communist, Catholic President Ngo Dinh Diem, since its foundation in 1956, against the communist revolutionary Ho Chi Minh, who was the leader of the North Vietnamese 'Democratic Republic of Vietnam' (DRV). In accordance with the Geneva Accords from 1954, Ho Chi Minh still demanded free elections to overcome the division of Vietnam, and attempted to overthrow the regime in South Vietnam with support from the Viet Minh – a communist coalition for national independence in North Vietnam – and the Viet Cong, who were South Vietnamese insurgents, representing the military arm of the 'National Liberation Front' (NLF), founded in 1960. Out of fear lest communism would spread from North Vietnam all through Asia, and cause a 'domino' effect, the US Army became involved in supporting the South Vietnamese government and liquidating the communist NLF.[8]

A common Sino-Soviet stance in the Vietnam War was all the more pressing since US President Lyndon B. Johnson, who had been re-elected in

November 1964, decided on a massive expansion of the fighting in early December. This involved retaliatory airstrikes and aerial bombing in North Vietnam as well as sending American ground troops to South Vietnam. After Johnson had already ordered the first direct military attacks on North Vietnam in August 1964, when two American destroyers had reportedly been attacked in the Gulf of Tonkin, he used his massive election victory to justify another escalation, which heralded the 'Americanisation' of the Vietnam War. Although this was meant to counteract Chinese hostility and potential 'Soviet adventurism', it drove the Soviet leadership into Chinese arms to unite in the face of American aggression, after it had kept a low profile in the war during the Khrushchev era.[9] Brezhnev was, accordingly, under increasing pressure to repair the Sino–Soviet split.

In addition to an escalation of the war due to American bombings and troop increases, the Kremlin had decided to reverse Khrushchev's hands-off policy, and from February 1965 onwards the Soviets began to aid the North Vietnamese substantially. This coincided with the fact that Johnson had ordered a bombing programme, 'Operation Rolling Thunder', which continued almost unabated from February 1965 to October 1968, as well as significantly increasing the number of American troops from more than 180,000 by the end of 1965 to 536,100 in 1968.[10] Although Mao and Brezhnev agreed on the need to support the North Vietnamese, the Soviets aimed for a short war that would be decided in favour of the North Vietnamese, whereas the Chinese favoured a prolonged battle that could enhance the revolutionary zeal against the imperialists. Moreover, since Mao was purging all revisionists *within* China, he could ill afford to side with the Soviet revisionists outside China.[11]

The factors that had caused the Sino–Soviet split therefore made it almost impossible for the Kremlin to reach an understanding with the Chinese leadership on the Vietnam War. Although the Soviet leadership favoured negotiations between Hanoi and the American government so as to salvage its policy of peaceful coexistence instead of risking détente, the increasingly radicalising Chinese Communist Party (CCP) under Mao intended to 'fight till the last Vietnamese', and warned the DRV against reaching a compromise.[12] In the summer of 1966 Mao's radicalisation culminated in the 'Great Proletarian Cultural Revolution', usually known as the 'Cultural Revolution', which was launched in order to extricate any capitalist elements from Chinese society by force and firmly establish Maoism. Negotiations between North Vietnam and the US Administration were accordingly out of the question for the CCP. As the former Polish ambassador to Beijing, Professor Rowiaski, put it, 'China's Vietnam policy was primarily a logical consequence of Mao Zedong's new strategy to transform his country into 'a centre and an armoury of the world revolution', and to take up a fight on two fronts, against US imperialism and Soviet revisionism'.[13] For the Chinese the Vietnam War represented a struggle *against* rather than *with* the Soviet leadership.

At the same time the Soviet leadership wanted to negotiate a way out of the Vietnam War *with* the support of the Chinese leadership. According to the Chinese ambassador to Moscow, Li Fenglin, the Chinese side 'regarded Vietnam as a predicament for the United States and wanted the United States to be caught in it', whereas the Soviet side 'wanted to help the United States to find a way out in order to avoid a superpower confrontation and, on the other [hand] supported Vietnam'. Caught in this 'contradictory situation', the Kremlin not only strove to assist the North Vietnamese and appease the Americans, but also aimed to do so without further antagonising the Chinese communists.[14] Meanwhile, the Chinese feared the growth of Soviet influence in North Vietnam, as Hanoi had grown more dependent on Soviet aid throughout 1966.[15] The Vietnam War thus also turned into a Soviet *and* Chinese predicament.

The nuclear question

The Sino-Soviet predicament was further complicated by the fact that the Chinese had detonated their first nuclear weapon on 16 October 1964, two days after Khrushchev's ouster. This confirmed Mao's belief that the Chinese had an equal right to lead the communist movement, and that the Sino–Soviet split could only be mended on his terms. He therefore demanded 'complete Soviet capitulation and recognition that Mao was right all along'.[16] China's new status as a nuclear power also reinforced Mao's refusal to participate in an editorial committee meeting on 15 December 1964 – later postponed to 1 March 1965 – to prepare the next international communist conference, after the one in November 1960.

Meanwhile, both the Soviet and American leaders shared the premise that Chinese nuclear ambitions should be curbed at all times. The US Administration was particularly concerned that 'China's test [...] could initiate a nuclear domino effect if vigorous action were not taken', and established the blue ribbon Committee on Nuclear Proliferation (also called the 'Gilpatric committee') 'to construct a new US non-proliferation policy in the wake of the PRC's atomic test'.[17] For the Soviet leadership, the Chinese nuclear detonation was a particular threat, as it meant that the 'Cold War in the Communist World' could go nuclear, too.[18] The Chinese detonation therefore provided an extra impetus to the superpowers' ambitions to adopt measures for arms control. The process to do so had already resulted in the formation of the Eighteen Nations Disarmament Committee (ENDC) under the aegis of the United Nations (UN) in 1962. This committee was co-chaired by the American and Soviet leaders, and contained Bulgaria, Poland, Czechoslovakia, and Romania as its Eastern European members. Although the other members had had no input in the Limited Test-Ban Treaty, which was concluded by the Soviet Union, Great Britain and the United States in August 1963, the Chinese nuclear test stimulated both superpowers to consult their allies on non-proliferation.

The Warsaw Pact's concerns for the *hypothetical* programme of nuclear sharing within NATO, Multilateral Nuclear Forces (MLF), which had dominated the meeting of deputy foreign ministers on 10 December 1964, thus gradually became overshadowed by the *actual* fact that China had turned into a nuclear power.[19] In the WP, too, the need for non-proliferation became more pressing. It was therefore no coincidence that Walter Ulbricht, who had taken the initiative for the PCC meeting on 19 January 1965, which was supposed to deal with MLF, in a letter on 13 January suggested linking the discussion on MLF to non-proliferation. He had even appropriated the initiative by attaching a draft non-proliferation treaty.[20] Just as in the USA, which attempted to rally its NATO allies behind a programme on non-proliferation, the Chinese nuclear test had turned non-proliferation into a WP priority.[21]

The Kremlin faced the hard task of improving its contacts with China to create a united front against American aggression in the Vietnam War, while cultivating its relations with the US Administration to formulate a non-proliferation policy that would curb the Chinese threat. Meanwhile, the Soviet leadership was so afraid of exacerbating the Sino–Soviet split that it dared not mediate between Washington and Hanoi in order to avoid Chinese blame of collaborating with the USA, but allowed other Eastern European leaders instead to initiate negotiations.[22] The Polish and Romanian leaders were particularly eager to seize this opportunity for very different reasons, as will become clear later in this chapter. In both cases mediation in the Vietnam War nevertheless became a means to maintain scope for manoeuvre vis-à-vis Moscow, and the conflict therefore began to play an increasingly important role within the Warsaw Pact.

At the same time the Soviet leadership needed the support of its WP allies more than ever. If it failed to convince its allies to sail the same course, it could hardly succeed in sailing between the American Scylla and the Chinese Charybdis. The Romanian leadership was, however, acutely aware of the fact that it took little to rock the boat, and explored the Kremlin's precarious position to the full. Eager to develop a Romanian nuclear programme, the Romanian leadership had a particular interest in the discussions on non-proliferation. As the Romanian historian Eliza Gheorghe shows, the Romanians cultivated contacts at both sides of the Iron Curtain to provide them with nuclear energy.[23] The US Administration had to work hard to curb the Gaullist challenge within NATO, but the Romanian leadership had at least as much ammunition against its hegemon as General de Gaulle.[24] With the Sino–Soviet split as its trump, it was determined to push Soviet tolerance to its limits.

Bilateral preparations

The Romanian leadership was well aware of the fact that Khrushchev's ouster had heralded a period in which the new Soviet leadership would go to great lengths to mend Sino-Soviet relations. As long as the Kremlin courted China, it could hardly prevent its Romanian allies from playing the Chinese card. Since the Romanian attempts at mediating in the Sino–Soviet split in the spring of 1964, Sino-Romanian relations had intensified so much that representatives from the Romanian leadership met on an almost weekly basis with Liu Fan, the Chinese ambassador in Bucharest. It was, therefore, part of a grander strategy to ask the Chinese opinion of developments within the WP, although the Chinese leadership had already been fully excluded from the alliance since 1961, when it stopped participating as an observer. The Romanian leaders no longer wanted to go it alone, but wished to create a joint front with their Chinese comrades.

The Romanians were, accordingly, particularly keen to discuss their preparation of the PCC meeting on 19 January 1965 with the Chinese, and the Romanian politburo member Emil Bodnaras, who was the specialist on Asia, invited Liu Fan on the first day of the new year 'in order to discuss with the Chinese leadership the way in which we can manage matters better where there are problems of common interest'. He particularly hoped to close ranks with the Chinese on the participation of Albania within the WP, which had been invited to the PCC meeting under Romanian pressure, and of the Asian observers. If they were to attend the PCC meetings again, as they had done up to 1961, 'there would be five of us, two members, and three observers'.[25] The Romanian intention was clear: if Albania, China, North Vietnam and North Korea were to side with Romania within the WP, they could form a coalition against the five remaining Eastern European countries. The Romanians realised only retrospectively that the initial years of the WP had provided them with a missed opportunity. The reversed Romanian stance on Albania's participation in the WP marked the new position Romania intended to occupy in the WP.

According to Bodnaras the meeting of deputy foreign ministers in December 1964 had also stimulated the Romanians to 'change the framework in which we shall act in the scheduled session'. They had decided to 'no longer come along with a document that we give to someone else', but to take the initiative in discussions instead, e.g. by raising the topic of disarmament and supporting 'the proposal of the P.R. China [from October 1964] regarding the general prohibition and the total destruction of nuclear arms'.[26] The Romanians were thus prepared to take a risky stance during the Sino–Soviet split. They could kill two birds with one stone: this would both serve to underline the Romanian independence, and signal to the Chinese that the Romanians were prepared to do them a service. Hoping for support from the Chinese side within the WP, the Romanians were more than willing to support them in return.

The Chinese leadership greatly welcomed the Romanian support. Emphasising in a meeting a week later that China, too, was against MLF, which was the central topic of the agenda, Liu Fan also explained that the Chinese comrades feared that the Soviet leaders would use that as a 'pretext to [...]

take a coordinated stance with the USA and India to turn against the Chinese' and to propose non-proliferation. It was, in fact, the East German leader, Walter Ulbricht, who explicitly made the link between MLF and non-proliferation in a proposal on non-proliferation a few days later.[27] Because this would in turn favour a nuclear monopoly of the countries that already possessed nuclear weapons, the Chinese only favoured non-proliferation as 'a first step' for total disarmament. Liu Fan therefore expected a Romanian attempt to undermine 'the intention of the Soviet Union to direct this session on a course against China', and requested Romania to support the Chinese position in full, which Bodnaras promised to do.[28] The Chinese attitude was all the more striking as the Chinese side refused all the Romanian requests, both concerning the participation as observers at the PCC meeting, and regarding the consultation of their Albanian ally.[29] The Romanian attempt to create an Asian coalition within the WP had turned into a Chinese ploy to use the Romanian delegation as their proxy within the alliance.

In another meeting Bodnaras underlined that the Romanians also agreed with the Chinese opposition to the Soviet proposal to convene the editorial committee of communist parties on 1 March 1965, as it represented a ploy to re-establish Soviet hegemony over the communist movement.[30] Even though the Chinese were among a small minority of parties that refused to participate, the fact that the Romanian leaders closed ranks with their Chinese comrades was a severe blow to the Kremlin. The Sino–Soviet split was, as such, imported into the WP. Moreover, this enabled the Romanian leadership 'to keep all options open', which, as the East German allies observed, was also the reason why the Romanian leadership was so reluctant to participate in PCC meetings.[31] The Chinese stance in the communist world seemed a great source of inspiration for the Romanian stance within the WP. Asking the Chinese whether the Romanians needed to intervene on any other point, Bodnaras servility vis-à-vis the Chinese seemed an ironic inversion of the Romanian defiance of the Soviet Union.[32] It did nevertheless serve a clear purpose: the Romanians could use the Chinese position to mark their independence within the WP, and the Chinese angle on non-proliferation coincided with Romanian interests.

The Sino-Romanian collusion stood in stark contrast with the Romanian progress in bilateral meetings with their WP allies before the PCC meeting started. In a conversation that Gheorghiu-Dej and Maurer had requested with Gomulka to discuss Ulbricht's proposal on non-proliferation, the Albanian question came to haunt the Romanians. Unbeknown to the Romanians, the Albanians had sent a letter to the Polish leadership in Warsaw, as Warsaw was the official depository of the Warsaw Treaty, in which they made their participation in the alliance conditional upon a number of impossible requests, such as Soviet self-criticism on its past attitude towards Albania, a revision of the nuclear test-ban treaty and a peace treaty with both Germanys.[33] The Romanian proposal to invite Albania thus backfired: the Albanian reply itself was so far-fetched that the Romanians could hardly continue to support them. Moreover, Gomulka severely criticised the Romanian opposition on convening an editorial committee to prepare another communist conference, and accused the Romanians of 'submitting to the Chinese'.[34] The Romanian leadership now faced a party that occupied the opposite end of the spectrum within the Sino–Soviet split. Instead of patching up the differences, the Romanian delegation began to realise that it would be confronted with strong opposition from its Polish comrades.

On the same day the Romanian delegation paid a visit to Walter Ulbricht, at his request. The East German leadership was fully aware of the Romanian collusion with China on its detonation of an atom bomb, disarmament and the communist conference, and desired to defend its own proposal on non-proliferation. Ulbricht wanted the issue to be raised at the UN, and hoped that the East German proposal would necessitate the unprecedented participation of the GDR at the UN. He thus tried to use the WP as a direct instrument for *de facto* East German recognition, by transmitting his proposal to the UN through the WP. The Romanian leadership nevertheless warned Ulbricht that 'we would make a grave mistake' if the problem were raised at the UN, as it could be used 'in order to condemn China', and thus undermined his transmission belt approach.[35] Although Gomulka had succeeded in checkmating his Romanian comrades, Gheorghiu-Dej and Maurer had called Ulbricht's bluff: on non-proliferation they would continue to side with the Chinese.

In bilateral meetings without the Kremlin the Romanians had to give way to their Polish comrades on the Albanian issue, but had managed to stand their ground with their East German allies on the non-proliferation treaty. The difference between these two meetings was striking: whereas Gomulka had managed to seize the initiative by using the Albanian reply as leverage over his Romanian comrades, Gheorghiu-Dej had succeeded in using potential Chinese condemnation at the UN as leverage over Ulbricht. The fact that the meeting with Gomulka took place at Romanian request, whereas Ulbricht met the Romanian leaders at his own request, already testifies to the hierarchy within the WP, according to which Poland ranked very high and the GDR considerably lower. Thus the position of the main protagonists of the PCC meeting had already been defined through bilateral meetings behind the scenes and without the Soviet Union, before the PCC meeting even started.

Playing the Chinese card

During the actual meeting the protagonists did not budge. All leaders apart from Gheorghiu-Dej united in their strong condemnation of the Albanian stance and in their support for Ulbricht's proposal to present a non-proliferation treaty to the UN, which he considered a logical and effective way to counter MLF. Brezhnev was the first strongly to voice his 'total support', but also offered an opening to the Chinese by arguing that 'concerning the struggle for [...] the non-proliferation of nuclear weapons it would be extremely desirable to coordinate our efforts with the People's Republic of China'. Supporting the Chinese proposal for a disarmament conference, Brezhnev accordingly underlined that he still hoped to repair relations with the Chinese.[36] Brezhnev thus trod his ground carefully and attempted to defuse Chinese and Romanian antagonism.

Gheorghiu-Dej cleverly used the window of opportunity in Sino-Soviet relations after Khrushchev's ouster by concentrating on the Chinese aspect in his speech. He was the first WP leader to welcome the Chinese nuclear detonation as 'an important triumph [...] for the socialist camp', and strongly supported the Chinese proposal for a conference on 'the total destruction of nuclear weapons'. Ignoring the East German proposal on non-proliferation altogether, the Romanian leader clearly emphasised the importance of unity between *all* socialist countries. At the end of his speech Gheorghiu-Dej even returned to Brezhnev's proposal to coordinate efforts with China, which had pleasantly surprised him, and suggested 'collaboration on all major international problems' with non-WP countries.[37] This was, in fact, an insidious move to rob the WP of its relevance. Refusing to allow the WP to act as a body to represent the socialist countries, Romanian Foreign Minister Manescu added in a later meeting that a non-proliferation treaty could lead to a nuclear monopoly of the already existing nuclear powers to keep their weapons.[38] This argument had a particularly interesting dimension to it, as the Romanian leaders seriously intended to keep the option open of developing their own nuclear programme.[39] Although no agreement was reached on a non-proliferation treaty, the Romanian leadership proved more pliable concerning the Albanian issue, in which the Chinese had not expressed great interest anyhow, and agreed on a resolution against Albania.[40]

The Romanian stance during the discussion between first secretaries echoed the conversations between Bodnaras and Liu Fan. Gheorghiu-Dej and Maurer insisted that the East German draft non-proliferation treaty could be used by India to condemn China at the UN, and reiterated the Chinese point of view that non-proliferation was only useful as a first step in the process towards disarmament. Gomulka was the first to target the Romanian objections, by arguing that 'the idea of non-proliferation' was no longer 'levelled directly against the Chinese Republic', as it had been before the 'experimental detonation' of a Chinese nuclear device.[41] He also undermined the proposal for total disarmament, as the West would never accept it, whereas 'the problem of non-proliferation is the easiest to solve'.[42] The Sino-Romanian collusion nevertheless turned non-proliferation, too, into a thorny issue.

The Romanians were not sensitive to the argument of their Czechoslovak comrade Novotny either, who argued that '[t]he Western press expects Romania to adopt a diverging position [...] at this meeting. If we do not include the issue of non-proliferation in the communiqué, it will be clear to everybody that Romania disagreed'.[43] This might, however, have been exactly what the Romanian leadership hoped for. As Gheorghe shows, the Romanians' status as 'maverick' could help them to obtain certain concessions, even concerning nuclear equipment, from the West.[44] Maurer accordingly underlined that 'Romania has the right to justify its position anywhere and at any time it chooses, using whatever arguments it deems suitable for the purpose'. Appealing to the Romanian lust for autonomy, Gomulka cleverly added that he did not mind the Romanian conversations with the Chinese, 'but don't we have our own minds, can't we evaluate the situation?'[45] However, for the Romanians WP unity was obviously subordinate to contact with the Chinese. Moreover, the Chinese stance on non-proliferation suited Romanian purposes.

Brezhnev was also wondering whether Gheorghiu-Dej and Maurer were expressing 'the personal opinion of the Romanian Workers Party, or whether you are subordinating [it] to an understanding with the Chinese comrades?'[46] The extent to which the Romanian delegation had coordinated its opinion with the Chinese was obviously unbeknown to Brezhnev. During a final meeting of first secretaries to fine-tune the communiqué, Gomulka managed to formulate a compromise that satisfied his Romanian comrade. Gheorghiu-Dej agreed to the formulation that '[t]he creation of MLF, in any form, means the proliferation of nuclear arms and, especially, the access of those arms to West German militarists'.[47] The Romanian delegation had thus succeeded in limiting any mention of proliferation to MLF, while undermining the East German attempt to use a WP proposal for a non-proliferation treaty to raise the status of the WP, and indirectly the GDR, at the UN. The Romanian leadership had accordingly managed to increase its own scope for manoeuvre on foreign policy issues while decreasing the importance of the WP. It had, at the same time, ensured that 'no document would be adopted against China', as Bodnaras had promised Liu Fan. The potential condemnation of China at the UN had provided the Romanians with a useful argument to achieve their own foreign policy objectives.

The Romanian collusion with the Chinese stance nevertheless resulted in a secret meeting of their six allies to discuss the convention of the editorial committee of the international communist conference, which was scheduled for 1 March. Gomulka himself used this opportunity to take the lead again, and suggested calling the 'editorial committee' a 'consultative session' instead, to signal clearly that it was not intended to determine the outcome of the meeting and to accommodate Romanian criticism of the term 'editorial'.[48] Without Romanian dissent, the other allies quickly agreed to Gomulka's proposal, and thus the only measure that was decided upon was ironically sealed outside the official confines of the WP. Although the Romanians had succeeded in reducing the relevance of the WP during the meeting itself, while also resisting the East German proposals on reforms, as we have seen in the previous chapter, their WP allies had managed to reduce the relevance of Romania by making decisions outside the confines of the alliance. The decision of the six remaining delegations to bypass Romania paved the way for a new trend within the alliance. After the Romanian attempt to create an Asian coalition in the WP had come to nothing, the division of 'the six' – as they

The alliance inside out

The way in which the Sino–Soviet split had turned the WP inside out was illustrated by the fact that Romania's exclusion from the final meeting coincided with another meeting between the Romanian and Chinese comrades. At Liu Fan's request, Bodnaras hurried to the Chinese ambassador to report in great detail on the manner in which the Romanians had used the WP meeting to defend Chinese interests.[49] Bodnaras even suggested that the draft non-proliferation treaty had been approved by the USA, which he confirmed the next day with information from Washington.[50] It was indeed the case that the non-proliferation discussion at the PCC meeting almost exactly coincided with a report by the Gilpatric Committee on Nuclear Proliferation in which it urged the US Administration to '"substantially increase the scope and intensity" of its non-proliferation efforts', which was issued on 21 January 1965.[51] Bodnaras thus emphasised that the WP members were uniting against China with the imperialists. After the Romanian attempt to 'mediate' in the Sino–Soviet split, this seemed an attempt to escalate it.

Adapting his speech to the antagonistic rhetoric of the Chinese, Bodnaras described the PCC meeting as a 'battle' in which a 'massive attack' was carried out against the Romanian delegation, in which Gomulka had 'the most combative attitude'. Moreover, he explained that the 'principal battle' was not about MLF, but about the nuclear monopoly of the 'monstrous club' of the traditional nuclear powers. Underlining that all Romanian objections were taken into account in the communiqué, Bodnaras used the PCC meeting to emphasise Romania's successful struggle for the defence of Chinese interests *and* for emphasising Romanian autonomy to the outside world.[52] One day later the Romanian delegation had prepared the minutes for the Chinese and had taken all the top secret documents, such as Ulbricht's letter, the draft communiqué and the draft non-proliferation treaty, from the PCC meeting to Liu Fan. The delegation was led by Maurer himself, who dwelt at length on Gomulka's role:

> In the scope of the discussion [on non-proliferation] the principal leader, the most active and most 'shrewd' instrument was Gomulka; not only the most 'shrewd' leader, but also the most perfidious and able to advocate for the cause defended by the others. None of the participants was so active, inventive and obstinate about those ideas as Gomulka [...] Neither Ulbricht, nor Brezhnev, and even less the others were anywhere near the level of Gomulka in terms of supporting those common proposals, which were probably decided beforehand [...] The discussions lasted 4 hours. They took place between the Romanian part and all the others.[53]

It was indeed striking that the discussions on non-proliferation seemed to be determined by Gomulka on the one hand and Maurer and Gheorghiu-Dej on the other hand. Brezhnev was at most reduced to an arbiter, but did not seem able to seize the initiative. Nor was he able to push through the East German proposals, which he vehemently supported. As Maurer emphasised, 'no decision was taken, because we opposed it'.[54] Liu Fan was duly impressed by the Romanian attitude and thanked Maurer and Bodnaras profusely for the detailed information. The Romanians had thus become extremely useful informers within the WP, while ensuring that the Sino–Soviet split also weakened the Kremlin within its own alliance.

Meanwhile, a Soviet delegation led by Premier Kosygin had just returned from a disastrous trip to China, where Mao Zedong had flatly refused to participate in the editorial committee on 1 March, while cold-shouldering everyone who did.[55] Mao had called the Soviet delegates 'traitors of Marxism' and had promised that 'the polemics would go on for another 9–10 thousand years'.[56] This was not far from the truth: it proved to be the last meeting ever between any Soviet leader and Mao.[57] Kosygin had also visited China's traditional allies North Korea and North Vietnam, which welcomed the Soviet leader and did not oppose the meeting on 1 March, although they would not attend it either out of deference to China. Romanian participation in the committee thus became particularly important for Brezhnev, who asked Gheorghiu-Dej in a letter to consider participating in the conference after all.[58] The Kremlin would rather gain an obstinate Romania, than lose it altogether.

The Soviet leadership even sent foreign ministry official Tolkunov to Bucharest at the end of February in an attempt to win the Romanian comrades over. In a conversation with Bodnaras and Ceausescu he emphasised that the RWP and the Kremlin shared 'the same point of view […] concerning the development of relations between fraternal parties', as had become clear at the PCC meeting. Emphasising the 'good opinion about the Romanian comrades' and the 'admiration of [their] experience', Tolkunov stressed that 'our Central Committee has displayed a total proof of tact and self-control concerning the positions of the Romanian Workers Party', as well as 'a complete understanding of the politics and position of the Romanian Workers Party', and requested 'a similar understanding' of the Soviet position in return.[59] This nevertheless fell on deaf ears: Bodnaras duly reported his entire conversation with Tolkunov a day later to the Chinese diplomat Van Tung, and regarded the Soviet overture as a 'manoeuvre to attempt […] to salvage the old orientation'. Refusing to cooperate with the Soviets on this delicate issue, the Romanians emphatically told the Chinese that they were eager to communicate their decision 'in the context of our collaboration'. The Romanian dissidents within the WP had tightened their bond with China, instead of deepening their 'understanding' of the Soviet Union.[60]

Meanwhile, the meeting on 1 March in Moscow, 'which was initially "intended to have a decisive importance for the destiny of the revolutionary movement", had turned into a miscarriage' according to the Romanian ambassador in Beijing.[61] The Chinese stuck to their guns, and the countries that participated – which included all WP members except Romania and Albania – had issued a half-hearted communiqué for the sake of unity, in which their support for Moscow remained ambivalent.[62] Moreover, the East German and Polish delegates had openly turned against some Soviet proposals.[63] The Kremlin was, accordingly, forced to compromise, and the conference had stimulated a new *modus operandi*, with more 'respect for the equality and autonomy' of each party, as 'an international monolithic organisation does not and cannot exist', as a Polish delegate put it.[64] The Soviet monolith had become an anachronism.

Closing ranks on Vietnam?

In April 1965 the Soviet leaders intensified their attempts to close ranks with the Chinese on the Vietnam issue. On 3 April Brezhnev and Kosygin wrote a letter to Mao and Zhou Enlai, in which they proposed a meeting between Chinese, North Vietnamese and Soviet representatives at the highest level of representation in order to 'discuss together the measures that should be taken in future for the defence of the security of the Democratic Republic of Vietnam'.[65] The Soviets warned that 'the aggressor can go still further', if no 'common action' was undertaken. The Chinese leadership replied that it already met frequently with the Vietnamese comrades to 'support' them 'in the struggle against the aggression of American imperialism'. They called the Soviet 'assistance up to the present [...] very insignificant', and advised the Soviets to discuss 'this problem' bilaterally with the Vietnamese.[66] The Kremlin forwarded both letters to the Romanian Workers Party, which had been led by Nicolae Ceausescu since Gheorghiu-Dej's death in March 1965.[67] The Soviet leaders intended to show their willingness to find a way out of the Sino–Soviet split while also expressing their indignity about the fact that the Soviet help had been considered 'very insignificant'.[68] In contrast to the lengthy conversations with Chinese Ambassador Liu Fan, Soviet Ambassador I.K. Jegalin was allocated ten minutes to hand over the letters to Ceausescu and to convince him that the 'the Soviet aid' was, in fact, 'sufficient'.[69] The Soviet attempts to win both the Romanians and the Chinese over remained unrequited.

Matters between Moscow and Beijing had escalated to such an extent that the Soviets complained to the Romanians that 'the Chinese refused to allow Soviet planes to cross their territory' on the way to Vietnam.[70] A top-level Chinese delegation, consisting of Deng Xiaoping, Kang Sheng and Liu Fan, meanwhile complained to Maurer and Ceausescu that 'the Soviets do not respect the sovereignty of our country', which they 'consider a province of the Soviet Union'. According to the Chinese, the 'real purpose' of closing ranks on Vietnam was to enable 'collaboration between the United States of America and the Soviet Union'. In Chinese eyes the Kremlin was ready to sacrifice Vietnam for the sake of détente. Deng Xiaoping insidiously added to this: 'Their real purpose is to isolate China [...] As we see, you, too, have this experience.' Maurer responded: 'But we fight it.'[71] Praising Romania's independent stance in the Vietnam War, the Chinese obviously hoped to break through their own isolation by creating a united Sino-Romanian front against the Soviet Union.

The Kremlin was also keen not to isolate Romania, as it needed Romanian support in the Sino–Soviet split. When Brezhnev invited a Romanian delegation led by Ceausescu to Moscow in September 1965, he therefore tried to close ranks on the Vietnam War. However, when he suggested signing a common declaration to support Vietnam, the Romanian delegation flatly refused, as it demanded the approval of China and Vietnam, as Ceausescu himself proudly reported to Liu Fan.[72] Meanwhile, the Romanian leadership had attempted to maintain an independent stance in the Vietnam War by supporting the Vietnamese independently. From January 1965 onwards there had been many manifestations in favour of the Vietnamese people in Romania,[73] although the Vietnamese complained halfway through the year that the Romanian assistance to Vietnam had 'almost exclusively a moral character'.[74] The Vietnamese communists were particularly popular in Romania, as the Romanian people identified the Vietnamese struggle against the Americans with 'their resistance to the other big power [the Soviet Union]', and the Romanian leadership gladly capitalised on this sentiment.[75]

The Romanian leadership nevertheless stepped up its support in the summer, and after it had signed a declaration against the American military intervention in Vietnam in August,[76] it also invited a delegation of the NLF of South Vietnam to Romania in November, which it provided with maximal *material* support.[77] By 1967 Romania had in fact become the third largest supporter of Vietnam after the Soviet Union and China.[78] The other WP allies were nevertheless sceptical about Romania's ulterior motives, as the Romanians cherished particularly cordial relations with the American ambassador, too.[79] As will become clear later in this chapter, the Romanians strove to remain good relations with as many actors as possible in order to be able to play them off against one another when necessary. Although this enabled Romania to cultivate an autonomous stance in the Vietnam War without defining its position in the Sino–Soviet split, the Romanian leadership was increasingly turning into a pawn in its own game.

During the assembly of the UN in October 1965 it became painfully evident that the Kremlin had failed to win the Romanians over to its side: although the Soviet leadership attempted yet again to put a non-proliferation treaty forward with the support of its allies, it was under so much pressure from the Romanians that it could only do so in its own name.[80] The Romanian delegation was furious that the Kremlin put the treaty on the agenda, but it had successfully prevented it from legitimising it in a WP framework. The Romanian delegation ironically used the PCC meeting in January 1965 to undermine the Soviet stance: since the treaty had been vetoed there, the

Soviets had no right to present it in their allies' name at the UN. The Soviets succumbed and had thus been checkmated by the machinations of their own alliance.

The Polish move

The Romanian leadership diverged within the WP just as much on the Vietnam War as on non-proliferation, and in the issue on Vietnam it also found Gomulka its most mighty opponent. Gomulka was extremely critical of the Chinese uncooperative stance in the Vietnam War, and his support for a conference to resolve it was even such that it caught the attention of the US Administration, whose top diplomat W. Averell Harriman asked Gomulka in December 1965 to mediate between the Soviet, Chinese and North Vietnamese leaderships to attain a negotiated peace. The Poles were assured that the Americans would not approach the Romanians with the same request, as the Romanians would fear Chinese disapproval of mediating in the Vietnam War.[81] The Romanian refusal to take sides in the Sino–Soviet split thus prevented it from resuming the role as mediator, and the Polish leadership decided in the end to accept the American request. This started a grand-scale operation of Polish mediation, later known as 'Operation Marigold'.[82]

The Polish leadership had a vested interest in the peaceful resolution of the Vietnam War, as it feared that the Vietnam War 'could exacerbate East-West relations, pose a threat to détente, and relegate to the back seat the questions of key importance to Warsaw, namely those pertaining to European security', and therefore attempted to mediate in 1966. It also feared that an exacerbation of the Sino–Soviet split through the Vietnam War might 'lead to a greater Soviet control in Central and Eastern Europe', and a rapprochement with Bonn 'at the expense of Warsaw's interests'.[83] The same motive that drove Gomulka and Rapacki to force their allies to accept the 'Warsaw Package' during the conference of WP foreign ministers in February 1967, inspired them to adopt an active stance in the Vietnam War too.[84]

Gomulka accordingly sent a letter to the Chinese leadership in December 1965 in which he suggested a conference of the Asian communist parties and those of the WP at the highest level of representation in order to reach an agreement on aid to Vietnam. Arguing that the lack of unity within the socialist camp strengthened the 'American aggression', the Polish leader succeeded in pretending to act on his own initiative.[85] He also sent a cover letter to all his WP comrades, in which he asked them to 'examine the proposals contained in our letter'.[86] Most WP members welcomed the Polish initiative, as did the Vietnamese Communist Party,[87] but the Romanian leaders were predictably furious at the way in which they had been presented with another *fait accompli* by a WP ally. Whereas they had attempted to include the Asian observers again to strengthen their hand within the WP, Gomulka tried to involve the Asian communist parties for the sake of unity. Gomulka's proposal placed them in a difficult position, as it forced them to side openly with either the Soviet leaders, who were likely to accept it, or the Chinese, who would probably reject the proposal. The Sino–Soviet split had escalated to such an extent that the Vietnam War had also turned into a battleground of communism against communism. According to Bodnaras there were 'two wars in Vietnam – Vietnam with the USA, and China with the SU'. He nevertheless added that 'our friendship with China is useful so long as the rest has to take China into account. At the moment when they no longer take it into account, that friendship disappears'.[88] The Romanian relations with the Chinese were, accordingly, merely of an instrumental kind.

The Romanian balancing act thus became particularly difficult to sustain. Maurer therefore wanted to treat the letter 'with the greatest possible caution', as he regarded 'good relations with the Chinese' as 'one of the fundamental elements of our foreign policy'. Ceausescu agreed that 'we cannot support that letter', but emphasised that the situation was critical, and even feared that the 'extension of this war' could lead to 'very serious repercussions, not just in Asia, but also in Europe', as it could provoke 'extreme measures on behalf of the USA', including even the use of nuclear weapons. Ceausescu therefore suggested becoming 'more active' in the Vietnam War, *inter alia*, by visiting Vietnam. Rightly sensing that the Polish initiative was welcomed elsewhere, Ceausescu argued for becoming 'more active with the neighbouring socialist countries, in order to explain our point of view', and preventing further isolation of China, while also intensifying 'relations with capitalist countries' so as to 'unmask and isolate the USA'.[89] The other politburo members stressed that they should visit Vietnam before the next session of the PCC in order to strengthen their hand and avoid being isolated themselves within the WP. Competing with the Poles for the position of most influential NSWP member, the Polish move had stimulated the Romanians to move even faster.

The Romanian countermove

At roughly the same time the visit from French Foreign Minister Couve de Murville to Romania in April 1966 considerably strengthened the Romanian hand. It was the first visit of a French foreign minister to Romania during the Cold War, and it took place within a month of France's announced withdrawal from the military structures of NATO.[90] Ceausescu accordingly displayed a particular interest 'in the French position within NATO', and argued 'that the French politics supports the Romanian position within the Warsaw Pact', as it was an example of the politics of all states that strove after independence.[91]

Meanwhile, the Romanian leaders appropriated the Polish initiative by sending a Romanian delegation to Hanoi in May 1966 'concerning the possibility of some common actions of all socialist countries to support the struggle of the Vietnamese people against the imperialism of the USA'.[92] The Romanian effort to support Vietnam nevertheless served a further purpose. In a conversation with Hoang Tu, the extraordinary ambassador of North

Vietnam in Bucharest, Bodnaras talked at length about the impending PCC meeting that would take place in July 1966 in Bucharest, and about the Soviet attempts to turn the WP into a supranational institution.[93] In order to prevent this, he suggested using the Romanian position as hosts to invite the North Vietnamese, North Koreans and Chinese again as observers in another attempt to create a Romanian-Asian coalition.

The Romanian leadership thus tried to use the Vietnamese 'extraordinary appreciation' of their visit to Vietnam to gain support for its stance in the WP, and to broaden the scope of the WP through another attempt to include Asian observers.[94] Meanwhile, Bodnaras reported at great length to both the American and the Chinese ambassadors about his visit to Vietnam, carrying with him several proposals to improve the situation. The East German diplomat in Bucharest duly reported that Romania now unequivocally posed as a 'mediator' in the Vietnam War, too, thus reversing its previous stance, and bypassing the Poles.[95] The Romanian visit to Vietnam in May 1966 is, indeed, generally regarded as the 'start' of the Romanian mediation, even though the 'Chinese were obviously unenthusiastic about the Romanian discussions with the Vietnamese and with the Romanian position'.[96] The Polish move had forced the Romanians to jeopardise their relations with the Chinese.

The Romanian leaders ironically intended to use the WP to outwit their Polish comrades on the Vietnam issue, and decided that at the PCC meeting the Romanian delegation would propose 'to adopt […] a common position in the problem of supporting the struggle of the Vietnamese people'.[97] Romanian Foreign Minister Manescu was ordered to prepare a separate declaration or a text that could be included in the final communiqué.[98] During the conference of WP foreign ministers in Moscow in June 1966, which served to prepare the declaration on European security of the impending PCC meeting, Brezhnev asked Manescu in a private interview to support 'the Soviet proposal to adopt a Declaration on Solidarity with Vietnam in the context of the conference of the Political Consultative Committee'. Playing for time, Manescu suggested consulting the Vietnamese before discussing it within the WP, which Brezhnev considered 'really useful'. He even wondered 'who should take that initiative', as the time before the PCC meeting was short. Although Gromyko hastened to add that the Soviet comrades could 'undertake that task', Brezhnev was so keen to involve his Romanian comrades that he promised to phone Ceausescu to discuss the matter after a CPSU politburo meeting, which would take place in the afternoon.[99] Since the Vietnam War had become such a sensitive issue in the relations with China, Brezhnev was eager to side with the Romanians in order to avoid further antagonising the Chinese.

Brezhnev also questioned Manescu about the impending visit of Zhou Enlai to Romania from 16 June to 24 June. The Chinese refusal to close ranks on the Vietnam War threatened to seal the Sino–Soviet split. The Soviet leadership was therefore particularly nervous about Zhou Enlai's impending visit to Romania. Visibly 'agitated' and occasionally 'raising his voice', he expressed his concern about potential 'anti-Soviet discussions', which Ceausescu had promised 'not to allow'.[100] Brezhnev's agitation was, however, justified: in his announcement of Zhou Enlai's impending visit, the new Chinese ambassador, Tzen Iun-ciuan, started by assuring that '[w]e decisively support Romania in defence of its independence and sovereignty, against the Soviet use of the organisation of the Warsaw Treaty and COMECON for the control over its member states'.[101] Adding that the Chinese delegation would continue to Tirana after visiting Romania, it was quite clear that the Chinese regarded the Romanians as another ally in the Sino–Soviet split.

The Romanians had nevertheless overplayed their hand in their attempt to mediate between Hanoi and Washington. Zhou Enlai was not at all enchanted with Ceausescu's suggestion to engage in a 'multilateral discussion' with other governing communist parties on the Vietnam War, and he was not sensitive to Ceausescu's argument to reach a coordinated stance before the PCC meeting in July, so that 'neither country was left isolated in the Communist camp'.[102] Responding that the Chinese did not 'feel isolated', Zhou Enlai called the Soviet desire for a negotiated peace in Vietnam a 'betrayal of the Vietnamese liberation forces', and thus indirectly condemned the Romanian mediation too.[103] The Chinese obviously had no desire to contribute to a united Asian front within the WP.

Figure 5.1 Nicolae Ceausescu and his wife on a state visit to the PRC with Zhou Enlai (right), June 1971
Source: ANIC, fototeca online a comunismului românesc, photo #37058X9X66; upload.wikimedia.org/wikipedia/commons/7/7a/Vizita_oficială_a_lui_Nicolae_Ceauşescu_şi_a_Elenei_Ceauşescu_în_Republica_Populară_Chineză._Vizita_protocolară_la_Ciu_En_Lai.%28_iunie_1971%29.jpg

'One' against 'six'

The stakes were accordingly high for the PCC meeting from 4 to 6 July 1966 in Bucharest. Although the agenda was partly similar to the one in January 1965, as it also featured a declaration on European security and WP reforms, the Chinese aspect returned in the guise of a declaration on Vietnam instead of non-proliferation.[104] Meanwhile, Bucharest was swamped by Western journalists, who were curious to learn more about Romania's attitude vis-à-vis the WP. According to their Eastern European allies the Romanian leaders did not seem to mind at all that they were perceived as diverging from the rest of the alliance.[105] Thus the presence of Western press in their own capital also worked in Romanian favour by underscoring the image of the Romanian 'maverick'.[106]

As in 1965, the Romanian leaders arranged a number of bilateral meetings before the PCC session started in order to define their position. They first met with the Soviet leadership, which showed a great willingness to accommodate Romanian wishes. Brezhnev suggested adopting a declaration on Vietnam 'on the first day' so that it would have 'a good political resonance'.[107] The Soviet leaders had composed their own declaration after consulting the Vietnamese, as Manescu had recommended in Moscow in June.[108] This time the Romanian leaders came clean, however, and presented their Soviet comrades with their own version.[109] Since the Romanians had also consulted the Vietnamese, Ceausescu suggested asking the Romanian and Soviet ministers of foreign affairs to merge the two 'into one single proposal so as to ease tomorrow's discussions'.[110]

Brezhnev reacted enthusiastically, although he regretted that the East German and Polish ministers were not there yet 'so that we could work with the four of us'. It was, however, again Gromyko who severely intervened by claiming that '[a] Soviet-Romanian proposal will not be published, because we had agreed in Moscow that the Soviets would present a proposal'. As in Moscow in June, Brezhnev seemed much more willing than his Foreign Minister Gromyko to allow the Romanian comrades to take the initiative. Ceausescu nevertheless conceded that he would not call it 'a Soviet-Romanian proposal', and appeased the Kremlin by stressing that he had 'the same thoughts' on Vietnam.[111] Ceausescu's next mission was to see if he could also gain the support of the Polish comrades. The Polish delegation was, however, not at all enchanted with the Romanian suggestion to publish a 'Soviet' declaration on Vietnam the next day. It would give the impression 'that we have met here only for the problem of Vietnam', when the *raison d'être* of the PCC meeting was in fact the adoption of a declaration on European security.[112] Gomulka in particular was loth to allow Ceausescu to undermine his campaign for European security after he had already appropriated his initiative on Vietnam.

The customary disagreement between the Polish and Romanian delegations gained an interesting dynamic during the first session of the first secretaries.

Presumably aiming to forestall the Romanian-Soviet attempt to publish a Vietnam declaration on the first day, the Polish delegation had quickly prepared its own draft, in which it had suggested some considerable changes to the Soviet one.[113] The Romanian delegation had, in turn, decided to present a separate proposal after all, in addition to the 'Soviet' declaration that the party leaders had received just before the meeting. The first secretaries were thus suddenly confronted with *three* different proposals of the Vietnam declaration, two of which they had not even received. The champion of surprise proposals, Walter Ulbricht, was particularly annoyed by this course of events, and suggested 'taking the Soviet draft as the basis', since '[w]e only possess the Soviet draft'. Gomulka and Ceausescu nevertheless wanted all three drafts to be considered, which was supported by Brezhnev, who stated that 'all delegations have the right to submit their own drafts'.[114] Although all other allies were equally indignant about being surprised with two more drafts, they concurred with the suggestion that the foreign ministers should take all three proposals as a basis.

During the ensuing meeting of foreign ministers the impasse on the proposals was such that the only decision that was reached was to create a working party to resolve the issue.[115] Ceausescu, meanwhile, was keen to keep the initiative on Vietnam, and convened the first secretaries the next morning to discuss the matter again. Gomulka explained that the declaration needed to have 'a very serious character', the tone of which should be 'closer to a note instead of a resolution'. When Ceausescu objected that it 'should be a firm Declaration, not with the character of a diplomatic note', Gomulka replied that he was 'surprised' that the Romanian proposal seemed more appropriate for 'a dinner party' or 'a newspaper article' than for 'such an elevated institution' as the Warsaw Pact. With this remark, all hell broke loose: echoing Chinese and Vietnamese rhetoric on an inclination to negotiate, Ceausescu responded that he 'had not wanted to characterise the Polish draft', but that it in fact represented 'a stimulus for capitulation in the face of aggression'. Gomulka strongly rebuked Ceausescu for 'not controlling his words', in 'his position as a host', and added that the Polish delegation had felt compelled to compose its own draft after it had been suddenly confronted with the Romanian one.[116]

Brezhnev, meanwhile, had lost control of the conversation, and only succeeded in intervening with the apology that he 'did not want to enter in these polemics', and that it was 'incorrect' to blame the Polish draft for 'capitulation in the face of American imperialism'.[117] Brezhnev's reference to 'polemics' was unwittingly apt, as it did indeed seem as though the Sino–Soviet polemics had been imported once more into the WP through the Romanian and Polish delegations. The crux of the different drafts was indeed that the Romanians sided with the Chinese in emphasising American 'aggression', while the Poles agreed with the Americans that the option for a 'peaceful resolution', and indirectly Polish mediation, should be left open.[118] The WP dynamics had thus once again been determined by Polish and Romanian disagreement on the Sino–Soviet split, which had reduced Brezhnev to the role of a bystander. The irony resided nevertheless in the fact that the Romanian delegation had managed to coordinate its draft with the Soviets, even though the Soviets had been much closer to the Polish position in the run-up to the PCC meeting.

The acrimony of the meeting of the first secretaries spilled over into the foreign ministers, who disagreed on two versions of a draft by the above-mentioned working party, one *with* and one *without* Polish amendments. When the other foreign ministers conceded that they favoured the former, Gromyko remarked that 'six participants could not accept the procedure of one', to which Manescu replied that 'six parties cannot impose their will on one party either'. As the foreign ministers found themselves in 'an impossible situation', it was decided 'to report to the first secretaries [...] that this document was accepted by six ministers as a basis'.[119] The Romanian delegation had emphatically failed to reap the fruits of its coordination with the Soviet comrades. The Poles were, once more, ahead on the Vietnam issue. Meanwhile, the meeting had painfully revealed a complete failure to deal with disunity. In the tradition of democratic centralism, there was little experience on reaching a compromise.

In the meeting of first secretaries and prime ministers Maurer and Ceausescu insisted that the latest version was 'unacceptable' as a basis. This time Brezhnev lost his patience, 'stood up – as he does when he wants to seem imposing',[120] and added that '[i]f the worst comes to the worst, the declaration can be signed by six countries'. This infuriated Ceausescu, who strongly condemned 'this kind of pressure', and claimed that the Romanians would write 'a letter to all [communist] parties' to explain their stance, and that they, too, would publish a separate declaration. Gomulka angrily replied that '[w]e, comrades, do not exercise pressure on you, [...] but you attempt to exercise pressure on us, on all other six delegations', and Brezhnev 'categorically rejected the accusation', while blaming the Romanian delegation for 'the threat' of writing to all other communist parties.[121] This was, indeed, a serious threat, as it would mean an open break within the WP after the one within the communist movement. During the final discussions Ceausescu withdrew most of his objections, but the Romanian delegation had the last word after all, by forcing Gomulka to erase the Polish amendment that the communist countries would cultivate 'permanent contacts' with each other considering their support to Vietnam.[122] Ceausescu clearly wanted to undermine another Polish attempt at mediation. The Vietnam declaration had taken up so much time that the Kremlin had to postpone the discussion on reforms, which the Romanian delegation had compelled it to do, anyhow, as we have seen in the previous chapter.[123]

The Kremlin was, however, not at all pleased with the course of events. According to the Romanian participants, the Soviet delegation had been in 'a permanent condition of nervousness and irritation', and had displayed 'a lack of tact and politeness vis-à-vis the Romanian part'. Moreover, Gromyko's personal secretary was overheard to say to a translator of the Soviet delegation, 'that it is presently very difficult to work with the socialist countries and realise a unity of views'. Referring to the Vietnam declaration in particular, he said: 'It used to be very easy [...]: the SU proposed something, and the other socialist countries adopted it without discussions. Now it is no longer that simple. Every [country] has its own opinions.' He added that 'this is very good, [...] but we lose too much time'. The conversation was 'bluntly interrupted' when a Soviet delegate approached.[124] The emancipatory process within the alliance could, however, not be stemmed so easily. The views of the NSWP members began to overshadow those of the Soviet leaders, who failed to formulate an adequate response to the lack of unity.

Lessons for the future

Not only were the Soviet leaders ill at ease with the way in which the PCC meeting proceeded, but several NSWP members, too, felt that the Romanian position had left little space for their own point of view. The East German delegation had withdrawn all its amendments on the Vietnam declaration, because so much time was spent on the Romanian ones.[125] The Hungarian delegation found the way in which 'the documents came into being' extremely unsatisfactory, and concluded that the Romanian delegation was particularly obstinate in 'procedural matters'.[126] Kadar commented on the fact that 'the Romanian comrades were a step closer to the demagogic position of the Chinese', and they saw this reflected 'in their being extremely anti-American'. Moreover, they 'were waiting for an opportunity to be insulted' in order to pick a quarrel on the Vietnam declaration. The fact that the party leaders managed to reach a compromise on the Vietnam declaration was, according to Kadar, due to the unity of the 'six':

> It also played a role to some extent that there was a unified front against the Romanians without any kind of 'conspiracy'. This influenced the Romanians to a certain degree. They are retreating and coming closer without surrendering their independence. We do not know what impact this will have in the future, but it is certain that the Romanians will deliberate on their experiences as we have done and will reach certain conclusions.[127]

The Romanians did, indeed, deliberate on their experiences, and reached very different conclusions. Ceausescu emphasised the Romanian input in the Vietnam declaration, and stressed that the Poles 'were the ones who fought for every single issue', whereas 'the others [...] supported our position'. Although the support for the Romanian position did not conform to reality, Ceausescu rightly underlined that 'the most zealous proponents of a different position [...] were the Poles'. Another Politburo member added that the Soviets 'were easily persuaded, until the Polish [delegation] showed up'. The

192 *The dynamics of dissent, 1965–68*

Polish opposition was a real setback for the Romanian delegation, whose Romanian-Soviet declaration would probably have been easily approved if there had not been a Polish alternative. It is striking that the Soviet position seemed so susceptible to input from NSWP members, who once again determined the dynamics of the debate. The Romanian delegation was greatly pleased about this, and Bodnaras considered 'this conference [...] a turning point', since it was 'the first time that, at such a high level Summit, divergent points of view were discussed and presented by the most authorised decision makers'. He added that '[f]rom here [we should] draw conclusions about how [such] discussions should be handled in the future'.[128]

The Bucharest conference was a turning point in a number of ways. Whereas the Romanian leaders considered it a 'great victory', and intended to stretch further their room for manoeuvre within the WP, the other WP members were musing on ways to neutralise Romanian dissent. The acrimonious debates on the Vietnam declaration had made all participants more self-conscious about their role in the WP, and stood in sharp contrast to the successful conclusion of the declaration on European security, which has been treated in the previous chapter. The discussions on Vietnam were a severe blow to the Kremlin, as it had failed to seize the initiative between the Romanian and Polish polemics, and had thus been reduced to an arbiter. The WP had enabled the Romanians to undermine the hegemonic position of the Soviet Union to such an extent that only the Poles rose to the challenge of fundamentally opposing the Romanians. With the Romanians defending Chinese antagonism in the Vietnam War, and the Poles supporting attempts at negotiation, the Sino–Soviet split had been imported into the WP. Meanwhile, the alliance ran the risk of being hijacked by Romanian dissent instead of Soviet hegemony. This looming fate forced the NSWP members to define their position all the more clearly.

Vietnam revisited

A month after the PCC meeting Mao launched his Cultural Revolution, which was intended to provide the Chinese people with a shortcut to communism. After the Great Leap Forward had failed, this was the second concrete policy of radicalisation, in which the propaganda against Soviet revisionism served as a pretext to persecute any 'revisionist' within China. After the refusal to coordinate aid for Vietnam with the Soviet Union had already cost the Chinese leadership several allies, and had exhausted the patience of North Vietnam, the launch of the Cultural Revolution was a further step towards complete Chinese isolation. It was, moreover, another indication that the Sino–Soviet split had reached the point of no return. The Romanian leadership therefore became more cautious in condemning the American aggression in Vietnam, and did not even mention it in any speech after the PCC meeting. Although Maurer went on a secret mission to Hanoi in September 1966, his lunch appointment with Zhou Enlai in Beijing on his return took place in 'a cool atmosphere'.[129] According to the East German diplomat in Bucharest, the Romanian leadership intended to attempt to mediate again.[130]

The East German observation was very perceptive.[131] With the launch of the 'Cultural Revolution' the 'friendship' with the Chinese had become less useful, as it had become increasingly hard to take China seriously as a global player. After the Romanian leadership had already gone it alone within the WP by establishing diplomatic relations with the FRG in January 1967, and by refusing to break off diplomatic relations with Israel after it had taken control in the Six-Day War of the Syrian Golan Heights, the Egyptian Gaza strip, and the West Bank of Jordan in a pre-emptive strike in early June 1967, it needed to develop another initiative so as not to leave itself isolated on all fronts. Moreover, the Romanian lack of support for the Arab cause had jeopardised the prospects of Romanian oil imports from the Middle East, and had prompted the Romanian leadership to concentrate on the development of its nuclear programme instead, by turning once again to the Americans.[132] The Romanian stance in the Vietnam War had, however, compromised American support of the Romanian nuclear programme, and the Romanian leadership had to find a way to 'remain relevant in a context in which the maverick image was no longer enough'.[133] With the Sino-Romanian friendship a spent force, the Romanian leadership no longer had to worry about antagonising Mao. Mediation between Washington and Hanoi thus seemed the most promising way out of the Romanian predicament.

On 26 June 1967 Romanian Prime Minister Maurer met with US President Johnson in the wake of a meeting of the UN General Assembly. American support had become particularly imperative as the Romanian minister of foreign affairs, Corneliu Manescu, was lobbying for the position of president of the General Assembly of the UN.[134] Such support was considerably facilitated by the fact that both Romania and the USA had sided with Israel after the Six-Day War. Maurer explained that Romania had a 'special interest in settling the Vietnamese question', because 'when there is a crisis or tension in the world [...] countries are told to get together, to renounce some of their sovereignty and some of their independence and to obey the command of another state', and that 'it is this consideration which causes Romania to interfere in problems which really are beyond her and to try to settle them'.[135] Romanian mediation thus primarily served to maintain Romania's scope for manoeuvre in the international arena, which also explains the Romanian attempt to mediate between China and the Soviet Union in 1964. A negotiated settlement in Vietnam would diminish Soviet pressure to close ranks within the WP. Negotiating between Hanoi and Washington was, however, not sufficient to decrease international tension. For that purpose, Romania needed to keep China on board.

The Romanian leadership therefore continued to play the Chinese card a little longer, and in July 1967 Maurer led a delegation to Beijing. The discussion between Maurer and Zhou Enlai began with the habitual condemnation of the Warsaw Pact, in which 'forms of relations had taken root that do not correspond to the principles of equality among sovereign states'. Maurer even added that de Gaulle had said that he was 'convinced' that within the WP 'the same would happen [as within NATO]', namely that 'the example of Romania would be followed by other countries'.[136] The rest of the conversation ran somewhat less smoothly, because Maurer had to explain the motives for establishing diplomatic contacts with the FRG in January 1967, which could count on little sympathy with the radicalised Chinese leadership.

On the second day, the discussions took a more complicated turn, as Maurer proposed to participate in a conference of all communist countries to coordinate support for Vietnam and to prepare negotiations between the Vietnamese and the Americans for a peaceful resolution of the Vietnam War. This conference was an initiative from the Polish and Soviet leaders, who had asked their Romanian comrades to sign a collective letter to the Chinese communist party that contained the proposal for such a conference. Although Romania was the only WP member (other than Albania) that refused to sign, Maurer and his aide Niculescu-Mizil were extremely insistent on defending the convention of such a conference in their meeting with Zhou Enlai. Having just begun to pose as a mediator between North Vietnam and the USA, the Romanian leadership was compelled grudgingly to approve of the Polish-Soviet initiative to pave the way for a negotiated peace.

This course of events was particularly striking in a number of ways. On the one hand the Romanians had stressed their independence by refusing to sign the letter, and had sealed the division of 'six against one' that had dominated the Bucharest PCC meeting. On the other hand, they had abandoned their principled opposition to a conference of communist parties, which had previously resulted in their boycott of the consultative meeting on 1 March 1965, and in their anger about the Polish initiative for such a convention in January 1966. The Polish leadership had continued to strive after a position as a mediator in negotiations between the USA and Vietnam with Soviet support, but the Romanians had made a U-turn in their opposition to a negotiated resolution of the Vietnam War. To the Chinese leadership the Romanian delegation nevertheless argued that both China and Romania should participate in such a conference, as its contributions could be decisive, as the Romanians had experienced within the WP:

> Our experience has shown that when we have fought with clarity and firmness for our point of view in those meetings, we have achieved that a series of unjust points of view that had been prepared, were neither accepted nor put into practice.[137]

Maurer stressed that 'a single country' could achieve so much, to which Niculescu-Mizil added that it could achieve even more 'together with many more socialist countries'. Although the Romanian delegation attempted to depict 'the extraordinarily important role that the active presence of the PRC would have at socialist conferences' in the most flattering terms, the real motive behind inviting China seemed less congenial:

> Of the countries of the socialist system those countries who meet within the WP meet relatively frequently; the others very rarely. The Asian socialist countries do not come to combat the negative tendencies there where they manifest themselves most actively, nor do they come to contribute to the clarification of the problems of the relations between socialist countries. And this whole battle is waged only by Romania.[138]

The Romanian delegation seemed, in short, fed up with the way in which it had been defending Chinese interests, when the pay-off for their support was nil: the Chinese refused to participate in anything. The Romanians were, at least, actively engaged in the same questions as the Kremlin, though frequently disagreeing. Their campaign to involve the Asian countries in a coalition against Soviet hegemony had proven a great disappointment.

The Romanian U-turn on the Sino–Soviet split came too late. The Romanian meeting with the Chinese ironically coincided with a Polish proposal to organise an international conference of the 'six' WP countries to 'harmonise their opinions on China'.[139] The Soviet leaders had, already, given up on reaching a coordinated stance on the Sino–Soviet split together with Romania, and gladly endorsed the Polish proposal, which served to isolate Romania further. From 14–21 December 1967 delegations from the six communist parties met in Moscow, together with a delegation from Mongolia, in order to reach a common stance to 'confront the policy and ideology of the Mao Zedong Group [...] for the defence of Marxism-Leninism'.[140] This conference retrospectively represented the foundation of a new institution, the so-called 'China International' or 'Interkit' in Russian, to deal with the Chinese threat. Representing a kind of ideal Warsaw Pact – without Romanian dissent, but with Mongolian support – these countries would continue to meet until 1986.[141] Through the foundation of the Interkit, the Romanian isolation within the WP had been institutionalised.[142]

The Romanian mediation between Washington and Hanoi nevertheless paid off, when on 19 September 1967 Romanian Foreign Minister Manescu was elected as the first communist president to the General Assembly of the United Nations.[143] Romania's turn Westward proved more beneficial than its orientation towards China. The Romanian leadership therefore turned again to the Soviet comrades. After a delegation led by Maurer had visited Vietnam in order to convince the Vietnamese leaders of the importance of negotiations with the Americans at the end of September 1967, the delegation stopped in Moscow on its way to Romania.[144] Maurer emphasised that he agreed with his Soviet comrades on the necessity of a communist conference, and even thanked them for 'the powerful support' they provided, which enabled the Vietnamese to maintain 'great independence [...] in their position'.[145] Thus the Chinese rigidity in the Sino–Soviet split had ultimately driven the Romanians into the arms of their Soviet comrades.

Between November 1967 and February 1968 the Romanians embarked on a kind of shuttle diplomacy between Washington, Hanoi, Moscow and Beijing in an attempt to get all parties round the negotiating table. In line with their strategy to 'fight while negotiating', the North Vietnamese nevertheless launched their 'Tet Offensive' on 30 January 1968, which nipped the negotiations in the bud. The Romanian mediation was, however, duly rewarded, and in April 1968 US Secretary of State Dean Rusk proposed to pass a West-East Trade Bill, which would also facilitate a nuclear deal with the Romanians, at a National Security Council meeting.[146] The Romanian mediation had once again primarily succeeded in serving Romanian interests.

Consultations on non-proliferation

The Soviet leadership, meanwhile, proved amenable to Romanian interests in nuclear terms too, and it showed increasing good will towards the Romanian stance on non-proliferation. As Maurer had already told Zhou Enlai in the abovementioned conversation, the Kremlin agreed with the Romanian objections to the non-proliferation treaty, but 'had not been able to obtain much in the negotiations with the U.S.A.' Romanian and Soviet foreign ministry officials had even collaborated for several weeks on Romanian proposals 'for the improvement of the draft treaty', although 'concrete results were not obtained'.[147] The Romanian leadership had, however, become so confident about its influence within the WP, that it had formally requested the convention of a PCC meeting on 17 May 1967. Thus the Romanian leadership had made a U-turn on the WP too: after trying time and again to thwart the convention of such meetings, it had in fact taken the initiative in convening a PCC meeting itself. Despite its obstructive use of the WP, the Romanian leaders had begun to see that the alliance provided them, too, with an opportunity to make their voices heard.

The Kremlin had, in fact, trodden its ground extremely carefully regarding the non-proliferation treaty. Throughout the negotiations with the US leadership, the Soviet leaders had asked their WP allies for input into the treaty. This was a stark contrast with the Limited Nuclear Test-Ban Treaty, which had been concluded between the Soviet and US leaders without any input from their respective allies in August 1963. The Kremlin had consulted with the socialist countries in October 1966. In February 1967, less than a month after the Romanian *Alleingang* on diplomatic relations with the FRG, the Soviet foreign policy official A. Soldatov even consulted Romanian Foreign Minister Manescu in Bucharest on the latest version of the non-proliferation treaty, while emphasising that 'he was "ready to respond to any question, to register any observation, now or later, and, if you consider it necessary, to explain to other comrades of the Romanian leadership the Soviet position in this problem"'.[148] He also underlined that the Soviet Union had already supported several proposals on nuclear disarmament, as the Romanians had wished.

The US government had proposed that the current draft of the non-proliferation treaty be presented at the ENDC in Geneva, of which Romania was a member, but the Soviet leaders had responded that they would only do so 'after consultations with the fraternal countries'. Soldatov stressed that it 'depended only on the Romanian reply', when it would be presented in Geneva.[149] After the Romanian leadership had kept its Soviet comrades in the dark for another ten days on its judgement, Soldatov requested another meeting with Manescu in Bucharest, as the other five WP countries had 'already communicated their reply'.[150] The Soviet leadership thus went out of its way to include the Romanian comrades in the process, which was a stark contrast with the Chinese disinterest in any Romanian initiative.

Brezhnev also welcomed the Romanian proposal to convene a PCC meeting to discuss the non-proliferation treaty, as he told Ceausescu and Maurer during their bilateral summit meeting in Moscow in March 1967.[151] He emphasised the importance of socialist unity, especially considering the disunity in the West on non-proliferation, where France and the FRG still strongly disagreed with the treaty. In April 1967 Soviet and Romanian foreign ministry officials collaborated in Moscow on a draft treaty, and in May 1967 the Soviet and American leadership represented a new draft treaty at the ENDC disarmament conference in Geneva, which also contained several Romanian proposals. The other WP members were, however, less enthusiastic about the Romanian proposal to convene the PCC.[152] Although the Kremlin seemed relieved about the fact that Romania stayed firmly in the WP fold, Romania's allies apparently wanted to prevent another Romanian attempt to hijack the WP. Just as the Romanian leadership had prevented Ulbricht from convening PCC meetings three years earlier, so the other NSWP leaders were not enchanted about Romanian attempts to dominate the alliance either.

Non-proliferation under pressure

The Romanian leaders nevertheless maintained a very ambivalent attitude towards the Kremlin, and continued to inform the Chinese about their stance on non-proliferation, while also requesting a summit meeting with the Chinese leadership.[153] At the same time Ceausescu explicitly proposed to convene the PCC to discuss the treaty in a letter on 31 January 1968, two weeks after the ENDC had begun to examine the treaty's new draft.[154] Ceausescu was particularly 'vexed that the question of non-proliferation had not been discussed between the states of the Warsaw Pact', whereas 'the question had already been discussed several times in the NATO framework'.[155]

The other WP members agreed with the East German leaders that they 'did not see its utility', as they 'agreed with the treaty as it is', but they ultimately supported the proposal.[156] They probably acted on the same motive as the Hungarian leader, Janos Kadar, who did not consider it 'expedient to reject the Romanian comrades' proposal, because it would make it harder to convene the Political Consultative Committee of the Warsaw Pact on other occasions'.[157] Matters were accordingly turned upside down, with the East German leadership attempting to thwart a PCC meeting proposed by their Romanian comrades. To pressurise their allies further, the Romanians had already 'sharply attacked' the current draft treaty at the ENDC in Geneva on 6 February.[158]

Ceausescu nevertheless had 'strictly necessary amendments' to the current draft of the non-proliferation treaty, which he wanted to discuss before it was presented for approval at the ENDC on 15 March. Apart from including 'a new article' on 'continuing efforts for nuclear disarmament', the Romanian leadership also proposed a conference after five years to analyse 'what has been done' and 'what must be done in future', and a guarantee of nuclear countries not to attack non-nuclear countries. Although Ceausescu was aware that the other WP members would argue that 'everything that has been proposed now is everything that can be obtained', since 'the Americans will not want any more', he insisted that 'we should fight and we should not sign a treaty at any price'. The price for a good treaty was so high that Ceausescu already informed his comrades before the PCC meeting took place that a communiqué would probably be adopted on 'the Vietnamese problem', with which he was planning to agree.[159] After the Romanian delegation had entrenched itself on the Vietnamese issue during the PCC meeting in July 1966, it was now prepared to sacrifice its principled position on Vietnam for the sake of maintaining its own nuclear scope for manoeuvre.

At a meeting of deputy foreign ministers in Berlin on 26–27 February 1968 it became clear that the Romanian delegation would have to fight a hard battle to get anywhere with its proposed amendments on the non-proliferation treaty. All other delegations strongly supported the draft treaty, in which a great number of Romanian amendments were already included, as the Soviet delegate, Kuznetsov, emphasised. The Romanian deputy foreign minister attempted to blackmail his allies into concurring by stating that it was the 'sovereign right of every country' to decide when to present its separate proposals to the ENDC in Geneva.[160] The meeting of deputy foreign ministers thus amounted to nothing more than an exchange of opinions, in which the division of six against one was sealed yet again.

At the same time, the Romanian U-turn on a communist conference had resulted in deteriorating relations with the Kremlin after all. Although the Romanian leadership was disappointed with the Chinese refusal to participate, it was eventually more disillusioned with the consultative meeting about the conference, which took place in Budapest in February–March 1968. Instead of 'an exchange of opinions', the consultative meeting confronted the Romanian leadership with 'a fait accompli', as it '[w]as immediately proposed that the conference would be convened in Moscow, in the autumn of this year', which seemed a pretext to establish the CPSU once again as 'leading centre of the communist movement'.[161] Moreover, the Polish delegation, 'which had been the most harsh', had already attacked the Chinese comrades on the first day, and so did the Soviet and other delegations.[162] The Romanian delegates themselves were particularly violently attacked by a delegate from Syria, who blamed them for being the only communist party to continue siding with Israel after the crisis in the Middle East.[163]

The Romanian delegation decided to leave halfway through the conference in protest, which allegedly resulted in a proposal, *inter alia* supported by the Polish and East German delegations, to condemn Romania.[164] According to the Italian communists, who supported the Romanians, 'the Soviets were much more moderate than the East Germans and Poles', which anticipates the East German and Polish hard line in the Prague Spring, which will be discussed in the next chapter. The Italian party leader, Enrico Berlinguer, even contrasted the 'East German-Polish extreme point of view' with 'the Soviet position', which 'proves incapable of assuring mediation and hegemony'.[165] The East German and Polish proactive stance at the consultative conference on 1 March 1965 had thus turned into extremism, whereas Soviet hegemony had been undermined altogether. The consultative meeting, which could have served to conceal the differences between Romania and its WP allies, thus resulted in another split.

Romania under pressure

This debacle hardly boded well for the PCC meeting, which was to take place in Sofia on 6–7 March 1968. The other WP delegations had drawn their conclusions from the PCC meeting in Bucharest in July 1966, and they had carefully studied the Romanian proposed amendments to the non-proliferation treaty in order to refute them with success. Under the pretext of 'sovereign equality' and 'non-interference in domestic affairs', the Romanian proposals on limited inspections and on opting out of the treaty clearly served to keep all options open for developing a Romanian nuclear programme unhampered. It was no coincidence that 'the Romanian comrades' approach lends support to the opponents of the Nuclear Non-proliferation Treaty', as the Bulgarian leadership observed.[166] Meanwhile, the Romanian leaders themselves were convinced that they 'should not sign a treaty at any price'.[167]

The East German leadership was particularly worried about the fact that the Romanian amendments could thwart the non-proliferation treaty altogether, since that would lead to 'a strengthened position of Bonn', which 'attempted to prevent the conclusion of such a treaty by all means'. The treaty was of particular importance to the GDR, because it would mean the final blow to MLF, and therefore weaken the position of the FRG. The Romanian proposal that nuclear powers should never attack a non-nuclear power would nevertheless undermine East German security, as 'this guarantee would also [apply] to those states, on whose territories nuclear weapons are stationed', such as West Germany.[168] The other WP members agreed with this analysis, and Brezhnev even emphasised in a private conversation with

Ceausescu that 'West Germany would thank us' if Ceausescu's proposals were accepted.[169]

During the actual meeting the 'six' attempted to avoid antagonising the Romanian delegation by emphasising that their proposals 'correspond to the interests of the socialist countries', but are 'maximalist and unrealistic, because there is no way that the other side could be compelled to accept them'. Brezhnev even repeated time and again that a lot of Romanian proposals had already been included in the draft treaty. The atmosphere nevertheless soon turned sour, as Ceausescu declared that the Romanian leaders 'would present their proposals [...] in Geneva, [...] at the forthcoming session of the UN, in their whole foreign policy and in their public programme as well', whereas the 'six' feared that the amendments 'could lead to the postponement or even failure of the treaty'. The Romanian dissidents thus threatened to undermine a treaty, which the other WP members considered 'a victory for the socialist states, primarily for the Soviet Union, and a new phase in our offensive against imperialism's positions'.[170] Not only had the treaty been negotiated at length with all WP members, but the Soviet leadership had also succeeded in drafting a treaty that was acceptable to the USA and most of its allies, even though it would definitively prevent any projects on nuclear sharing, such as MLF. The treaty thus represented a peaceful solution to an issue that had caused so much unrest in the WP in the first half of the 1960s.

This time 'the six' were resolved not to yield to Romanian pressure. The Romanian leaders might have concluded from the Bucharest meeting in July 1966 that they could force their allies into submission, but the other WP members had also become more self-conscious about dealing with Romanian dissidence. The Romanian *Alleingang* on nuclear issues exhausted its allies' patience. Gomulka and Zhivkov even suggested expelling Romania from the WP in order to 'get rid of the factors impeding our organisation's work'. 'The six' now decided to live up to their threats from July 1966 by signing a declaration *without* Romania, in which they strongly supported the Soviet draft for a non-proliferation treaty.[171] Although they did not sign the declaration in the name of the Warsaw Pact, but as six individual states, it clearly signalled to the West that the vast majority of the alliance did *not* support the Romanian amendments. Meanwhile, the non-proliferation discussion had eclipsed the other issues to such an extent that a declaration on Vietnam was discussed and signed during a break. The same applied to the communiqué, which only mentioned that non-proliferation had been discussed in an atmosphere that was 'frank and comradely'.[172] Or, in the words of the Hungarian delegation, 'the atmosphere at the meeting was not exactly like a wedding feast'.[173]

It was, of course, a blow to the WP that the disagreements between Romania and the rest were made public for the first time in the history of the alliance, but the declaration of 'the six' had also served to undermine the Romanian position. Although Ceausescu triumphantly stated upon his return that the PCC 'must be satisfied with this role, and not the role up to now, to approve everything the Soviet Union does', his allies were not at all pleased with the way Ceausescu intended to undermine everything the Soviet Union did.[174] Without any Soviet pressure the other NSWP members rallied behind the Kremlin in supporting a treaty that they genuinely deemed to be in their interests. According to Hungarian Premier Jeno Fock, the separate declaration might enable 'the six' to 'have a greater impact on the Romanians [...] without causing a schism in the Warsaw Treaty'.[175] In the eyes of the other WP members, it was not the Soviet leadership, but the Romanian leadership that threatened to undermine their interests. On a great number of issues the interests of the communist countries coincided, and the maverick position of Romania was perhaps a boon to the West, but a nuisance to the East.

The main gain of the PCC meeting ironically consisted in the fact that 'the six' had found a way to bypass Romanian dissidence. Ceausescu was, accordingly, not amused when Zhivkov told him about the separate declaration.[176] The discussion in which the six had agreed on the declaration even went so smoothly that Kadar suggested that 'at some point, under calmer circumstances, when daily matters are not overwhelming, the first secretaries and prime ministers of the six countries should get together for the sake of unfettered, comradely talks'.[177] The Prague Spring was, at that stage, no topic for discussion at all, and the new Czechoslovak party leader, Alexander Dubcek, was an undisputed part of 'the six'. Although Kadar suggested meeting no later than June, the next meeting would, in fact, take place much sooner and under very different circumstances. However, by that stage, 'the six' would have turned into 'the five'.

Meanwhile, Ceausescu already sensed that Dubcek might be a potential ally, and reported to the politburo that '[t]he discussions with the Czech were good'.[178] In a private conversation during the conference Dubcek had expressed his regret that he had been unable to meet Ceausescu earlier, as he had been 'greatly occupied by our internal problems', which was the only reference to the Prague Spring. He added that the Romanian proposals were 'right, rational', but that he 'feared that we cannot obtain more from the Americans', and that he preferred 'such a treaty instead of nothing'. After Dubcek had confessed that he 'did not know those problems too well', Ceausescu inspired Dubcek with doubts by arguing that the American interest in concluding the treaty should be used to improve it still more.[179] The Czechoslovak report nevertheless strongly condemned the Romanian 'stubborn and unrealistic attitude', which lacked any 'willingness, no matter how small, to find a common standpoint with the [other] socialist countries regarding the treaty'.[180] At this stage 'the Czech' still intended to close ranks with the other five against Romania.

At the last moment the Romanian leadership decided to join 'the six'. After it had continued to argue that the treaty did not cater for the 'interests of non-nuclear states' during further negotiations at the UN, it radically changed its course in June 1968, when it became clear that an overwhelming majority of members supported the treaty.[181] The Romanian delegation suddenly contributed constructively to the negotiations, and attempted to pretend 'that Romania was never against the treaty, but had an active part in its perfection and improvement'.[182] When the conclusion of the non-proliferation treaty had become irreversible, the Romanian leaders wanted to share in its success. Unlike their French soul mates, the Romanian delegation ultimately decided to sign the non-proliferation treaty on 1 July 1968, together with 62 other states.[183]

Conclusion: Romania reconsidered

The Sino–Soviet split initially again provided the Romanian leadership with a useful instrument to increase its scope for manoeuvre in the second half of the 1960s: since Brezhnev and Kosygin hoped to repair Sino-Soviet relations, they had to tolerate the fact that Sino-Romanian relations could be cultivated at Soviet expense. Meanwhile the Romanian leadership could defend its own interests under the guise of defending those of the Chinese: thus the Chinese stance on non-proliferation conveniently served the Romanian purpose of keeping all options open in terms of its nuclear policy, as happened during the PCC meeting in 1965. With the Sino–Soviet split as leverage, Ceausescu had at least as many cards to play in the WP as de Gaulle had in NATO.

The Romanians' attempt to explore the Sino–Soviet split for their own interests coincided with their drive to expand the WP to include Asian countries as observers, so that the Romanian leadership could build a grander coalition. The Chinese leadership, for one, was, however, not interested in participating in WP sessions, and in that respect the Romanian courting of Asia was to no avail. The Vietnam War, too, complicated Romania's 'neutral' stance within the Sino–Soviet split. Unlike their Polish comrades, who did not have to worry about antagonising China, the Romanian leaders were not in a position to mediate. Meanwhile, China's refusal to coordinate assistance to Vietnam frustrated even its Asian allies, and the Romanian leadership was closer to the Soviet position than it dared to admit. The PCC meeting in July 1966 nevertheless still witnessed a sharp divide on the Vietnam War in which the 'one' maverick, Romania, attempted to pressurise its 'six' allies into submission. Meanwhile, the other WP comrades began to muse on effective ways to neutralise Romanian dissent.

Once the Sino–Soviet split was beyond repair, it could no longer be used as leverage over the Soviet comrades. With the advent of the Chinese Cultural Revolution in August 1966, Romanian foreign policy made another U-turn. Ceausescu and his cronies suddenly backed an initiative on convening a conference on Vietnam, and blamed their Chinese and other Asian allies for leaving the Romanians alone to do all the hard work. They even decided again to adopt the posture of mediator themselves, but their balancing act between the Soviet Union, China and the USA became increasingly difficult to sustain, and Romania ran the risk of isolation. It now seemed to dawn on the Romanian leadership that its Eastern European allies were more reliable than the Asian ones. The *flexible* foreign policy thus turned into an *inconsistent* one, and the scope for manoeuvre robbed the Romanian leaders of a rudder to steady their course: manoeuvrability had turned into vulnerability.

The Romanian reorientation towards Eastern Europe culminated in their attempt to convene a PCC meeting on non-proliferation in 1967. Although de Gaulle had withdrawn France from the integrated structures of NATO, Ceausescu seemed to follow the opposite course. The Romanian leadership had obviously begun to see the benefits of the alliance as an instrument for asserting its independence. By expanding their own room for manoeuvre, the Romanian leaders had nevertheless decreased the manoeuvrability of their allies. It therefore took the Romanian leaders almost a year to gain their allies' consent, and 'the six' were determined not to allow the Romanians to hijack the meeting as they had done in July 1966. The PCC finally convened in March 1968, and ended in a defeat for Romania. This time 'the six' closed ranks and decided to declare their support for non-proliferation without Romania. This was a bold move, in which 'the six' unprecedentedly took a public stance against Romania. The Romanian leadership was, accordingly, already excluded from decision making before the Prague Spring began to play a role in the Soviet bloc. Although Romania could be independent with impunity, it could no longer do so within the WP.

The Romanian signature on the non-proliferation treaty in July 1968 therefore does not testify to any Soviet pressure, but to a genuine desire to avoid further isolation. Moreover, the evolution of the treaty illustrated a new course in Soviet foreign policy: whereas the NSWP allies had not been involved at all in the Limited Nuclear Test-Ban Treaty that was concluded in August 1963, they had been elaborately consulted on non-proliferation. Since the actual treaty contained a great number of Romanian proposals, Romania would undermine its own interests if it refused to sign at the last moment. The Romanian signature should therefore be regarded as an acknowledgement of its input, rather than a confirmation of Soviet hegemony.

Contrary to conventional wisdom, Romanian pressure was considered a much greater threat to the NSWP members than Soviet hegemony. Although the Kremlin is usually depicted as the autocratic hegemon, one should bear in mind that on many issues Soviet and Eastern European interests coincided, whereas the Romanian position was a genuine anomaly. No other Eastern European country apart from Albania prioritised contacts with Asia over Eastern Europe, nor did any other NSWP country share an interest in preventing non-proliferation. Democratic centralism turned upside down resulted in a tendency that was also far from democratic, and according to which the minority attempted to dictate to the majority. Romanian interests were often diametrically opposed to NSWP interests; where most NSWP members relished cooperation within the WP as a safe bulwark in the Cold War inside and outside the communist world, the Romanian leadership cultivated its position as free rider by using its 'independence' within the WP to court unlikely allies in Asia and the West, while siding with its WP allies when it feared isolation.

The Romanian quest for independence should not be examined by merely analysing Romanian-Soviet relations, as they do not constitute the whole story. In fact, the Soviet leadership was often more amenable to Romanian wishes than its WP allies. Although the Kremlin was keen not to lose an ally, the other allies feared being stifled by Romania's quest for independence. The real freedom fighter in this respect was Gomulka, as he did his allies the favour of withstanding Romanian pressure. The Romanian *Alleingang* was a much greater threat to the NSWP members' interests than the Kremlin's authority, which was time and again undermined by the Romanian comrades. The Romanian leaders only did their allies an inadvertent favour: they compelled them to define their own stance in the WP more clearly in order to withstand Romanian dissent. Thus they ultimately emancipated their allies at their own expense: by 1968 they had to choose between isolation or integration.

Dissent again proved more dynamic than is often assumed. While paralysing the WP on the surface, it actually spurred the other WP leaders into action so as to prevent it from eclipsing *their* foreign policy goals. Whereas the Romanian leaders played chess on too many boards simultaneously, the Romanian dissent compelled the other WP members to play the game with increasing skill. Although Ulbricht was checkmated on the German question in the previous chapter, Gomulka occasionally succeeded in calling the Romanians' bluff in terms of the Sino–Soviet split. Romania's position as maverick should therefore be studied within the context of the Warsaw Pact, as that sheds an altogether different and far more realistic light on its *modus operandi*: Romanian independence left little scope for the independence of others, and therefore had to be isolated. One should avoid the trap of regarding Romanian foreign policy up to March 1968 through the lens of the Prague Spring: Ceausescu was by no means a hero before he got the unique opportunity to defy the other WP allies by siding with 'the Czech'. The Prague Spring may have come as a godsend for the Romanian leadership, as it enabled them to turn their isolation once again into independence.

Notes

1 'Informative note on the Bucharest conference', Bucharest, 12 July 1966, ANIC, RCP CC, IR, 95/1966, 257.
2 'Information File, Romanian People's Republic', Berlin, July 1965, SAPMO-BArch, DY 30/IVA2/20/364, 364.
3 Brezhnev quoted in S. Radchenko, 'The Sino-Soviet Split', in M. Leffler and O.A. Westad (eds), *The Cambridge History of the Cold War. Volume II: Crisis and Détente* (Cambridge, 2010), 358.
4 Cf. S. Radchenko, *Two Suns in the Heavens: The Sino-Soviet Struggle for Supremacy, 1962–1967* (Stanford, 2009), 120–40, for a further explanation of the failed rapprochement.
5 See L.M. Lüthi, *The Sino-Soviet Split: Cold War in the Communist World* (Princeton, 2008), 302, on the 'overhaul in Soviet policy toward the war in Indochina'.

6 Cf. Q. Zhai, *China and the Vietnam Wars, 1950–1975* (Chapel Hill, 2000) for the Chinese perspective; O.A. Westad, *The Global Cold War* (Cambridge, 2005), 158–70, for the Asian perspective.
7 Cf. D.E. Kaiser, *American Tragedy. Kennedy, Johnson, and the Origins of the Vietnam War* (Massachusetts, 2000); and G.C. Herring, *America's Longest War. The United States and Vietnam, 1950–1975* (New York, 1979), for the American perspective.
8 See Herring, *America's Longest War*, on the American involvement. See X. Liu and V. Mastny (eds), *China and Eastern Europe, 1960s–1980s. Proceedings of the International Symposium: Reviewing the History of Chinese-East European Relations from the 1960s to the 1980s. Beijing, 24–26 March 2004*, Zürcher Beiträge zur Sicherheitspolitik und Konfliktforschung Nr. 72 (Zurich, 2004); and I.V. Gaiduk, *The Soviet Union and the Vietnam War* (Chicago, 1996), for the Soviet stance.
9 Cf. F. Logevall, 'The Indochina Wars and the Cold War, 1945–75', in Leffler and Westad (eds), *The Cambridge History of the Cold War II*, 281–304, for more information on the Vietnam War.
10 Logevall, 'The Indochina Wars', 296.
11 Lüthi, *The Sino-Soviet Split*, 285 and 300.
12 Reply to B. O'Flaherty, 'How Vietnam sees China', *The Diplomat*, 18 October 2011, thediplomat.com/asean-beat/2011/10/18/how-vietnam-sees-china/ (accessed 18 September 2013).
13 Rowiaski, Polish ambassador to Beijing, in X. Liu and V. Mastny (eds), *China and Eastern Europe, 1960s–1980s. Proceedings of the International Symposium: Reviewing the History of Chinese-East European Relations from the 1960s to the 1980s. Beijing, 24–26 March 2004*, Zürcher Beiträge zur Sicherheitspolitik und Konfliktforschung Nr. 72 (Zurich, 2004), 80.
14 Li Fenglin, in Liu and Mastny (eds), *China and Eastern Europe*, 67–68.
15 O.A. Westad, C. Jian, S. Tonnesson, N.V. Tung and J.G. Hershberg (eds), *77 Conversations between Chinese and Foreign Leaders on the Wars in Indochina, 1964–77*, CWIHP Working Paper No. 22 (Washington, 1998), 10–11.
16 Radchenko, *Two Suns in the Heavens*, 129.
17 F.J. Gavin, 'Nuclear Proliferation and Non-proliferation during the Cold War', in M. Leffler and O.A. Westad (eds), *The Cambridge History of the Cold War. Volume II: Crisis and Détente* (Cambridge, 2010), 405.
18 Cf. the subtitle of Lüthi's book, *The Sino-Soviet Split. Cold War in the Communist World*.
19 GDR report of the deputy foreign ministers meeting, December 1964, SAPMO-BArch, DY 30/3393, 13–25.
20 Letter from Ulbricht to WP leaders, 13 January 1965, SAPMO-BArch, DY 30/3388, 69–71.
21 Cf. for a discussion of the non-proliferation debate 'on both sides of the Iron Curtain': H. Brands, 'Non-Proliferation and the Dynamics of the Middle Cold War', *Cold War History* 7:3 (2007), 391.
22 Hershberg, in Liu and Mastny (eds), *China and Eastern Europe*, 68.
23 Cf. R.E. Gheorghe, 'Atomic Maverick. Romania's Negotiations for Nuclear Technology, 1964–70', *Cold War History* 13:3 (2013), 373–92.
24 Cf. F. Bozo, 'France, "Gaullism", and the Cold War', in Leffler and Westad (eds), *The Cambridge History of the Cold War II*, 158–78.
25 Meeting between Bodnaras and Liu Fan, 1 January 1965, ANIC, RWP CC, IR, 4/1965, 1–12.
26 Ibid.
27 Letter from Ulbricht to Gheorghiu-Dej and Maurer, 13 January 1965, ANIC, RWP CC, IR, 15/1965, 164–65.

28 Meeting between Bodnaras and Liu Fan, 9 January 1965, ANIC, RWP CC, IR, 4/1965, 15–19.
29 Meeting between Bodnaras and Liu Fan, 14 January 1965, ANIC, RWP CC, IR, 4/1965, 20–31.
30 Letter from RWP CC to CPSU CC, 4 January 1965, SAPMO-BArch, DY 30/3655, 179–90.
31 Estimate from the East German Embassy in Bucharest on Romanian economic, political and cultural development in 1964, 7 January 1965, SAPMO-BArch, DY 30/IVA2/20/369, 21.
32 Meeting between Bodnaras and Liu Fan, 14 January 1965, ANIC, RWP CC, IR, 4/1965, 20–31.
33 Note by the Albanian government to the PCC, Tirana, 15 January 1965, SAPMO-BArch, DY 30/3388, 347–71.
34 Meeting between Gheorghiu-Dej, Maurer and Gomulka, 18 January 1965, ANIC, RWP CC, IR, 15/1965, 92–102.
35 Meeting between Gheorghiu-Dej, Maurer and Ulbricht, 18 January 1965, ANIC, RWP CC, IR, 15/1965, 103–11.
36 Cf. minutes of the PCC, 19–20 January 1965, ANIC, RWP CC, IR, 15/1965, 29, for the altered and erased paragraph.
37 Ibid., 77.
38 First session of the editorial committee, 19 January 1965, ANIC, RWP CC, IR, 16/1965, 224.
39 Cf. for the Romanian nuclear programme: Gheorghe, 'Atomic Maverick', 373–92.
40 See 'PCC Resolution on Nonparticipation of Albania in the Warsaw Pact', 19 January 1965, PHP, www.php.ethz.ch/collections/colltopic.cfm?lng=en&id=17922&navinfo=14465 (accessed 26 August 2013), and second session of the editorial committee, 20 January, ANIC, RWP CC, IR, 16/1965, 231–36.
41 'Polish Minutes of Discussion at the PCC Meeting in Warsaw', 20 January 1965, PHP, 5, www.php.isn.ethz.ch/collections/colltopic.cfm?lng=en&id=17921&navinfo=14465 (accessed 26 August 2013).
42 'Romanian Minutes of the PCC Meeting', 20 January 1965, PHP, 5, www.php.isn.ethz.ch/collections/colltopic.cfm?lng=en&id=17920&navinfo=14465 (accessed 26 August 2013). Cf. minutes of the PCC, 19–20 January 1965, ANIC, RWP CC, IR, 15/1965, 3–91.
43 Ibid., 11.
44 Gheorghe, 'Atomic Maverick', 375.
45 'Polish minutes', 20 January 1965, PHP, 7.
46 Ibid., 9.
47 Minutes of the PCC, 19–20 January 1965, ANIC, RWP CC, IR, 15/1965, 88.
48 'Hungarian Report on the Warsaw Pact Political Consultative Committee Meeting of 19–20 January 1965', 25 January 1965, PHP, www.php.isn.ethz.ch/collections/colltopic.cfm?lng=en&id=17915&navinfo=14465 (accessed 26 August 2013).
49 Meeting between Bodnaras and Liu Fan, 27 January 1965, ANIC, RWP CC, IR, 4/1965, 34–40.
50 Meeting between Maurer, Bodnaras and Liu Fan, 28 January 1965, ANIC, RWP CC, IR, 4/1965, 43.
51 Gavin, 'Nuclear Proliferation', 405–6.
52 Meeting between Bodnaras and Liu Fan, 27 January 1965, ANIC, RWP CC, IR, 4/1965, 36–38.
53 Meeting between Maurer, Bodnaras and Liu Fan, 28 January 1965, ANIC, RWP CC, IR, 4/1965, 50.
54 Ibid., 49.
55 Minutes of discussion between A.N. Kosygin and Mao Zedong, 11 February 1965, ANIC, RWP CC, C, 12/1965, 14–15. In this discussion Mao Zedong also

blames the Soviet leadership for its actions against Albania; thus a WP matter also became a bone of contention within the Sino–Soviet split.
56 Meeting between Bodnaras and Liu Fan, 5 February 1965, ANIC, RWP CC, IR, 4/1965, 62.
57 See Radchenko, *Two Suns in the Heavens*, 144–48, for Kosygin's visit to Mao.
58 Letter from Brezhnev to Gheorghiu-Dej, 18 February 1965, ANIC, RWP CC, C, 15/1965, 41–42.
59 Minutes of discussions between comrades Nicolae Ceausescu and Emil Bodnaras with L. N. Tolkunov, Bucharest, 23–24 February 1965, ANIC, RWP CC, C, 15/1965, 17, 28.
60 Meeting between Bodnaras and Van Tung, 24 February 1965, ANIC, RWP CC, IR, 4/1965, 91–99.
61 'Information about some aspects on Sino-Soviet relations', 3 June 1965, ANIC, RWP CC, IR, 1/1965, 17–21.
62 Communiqué of the Moscow Meeting, March 1965, FIG ACP, 802/I, International meetings, mf 0528, 0814–18.
63 'Material relating to the Moscow meeting', FIG ACP, 802/I, International meetings, mf 0528, 0883.
64 Discussion at the 3rd plenum of the Polish United Workers' Party, 7 April 1965, FIG ACP, Poland, mf 0528, 51–52.
65 Letter from Brezhnev and Kosygin to Mao Zedong and Zhou Enlai, 3 April 1965, ANIC, RWP CC, IR, 50/1965, 11–12.
66 Letter from CPC CC to CPSU CC, 11 April 1965, ANIC, RWP CC, IR, 50/1965, 9–10.
67 See Chapter 4 of this book.
68 Letter from CPSU CC to CCP CC, 20 April 1965, ANIC, RWP CC, IR, 50/1965, 6–8.
69 Minutes of the discussions between Jegalin and Ceausescu, 23 April 1965, ANIC, RWP CC, IR, 50/1965, 2.
70 Conversation between Romanian ambassador Rosianu and Soviet ambassador Denisov, 23 April 1965, ANIC, RWP CC, IR, 1/1965, 12.
71 Minutes of discussions with a delegation of the CCP, which participated to the works of the IXth congress of the RCP, 26 July 1965, ANIC, RCP CC, C, 105/1965, 5, 7.
72 Meeting between Ceausescu and Liu Fan, 21 September 1965, ANIC, RCP CC, IR, 4/1965, 199–212.
73 Diplomatic report from Bucharest, 4 February 1965, SAPMO-BArch, DY 30/IVA2/20/369, 52–75.
74 Ibid., 24 June 1965, Bucharest, SAPMO-BArch, DY 30/IVA2/20/369, 228.
75 Budura, Romanian ambassador to Beijing, in Liu and Mastny (eds), *China and Eastern Europe*, 70.
76 Diplomatic report from Bucharest, 19 August 1965, SAPMO-BArch, DY 30/IVA2/20/369, 313.
77 Ibid., 25 November 1965, SAPMO-BArch, DY 30/IVA2/20/369, 480.
78 R.E. Gheorghe, 'Romania's Nuclear Negotiations Postures in the 1960s. Client, Maverick and International Peace Mediator', *Romanian Nuclear History Project Working Paper* No. 1 (2012), 25, www.roec.ro/romanias-nuclear-negotiations/ (accessed 27 August 2013).
79 'Information Report, 5.8.1965–19.8.1965', Bucharest, DY 30/IVA2/20/369, 312–34.
80 Meeting between Bodnaras and Liu Fan, 28 October 1965, ANIC, RCP CC, IR, 4/1965, 222. The Romanians also wrote a report on their position on non-proliferation in which they expressed their satisfaction with the Chinese position. Cf. Memorandum on a non-proliferation treaty, August 1965, ANIC, RCP CC, IR, 38/1965, vol. I, 99–107.

208 *The dynamics of dissent, 1965–68*

81 'Information Report, 26.11.1965–9.12.1965', Bucharest, DY 30/IVA2/20/369, 503–24.
82 J.G. Hershberg, *Who Murdered 'Marigold': New Evidence on the Mysterious Failure of Poland's Secret Initiative to Start US-North Vietnamese Peace Talks, 1966*, Cold War International History Project Working Paper no. 72 (Washington, April 2000). Cf. for mediation in the Vietnam War in general: G.C. Herring, *The Secret Diplomacy of the Vietnam War. The Negotiating Volumes of the Pentagon Papers* (Austin, 1983).
83 Rowiaski, Polish ambassador to Beijing, in Liu and Mastny (eds), *China and Eastern Europe*, 79; see also J.G. Hershberg, *Marigold. The Lost Chance for Peace in Vietnam* (Stanford, 2012); and *Who Murdered 'Marigold'*, for a minute account of the Polish negotiations during the Vietnam War.
84 See Chapter 4 for the Warsaw Package, which conditioned potential diplomatic relations with the FRG on recognition of the Oder-Neisse border and the GDR.
85 Letter from PUWP CC to CCP CC, 28 December 1965, ANIC, RCP CC, C 5/1966, 31.
86 Letter from Gomulka to Ceausescu, 5 January 1966, ANIC, RCP CC, C, 5/1966, 25.
87 See e.g. Letter from Kadar to Gomulka, 12 January 1966, SAPMO-BArch, DY 30/3389, 17a–18; and ibid., Letter from Novotny to SED CC, 20 January 1966, 26–27; and ibid., Letter from Vietnamese CC to PUWP CC, 14 April 1966, 120–22.
88 Minutes of the session of the RCP permanent presidium, 19 January 1966, 18.
89 Ibid., 7–21.
90 Bozo, 'France, "Gaullism", and the Cold War', 172.
91 Information about the visit of the French Foreign Minister Couve de Murville from 25–28 April 1966 in Romania, Bucharest, 6 May 1966, SAPMO-BArch, DY 30/IVA2/20/365, 11.
92 Protocol Nr. 25 of the session, of the Permanent Presidium of the RCP CC, 24 May 1966, ANIC, RCP CC, C, 81/1966, 3.
93 Cf. Chapter 4 of this book.
94 Conversation between Emil Bodnaras and Hoang Tu, Top Secret, 2 June 1966, ANIC, RCP CC, C, 181/1966, 102–7.
95 Diplomatic report from Bucharest, 9 June 1966, SAPMO-BArch, DY 30/IVA2/20/370, 253.
96 M. Munteanu, 'Over the Hills and Far Away: Romania's Attempts to Mediate the Start of U.S.-North Vietnamese Negotiations, 1967–68', *Journal of Cold War Studies* 14:3 (2012), 73.
97 Protocol Nr. 25 of the session of the Permanent Presidium of the RCP CC, 24 May 1966, ANIC, RCP CC, C, 81/1966, 3.
98 Decision of the presidium, 3 June 1966, ibid., 51.
99 Discussion between L.I. Brezhnev and C. Manescu, Top Secret, Extremely Important, Single Copy, 11 June 1966, ANIC, RCP CC, C, 73/1966, 38.
100 Ibid., 39.
101 Meeting between Emil Bodnaras and Tzen Iun-ciuan, 7 June 1966, ANIC, RCP CC, IR, 82/1966, 3.
102 Munteanu, 'Over the Hills', 74.
103 Ibid.
104 See for European Security and WP reforms Chapter 4 of this book.
105 Diplomatic report from Bucharest, 26 May 1966, SAPMO-BArch, DY 30/IVA2/20/370, 228.
106 See for this image: Gheorghe, 'Atomic Maverick', 375.
107 Minutes of the discussions with the Soviet delegation, 3 July 1966, ANIC, RCP CC, IR, 94/1966, vol. II, 138.
108 Soviet draft of the declaration on Vietnam, ANIC, RCP CC, IR, 95/1966, 115–20.

109 Romanian draft of the declaration on Vietnam, ANIC, RCP CC, IR, 95/1966, 101–7.
110 Minutes of the discussions with the Soviet delegation, 3 July 1966, ANIC, RCP CC, IR, 94/1966, vol. II, 143.
111 Ibid.
112 Minutes of the discussions with the delegation of the P. R. Poland, 3 July 1966, ANIC, RCP CC, IR, 95/1966, 9.
113 Polish draft of the declaration on Vietnam, ANIC, RCP CC, IR, 95/1966, 121–23.
114 Minutes of the meeting of the Political Consultative Committee, 4–6 July 1966, session of 4 July 1966, ANIC, RCP CC, IR, 94/1966, vol. I, 11–12.
115 Minutes of the session of foreign ministers, Top Secret, 4 July 1966, ANIC, RCP CC, IR, 94/1966, vol. II, 24.
116 Minutes of the meeting of the Political Consultative Committee, 4–6 July 1966, session of 5 July 1966, ANIC, RCP CC, IR, 94/1966, vol. I, 150–54.
117 Ibid., 156.
118 Minutes of the session of foreign ministers, Top Secret, 4 July 1966, ANIC, RCP CC, IR, 94/1966, vol. II, 24.
119 Minutes of the session of foreign ministers, morning session, 6 July 1966, ANIC, RCP CC, IR, 94/1966, vol. II, 50–75.
120 Minutes of the Romanian Party Politburo Meeting, Report on the PCC Meeting by the General Secretary of the PCR (Nicolae Ceausescu), 12 July 1966, PHP, 5, www.php.isn.ethz.ch/collections/colltopic.cfm?lng=en&id=17947&navinfo=14465 (accessed 26 August 2013).
121 Minutes of the meeting of the Political Consultative Committee, 4–6 July 1966, session of 6 July 1966, ANIC, RCP CC, IR, 94/1966, vol. I, 186–88. See also the 'Polish Minutes', 5 July 1966, PHP.
122 Minutes of the meeting of the Political Consultative Committee, 4–6 July 1966, session of the afternoon of 6 July 1966, ANIC, RCP CC, IR, 94/1966, vol. I, 195–96.
123 See Chapter 4 of this book.
124 'Informative note on the Bucharest conference', Bucharest, 12 July 1966, ANIC, RCP CC, IR, 95/1966, 255–58.
125 'East German Substantive Summary of the PCC Meeting', 8 July 1966, PHP, www.php.isn.ethz.ch/collections/colltopic.cfm?lng=en&id=17955&navinfo=14465 (accessed 26 August 2013).
126 Minutes of the Hungarian Party Politburo Session – Report on the PCC Meeting by the First Secretary of the Hungarian Socialist Workers Party (János Kádár), 12 July 1966, PHP, 1, www.php.isn.ethz.ch/collections/colltopic.cfm?lng=en&id=17949&navinfo=14465 (accessed 26 August 2013).
127 Ibid., 5.
128 Minutes of the Romanian Party Politburo Meeting, 12 July 1966, PHP.
129 Diplomatic report from Bucharest, 13 October 1966, SAPMO-BArch, DY 30/IVA2/20/372, 192.
130 Embassy, Bucharest, 13/9/1966, PAAA, MfAA, A 5394, 46.
131 See Munteanu, 'Over the Hills', for a detailed account of the Romanian attempts at negotiations.
132 Gheorghe, 'Romania's Nuclear Negotiations Postures', 28–29.
133 Ibid., 25.
134 Munteanu, 'Over the Hills', 76.
135 Maurer, quoted by Munteanu, 'Over the Hills', 75–76.
136 Minutes of the discussions on the occasion of the visit in China by the delegation led by Ion Gheorghe Maurer, 5 July 1967, ANIC, RCP CC, IR, 49/1967, 41–42.
137 Minutes of the discussions on the occasion of the visit in China by the delegation led by Ion Gheorghe Maurer, ANIC, RCP CC, IR, 49/1967, 6 July 1967, 62.
138 Ibid., 63, 71.

139 Document 4, 18 July 1967, in J.G. Hershberg, D. Wolff, P. Vámos and S. Radchenko (eds), *The Interkit Story: A Window into the Final Decades of the Sino-Soviet Relationship*, CWIHP Working Paper No. 63 (Washington, 2011), 48–49.
140 Document no. 6, in Hershberg *et al.*, *The Interkit Story*, 52–56.
141 Ibid., 8.
142 Cf. L. Watts, *A Romanian INTERKIT? Soviet Active Measures and the Warsaw Pact 'Maverick', 1965–1989*, CWIHP Working Paper No. 65 (Washington, 2012), 1.
143 L. Betea, 'Convorbiri neterminate cu Corneliu Mănescu', in L. Betea (ed.), *Partea lor de adevăr* (Bucharest, 2008a), 559.
144 Cf. Q. Zhai, *Beijing and the Vietnam Peace Talks, 1965–1968: New Evidence from Chinese Sources*, CWIHP Working Paper No. 18 (Washington, 1997), for the Chinese and Vietnamese views on negotiations.
145 Minutes of discussion between Gheorghe Maurer and the Soviet leadership, 2 October 1967, ANIC, RCP CC, IR, 82/1967, 122.
146 Gheorghe, 'Romania's Nuclear Negotiations Postures', 31.
147 Minutes of the discussions during Maurer's visit in China, ANIC, RCP CC, IR, 49/1967, 6 July 1967, 67.
148 'Top Secret. Information on discussions with A.A. Soldatov, deputy of the minister of foreign affairs of the USSR, on the problem of nonproliferation of nuclear arms', 27–28 February 1967, ANIC, RCP CC, IR, 113/1967, 21. The ENDC had again resumed its work on 21 February 1967.
149 Quoted in ibid., 27.
150 Meeting between Soldatov and Manescu, 6 March 1967, ANIC, RCP CC, IR, 113/1967, 28–29.
151 Minutes of the discussions at the highest level between the CPSU and the RCP, Moscow, 17–18 March 1967, ANIC, RCP CC, IR, 14/1967, 38.
152 Note on Romanian intervention in the ENDC committee, 22 June 1967, ANIC, RCP CC, C, 104/1967, 66–69.
153 'Protocol Nr. 8 of the session of the Permanent Presidium of the RCP CC of 19 February 1968, ANIC, RCP CC, C, 24/1968, 1–3.
154 Letter by the General Secretary of the PCR (Nicolae Ceaușescu) to the First Secretary of PZPR (Władysław Gomułka) Proposing to Summon the PCC, 31 January 1968, PHP, www.php.isn.ethz.ch/collections/colltopic.cfm?lng=en&id=18012&navinfo=14465 (accessed 26 August 2013).
155 'East German Criticism of the Romanian Amendments to the Soviet Draft of a Non-proliferation Treaty', 4 March 1968, PHP, 13, www.php.isn.ethz.ch/collections/colltopic.cfm?lng=en&id=17992&navinfo=14465 (accessed 26 August 2013).
156 Minutes of the extraordinary plenary session of the Central Committee of the Romanian Communist Party, 1 March 1968, ANIC, RCP CC, C 31/1968, 40.
157 'Memorandum by the Hungarian Foreign Minister (János Péter) on the Romanian Proposal to Convene the PCC', 5 February 1968, PHP, 1, www.php.isn.ethz.ch/collections/colltopic.cfm?lng=en&id=18010&navinfo=14465 (accessed 26 August 2013).
158 'Memorandum about the conversation between comrade Walter Ulbricht and comrade diplomat Abrassimov', 13 February 1968, SAPMO BArch, DY 30/3390, 41–43.
159 Minutes of the extraordinary plenary session of the Central Committee of the Romanian Communist Party, 1 March 1968, ANIC, RCP CC, C 31/1968, 43, 45.
160 East German Minutes of the Berlin Meeting of Deputy Ministers of Foreign Affairs Preparatory to the PCC Meeting, 26 February 1968, PHP, www.php.isn.ethz.ch/collections/colltopic.cfm?lng=en&id=17996&navinfo=14465 (accessed 26 August 2013). Cf. PA AA, MfAA, G-A 552.
161 Minutes of the extraordinary plenary session of the Central Committee of the Romanian Communist Party, 1 March 1968, ANIC, RCP CC, C 31/1968, 6–7.

162 Minutes of the session of the Permanent Presidium of the RCP CC of 29 February 1968, ANIC, RCP CC, C, 30/1968, 4.
163 'Meeting of the [PCI] leadership', 15 March 1968, FIG ACP, Leadership, 1968, mf 020, 0596–97.
164 Letter from RCP CC to PCI [Partito Comunista Italiano] CC, 5 March 1968, FIG APC, mf 0552, 2296.
165 'Meeting of the [PCI] leadership', 15 March 1968, FIG APC, Leadership, 1968, mf 020, 0596–97.
166 'Draft Commentary on Romanian Position at the PCC Meeting to the CC of the Bulgarian Communist Party Plenary Meeting', 6 March 1968, PHP, 8, www.php.isn.ethz.ch/collections/colltopic.cfm?lng=en&id=17988&navinfo=14465 (accessed 26 August 2013).
167 Minutes of the extraordinary plenary session of the Central Committee of the Romanian Communist Party, 1 March 1968, ANIC, RCP CC, C, 31/1968, 45.
168 'East German Evaluation of the Romanian Position on the Soviet Proposal of a Non-proliferation Treaty', 26 February 1968, PHP, 2, www.php.isn.ethz.ch/collections/colltopic.cfm?lng=en&id=17994&navinfo=14465 (accessed 26 August 2013).
169 'Discussion between comrades Nicolae Ceausescu and Ion Gheorghe Maurer, and comrades Leonid Brezhnev and Alexei Kosygin, 6 March 1968', ANIC, RCP CC, IR, 38/1968, 115.
170 'Report to the Hungarian Party Politburo and Council of Ministers on the PCC Meeting', 9 March 1968, PHP, 4, www.php.isn.ethz.ch/collections/colltopic.cfm?lng=en&id=17967&navinfo=14465 (accessed 26 August 2013).
171 'Statement Supporting Soviet Draft Non-Proliferation Treaty', 9 March 1968, PHP, www.php.isn.ethz.ch/collections/colltopic.cfm?lng=en&id=17974&navinfo=14465 (accessed 26 August 2013).
172 'Communiqué on Soviet Draft Non-Proliferation Treaty', 9 March 1968, PHP, www.php.isn.ethz.ch/collections/colltopic.cfm?lng=en&id=17970&navinfo=14465 (accessed 26 August 2013).
173 Minutes of the Hungarian Party Politburo Session, 8 March 1968, PHP, 4.
174 'Protocol Nr. 10 of the session of the Executive Committee of the RCP on 8 March 1968', ANIC, RCP CC, C, 34/1968, 11.
175 Minutes of the Hungarian Party Politburo Session, 8 March 1968, PHP, 5.
176 'Note about a conversation between comrade N. Ceausescu and T. Zhivkov on the evening of 7.III.1968 (Sofia)', ANIC, RCP CC, IR, 38/1968, 91.
177 'Report to the Hungarian Party Politburo', 9 March 1968, PHP, 8.
178 'Protocol Nr. 10 of the session of the Executive Committee of the RCP on 8 March 1968', ANIC, RCP CC, C, 34/1968, 11.
179 'Note on a discussion between comrade N. Ceausescu and A. Dubcek in Sofia', 6–7 March 1968, ANIC, RCP CC, IR, 38/1968, 92.
180 'Czechoslovak Report on the PCC Meeting', 26 March 1968, PHP, 4–5, www.php.isn.ethz.ch/collections/colltopic.cfm?lng=en&id=17969&navinfo=14465 (accessed 26 August 2013).
181 Diplomatic report from Bucharest, SAPMO-BArch, 23 May 1968, DY 30/IVA2/20/374, 322.
182 Ibid., 20 June 1968, SAPMO-BArch, DY 30/IVA2/20/374, 419.
183 Gavin, 'Nuclear Proliferation', 410.

Part III
Crisis and consolidation, 1968–69

6 The limits of emancipation
The Prague Spring

> We consider it necessary to put an end to the interference in the affairs of other states, of other parties, once and for all, in order to establish relations among socialist countries, among communist parties, on a truly Marxist-Leninist footing.[1]
> (Ceausescu's speech after the invasion of Czechoslovakia, 21 August 1968)

In the second half of the 1960s the Warsaw Pact threatened to be paralysed by the division between the 'one' (Romania) and 'the six' (the rest). The dynamics between the 'six' on the one hand and Romania on the other took an altogether different turn in the course of 1968. Although Romania was clearly isolated during the PCC meeting in Sofia in March 1968, since it was the only country at that meeting that did not support the non-proliferation treaty, there was another country that tended to develop into an anomaly within the WP: Czechoslovakia. However emphatically the new Czechoslovak leader, Alexander Dubcek, still stuck to the position of the other five at the beginning of March 1968, the Czechoslovak leadership had begun to develop its own idiosyncratic kind of communism from its plenum in January 1968 onwards, which culminated in a process of internal reforms usually known as 'the Prague Spring'.

In this chapter the Prague Spring will be analysed from the perspective of the multilateral decision making of the five WP countries that eventually agreed to invade Czechoslovakia to put an end to the reforms on 21 August 1968. This chapter will accordingly distinguish itself from the previous ones, as it deals with most of the protagonists from the Warsaw Pact, but not explicitly with the institution in itself. An understanding of the multilateral decision making during the Prague Spring is, however, essential in gauging the evolution of the WP in the period afterwards, and a detailed examination of the decision making might also serve to debunk conventional wisdoms on the alleged role of the alliance in this critical period.

In most historiography to date the international ramifications of the Prague Spring are viewed from the perspective of *bilateral* Czechoslovak-Soviet relations.[2] Although a tendency has developed quite recently to view the decision making in a somewhat broader perspective, especially in some excellent rticles by the Harvard historian Mark Kramer, the latest historiography has still failed to distinguish between *multilateral* decision making by several WP countries, and *Warsaw Pact* decision making.[3] This perhaps explains why it is often assumed that the invasion in Czechoslovakia was in fact a '*Warsaw Pact* invasion'.[4] This distinction is, however, crucial. The Warsaw Pact owes much of its reputation as a Soviet instrument to its alleged involvement in the invasion in Czechoslovakia. Immediately after the invasion in Czechoslovakia, US President Lyndon B. Johnson and his top aides even assumed in a National Security Council meeting that the invasion was conducted by the Warsaw Pact, and concluded that '[t]here is a great difference between the Warsaw Pact and NATO with respect to internal affairs of members', as 'NATO is operative only in the event of international aggression and grants no rights to a member to intervene in the affairs of another'.[5] An analysis of the hypothetical role of the WP in the Prague Spring is therefore crucial in order to examine whether the invasion in Czechoslovakia verily revealed a fundamental distinction between NATO and the WP.

The historical context

The year 1968 is often considered the year 'that rocked the world'.[6] Students revolted in West Germany, Italy and France, the American civil rights activist Martin Luther King was murdered, and American prestige was under pressure after the broadly televised North Vietnamese Tet Offensive in the Vietnam War.[7] Revolutionary tendencies spread beyond the Iron Curtain,[8] where both students and the society at large 'began to challenge Cold War certainties'.[9] This process erupted in Czechoslovakia, where the Stalinist leader Antonin Novotny had led the Communist Party of Czechoslovakia (CPCz) since Stalin's death in 1953, while resisting the tendencies in Eastern Europe towards de-Stalinisation. His regime had, as such, turned into an anachronism, and criticism of Novotny and his autocratic way of leading the party rose within the CPCz, and within Czechoslovak society at large. As in Western Europe, students were particularly critical of the establishment, and the Slovak First Secretary Alexander Dubcek echoed their concerns within the CPCz.

The more reform-minded CPCz members therefore centred around Dubcek, who clashed severely with Novotny during a CPCz CC plenum from 30–31 October 1967, when Dubcek promoted equal rights for Czechs and Slovaks, a more democratic kind of political leadership, and a division of the posts of first secretary and president, which Novotny had held simultaneously.[10] In a desperate attempt to remain in power, Novotny invited Brezhnev over to Prague in early December, but Brezhnev's exclamation 'this is your affair' did little to consolidate Novotny's power.[11] After Novotny also lost support within the CPCz, he was asked to step down as first secretary during a CPCz CC meeting from 19–21 December 1967.

During the meeting of the Central Committee of the Communist Party of Czechoslovakia, which lasted from 3–5 January 1968, Dubcek was elected first secretary of the CPCz.[12] At the January plenum, when Dubcek succeeded Novotny as first secretary, an Action Programme was nevertheless launched that would pave the way for democratisation within the party and within society. This heralded the beginning of a period of liberalisation: the 'Prague Spring'. United in their criticism of Novotny, Dubcek's supporters nevertheless held conflicting interests, supported reforms in different degrees, and hardly formed a stable faction.[13] The political foundation for the reforms was, accordingly, thin

However, Czechoslovakia was not the only country in Eastern Europe that was subject to reforms in 1968. Hungary had also embarked on a programme of reforms at the beginning of 1968, when Kadar's 'New Economic Mechanism' was approved, which heralded a process of economic decentralisation to remedy the inefficient system of central planning, and unprecedentedly introduced a degree of free market economy.[14] It was, therefore, in Kadar's interest that the reforms within Czechoslovakia would not spin out of control, since he did not want his own reforms to arouse suspicion within Eastern Europe. Meanwhile, the Romanian leader Ceausescu greatly valued the Czechoslovak process of reforms exactly because they *could* spin out of control: he considered this a way to break through Romanian isolation, because it could lead to a cleavage between Czechoslovakia and the rest of the WP.[15]

Gomulka, Ulbricht and Zhivkov indeed had no sympathy for reforms at all, and watched the developments in Czechoslovakia with great apprehension, out of fear lest the reform-minded spirit might infect the people in their countries. The Polish leader, Gomulka, warned Dubcek on 7 February that the Czechoslovak reforms could be 'a catalyst for further protests in Poland'.[16] When student protests erupted in Warsaw in March 1968, while the Polish leadership was at the PCC meeting in Sofia, Polish students did, indeed, chant 'Poland awaits her own Dubcek'.[17] This was particularly painful to Gomulka, who was genuinely popular when he came to power in October 1956. Despite Gomulka's initial reputation as a reformer within Eastern Europe, the Polish protests were quenched with force. Gomulka thus sacrificed a potential reform process for the consolidation of his power, which was a choice that Dubcek would refuse to make.

Dubcek was, however, confronted with a larger challenge than Gomulka. In the course of March the CPCz Presidium had begun to abolish censorship, freedom of speech had radicalised the mass media, and Novotny had been forced to resign as president by public protests from the citizens. Through the liberalisation of the media, Dubcek was, accordingly, not only under pressure from thousands of university students, as in Poland, but from the Czechoslovak society at large. According to the British historian William Shawcross, Czechoslovakia 'underwent, in 1968, the emotional breakdown that Hungary and Poland had endured twelve years before', with the difference that '[i]n those twelve years enormous frustration had built up', which would have confronted any leader of the reform movement with an almost impossible task.[18]

When Dubcek subsequently failed to stem the demands of 'an ever more excited and extremist public',[19] the leaders of the Soviet Union, the GDR, Poland, Bulgaria and Hungary decided to offer 'fraternal assistance' in the form of a military intervention on 21 August 1968. This invasion was retrospectively justified with the so-called 'Brezhnev doctrine', according to which a socialist country was only sovereign to the extent that it was socialist. Foreign intervention was, as such, legitimate if socialism was under threat. As Mastny puts it, this doctrine 'merely expressed verbally what the Kremlin had practised before – but would never again practise in the region',[20] and explains, *inter alia*, the Soviet invasion in Hungary in 1956. Although WP troops had already been stationed in the GDR, Poland and Hungary, they had so far been absent from Czechoslovakia. Novoty had, however, agreed to the placement of Soviet nuclear warheads on Czechoslovak soil 'under strict Soviet control' in 1965, but due to delays, the Czechoslovak storage sites had not been completed yet.[21] This also put Czechoslovakia geopolitically in a vulnerable position: it was the only WP country whose border with the FRG was fully exposed.

The six in Dresden

At the beginning of March events in Czechoslovakia were still sufficiently under control for non-proliferation to take priority over internal Czechoslovak developments during the PCC meeting in Sofia, but by the end of March, Brezhnev decided to convene a meeting of 'the six' in Dresden in order to discuss the situation in Czechoslovakia. Consulting all WP members apart from Romania on the convention of the meeting, Romanian isolation had now become irreversible: Romania was not even invited. Kadar's suggestion at the PCC meeting that 'the first secretaries and prime ministers of the six countries should get together for the sake of unfettered, comradely talks', thus materialised earlier than anticipated.[22] The meeting took place outside the institutional confines of the Warsaw Pact, which made it possible to bypass Romania. 'The six' had turned into a parallel reality.

The convention of the Dresden meeting on 23 March differed significantly from usual procedures within the WP. The Soviet leadership had unilaterally convened the meeting, albeit with explicit approval from the East German, Polish, Hungarian and Bulgarian leaders, and one member was excluded altogether. Moreover, the meeting in Dresden was convened under a false pretext: the Czechoslovak leadership was invited for a meeting on economic cooperation within Eastern Europe, even though all the other leaders knew perfectly well that the meeting was intended to discuss the political developments within Czechoslovakia. The participants thus started on an unequal footing, even though Dubcek himself was the only member of the Czechoslovak delegation who *was* informed of the actual topic of the meeting. He had in fact explicitly agreed to the smokescreen, since he was afraid that his comrades would otherwise accuse him of bowing to Soviet wishes.[23] Even in the early stage of the Prague Spring Dubcek had to find a balance between not seeming too anti-Soviet in Soviet eyes, and not seeming too pro-Soviet in Czechoslovak eyes.

The Dresden meeting did resemble a WP meeting in the position of its participants. In the absence of Romania, Gomulka put the biggest stamp on the meeting by eloquently legitimising interference in internal affairs in 'situations when so-called domestic affairs naturally become external affairs, thus affairs of the entire socialist camp'. Gomulka thus neatly formulated the Brezhnev doctrine *avant la lettre* by legitimising interference in domestic affairs when they have external repercussions. Both Brezhnev and Gomulka characterised the situation as a counterrevolution, although Gomulka was more explicit about the need for immediate measures and external interference than Brezhnev.[24] Since the threat of contagion in Poland was much more immediate than the potential collapse of the Soviet bloc,[25] Gomulka had more reason to call for immediate measures and foreign interference than Brezhnev, for whom 'the security of the socialist countries' was paramount.[26] Brezhnev therefore emphasised that the salvation of socialism in Czechoslovakia was not optional. The Czechoslovak leaders were thus under increasing pressure to agree to a change of course in Dresden. Through the convention of the Dresden meeting the formula that domestic affairs could become external affairs had already become a self-fulfilling prophecy.

Ulbricht was as extreme as usual, and added the threat of West German imperialism to the interpretation of a counterrevolution in Czechoslovakia. For him, too, the situation was critical: the Czechoslovak rapprochement to the FRG seemed to threaten the legitimacy of the GDR. Since Czechoslovakia shared a border with West Germany, it could prove to be the weakest link within the WP. By appealing to the need for unanimity within the WP, Ulbricht was directly defending the survival of his country. Meanwhile, the Bulgarian delegate agreed with the hardliners, and concentrated on the leading role of the party, which also reflected the conventional Bulgarian position: the Bulgarian leadership tended to side with the Kremlin,[27] as it cherished the maintenance of the status quo and the importance of the communist monopoly on power above all else.[28]

Only the Hungarian leader, Kadar, sided with his Czechoslovak comrades in categorically rejecting the assessment of the reforms in Czechoslovakia as a 'counterrevolution', while denouncing the interference in internal affairs. Kadar trusted the Czechoslovak leaders to control the situation themselves, and strove to avoid the equation of reforms with counterrevolution, as that would also endanger the reform process within Hungary. The same applied to legitimising interference in internal affairs: if that was allowed in Czechoslovakia, Hungary might well be next.[29] Kadar had to defend the Czechoslovak scope for manoeuvre, in order to safeguard his own. The Czechoslovak participants also attempted to maintain *their* scope for manoeuvre, and emphasised that 'the party is capable today of mastering the situation with principle and flexibility'.[30] The mere convention of the meeting nevertheless indicated that the *internal* scope for manoeuvre of a communist country was at stake.

In that respect the meeting differed significantly from those that were convened within the WP framework: purely domestic issues had never been at stake at all within the confines of the alliance. The alliance was officially an outward-looking institution, founded to deal with the *external* threat from NATO, and not an instrument for the control of its members' *internal* developments, which explains why Dubcek thought that allegiance to the WP was sufficient to safeguard the sovereignty of Czechoslovakia.[31] Moreover, the meeting could not have proceeded as it did within a WP framework. Not all allies had been consulted on its convention, nor on its agenda, and the Czechoslovak participants had not been able to prepare for the meeting. The Dresden meeting merely served to pressurise the Czechoslovak leaders into adopting a different course. The alliance ironically would have provided the Czechoslovak participants with much more leverage over their allies than this improvised setting.

Reflecting the ambivalent nature of the meeting, the Dresden meeting was concluded with a communiqué that bore no relation to the meeting itself. The choice not to use the institutional procedures of the alliance facilitated the disguise. Only mentioning economic problems that had not been central to the meeting, the communiqué concealed the fact that several of its allies had begun to attempt to interfere in internal Czechoslovak affairs. It was, ironically, the East German secret recording of the meeting that proved how much reality differed from appearance. Romania had been isolated in the WP before; 'the six' had already convened separately during the PCC meeting in Sofia. This meeting nevertheless served a further purpose that the alliance could not legitimise

Echoes from Dresden

The smokescreen used in Dresden backfired. Since the communiqué stated that economic cooperation within COMECON and several WP issues had been discussed by 'the six', Ceausescu was furious at being excluded, and he explained to the RCP CC that 'the discussions [...] in Dresden contradict the spirit of relations between Socialist states of the Warsaw Pact and the CMEA [COMECON]. Our opinion is that a group of countries, members of an international organisation, do not have the right to meet separately and discuss the activity of international organisations of which other countries are members as well'.[32] The meeting of 'the six' to discuss the developments in Czechoslovakia thus seemed to seal the Romanian isolation, although Ceausescu gradually realised from diplomatic reports from Prague that the meeting at Dresden had specifically been used to discuss the situation in Czechoslovakia, and strongly condemned the participating countries for 'exert[ing] pressure upon the Czechoslovaks regarding their internal situation'.[33] Thus 'the six' had already turned into 'the five'.

Meanwhile, Dubcek chose to keep his Czechoslovak comrades in the dark about the real nature of the Dresden meeting in order to prevent Czechoslovak-Soviet antagonism, and only stated *en passant* that his allies had voiced their 'specific concerns and advice' about the situation in Czechoslovakia.[34] The intention of the Dresden meeting did not, however, elude 134 Czechoslovak writers and cultural figures, who sent an open letter to the CPCz CC, in which they emphasised that 'the Dresden communiqué [...] has made it clear to us that the CPCz CC must stand up to pressure motivated by doubts about the nature and objectives of our internal measures'. The authors added that 'the need to maintain international solidarity among socialist states should not cause you to forget that your responsibility for this country is above all to its own people'.[35] Prioritising internal affairs over external duties, the authors thus turned the incipient Brezhnev doctrine on its head.

Shortly after the letter the CPCz Central Committee convened from 1–5 April to adopt an 'Action Programme' that would serve as a blueprint for a more democratic and liberal kind of socialism, also known as 'socialism with a human face'. One day later the government resigned in order to form a new government, led by Oldrich Cernik. The action programme aimed on the one hand to 'justify [the party's] leading role in society', while denying the communist monopoly on power, and called on the other hand for reforming 'the whole political system', including 'freedom of speech'. Stating that 'the basic orientation of Czechoslovak foreign policy [...] revolves around alliance and cooperation with the Soviet Union and the other socialist states', it simultaneously claimed that 'the CSSR [Czechoslovak Socialist Republic] will formulate its own position toward the fundamental problems of world politics'.[36] This dual policy of relaxing the grip on the Czechoslovak people and professing allegiance to the WP illustrates that Dubcek was well aware of the dilemma that confronted him. While he was 'under increasing pressure from his Warsaw Pact partners to slow down the process of reform and to muzzle the press', both the press and the 'ever more excited and extremist public' urged him 'to ignore the threats of the Russians and quicken the pace of change'.[37] His scope for manoeuvre was very limited.

The reference to 'alliance and cooperation' was clearly meant to assuage any Eastern European fears about a Czechoslovak *Alleingang*, but the statement that '[o]ur geographical position [...] compel[s] us to pursue a more active European policy aimed at the promotion of mutually advantageous relations with all states and with international organisations' had quite the opposite effect: this clearly implied an intended rapprochement with the FRG, which was as close to Czechoslovakia as the Soviet Union.[38] The Action Programme thus indicated that the Czechoslovak leadership would sail a course that was similar to Romania's in terms of foreign policy, but they embarked on a far more dangerous trajectory. The socialist's party monopoly of power had never been at stake in Romania, but in Czechoslovakia that, too, seemed under threat.

Meanwhile, the views of the hawks and doves within the five socialist countries gradually began to converge. The Hungarian politburo, too, began to fear that 'the communist party in the CSSR had lost control of events', and that Czechoslovakia would turn into a 'bourgeois democracy'. The role of the media was criticised and the Hungarian leaders feared 'a situation analogous to that in Hungary in 1956'. The Bulgarian leadership even suggested '[using] military force against the CSSR as a last resort'.[39] At the same time the CPSU CC was hastily convened in Moscow to deal with the situation. At this session it was decided 'to prevent the loss of socialist achievements in Czechoslovakia and its withdrawal from the "socialist camp"' by providing 'assistance to the healthy forces'.[40] Still considering Dubcek one of them, Brezhnev wrote him a letter in which he begged Dubcek to secure 'the leading role of the party', and added that the 'loyalty to the Warsaw Pact is the guarantee of national independence and the security of the Czechoslovak Republic and the entire socialist community'.[41] Brezhnev called him the same day to propose bilateral consultations.

Both within the 'five', and within the CPSU politburo, there remained, however, a division between 'hawks' and 'doves', whereas Brezhnev 'himself was still undecided'.[42] One of the Soviet hawks was politburo member Alexander Shelepin, who was also Brezhnev's most serious rival. The general consensus within the Kremlin during the month of April was still that the Czechoslovak leadership could control the situation itself.[43] At the same time both Ulbricht and Gomulka repeatedly called Brezhnev, and urged him to send in troops to the CSSR, as they 'were worried about the security of their own countries if Czechoslovakia broke away from the alliance'. Although Brezhnev remained 'extremely cautious' for a long time, he exclaimed during one session: 'If we lose Czechoslovakia, I will step down from the post of general secretary!'[44] Since his own fate was linked to the fate of Czechoslovakia, Brezhnev's scope for manoeuvre was limited still further. At the same time, Brezhnev had suddenly become the central figure in solving the Czechoslovak crisis. The developments in Czechoslovakia had inadvertently reinforced Soviet hegemony, after the WP's multilateralisation had limited Soviet power. A military solution was, after all, inconceivable without Soviet participation.

The positions of Ulbricht and Gomulka had become increasingly vulnerable, too. Gomulka explained to the Soviet ambassador Averki Aristov that 'the events developing there [have] an increasingly negative effect on Poland', where protesters chanted 'Long Live Czechoslovakia',[45] and added that Czechoslovakia was on the verge of being 'transformed into a bourgeois republic'. He therefore 'expressed the need for us to intervene immediately'.[46] His political fate, too, seemed linked to that of Czechoslovakia.

At the same time Ulbricht faced an equally great problem, since the Czechoslovak leadership was negotiating diplomatic relations with the

FRG.[47] This was a flagrant denial of the protocol signed at the WP foreign ministers meeting in February 1967, the so called 'Warsaw Package', in which it was agreed to refrain from following Romania's example in establishing diplomatic relations with the FRG unless the West German leaders fulfilled several criteria, such as recognising the GDR. The Czechoslovak commitment to the Warsaw Package had, however, been lukewarm from the start.[48] The talks with Egon Bahr also stimulated a different attitude within the WP, since 'the SPD believes that the CSSR has a real chance of pursuing a more active policy vis-à-vis its partners in the Warsaw Pact'. The West German *neue Ostpolitik* ('new Eastern policy') of intensifying its relations with countries in Eastern Europe thus posed a particular threat to the East German leadership. In its courting of Czechoslovakia the West German government ignored the existence of East Germany all the more emphatically. Ulbricht felt his grip on the German question weakening. The GDR itself was caught in a 'political pincer', with the reforms in Czechoslovakia on one side and the West German courting of Eastern Europe on the other.[49]

The Czechoslovak leadership, meanwhile, was particularly concerned about its relations with the Kremlin, and Foreign Minister Jiri Hajek proposed to ease the tensions by sending a Czechoslovak delegation to the Soviet Union as Brezhnev had requested. The delegation's mission would be to clarify issues such as 'the internal situation in the party, [...] the leading role of the party', and only mentioned in the seventh place, 'Czechoslovak foreign policy', including 'future policy toward the FRG'.[50] Although the Czechoslovak leadership had rightly sensed that it needed to tilt the balance in its favour, it seemed to ignore the significance of its other Eastern European allies.

The situation had thus become increasingly delicate on several fronts by the end of April. The Czechoslovak leadership felt misunderstood, but its rapprochement with the FRG did little to reassure its Eastern European allies about its foreign policy orientation. Meanwhile, Ulbricht and Gomulka both had their own compelling reasons to pressurise Brezhnev to come into action, whereas Brezhnev himself had to deal with CPSU and WP comrades who were more hawkish than him. However eager to safeguard Hungarian reforms, even the Hungarian leadership feared that the survival of socialism was at stake within Czechoslovakia. Eager to explain their position to the Kremlin, the Czechoslovak leaders agreed to send a delegation to Moscow in early May. If they could succeed in convincing their Soviet comrades that the loss of Czechoslovakia was not imminent, they hoped to prevent the sword of Damocles from falling.

Moscow in May

The Moscow summit, which took place on 4–5 May, did little to resolve the situation. The Soviet leadership was sceptical about Dubcek's control over the media, and Brezhnev was particularly concerned about the 'lack of [...] unity' in the presidium. The Czechoslovak reaction already demonstrated a lack of unity: whereas the Slovak First Secretary Bilak shared Soviet concerns, Dubcek emphasised the undiminished 'cooperation with the Soviet Union' instead, and argued that the rapprochement with West Germany only concerned 'the expansion of economic ties'.[51]

Dubcek nevertheless seemed to have downplayed the rapprochement with the FRG. Czechoslovak border guards had removed barbed wire and electric fences along the border with the FRG, and 40,000 Western tourists a day were travelling to Czechoslovakia. Arguing that the Czechoslovak 'border with the FRG is open', Brezhnev added that '[i]f such matters do not upset you, they do upset the GDR, Poland and the Soviet Union'. This was the crux of the conversation: in spite of 'the CPSU's principled position based on full respect for the independence of all fraternal parties and countries [...] not every question is a purely internal matter', as Brezhnev put it. Adding that 'Cdes. Gomulka, Ulbricht, Zhivkov, and the others [...] are prepared for [the defence of socialism in Czechoslovakia] as well', Brezhnev clearly indicated that the Czechoslovak question had become a question of the socialist camp.[52] It was not Czechoslovak loyalty to the WP as such that was at stake, but rather the repercussions of internal decisions on external developments.

Brezhnev's next step was to invite Gomulka, Ulbricht, Zhivkov and Kadar to Moscow on 8 May for a secret assessment of events in Czechoslovakia. Although Brezhnev repeated the need for 'joint measures' to defend socialism in Czechoslovakia, he agreed with Kadar, who still denied that there was a counterrevolution in Czechoslovakia.[53] Kadar strongly condemned the tunnel vision of some of his comrades:

> If we keep thinking that Mao Zedong and his comrades are not normal people, that Fidel Castro is a little bourgeois, that Ceausescu is a nationalist, and that the Czechoslovaks have all gone crazy, we cannot find any solution.[54]

Kadar nevertheless agreed with the other participants on the endeavour 'to get [Czechoslovak] consent to host joint military manoeuvres on [their] territory as soon as possible', so as to 'stabilise the situation in the country'. Brezhnev in turn agreed with Kadar to support the 'healthy forces in the Czechoslovak party', and concluded that 'we can agree, and I hope that Cdes. Ulbricht and Gomulka also agree, that at the given moment we will not mount an attack on the new CPCz leadership as a whole'.[55] The Polish and East German hard line seemed to be eclipsed by the Soviet-Hungarian duo.

Brezhnev was clearly under pressure from his East German and Polish comrades to take more decisive measures, but he stood his ground. Ulbricht and Gomulka seemed to have less scope for manoeuvre within this informal multilateral setting than within the checks and balances of the WP framework. Meanwhile, the new dynamics of the situation enabled Kadar to increase his influence by assuming a moderate position in between both extremes. Where Kadar used to side with Gomulka against Ceausescu, he now opposed Polish and East German extremism in the Czechoslovak case. Ceausescu's absence seemed to create more scope for manoeuvre for Kadar, whose moderation enabled Brezhnev to withstand the pressure from the hardliners within the CPSU and the WP. Brezhnev set such store by Kadar's mediating role that he called him at least once a week during the Prague Spring, and sometimes even twice a day.[56] Although Brezhnev could now call the shots, his shots were still significantly less far-reaching than some of its Eastern European allies might have wished.

The Romanian reaction

Meanwhile, Romania's forced exclusion from the decision making stood it in good stead in its relations with the West. Since rumours were increasing about a potential Soviet invasion of Czechoslovakia, the American Ambassador Goldberg asked Romanian Foreign Minister Manescu for information during a UN session in New York on 9 May. Manescu commiserated about the potential interference in Czechoslovak affairs, and proudly exclaimed that we 'firmly oppose any intervention to the last man'. Romania's foreign policy during the Czechoslovak crisis was praised in Washington, London and Paris, and the Romanian ambassador in Washington successfully purchased equipment and advanced technology from the USA, as well as resuming 'negotiations with representatives of General Electric in Canada to start a Romanian nuclear programme'.[57] Thus Romania's denunciation of its allies' decision making during the Prague Spring enabled its leadership once more to reap the benefits from its position as a maverick.

At the same time, the Romanian leaders were increasingly interested in intensifying the ties with their Czechoslovak comrades, and they seized the renewal of a bilateral friendship treaty on mutual assistance and cooperation as an opportunity to do so. Both sides negotiated on the treaty from 16–21 May in Bucharest. The Romanian delegates hoped to win the Czechoslovaks over to their position on the WP, and wanted to mention their desire for 'the simultaneous elimination of the two military blocs'. However, the Czechoslovak delegates remained loyal to the WP, and ultimately agreed to the stipulation that both countries were 'firmly determined to act in conformity with the Warsaw Pact as long as it is functional'.[58] Meanwhile, the other NSWP members were so sceptical about Romania's position within the WP that they decided 'to attempt to involve Romania' in the WP's development, but to continue, 'when that does not work, also without Romania'.[59]

On other aspects, too, the Romanians were still more extreme. The Czechoslovak leadership intended to include a reference to 'West German militarism', and reluctantly dropped the word 'West German' at Romanian request. With another epithet the Czechoslovak negotiators stood their ground: despite Romanian insistence on including 'the principle of national sovereignty' in the paragraph on relations between the socialist states, the

Czechoslovak side categorically rejected the epithet 'national', which the Romanian side wanted to use as a boost to its independent course.[60]

It is striking that the Czechoslovak delegates were not at all keen to model their foreign policy after the Romanian one. Despite reorienting its foreign policy towards the rest of Europe, including the FRG, they remained adamant about their loyalty to the WP, and were loth to downplay the West German threat. The Romanian leadership therefore hoped 'for a change in Czechoslovak foreign policy and an approach to the Romanian point of view, since this would signal the end of Romania's isolation', but Ceausescu's hope remained empty, and Dubcek turned down the RCP's invitation to visit Bucharest.[61] At this stage Dubcek still prioritised his relations with the Soviet Union over Romania, however extreme his foreign policy might have seemed to the 'five'.

The decline in relations

Czechoslovak relations with the Soviet Union became increasingly problematic, and the Soviet interpretation of events drew closer to the East German one.[62] During the CPCz CC plenum from 29 May to 1 June a schism arose between hardliners who copied Moscow's position and agreed with Bilak that the internal matters were 'not purely our own, Czechoslovak affair', and reform-minded members, who supported Dubcek.[63] As the party was confronted with fundamental changes, it was decided to bring the Extraordinary 14th CPCz Congress forward by two years, and to convene it on 9 September 1968. This move greatly worried Brezhnev, who feared the congress would be used to implement irreversible reforms and personnel changes. He immediately wrote to Dubcek to invite him to a bilateral meeting after Dubcek's scheduled visit to Hungary, at a location of his choice. Dubcek announced that he was 'at the present time [...] too busy', and was planning to return straight to Prague after visiting Kadar.[64] Dubcek's refusal to meet Brezhnev was a severe blow to the latter's faith in him.

Meanwhile, Kadar's relations with Dubcek were closely watched by the Romanian Ministry of Foreign Affairs, which somewhat enviously commented on 'Kadar's role as a mediator, with the Soviets on one side, and the Czechoslovaks on the other'.[65] Wont to mediate between great powers, Romania was pushed to the margins during the Prague Spring, and had so far even failed to win over Dubcek, who was much more interested in the reform-minded Kadar.[66] Having declined invitations to both Bucharest and Moscow, Dubcek eagerly travelled to Hungary on 13–14 June in the hopes of exchanging information about the meeting in Moscow and the developments in Czechoslovakia. Dubcek underscored the adverse effect of the Moscow meeting, which had led both Czechoslovak and Western newspapers to conclude that '[a]nother country has distanced itself from the camp', whereas Kadar explicitly warned Dubcek against succumbing to Romanian advances:

As far as we know, it seems to us that democracy is not the main concern of the Romanian leaders. Still, they welcome the events happening in Czechoslovakia, since they suppose that they might find allies against the Soviet Union, against CMEA (COMECON), and against the Warsaw Pact there.[67]

Kadar hit the nail on the head, since the reforms in Czechoslovakia were quite the opposite from Romania's internal development. The RCP had an extremely firm grip on its people, did not allow any freedom of expression, and its united leadership had managed to elevate the party's monopoly of power beyond limits. It was exactly because the Czechoslovak leadership failed on all these fronts, that 'the five' feared the demise of socialism altogether. Socialism in Romania was not at stake, and despite its independent foreign policy, it was clear that for *internal* reasons Romania would remain a strong link in the WP. Its independent foreign policy even consolidated the RCP's dictatorial rule domestically, which indirectly strengthened the socialist camp. If the Prague Spring illustrates that internal matters can become external, it also explains why Romania was never threatened with invasion: its domestic developments would never be 'the first domino' in the collapse of the Soviet bloc.[68]

Two weeks after the meeting between Dubcek and Kadar, Czechoslovak freedom had spun so much out of control that the Czechoslovak author Ludvik Vaculik published a manifesto of 'Two Thousand Words' in four major newspapers, which was signed by nearly 70 prominent intellectuals. The manifesto strongly endorsed the 'regenerative process of democratisation' since the beginning of 1968, and praised the 'Action Programme', but asked for a better Central Committee to be elected at the Czechoslovak communist congress in September. It also 'demand[ed] the departure of people who abused their power', and the establishment of new committees and platforms, e.g. for the defence of free speech, which would enable the people to participate in politics, and, in short, create a civil society out of the control of the CPCz. Clearly encouraging Dubcek and the reform-minded communists within the party to liberalise society still further, and warning against 'the possibility that foreign forces will intervene in our development', the possibility of foreign intervention almost turned into a self-fulfilling prophecy. The remark that 'we can assure our allies that we will observe our treaties of alliance, friendship, and trade' did little to assuage its allies' apprehension.[69] The 'Two Thousand Words' proclaimed everything that 'the five' denounced, and did Dubcek an inadvertent disservice: it pre-empted any attempts to convince 'the five' that the situation was under control, and thus made Dubcek's situation still more untenable.[70]

The reaction from the 'five' was predictable. Dubcek received a series of letters that expressed great concern about the situation and put him under increasing pressure to gain control. Any fears about counterrevolution now seemed vindicated, as Brezhnev stressed in his letter. He was 'doubly and triply alarm[ed]' by the fact 'that all this is going on two months before the party's Extraordinary Congress begins its work'. Even Czechoslovak officials had joined the attacks on 'the positions of the socialist countries on vital issues', and had 'emphasise[d] the notion that the place of Czechoslovakia in foreign policy should be based on its geographical location, that is, on its being "between the USSR and Germany"'. Dubcek's claims about allegiance to the WP and the defence of socialism thus seemed increasingly hollow to 'the five'. Adding that the CPSU was 'ready to provide all necessary help to socialist Czechoslovakia', Brezhnev clearly indicated that he no longer expected Dubcek to control the situation on his own.[71]

At the same time, there were clear indications that 'all necessary help' might not be only political. As agreed at the Moscow meeting, the Kremlin had organised 'strategic-operational command-staff exercises' on Czechoslovak territory, in which 30–40,000 troops of 'the five' would participate. Although these military manoeuvres, called the 'Sumava Exercises', had already been planned in 1967, they had initially been scheduled for late 1968 or early 1969, but the Czechoslovak leadership had agreed to bring the date forward to mid-June. The Czechoslovak defence officials became increasingly apprehensive, however, because of the participation of additional Polish and East German troops, 'the [unusually high] number of combat units',[72] and the ad hoc and '[unilateral] decisions by [Soviet] Marshal Yakubovskii', the WP's supreme commander, who 'for unknown reasons [...] has sought to prolong the exercises'. The Czechoslovak leadership accordingly asked Brezhnev 'to terminate the exercises, carry out the final analysis, and withdraw all allied troops from CSSR territory'.[73] At this stage the Kremlin nevertheless wanted to keep all options open, by involving the Warsaw Pact on a military level, while ignoring it politically.

Meanwhile, a top secret Hungarian report about the Sumava Exercises vindicates the Czechoslovak concerns. According to the report, 'the exercise was organised essentially for political reasons and with political objectives', as a 'kind of camouflage' to demonstrate 'the strength and unity of the Warsaw Pact, [...] influence the Czechoslovak events, [...] and shore up the authority of the Soviet Union and the Warsaw Pact'. However, this strategy proved counterproductive. The Hungarian officials concluded that 'the experience of the entire exercise unfortunately confirmed that there are unacceptable shortcomings, irregularities, and inadequate provisions in the Warsaw Pact, [which] will erode the dignity of the Soviet Union and undermine the pact'. The Soviet side in turn regarded '[t]he repeated insistence [...] that the exercise be terminated' as a blemish on Soviet-Czechoslovak friendship,[74] and was surprised at the lack of 'the fraternal warmth and friendliness that had previously distinguished the Czechoslovak friends'.[75]

In the month of June trust was accordingly eroded on both sides: whereas Brezhnev suspected Dubcek's decision to reject another bilateral meeting, the Sumava Exercises exacerbated the apprehension of a Soviet intervention in Czechoslovakia. Meanwhile, the 'Two Thousand Words' seemed a clear indication that the counterrevolutionary situation in Czechoslovakia threatened to become irreversible, whereas 'the five' regarded the weak denunciation of the 'Two Thousand Words' by the CPCz as another indication that Dubcek had lost control. At the same time, the use of WP exercises as camouflage had weakened its position.

Warsaw: the point of no return?

During the month of July relations between Czechoslovakia and its allies took a new turn. The mutual erosion of trust necessitated further consultations, and Brezhnev decided to invite Dubcek to Warsaw for a meeting with 'the five'.[76] Dubcek nevertheless declined the invitation out of fear of being 'pilloried',[77] while stressing respect for 'the sovereignty of every party on questions of its internal policy'. In a conversation with Soviet Ambassador Chervonenko, Dubcek proposed 'bilateral negotiations [...] with representatives of the fraternal parties', including 'representatives of the Communist Party of Romania and the League of Communists of Yugoslavia' instead.[78] Thus Dubeck attempted to broaden the scope of negotiations to two more countries for which the concepts of sovereignty and non-interference were paramount, and which were prone to sympathise with Czechoslovak interests. Dubcek began to realise that he might now need Ceausescu's support. Echoing the rhetoric of national communists, Dubcek clearly undermined the five's prerogative to determine the Czechoslovak course of events, while also suggesting the inclusion of a non-WP member, which had officially broken with Moscow in 1948, in the negotiations. Whereas 'the five' had represented a reduced WP, Dubcek proposed to transcend the limits of the WP altogether, while also pre-empting the dynamics of multilateralism.

Chervonenko's reaction was accordingly far from enthusiastic, and emphasised that 'with this step the CPCz leadership, and above all Cde. Dubcek, are bringing their relations with the CPSU into a new phase'. Chervonenko showed little understanding for Dubcek's reference to sovereignty on internal matters, but explained instead that 'the problem was not only the internal situation in Czechoslovakia, but also whether the CPCz under his leadership would remain an internationalist component of the socialist camp'.[79] The problem with Czechoslovakia extended again further than the Romanian and Yugoslav insistence on national sovereignty, since communism itself was at stake. Dubcek's arguments were therefore bound to fall on deaf ears.

The Romanian leadership was far more susceptible to Dubcek's reasoning. Since the Kremlin witnessed the incipient rapprochement between Czechoslovakia and Romania with apprehension, the Soviet ambassador to Romania, Vladimir Basov, visited Ceausescu on 12 July to inform him about the situation in Czechoslovakia. Anticipating criticism on Soviet interference, Basov emphasised that the fraternal parties had explicitly asked the CPSU for assistance, since the 'situation in Czechoslovakia was becoming still more alarming', with anti-socialist forces intensifying the counterrevolution, the 'Two Thousand Words' undermining the CPCz, and the party itself reorienting its foreign policy in such a way that it would be 'determined by its geographical situation [...] "in between the SU and Germany"'.[80] Basov thus attempted to convince Ceausescu of the 'international duty of all fraternal parties to provide the C.P. of Czechoslovakia with all support that is necessary in this difficult moment'. Ceausescu nevertheless argued that 'the Czechoslovak party has the situation under control', and that he was 'greatly worried about possible actions of interference in internal affairs', which would have 'grave consequences in the world and the communist movement'. He strongly condemned 'the convention of a meeting of a group of parties from socialist countries, excluding other parties from socialist countries', and urged the Soviets 'to find other ways'.[81] The Romanian emphasis on non-interference clearly went beyond mere rhetoric.[82]

Dubcek's refusal to attend the meeting in Warsaw proved a *faux pas*. He had further antagonised the hardliners, while also greatly disappointing Kadar, who still believed in a multilateral solution. In another attempt to mediate, Kadar proposed a bilateral Soviet-Czechoslovak meeting before the multilateral one in Warsaw. When the CPCz presidium rejected this proposal too, Kadar's support for Dubcek began to evaporate. On a vain quest for sympathy, Dubcek asked Kadar to meet him secretly. The meeting took place on Hungarian territory on 13 July, one day before the meeting in Warsaw. It was, however, a cold shower for Dubcek and Cernik, as Kadar and Hungarian Prime Minister Jeno Fock severely rebuked them for turning down the invitation to Warsaw, and emphasised that their relations, too, had entered a new phase, in which they would be 'fighting on opposing sides'.[83] Dubcek's refusal to re-enter the multilateral setting severely undermined his own stance and offended his allies. Bilateralism had already become an anachronism.

The Hungarian politburo still denied the existence of a counterrevolution in Czechoslovakia, and sent Kadar to Warsaw with a resolution that a political solution should be sought instead of a military one.[84] During the meeting in Warsaw on 14-15 July Kadar nevertheless criticised Dubcek's 'refusal to take part in our meeting', and emphasised that it was 'both the right and the duty of the socialist countries to decide collectively' about Czechoslovakia.[85] His willingness to close ranks with the other four socialist countries failed to carry conviction. Both Ulbricht and Zhivkov strongly criticised Kadar for downplaying the situation, and Ulbricht even added that Hungary's internal problems might be the next to be remedied. Ulbricht predicted the abolition of the communist party in Czechoslovakia, and therefore suggested sending 'a joint open letter to the CPCz CC', which 'should draw a connection between the internal developments in Czechoslovakia and the general developments in the international arena'. Zhivkov went a step further, and argued that '[t]here is only one appropriate way out – [...] by relying on the armed forces of the Warsaw Pact'.[86] The arguments, too, had accordingly entered a new phase: the call to arms had now been voiced.

Brezhnev nevertheless remained far more moderate. He refrained from attacking Kadar, and dwelt on the most problematic aspects of the situation in Czechoslovakia, such as the 'counterrevolutionary process', the fact that 'the leading role of the communist party is being undermined', 'the demands [...] for a radical reassessment of foreign policy', and '[t]he party's relinquishment of control over the mass media'. Although he agreed to Ulbricht's proposal of a letter to the CPCz, he still preferred a political solution, while promising 'Czechoslovakia all necessary assistance':[87]

> If the threat that the political content of the CPCz will be transformed into some sort of new organisation is real [...] then this, I repeat, affects the interests not only of communists in Czechoslovakia and not only the people of Czechoslovakia, but the interests of the entire socialist system and of the whole world communist movement. Any attempt to thwart such a process cannot be considered interference in internal affairs.[88]

Thus Brezhnev eloquently legitimised *any* interference in Czechoslovak affairs, if it served the salvation of the socialist system. After Brezhnev had concluded the meeting, Kadar unexpectedly took the floor and praised Brezhnev's speech in particular, while emphasising his readiness 'to take part in all joint actions'.[89] Kadar's U-turn on the Czechoslovak crisis was complete. Ulbricht's remark on Hungary's internal situation may have prompted Kadar to tread his ground more carefully. Moreover, the fact that Brezhnev had not decided yet on a military solution, despite pressure from the hardliners, enabled Kadar to continue backing Brezhnev. His support for Dubcek had fully evaporated, and the balance thus began to tilt in favour of stronger measures.

The 'five' therefore decided to prepare a joint letter, in which they legitimised interference in Czechoslovak affairs along Brezhnev's lines. The letter primarily aimed at an internal, political solution of the situation by demanding that the CPCz leadership take 'decisive' measures against 'anti-socialist forces', end the activities of anti-socialist political organisations, reassert 'control over the mass media', and close ranks.[90] The letter was, as such, an ultimatum to the Czechoslovak leadership.

Meanwhile, the Polish delegation was entrusted with the draft of a communiqué that explicitly omitted any 'references to the Warsaw Pact', as Romania had not participated in the meeting.[91] The Warsaw Pact was, accordingly, not used as an instrument either to justify or organise any actions against Czechoslovakia: Brezhnev in particular was very careful to refrain from referring to the alliance. Although the WP had provided a useful training in multilateralism, it was not the WP framework that facilitated the decision making. Had the Warsaw meeting taken place within the confines of a PCC meeting, then the letter could never have been sent to Czechoslovakia, as the Romanian and Czechoslovak participants would not have agreed. The WP had turned into too mature an alliance to lend itself to the somewhat obfuscated decision making during the Prague Spring.

The Warsaw letter, meanwhile, did not go down well with either the Czechoslovak leadership or the Czechoslovak people. Its publication provoked huge condemnation of the Warsaw meeting, and the popular support for Dubcek and his comrades was greater than ever.[92] After Dubcek and Cernik had written a letter to Brezhnev in which they expressed their anger at the convention of the meeting, the CPCz presidium wrote another letter in which they stressed their disagreement with the assessment of the internal situation by 'the five'.[93] The letter categorically denied 'the assertion that our current situation is counterrevolutionary or the allegation of an imminent threat to the foundations of the socialist system', and emphasised that '[t]he overriding orientation of Czechoslovakia's foreign policy [...] is alliance and cooperation with the Soviet Union and the other socialist states', including active participation in the WP.[94] Dubcek's refusal to attend the Warsaw meeting nevertheless indicated that he was under internal pressure to prioritise the reform process to socialist cooperation.

Claiming that 'the political situation is consolidating and that the influence of the party [...] is growing stronger', the presidium members emphasised the 'respect for [...] non-interference in [...] internal affairs', as 'enshrined in the Declaration of the Government of the USSR of 30 October 1956'. The letter ended with another proposal 'to arrange bilateral negotiations', which could serve to 'consider' a possible multilateral meeting on Czechoslovak terms.[95] The Czechoslovak leadership clearly wanted to regain control over its relations with its allies, while avoiding another Dresden.[96] To some extent, the Czechoslovak leaders had a point: meetings within the WP had increasingly been prepared in a bilateral or multilateral setting, and the tendency to present the participants with a *fait accompli* had become outdated. The multilateralisation during the Prague Spring was, however, not institutionalised, and therefore hard to control. With the proposal for bilateral meetings the situation was, therefore, almost back to square one. Since the Czechoslovak leadership emphatically failed to accept the distinction between internal affairs *with* or *without* external repercussions, the allies were still arguing at cross purposes.

The Romanian interpretation

The deterioration in relations between Czechoslovakia and 'the five' was greatly welcomed by the Romanian leadership, which publicly condemned the Warsaw meeting, and began to develop an altogether new interpretation of the developments in Czechoslovakia. Although the Czechoslovak leadership still strove to prove its loyalty to the Soviet Union, the Romanian leadership was convinced that the Czechoslovak reforms were inspired by Czechoslovak 'discontent [...] with the prolonged situation of dependence [...] on the SU'.[97] Projecting Romanian interests on the CPCz, the Romanian leadership began to construe a new narrative of the situation in Czechoslovakia to escape from its own isolation.

The limits of emancipation: the Prague Spring 233

The Romanian leadership even turned again to its Chinese comrades, which it had largely ignored since the beginning of the Cultural Revolution in August 1966. The Romanian politburo member Bodnaras summoned the Chinese diplomat in Bucharest, Ma Siu Sen, in order to discuss the Warsaw letter and other letters by the 'five', and share his interpretation of the Czechoslovak situation. Bodnaras argued that Romania 'had encouraged other countries […] to adopt a course towards affirming their own political personality, independent from the Soviet Union', and that 'the Czechoslovak comrades, too, were influenced in that way'. According to Bodnaras, the Czechoslovak leadership no longer wanted to be 'an instrument of Soviet politics in Czechoslovakia', and he therefore concluded that 'socialism [was] not in danger in Czechoslovakia', but the 'dominance of the SU'. He even added that '[t]hey fear the emancipation of the Czechoslovak people, because this will encourage a process of general emancipation from the control of the CPSU in Hungary, in Poland, in the GDR, in Bulgaria'.[98]

With this remark Bodnaras had partly identified the crux of the issue. The Kremlin, and many of its Eastern European allies, indeed feared the domino effect of the Czechoslovak calls for reforms. Although the Romanian people might have secretly cherished similar hopes, Ceausescu's control was such that he did not have to fear Czechoslovak contagion. It was, however, not so much 'emancipation from the control of the CPSU' that was at stake; Ulbricht, Gomulka, and Zhivkov cherished more extreme views than Brezhnev, because they feared the Czechoslovak *people* would emancipate from the control of the Czechoslovak *party*, and that the people in the other WP countries would follow. That seemed to happen in Czechoslovakia, which explains why 'the five' were far more concerned about Czechoslovak developments than about the position of Romania. The Romanian leadership obviously had 'emancipated' itself far more from the Soviet grip than the Czechoslovak leadership. It could condemn the Warsaw meeting and other Soviet measures with impunity. However, the Romanian people had not been able to emancipate themselves from the party at all. Ceausescu's scope for manoeuvre within the WP was, as such, related to his control over the Romanian people. A Bucharest Spring was unthinkable; Ceausescu succeeded in ensuring that it would remain winter.

It did, however, serve Romanian public relations to equate Czechoslovak and Romanian developments; support of the Prague Spring became instrumental to the Romanian image. It made Ceausescu's regime seem all the more sympathetic, and confirmed Romania's role as maverick within the WP. Bodnaras's reference to 'emancipation' is particularly interesting, as this is a rare instance of its use in formal documents. It indicates again a mature kind of self-reflection and proves that Romania's role in the WP and its attitude within the Prague Spring – albeit partly forced by its exclusion – were part of a consciously developed strategy. According to Bodnaras, the Romanians owed their emancipation to the Chinese, which fully fits with earlier findings in this book:

The Romanians, who have enjoyed the privilege of having more contacts with the Chinese CP, including personal contacts, such as those by comrades Ceausescu, Maurer, Chivu, Bodnaras and Gheorghiu-Dej, have felt support and have had many things to learn from the very inspiring and useful exchanges with the leadership of the Chinese Communist Party, headed by Cde. Mao Zedong. This has contributed to the strengthening of our position, to our political orientation, to the defence of the principles of independence, to equality in rights, sovereignty, non-interference in internal affairs, to the leading role of the communist party, of the working class, of the construction of socialism.[99]

This assessment seemed much closer to the truth: the Chinese and Romanian autonomy vis-à-vis the Soviet Union, combined with a strict regime at home, indeed shared many features. In 1968, during the height of the Chinese Cultural Revolution, it was, however, more advantageous to the Romanian leadership to stress its support for Czechoslovakia. The Romanian leaders had therefore already arranged with their Czechoslovak comrades to meet them immediately after their meeting with the Soviets. Romania's public support of the Czechoslovak cause stood it in good stead in many European capitals: 'the emancipation of its foreign policy' was, in the very same words, praised in Paris, where a telegram from the Ministry of Foreign Affairs added that the Romanian leaders 'acted very wisely', as 'Romania's policy of independence is irreversible now, hence accepted by the Soviet Union and its other allies in the East'.[100] It is remarkable to note that both the Romanian leadership and its admirers in other European capitals began to use the rhetoric of 'emancipation' at exactly the same time. Although Czechoslovak foreign policy was still shrouded in ambiguities, the Prague Spring had enabled Romanian emancipation to be sealed.

Soviet-Czechoslovak estrangement

The Romanian interest in the Czechoslovak cause coincided with a further estrangement between the Czechoslovak leadership and the Kremlin. On the last day of the Warsaw meeting the Czechoslovak General Vaclav Prchlik had held a press conference in which he strongly condemned the Warsaw meeting, while denouncing 'the five' for the 'violations of the fundamental clauses of the Warsaw Treaty', such as the principles of sovereignty and non-interference.[101] The Soviet government was furious about this indictment, and accused Prchlik of 'undermining the Warsaw Pact', while expressing its increasing concern about the security situation in Czechoslovakia.[102] At the same time the 'five' decided to start preparing 'Operation Danube', which was the code name for a military intervention in Czechoslovakia.[103] Ulbricht and Zhivkov offered concrete military assistance on 21 July. Two days later Kadar finally decided that Hungary would participate, too, which earned him profound gratitude from the Kremlin.[104]

Unlike the Sumava Exercises, 'Operation Danube' was not an official WP exercise. It concerned military manoeuvres on Czechoslovak soil in which the participants constituted a kind of 'coalition of the willing'. Military intervention had, however, not yet become irreversible. As a Hungarian report notes, '[the Soviet generals] declared that although we will prepare for the exercises [...], it would be good if we did not actually have to go ahead with them. The political objective of the manoeuvres is to help the Czechoslovak people defeat the counterrevolution'.[105] The Rubicon had not yet been crossed.

Brezhnev still tried to find a political solution for the situation in Czechoslovakia. He therefore agreed to the request the CPCz presidium had made in its letter of 17 July, namely to meet bilaterally on Czechoslovak soil. On 29 July Brezhnev and Kosygin met Dubcek and Cernik in Cierna nad Tisou, a small railroad crossing town in Slovakia, to find a way out of the impasse. Brezhnev named all the usual arguments, while emphasising yet again that the salvation of socialism in Czechoslovakia was 'not purely an internal affair', but, instead, 'our international duty'. Adding that *'the threat of a counterrevolutionary coup in your country has become a reality'*, he blamed Dubcek for refusing to come to Warsaw, which amounted to negligence of *his* 'international duty': he had turned down 'fraternal' assistance for nothing less than the salvation of socialism.[106]

Dubcek nevertheless condemned 'the Warsaw meeting [...] as a means of external pressure on our party'. Still expressing Czechoslovakia's 'firm' and 'loyal' allegiance to the WP, he continued that '[t]he aim of the Warsaw Pact concerns defence preparations and foreign policy activity. The Pact would betray its aims and be seriously weakened if it were actually being used to try to influence internal developments in our state'. Dubcek's remark was explicitly targeted at a letter from Walter Ulbricht, which 'proposes to assist us via the Warsaw Pact – in other words by military action'.[107] Dubcek had rightly realised that the 'Warsaw Pact [...] cannot launch a campaign against a socialist country without that country's approval', but he had wrongly concluded that there would be *no* invasion: there could be an invasion, but there simply could not be a *Warsaw Pact* invasion.[108] The Warsaw Pact did not pose a threat to Dubcek's leadership, but the fact that the decision making took place *outside* its institutional confines did.

Soviet Premier Kosygin was not at all convinced by Dubcek's arguments, and thus the negotiations in Cierna nad Tisou, too, ended in stalemate. The Soviet side nevertheless agreed to convene another multilateral meeting on Czechoslovak conditions: it would take place on Czechoslovak territory, and neither the Warsaw meeting, the Warsaw letter, nor the situation in Czechoslovakia would be mentioned. The Kremlin had agreed to this under the condition that the Czechoslovak leadership would regain control over the situation by removing certain officials as well as taking '[r]adical measures vis-à-vis the mass media'.[109] For the time being, Dubcek and his comrades seemed to have gained the upper hand in the negotiations.

A multilateral solution?

A multilateral conference was scheduled in the Slovak capital Bratislava on 3 August. Brezhnev was still eager to find a political solution, but most of his allies were impatient to undertake military measures. Gomulka 'voiced a certain discontent that the Soviet comrades had agreed to the Bratislava meeting',[110] the East German leadership could not wait 'to deal a collective blow',[111] and the Bulgarian leader Zhivkov also referred to 'all possible and necessary means, including the armed forces of the Warsaw Pact if the situation so demands'.[112] Mentioning the break with China and Albania, and the delicate relations with Cuba, Romania and Yugoslavia, Zhivkov argued that 'if […] Czechoslovakia leaves the Warsaw Pact or remains in it and behaves like Romania or some other revisionist state, the forces of the Warsaw Pact will be severely weakened and this will pose a great threat to the GDR, Hungary, and Poland'.[113] The concerns about Czechoslovakia's internal situation were thus exacerbated by worries about its actual loyalty to the Warsaw Pact. Czechoslovakia's incipient 'emancipation' from Soviet control was not at all welcomed by most of the NSWP members.

Thus the Kremlin had convened a multilateral meeting against the wishes of most participants. This, too, would not have been possible if it concerned an official PCC meeting. All Czechoslovak conditions were nevertheless fulfilled: Czechoslovakia was not specifically mentioned, and a declaration was prepared concerning 'the current international situation' in general.[114] Brezhnev was obviously keen to keep Dubcek on board. The actual composition of the document was, however, truly multilateral, and CPCz presidium member Bilak mentioned in his memoirs that '[t]his was the only meeting in my life […] where literally every word of the document, from A to Z, was written by the first/general secretaries of the parties and by the prime ministers'.[115] The crux of the declaration was the clause that 'defending these [socialist] gains […] is the common international duty of all the socialist countries'. Although the Czechoslovak participants succeeded in including the 'principles of equality, respect for sovereignty and national independence, territorial integrity, fraternal mutual assistance, and solidarity', despite vehement objections from the East German participants, they failed to convince their comrades to include the principle of 'non-interference in internal affairs' too.[116] This left open the option of 'fraternal assistance' for the salvation of socialism.

Meanwhile, a minority of five pro-Moscow hardliners within the CPCz, headed by Vasil Bilak, used the Bratislava conference to give the Soviet leadership a secret letter, which Bilak secretly gave to CPSU politburo member Pyotr Shelest in the men's lavatory. Echoing Soviet rhetoric, the letter underlined that '[t]he very existence of socialism is under threat', and that the 'Czechoslovak Socialist Republic' can only be saved from 'counterrevolution' with Soviet 'support and assistance with all the means at your disposal'. The letter concluded that 'our statement should be regarded as an urgent request and plea for your intervention and all-round assistance'.[117] The Bratislava conference had thus proved a Trojan Horse: it had facilitated an invitation for the Soviets to intervene, and its declaration, too, could be used to justify intervention.

The Czechoslovak presidium was, however, optimistic about its outcome, and considered it 'a fresh impetus for the promotion of mutually beneficial relations among the fraternal parties'.[118] Kadar fully agreed, and was particularly relieved that a political solution still seemed possible.[119] The Bratislava meeting seemed to have erased the negative consequences of the Warsaw meeting. Czechoslovak isolation appeared to have been overcome in Bratislava, and the unity of 'the five' restored. All this would, however, prove merely cosmetic, if the internal situation in Czechoslovakia, where Dubcek was still under a lot of pressure to continue the reforms, did not change. The five socialist countries still had their 'internationalist duty' to consider.

Casting the die

The Kremlin was not so optimistic about the situation, as Dubcek still failed to gain control over the party, the press and 'the rightist forces' after Bratislava.[120] Brezhnev subsequently embarked on a campaign of telephone conversations, messages from the CPSU and letters in order to urge Dubcek to fulfil 'the agreements reached at Cierna nad Tisou'.[121] The telephone calls symptomised the increasingly untenable situation. While Brezhnev concluded that the Czechoslovak 'presidium in general has lost all its power', and referred to 'new, independent measures', Dubcek emphasised that he was 'running out of steam', and 'thinking of giving up this work', and pleaded for 'more time [...] to fulfil the agreement we reached in Cierna nad Tisou'.[122] Although Brezhnev's phone calls were reinforced by a personal letter and by another conversation with Chervonenko, the internal situation did not seem to change.[123] As the British historian William Shawcross aptly puts it, 'Dubcek was forced to play the part of flustered referee in a savage game between an excited chauvinistic Czechoslovak public and angry frightened Warsaw Pact allies'.[124] 'Internationalist duty' became all the more important to ensure that Czechoslovakia and the WP continued playing the same game.

Brezhnev still hoped to avoid an intervention, and asked for his allies' support in finding a political solution. Brezhnev accordingly decided to meet with a kindred spirit, and invited Kadar to a meeting in Yalta on 12–15 August. Kadar's optimism after Bratislava had evaporated, and although he emphasised that 'political problems require political solutions', he also added that 'we have seen and recognised that military assistance may prove necessary on our part'. Kadar and Brezhnev agreed that a political solution was still preferable, but that a military one might be inevitable. In order to prevent the latter, Brezhnev asked Kadar 'to have one more talk with Dubcek', as 'apart from the Soviet Union, the HSWP [Hungarian Socialist Workers Party] is the only party that can make some impression on them'.[125]

Brezhnev was nevertheless under mounting pressure to invade by the hardliners within the CPSU, such as Minister of Defence Andrei Grechko and politburo member Alexander Shelepin, who vied for Brezhnev's position within the politburo. The Czechoslovak ambassador to the UN told his Romanian colleague a month *after* the invasion that Brezhnev and Kosygin 'had been against a military invasion in Czechoslovakia and had militated for political solutions'.[126] Although Ulbricht, Gomulka and Zhivkov also pressed Brezhnev to give the green light for intervention, Brezhnev preferred to discuss the matter once more with the more moderate Kadar. He thus attempted to withstand the pressures from the hardliners both domestically and internationally.

Dubcek, meanwhile, chose to discuss the situation with Ceausescu instead, who had arrived in Prague with a delegation at the highest level of representation on 15–16 August. Romanian support had become increasingly welcome as the pressure from 'the five' grew. Dubcek accordingly used this meeting to emphasise that the Czechoslovak contacts with 'the five' had radically changed for the worse, even though Czechoslovak foreign policy had not changed significantly and Czechoslovakia would remain loyal to the WP. The Czechoslovak prime minister added that the situation in Czechoslovakia was not 'counterrevolutionary' anyhow, and that 'every communist party should be responsible for its own fate'.[127] The Czechoslovak optimism after Bratislava also seemed to have evaporated.

Dubcek's and Cernik's arguments must have sounded like music to Ceausescu's ears. With their defiance of the 'five' and their emphasis on the right to conduct affairs as they saw fit, the Czechoslovak leaders began to draw increasingly near to the Romanian position. Ceausescu therefore emphasised his fundamental disagreement with 'the five' and strengthened the Czechoslovak resolve to act independently, while praising the Czechoslovak course since the January plenum. He also stressed that he was against 'any kind of interference in internal problems', and that he had warned the Kremlin against armed intervention, too. The escalation of tensions between Dubcek and 'the five' thus enabled Ceausescu to present himself as a staunch supporter of the Czechoslovak right to independence, while defying the pressure of 'the five'. Dubcek had lost five allies, but Ceausescu had now gained an ally for whom the Romanian insistence on 'non-interference in internal affairs' had come as a godsend.[128] Dubcek underscored the unity of views and his 'profound sympathy [...] for Ceausescu personally' during the toasts after the meeting. His faith in Ceausescu nevertheless definitively sealed the deterioration of relations with 'the five'.[129]

Dubcek's meeting with Ceausescu therefore stood in sharp contrast to the one with Kadar, which took place one day later, on 17 August. Kadar and Dubcek strongly disagreed in their assessment of the Warsaw meeting, although both considered the Bratislava declaration constructive. Dubcek nevertheless explained 'that Czechoslovakia's internal political situation is more complicated than it was before the Warsaw meeting', whereas Kadar

The limits of emancipation: the Prague Spring 239

seemed to have lost faith in Dubcek's ability to act.[130] Instead of promising to undertake action, Dubcek was justifying his failure to act. The meeting was to no avail, since Dubcek had already switched allegiance to Ceausescu.

The intervention

Meanwhile, the necessity to act had been unanimously agreed at a lengthy politburo meeting in Moscow, which had convened on 15–17 August. Considering the fact 'that all political means […] have already been exhausted', the Soviet politburo had 'unanimously decided to provide help and support to the Communist Party and people of Czechoslovakia with military force'.[131] The politburo had also drafted a letter to the CPCz presidium, with an ultimate warning to 'adopt the necessary, urgent measures', in order to fulfil 'the commitments undertaken by you' at Cierna nad Tisou.[132] Emphasising that '[a]ny delay in this matter would be extremely dangerous', the Kremlin clearly implied military intervention, although the letter was not interpreted as such in Prague.[133] Since the Kremlin had definitively lost faith in Dubcek,

Figure 6.1 Nicolae Ceausescu (right) on his visit to Alexander Dubcek (left), 15–16 August 1968
Source: ANIC, fototeca online a comunismului românesc, photo #G539, 202/1968; upload.wikimedia.org/wikipedia/commons/c/cd/IICCR_G539_Ceausescu_Dubcek_Svoboda.jpg

Chervonenko immediately arranged a secret meeting with the Czechoslovak President Ludvik Svoboda on 17 August, and warned him 'that the CPSU CC Politburo will do what is required by the circumstances, but will never permit the socialist gains in fraternal Czechoslovakia to be damaged'.[134] Although Svoboda begged him not to 'resort to military means', Chervonenko concluded 'that at the most trying and critical moment, Svoboda will stand with the CPSU and the Soviet Union'.[135]

At the same time, in Moscow, General Ivan Pavlovskii, the Soviet deputy minister of defence, was appointed supreme commander of the invasion.[136] Thus the control over the invasion was at the last moment transferred from Warsaw Pact Supreme Commander Yakubovskii, who had coordinated the Sumava Exercises, to the deputy defence minister. It is important to note that the intervention in Czechoslovakia was *not* carried out under WP command, but under Soviet command, while the decision of the other four socialist countries to employ *their* armies was made within the framework of the respective governments, and *not* the Warsaw Pact. The alliance accordingly did not even enter the equation on an operative level.

On 18 August Brezhnev convened his four allies to inform them about the politburo's decision. Emphasising the failure of the Czechoslovak leadership to fulfil its commitments, Brezhnev explained that 'we had no other choice in handling things'.[137] On the same day the Kremlin sent a letter to the CPSU CC members to explain the need for 'active measures in defence of socialism in the CSSR'. Referring again to the 'internationalist duty' of 'the five', the letter stated that 'the governments of the five countries have ordered their military units to take all necessary measures on 21 August'. Thus the Warsaw Pact was explicitly not used in order to legitimise the intervention: the emphasis was on the consent of the *governments*, turning the invasion into an intergovernmental venture instead. The letter concluded that '[t]he troops of our countries will not interfere in the internal affairs of fraternal Czechoslovakia. They will be withdrawn from its territory as soon as the danger to the independence and security of Czechoslovakia and to the socialist future of the Czechoslovak people is eliminated'.[138] Again the salvation of socialism was paramount.

However hollow the phrase 'the salvation of socialism' may seem, it was of course not at all the armies' intention to wage a war on Czechoslovak soil, and measures were therefore taken to avoid any bloodshed. Soviet soldiers were ordered to 'exercise maximum restraint', and to concentrate on the defence of socialism instead.[139] Meanwhile, Chervonenko arranged a meeting with President Svoboda on the eve of the invasion to explain the reasons for intervening and to 'appeal to the army and people of Czechoslovakia not to resist the troops of the fraternal countries'. Although Svoboda objected to the intervention of troops, he agreed with Chervonenko's request in order to avoid bloodshed, and added that he 'would never cut his ties with the USSR'.[140] Defence Minister General Martin Dzur made the same decision, and ordered all troops 'to remain in their barracks', to refrain from using weapons, and to give 'maximum all-round assistance' to the Soviet troops.[141] On the night of 20–21 August, approximately 170,000 Soviet troops entered Czechoslovak territory, supported by Polish, Bulgarian and Hungarian combat units, and an East German liaison unit.[142] The Czechoslovak people and soldiers offered, indeed, no armed resistance. From a military point of view, the salvation of socialism seemed to go according to plan.

From a political point of view, however, the 'salvation of socialism' was not quite so easy. Although the 'five' had counted on the 'healthy forces' within the CPCz presidium, led by Bilak, to take care of the political side of affairs, they turned out to be in the minority. Shortly after the foreign troops had entered Czechoslovak territory, the presidium voted with a majority of seven to four to adopt a statement in which it emphasised that 'the border crossing not only contravenes all principles governing relations between socialist states, but also violates the fundamental provisions of international law'. The CPCz presidium nevertheless also asked the citizens to 'remain calm and to refrain from putting up any resistance against the advancing troops, since it would now be impossible to defend our state borders'.[143] Although the troops of 'the five' accordingly entered Czechoslovak soil with hardly any resistance, the invasion turned into a Pyrrhic victory: however successful militarily, political legitimation was conspicuous by its absence.

Paving the way for 'normalisation'

The 'five' went to great lengths to legitimise their course of action in international terms. They sent the Romanian politburo a letter in which 'the immediate help in the struggle against forces of the right' and against 'counterrevolution' was justified as follows:

> The defence of socialism in Czechoslovakia is not only an internal affair of the people of that country, but it is, as you understand, the problem of preserving the security of our countries, the problem of defending the positions of global socialism.[144]

Thus clearly formulating a theory that would later be known as 'the Brezhnev doctrine', the 'five' continued to stress that 'interference in internal affairs' was out of the question, since the allied armies would withdraw as soon as socialism was consolidated.[145]

The Romanian politburo, which Ceausescu had convened at 6.30 in the morning, as soon as he had been informed about the intervention, was, however, not so easily convinced. Its members unanimously decided to send a letter to 'the five', in which their action was defined as 'the occupation of Czechoslovakia', and in which the Romanian leadership emphasised their 'disapproval' of the 'flagrant transgression of the national sovereignty' and the 'interference in internal affairs'. The politburo members categorically rejected the assessment of the situation in Czechoslovakia as 'counterrevolutionary', and demanded 'a speedy withdrawal of the troops of those five countries'.[146] They thus carefully distinguished between the course of action by 'the five' and the Warsaw Pact.

The Romanian politburo nevertheless decided to mobilise the Romanian people to defend 'the national independence and sovereignty' of Romania, since '[w]e have no guarantee that what happened in Czechoslovakia tonight cannot happen in Romania in another night'. The presence of 'allied' troops near the Romanian border was further cause for anxiety.[147] The invasion in Czechoslovakia allowed Ceausescu and his comrades to provide their independent course with extra pathos, since they could now *claim* that sovereignty was really under threat, even though 'they did not feel directly threatened'.[148] With the intervention as a sword of Damocles, the Romanian defiance of the Kremlin seemed fully justified. Thirteen other European communist parties joined the Romanian politburo in condemning the invasion and sympathising with Czechoslovakia. Thus the intervention of 'the five' in Czechoslovakia enabled the Romanian leaders to occupy the moral high ground. Instead of being isolated by 'the six', the Romanian leaders rose above 'the five' in unequivocally calling 'the military intervention a grave mistake'.[149]

The Romanian leaders were so successful in using the possibility of an invasion in Romania as an instrument to stir national sentiments that there were large demonstrations on Bucharest's Palace Square on 21 August, where Ceausescu held a speech in which he openly condemned the invasion and professed his support for the legal Czechoslovak government.[150] Ceausescu was, for once, the hero of the liberty of the people, while supporting reforms that he would never have allowed in Romania. He managed, however, to gain a considerable degree of genuine popularity, as he could now show that the Romanian 'declaration of independence' was not mere rhetoric, but that the politburo had indeed defied the Kremlin at the risk of being its next victim. Ceausescu's condemnation of the invasion in Czechoslovakia thus served his 'personality cult', by capitalising on the people's nationalist feelings.[151] Meanwhile, the Romanian leaders were assured via various channels that they had no reason to fear the Czechoslovak fate.[152] The initial fears within the Romanian politburo proved unfounded: however detrimental Brezhnev's doctrine was to Czechoslovakia, it also implied that Romania was safe, as socialism was by no means under threat in Romania.[153]

The fate of Czechoslovakia was still undecided. Soviet commanders reported from Prague that 'the "healthy forces" have gone to pieces', and that there was no alternative government left to govern Czechoslovakia, since Dubcek and Cernik had been arrested and transferred to Moscow immediately after the invasion.[154] The situation was so different from that anticipated that the Kremlin immediately started an inquiry into 'the work of the Ministry of Foreign Affairs', because the 'Soviet leadership had not been well informed'.[155] Chervonenko was forced to establish an alternative course of action with the remaining members of the CPCz presidium, including President Svoboda, at the Soviet embassy in Prague, where the CPCz members insisted on Dubcek's release from Moscow.[156] Brezhnev, in turn, attempted to involve Dubcek in a solution for 'normalising' the situation in Czechoslovakia, while underscoring time and again that 'we don't intend to keep it under "occupation"', but that 'the Kremlin merely wanted the Communist Party of Czechoslovakia' to 'act normally and independently in accord with the principles contained in the Bratislava Declaration'.[157]

Dubcek nevertheless inadvertently echoed the Romanian rhetoric by calling 'the use of troops [...] the greatest political mistake',[158] and stuck to this line when President Svoboda arrived in Moscow with a delegation to ask for the return of Dubcek and Cernik to Czechoslovakia. The Kremlin entered into several days of negotiations with all Czechoslovak officials in Moscow, during which Brezhnev stressed the need for 'a political solution'. Conceding that 'the troops will leave' and that Dubcek and Cernik could return home if they guaranteed to 'fulfil the pledges made at Cierna nad Tisou', Brezhnev and Kosygin distributed a draft protocol in which the Cierna nad Tisou agreements were committed to paper, so as 'to solve [the Czechoslovak] problems together with our army'.[159] This draft protocol thus constituted a kind of Cierna nad Tisou at gunpoint. Dubcek did, however, succeed in removing any reference to 'counterrevolution' or the Warsaw letter, and five days after the invasion he signed a protocol that enshrined the 'principles [...] of the talks in Cierna nad Tisou and the conference in Bratislava'.[160]

A crumbling coalition

The 'Moscow Protocol', as it was subsequently called, thus constituted a blueprint for the process of 'normalisation' in Czechoslovakia, according to which the CPCz leadership would finally establish 'control of the mass media' and would carry out the 'personnel changes' that the Kremlin had so long requested. The foreign troops would remain until 'the threat to the gains of socialism in Czechoslovakia and the threat to the security of the countries of the socialist commonwealth have been eliminated', and '[a]ll outstanding [military] problems will be decided at the level of the ministers of national defence and foreign affairs'.[161] The process of 'normalisation' would thus be organised through intergovernmental channels, and the WP was nowhere mentioned either to justify or regulate the current state of affairs. The Moscow Protocol was necessary exactly because the Warsaw Treaty did not cater for such a situation.

The 'five' did not play a role in establishing the ground rules for post-invasion Czechoslovakia either. Although the other four leaders were invited to Moscow in the middle of the negotiations about the Moscow protocol on 24 August, the arguments of Ulbricht, Gomulka and Zhivkov to establish a 'military dictatorship in Czechoslovakia' did not carry conviction. The hardliners regarded the Soviet plea for 'normalisation' under Dubcek's lead as a 'compromise' with 'the counterrevolution', and were not at all enchanted with Brezhnev's course.[162] Brezhnev, meanwhile, paved the way for normalisation bilaterally with his Czechoslovak comrades. He thus seemed to have sacrificed multilateralism to moderation. The coalition of the 'five' began to crumble.

Brezhnev's moderate course was, however, welcomed in Romania, where Soviet Ambassador Basov discussed the situation with Ceausescu one day after Brezhnev's consultations with the five. After Ceausescu had greatly boosted his popularity with his public condemnation of the invasion on 21 August, he now trod his ground more carefully. Ceausescu still questioned why Romania, as a WP member, was not included in the decision making concerning the situation in Czechoslovakia, and criticised the fact that it was not resolved by peaceful means, but emphasised that 'these differences of opinion are temporary and we want them to be liquidated as soon as possible'. Praising the fact that the Kremlin had begun negotiating with the Czechoslovak comrades, he stressed the importance 'that the situation in Czechoslovakia normalises as soon as possible'.[163] Ceausescu's plea for 'normalisation' was, paradoxically, much more in line with Brezhnev's thinking than the plea of the hardliners for military dictatorship. It might even have tilted the balance in favour of normalisation: Ceausescu's conversation with Basov took place, after all, one day *before* the Moscow Protocol was concluded.

Moscow's moderation was a genuine relief to the Romanian leadership. In contrast to the first Romanian politburo meeting since the intervention in Czechoslovakia, the second one, which took place straight after Ceausescu's meeting with Basov, focused on the 'normalisation' in Czechoslovakia and the friendship with the Soviet Union. Ceausescu repeated the temporary nature of the differences of opinion with the Soviet leadership, and Maurer suggested meeting the Soviet leadership at the highest level of representation. The Romanian politburo members also proposed bilateral meetings with the Bulgarians and the Hungarians. They clearly wanted to forestall further actions by the coalition of the five, and were confident that Ceausescu's plea for normalisation would reach the Kremlin via Basov.[164] Considering the nature of the Moscow Protocol, the Romanian leaders seemed to have succeeded on both counts. The dynamics of relations between the WP members had thus shifted significantly *after* the invasion on 21 August. The Soviet-Romanian agreement that normalisation was the way forward stood in stark contrast to the division of the 'five' on the future of post-invasion Czechoslovakia.

Normalisation under pressure

The Romanian request for a bilateral meeting was categorically rejected by the Kremlin, which stated that such a meeting 'required another atmosphere'.[165] The Soviet leaders were particularly vexed by the Romanian use of the term 'occupation', which totally undermined their attempts to legitimise their course of action.[166] Meanwhile, the Romanian leaders continued to tone down their criticism, and were so pleased with the Soviet negotiations with the Czechoslovak leaders in Moscow and their return to Prague that they began to use the term 'penetration' instead.[167] Although NATO circles alluded to a break between Romania and the WP, the Romanian side openly emphasised 'the willingness to cooperate with the Warsaw Pact countries and the loyalty to the treaty'.[168] The Albanian reaction to the invasion in Czechoslovakia was quite the opposite: the Albanian leadership decided to withdraw formally from the WP on 13 September 1968 in protest.[169] Meanwhile, Romanian diplomats in various countries began to court their Soviet colleagues, while stressing the 'necessity of friendship and cooperation' time and again.[170] The Romanians, as usual, knew exactly what the limits of emancipation were.

However loth to meet the Romanian leadership, the Kremlin was nevertheless keen to underline that it never intended to invade Romania. The Soviet ambassador to Washington, Anatoly Dobrynin, even assured the US Secretary of State Dean Rusk that 'reports of an invasion of Romania were without foundation'.[171] US President Johnson and his top aides rightly concluded in the ensuing National Security Council meeting that '[t]he Soviets are unlikely to invade Romania', because '[t]here is no current threat to the communist system in Romania'.[172] The WP, however, granted no right to intervene in the affairs of one of its members anyhow, which is exactly why Brezhnev had to conceive another doctrine to legitimise the invasion.

The doctrine in question had been in the making since the Dresden meeting in March 1968, when Gomulka had explicitly legitimised interference in internal affairs if they had external ramifications. It had already been enshrined in the Bratislava declaration, which emphasised the 'internationalist duty' to defend socialism. It was elaborated in the Soviet newspaper *Pravda* five weeks after the invasion, where it was explicitly stated that '[e]ach communist party is free to apply the principles of Marxism-Leninism and socialism in its own country', but any of its decisions 'must not be harmful either to socialism in [its] own country or to the fundamental interests of other socialist countries'. Since 'the national *in*dependence' of one socialist country *de*pended on 'the power of the socialist commonwealth', the 'actions taken in Czechoslovakia by the five socialist countries' were not only 'aimed at safeguarding the vital interests of the socialist commonwealth', but 'especially at defending the independence and sovereignty of Czechoslovakia as a socialist state'.[173]

Instead of trampling on Czechoslovak sovereignty as the Romanians claimed, the invasion of Czechoslovakia had, according to this doctrine, salvaged the sovereignty of Czechoslovakia *as a socialist state*. This doctrine, later known as the 'Brezhnev doctrine', thus justified interference in WP members' internal affairs in a way that the Warsaw Treaty never could. It also based its justification on criteria that were extraneous to the WP: not loyalty to the WP, but the application of Marxist-Leninist principles was the central tenet. The Brezhnev doctrine explained retrospectively why Romania was never under threat from an invasion. It did, however, contain a warning for the Romanian leadership, too, as '[i]t must be emphasized that even if a socialist country tries to adopt a position "outside the blocs", it in fact retains its national independence only because of the power of the socialist commonwealth'.[174]

The Brezhnev doctrine was published unilaterally by the Soviets one day *before* Brezhnev convened the leaders of the other four socialist countries for another meeting in Moscow. The publication was particularly timely, as Dubcek had allegedly failed to carry out the provisions of the Moscow Protocol, and Brezhnev needed to convince his allies that he had not grown soft after he had refused to implement the military dictatorship that most of them demanded. Brezhnev used the multilateral framework once again to discuss Dubcek, and emphasised the necessity 'of the conclusion of a treaty providing for the deployment of units of our troops on Czechoslovak territory'. Brezhnev hoped that the conditional troop withdrawal would have 'a certain positive influence on the entire political situation in Czechoslovakia', and would motivate Dubcek to abide by the Moscow Protocol.[175]

The Soviet-Czechoslovak negotiations on the deployment of troops went smoothly. Since the troops were already stationed in Czechoslovakia, the Czechoslovak leadership had little choice. Brezhnev still promised to 'withdraw troops in stages as normalisation progresses'. Arguing that 'it is essential for the security and defence of the borders', the Soviet leaders convinced their Czechoslovak comrades to keep 70,000 to 80,000 Soviet troops on Czechoslovak territory for a 'temporary stay, without any fixed time limits'. Hungary, the GDR and Poland already had Soviet troops on their soil, so the presence of Soviet troops in a WP country was not an anomaly. Moreover, the presence of Soviet troops in Czechoslovakia did indeed serve to remedy a remarkable lacuna in safeguarding the security of the Eastern European border with Western Europe. Both the Soviet and the Czechoslovak sides therefore agreed to stipulate the number of remaining troops 'to ensure the safety of the whole socialist community' within 'the framework of the Warsaw Pact'.[176] The WP could now be used to legitimise the deployment of troops, as the remaining troops served the '*protection against foreign enemies*', as a Czechoslovak assessment emphasised, and 'they protect not only our country, but also the territory of other Warsaw Pact states'.[177] The actual treaty was, however, concluded *bi*laterally, while explicitly mentioning the 'consent' of the Bulgarian, Hungarian, East German and Polish governments.[178] Although the unity of 'the six' seemed to be restored, 'normalisation' was not cast in a WP mould.

This time Romania was, however, no longer isolated. The Czechoslovak leadership was still keen to express its appreciation of the Romanian stance, as the Czechoslovak ambassador in Bucharest, Karel Kurka, emphasised in a conversation with the Romanian leadership in November 1968. He denounced Ulbricht's interpretation of the situation in Czechoslovakia in particular, and he stressed that '*the diplomats of those five countries* [...] *are in total isolation within the diplomatic corps of Bucharest*'. He nevertheless added that he also appreciated the Hungarian position, since 'the Hungarians have been the most serious, if one can say such a thing about invaders'. At the same time '[t]he ambassador underlined that the actual situation [...] is *very complicated*', since there were '*inevitable, serious clashes*' between those members of the Central Committee, who were elected during Novotny's reign, and the 'comrades from the Dubcek era', who were under *'powerful pressure'* from the CPSU *'to conduct self-criticism'* and to *'recognise* [their] *mistakes'* during the Prague Spring. Normalisation was, accordingly, under threat.[179]

Dubcek almost echoed his ambassador's words in a meeting with the Soviet leadership in Kiev on 7–8 December.[180] Since Dubcek had still failed to solve the personnel issues and gain complete control over the media, his power over some parts of the CPCz also began to erode. The pressure from Moscow on the one hand and the more conservative members of the CPCz on the other hand became too hard to bear. A significant group of CPCz members, headed by the Slovak politician Bilak, and backed by President Svoboda, decided to put the Slovak Deputy Prime Minister Gustav Husak forward as the new party leader instead.[181] He seemed the ideal candidate to 'normalise' Czechoslovakia, as he had been imprisoned during the Stalin era, denounced by Novotny, and was a moderate supporter of the Prague Spring, while he was also trusted by the Kremlin. Bilak and his comrades were scheming to execute this intra-party coup during the Central Committee session that would take place in April 1969. On 17 March 1969 Dubcek nevertheless still represented Czechoslovakia at the WP's PCC meeting in Budapest, where he nervously chaired the meeting.[182]

Soviet-Czechoslovak relations took an unexpected turn. After the Czechoslovak ice hockey team had defeated the Soviets twice during the World Ice Hockey Championship in Sweden on 21–28 March 1969, Czechoslovak discontent with the presence of Soviet troops spiralled out of control.[183] In a spirit of victory and provoked by agents of the Czechoslovak State Security, 100,000 citizens thronged the streets of the major towns in Czechoslovakia immediately after the final match, and severely insulted the Soviet Army and its leaders with slogans 'such as "occupiers", "fascists", "Brezhnev is a hooligan" and so on'.[184] The CPSU politburo met in an emergency session on 30 March to discuss the 'open attack by Czechoslovak counterrevolutionary forces', while 'the passivity of the Dubcek leadership' was severely criticised.[185] On 1 April Soviet Defence Minister Andrei Grechko arrived in Prague unannounced in order to discuss the situation with his Czechoslovak colleague Martin Dzur and some of his aides. Grechko was particularly disgruntled that the political leadership did not seem to have 'issued instructions' to restore order, and considered the 'situation [...] worse than on August 21, 1968'.[186] Meanwhile, the so-called 'healthy forces' within the CPCz had finally gathered the clout they had lacked on 21 August. During the CC session on 17 April 1969 Dubcek was removed and Czechoslovakia began to be 'normalised'.

Conclusion: irreversible multilateralisation

By 1968 the WP had integrated to such an extent that a unilateral Soviet move concerning the situation in Czechoslovakia was unthinkable. It was exactly because the WP had heightened the self-consciousness of *all* its members during the 1960s that Brezhnev had to consult his allies extensively. The multilateral dynamics that were developed within the WP enabled the multilateral decision making during the Prague Spring, but it was not the WP *as institution* that facilitated the invasion; on the contrary, the intervention would have been blocked within a WP framework, as the Warsaw Pact, like NATO, did *not* cater for a discussion of its allies' internal affairs, and the absence of Romania would make any WP meeting on this matter both illegal and impossible. Brezhnev could afford to bypass Romania by *not* using the WP framework, but he could ill afford to lose the support of his other Eastern European allies too.

The roles had even been reversed: Brezhnev was under more pressure from some of his junior allies to invade than vice versa. The multilateral decision making nevertheless enabled Brezhnev to slow down the process, and withstand the pressure from hardliners within the Kremlin. In stark contrast to the Soviet invasion in Hungary in the autumn of 1956, the decision-making process in 1968 lasted six months. Although Brezhnev ultimately faced such internal and external pressure that there was no alternative, the multilateral consultations had cushioned the decision making and had enabled an intervention without bloodshed.

Brezhnev had also used the multilateral decision making to gain time in searching for a political solution. His eagerness to avoid a military intervention is reflected by the faith he put in Kadar, whose position as mediator between the Czechoslovak leadership and the other five socialist leaders he greatly encouraged. Whereas Kadar had kept a low profile within the WP, where his stance was eclipsed by Romanian dissent, the multilateral decision making during the Prague Spring increased his scope for manoeuvre. Suddenly it was his opinion that served to tilt the balance, and to withstand the arguments of the hardliners, Ulbricht, Gomulka and Zhivkov, whose positions corresponded to their customary positions within the alliance. The sharp antagonism between the 'one' and 'six' others, however, did not exist, because Romania was – exactly for that reason – not invited to the consultations. The Czechoslovak refusal to join the meeting in Warsaw in July heralded the birth of 'the five', which now began to strive to solve the situation in Czechoslovakia definitively. The Czechoslovak withdrawal from the multilateral process in Warsaw came at a price: the salvation of socialism was no longer in Czechoslovak hands.

Meanwhile, the one WP ally that was threatened with isolation after the PCC meeting in Sofia in early March 1968 had suddenly found a new ally. The Czechoslovak defiance of Soviet imperatives enabled the Romanian leadership to cast the Prague Spring in a new narrative, according to which the reform process primarily served to emancipate Czechoslovakia from the Soviet grip after the Romanian model. The invasion of 'the five' in turn allowed Ceausescu to stir the nationalist feelings of the Romanian people and present himself as the staunch supporter of those leaders who were subdued by the Kremlin. The impending Romanian isolation in March 1968 had thus turned into a heroic quest for independence, which caused Ceausescu's finest hour. At the same time, Dubcek's acceptance of the Romanian friendship in June 1968 proved a turning point in the relations between Dubcek and 'the five'.

The invasion of 'the five' hardly proved to be Brezhnev's finest hour. A military success, it was a political failure, as the 'healthy forces' in Czechoslovakia had evaporated in the face of Soviet tanks. The salvation of socialism came at a price. The fact that 'the five' had to resort to military force highlights the limits of the Kremlin's political power: Brezhnev was too weak to enforce a political solution. Although the invasion in Czechoslovakia often serves to reinforce conventional wisdoms about the WP as a Soviet transmission belt that allegedly subdued unruly Eastern European allies, the evidence concerning the Prague Spring points in a different direction. The invasion was conducted by a 'coalition of the willing', which consisted of four countries in addition to the Soviet Union that had put more pressure on the Kremlin to invade than vice versa. Not only did the political decision making take place outside the WP framework, but the military intervention, too, was commanded by the Soviet Deputy Minister of Defence Pavlovskii, and not by the Warsaw Pact's Supreme Commander Yakubovskii. The members of the 'coalition of the willing' had gone to great lengths to avoid using the WP as an instrument to invade. It was accordingly not even a WP invasion in a military sense.

Brezhnev needed to invent his own doctrine exactly because nothing within the Warsaw Treaty could legitimise the invasion. Brezhnev's doctrine of 'limited sovereignty' at the same time indicates the limits of emancipation for the WP members: emancipation from the Soviet grip was only allowed if accompanied by the unquestionable communist monopoly on power. Sovereignty had as such become conditional on socialism. The Brezhnev doctrine thus gives a retrospective clue to the reasons why the Kremlin never even conceived of invading Romania: under Ceausescu's rule socialism was never at stake. The Romanian stance during the Prague Spring once again shows that the WP members had considerable scope for manoeuvre, as long as they did not push it to the limits. It was, indeed, not so much the Czechoslovak attitude to the Warsaw Pact that caused the invasion, as the fact that the process of reforms in Czechoslovakia spiralled out of Dubcek's control, exacerbated by a radicalising press. Although Dubcek was keen to improve his contacts with West Germany – which in itself was a sensitive issue – he never questioned his allegiance to the Warsaw Pact. The Prague Spring represented, in the first instance, an *internal* process of reforms, which only had *external* repercussions to the extent that socialism was under threat. The Brezhnev doctrine served to legitimise the intervention for exactly those reasons.

The mere existence of the Brezhnev doctrine also suggests that Brezhnev had more scope for unilateralism *outside* the confines of the WP than *within* the alliance. No foreign policy decision within the WP carries Brezhnev's name. Although the multilateral decision making during the Prague Spring was a clear effect of the multilateralisation within the WP, Brezhnev was able to convene meetings and dictate the agenda in a way that had become impossible within the alliance. By 1968 the WP had multilateralised too much to enable the kind of transmission belt approach that is often associated with the alliance. For unilateralism the Kremlin had to bypass the Warsaw Pact, instead of using it. The intervention in Czechoslovakia by the 'coalition of the willing' thus took place in spite of the Warsaw Pact's existence, although the fact that it was decided within a multilateral framework is a clear indication that the WP's multilateralisation had become irreversible.

Notes

1 Ceausescu's speech, 21 August 1968, FIG APC, Czechoslovakia 1968, mf 0552, 2378.
2 W. Shawcross, *Dubcek: Dubcek and Czechoslovakia, 1968–1990* (London, 1990); K. Williams, *The Prague Spring and its Aftermath* (Cambridge, 1997); and P. Windsor and A. Roberts, *Czechoslovakia 1968. Reform, Repression and Resistance* (London, 1969).
3 M. Kramer, 'The Kremlin, the Prague Spring, and the Brezhnev Doctrine', in V. Tismaneanu, *Promises of 1968: Crisis, Illusion, and Utopia* (Budapest and New York, 2010), 276–362; 'Die Sowjetunion, der Warschauer Pakt und blockinterne Krisen während der Breznev-Ära', in T. Diedrich, W. Heinemann and C.F. Ostermann (eds), *Der Warschauer Pakt. Von der Gründung bis zum Zusammenbruch 1955 bis 1991* (Berlin, 2009), 274–336; 'The Prague Spring and the Soviet Invasion in Historical Perspective', in G. Bischof, S. Karner and P. Ruggenthaler (eds), *The Prague Spring and the Warsaw Pact Invasion of Czechoslovakia in 1968* (New York and Plymouth, 2011), 35–58; 'New Sources on the 1968 Invasion in Czechoslovakia', in J.G. Hershberg (ed.), *Inside the Warsaw Pact*, CWIHP Bulletin No. 2 (Washington, 1992), 1, 4–13; and 'The Prague Spring and the Soviet Invasion of Czechoslovakia: New Interpretations', in J. G. Hershberg (ed.), *From the Russian Archives*, CWIHP Bulletin No. 3 (Washington, 1993), 2–13, 54–55. See also M.J. Ouimet, *The Rise and Fall of the Brezhnev Doctrine in Soviet Foreign Policy* (Chapel Hill, 2003).
4 Cf. for this term *inter alia*: J. Suri, 'The Promise and Failure of "Developed Socialism": The Soviet "Thaw" and the Crucible of the Prague Spring', *Contemporary European History* 15:2 (2006), 150; and A. Kemp-Welch, 'Eastern Europe: Stalinism to Solidarity', in M. Leffler and O.A. Westad (eds), *The Cambridge History of the Cold War. Volume II: Crisis and Détente* (Cambridge, 2010), 228.
5 'Summary Notes of the 590th Meeting of the National Security Council', 4 September 1968, in J. Navrátil (ed.), *The Prague Spring 1968* (Budapest and New York, 2006), 494.
6 M. Kurlansky, *1968: The Year that Rocked the World* (New York, 2004); cf. C. Fink, P. Gassert and D. Junker (eds), *1968: The World Transformed* (Cambridge, 1998), 193–216.
7 See J. Suri, *Power and Protest: Global Revolution and the Rise of Détente* (Massachusetts, 2003), for a lucid analysis of the 1960s on a global scale (162–212).
8 R. Gildea, J. Mark and A. Warring (eds), *Europe's 1968. Voices of Revolt* (Oxford, 2013).
9 A. Kemp-Welch, *Poland under Communism. A Cold War History* (Cambridge, 2008), 146.

10 See 'Speeches by Alexander Dubcek and Antonín Novotný at the CPCz CC Plenum', 30–31 October 1967, in Navrátil et al. (eds), *Prague Spring*, 13–17.
11 Navrátil et al. (eds), *Prague Spring*, 7.
12 See 'Resolution of the CPCz CC Plenum, January 5, 1968, Electing Alexander Dubcek as First Secretary', in Navrátil et al. (eds), *Prague Spring*, 34–36.
13 Shawcross, *Dubcek*, 121.
14 See C. Békés, 'Hungary and the Prague Spring', in G. Bischof, S. Karner and P. Ruggenthaler (eds), *The Prague Spring and the Warsaw Pact Invasion of Czechoslovakia in 1968* (New York and Plymouth, 2011), 371.
15 See for the link between 'full solidarity with the fraternal Czechoslovak people' and the Romanian desire to dissolve the WP, e.g. L. Betea, 'Primăvara de la Praga, vara de la București', in L. Betea et al. (eds), *21 august 1968. Apoteoza lui Ceaușescu* (Bucharest, 2009), 40.
16 Kemp-Welch, *Poland*, 152.
17 Ibid.
18 Shawcross, *Dubcek*, 121.
19 Ibid., 131.
20 V. Mastny, 'Was 1968 a Strategic Watershed of the Cold War?' *Diplomatic History* 29:1 (2005), 176.
21 Kramer, 'The Kremlin', 309; see also Chapter 4 of this volume.
22 Cf. 'Report to the Hungarian Party Politburo and Council of Ministers on the PCC Meeting', 9 March 1968, Parallel History Project on Cooperative Security, 8, www.php.isn.ethz.ch/collections/colltopic.cfm?lng=en&id=17967&navinfo=14465 (accessed 28 August 2013).
23 Cf. Navrátil et al. (eds), *Prague Spring*, 64, for the conventional reading, which is confirmed by Dubcek himself (S. Dubcek and A. Sugar, *Dubcek Speaks* (London, 1990), 42); and Békés, 'Hungary and the Prague Spring', 382, for the archival evidence, which proves that Dubcek was complicit in the smokescreen.
24 See 'Stenographic Account of the Dresden Meeting', 23 March 1968, in Navrátil et al. (eds), *Prague Spring*, 64–72.
25 Kemp-Welch, *Poland*, 148–57.
26 'Stenographic Account of the Dresden Meeting', 66.
27 Cf. for this trend throughout the 1960s, e.g. Information about the development of international relations of the People's Republic of Bulgaria, October 1966, PA AA, MfAA, C 838/77, 106.
28 Information about the positions of the communist parties vis-à-vis Czechoslovakia, Berlin, 26 July 1968, SAPMO-BArch, DY 30/IVA2/20/13, 12.
29 Cf. Békés, 'Hungary and the Prague Spring', 371–95, for Hungary's position during the Prague Spring.
30 See 'Stenographic Account of the Dresden Meeting', 64–72.
31 Dubcek and Sugar, *Dubcek Speaks*, 58.
32 M. Retegan, *In the Shadow of the Prague Spring: Romanian Foreign Policy and the Crisis of Czechoslovakia, 1968* (Oxford, 2000, 2008), 85–86.
33 Ibid., 88.
34 See 'Alexander Dubcek's Presidium Report on the Dresden Meeting', 25 March 1968, in Navrátil et al. (eds), *Prague Spring*, 73–75.
35 'Open Letter from 134 Czechoslovak Writers and Cultural Figures to the CPCz Central Committee', 25 March 1968, in Navrátil et al. (eds), *Prague Spring*, 76.
36 'The CPCz CC Action Program', April 1968, in Navrátil et al. (eds), *Prague Spring*, 92–95.
37 Shawcross, *Dubcek*, 131.
38 'The CPCz CC Action Program', April 1968, in Navrátil et al. (eds), *Prague Spring*, 92–95.

39 'Dispatch from Budapest Outlining Hungarian Concerns about Events in Czechoslovakia after the Dresden Meeting', 6 April 1968, in Navrátil et al. (eds), Prague Spring, 81–82.
40 Navrátil et al. (eds), Prague Spring, 84.
41 'Letter from Leonid Brezhnev to Alexander Dubcek Expressing Concern about Events in Czechoslovakia', 11 April 1968, in Navrátil et al. (eds), Prague Spring, 99–100.
42 'Memoir of Andrei Aleksandrov-Agentov on Internal Soviet Deliberations about Czechoslovakia', in Navrátil et al. (eds), Prague Spring, 102.
43 'Information report 12/1968', GDR embassy in Moscow, 9 April 1968, SAPMO-BArch, DY 30/IVA2/20/162, 261.
44 'Memoir of Andrei Aleksandrov-Agentov', 102.
45 Kemp-Welch, Poland, 163.
46 'Cable to Moscow from Soviet Ambassador to Warsaw Averki Aristov Regarding Wladislaw Gomulka's Views on the Situation in Czechoslovakia', 16 April 1968, in Navrátil et al. (eds), Prague Spring, 103.
47 See 'Report on Secret Discussions between the CPCz CC International Department and Egon Bahr of the West German Social Democratic Party', 17–19 April 1968, in Navrátil et al. (eds), Prague Spring, 108–11.
48 See Chapter 4 of this book.
49 M. Wilke, 'Ulbricht, East Germany, and the Prague Spring', in G. Bischof, S. Karner and P. Ruggenthaler (eds), The Prague Spring and the Warsaw Pact Invasion of Czechoslovakia in 1968 (New York and Plymouth, 2011), 354.
50 '"Proposal for a Number of Major Political Measures to Facilitate the Process of Mutual Understanding in Relations with the USSR," by Czechoslovak Foreign Minister Jirí Hájek', 17 April 1968, in Navrátil et al. (eds), Prague Spring, 106–7.
51 'Stenographic Account of the Soviet-Czechoslovak Summit Meeting in Moscow', 4–5 May 1968, in Navrátil et al. (eds), Prague Spring, 114–25.
52 Ibid., 124.
53 'Minutes of the Secret Meeting of the "Five" in Moscow', 8 May 1968, in Navrátil et al. (eds), Prague Spring, 132–43.
54 Retegan, In the Shadow of the Prague Spring, 134.
55 'Minutes of the Secret Meeting of the "Five" in Moscow', 8 May 1968, in Navrátil et al. (eds), Prague Spring, 132–43.
56 Békés, 'Hungary and the Prague Spring', 380.
57 Retegan, In the Shadow of the Prague Spring, 135 and 109.
58 Ibid., 101.
59 Information about conversations between inter alia Gomulka, Kadar, Axen and Winzer, 28 May 1968, SAPMO-BArch, DY 30/IVA2/20/429, 267.
60 Retegan, In the Shadow of the Prague Spring, 102.
61 Ibid., 115.
62 'Information report 17/1968', GDR embassy in Moscow, 28 May 1868, SAPMO-BArch, DY 30/IVA2/20/162, 331.
63 See 'Alexander Dubcek's Speech to the CPCz CC Plenary Session, May 29–June 1, 1968, with Discussion by Vasil Bil'ak', in Navrátil et al. (eds), Prague Spring, 152–55. This schism had been incipient from the beginning, cf. Shawcross, Dubcek, 121.
64 See 'Letter from Leonid Brezhnev to Alexander Dubcek Proposing Another Bilateral Meeting', 11 June 1968, in Navrátil et al. (eds), Prague Spring, 158–59.
65 Retegan, In the Shadow of the Prague Spring, 124.
66 Dubcek and Sugar, Dubcek Speaks, 57: 'I thought it would be Kádár who would say no.'
67 Retegan, In the Shadow of the Prague Spring, 140.

68 See for this term: J. Granville, *The First Domino. International Decision-making during the Hungarian Crisis of 1956* (Texas, 2004).
69 'The "Two Thousand Words" Manifesto', 27 June 1968, in Navrátil *et al.* (eds), *Prague Spring*, 179–81.
70 Cf. Shawcross, *Dubcek*, 134–35.
71 'Letter of the CPSU CC Politburo to the CPCz CC Presidium', 4 July 1968, in Navrátil *et al.* (eds), *Prague Spring*, 194–98.
72 '"Status of the Šumava Allied Exercise," Report to Alexander Dubcek by CSSR Defense Minister Martin Dzúr', 17 June 1968, in Navrátil *et al.* (eds), *Prague Spring*, 161.
73 'Briefing on the Šumava Exercises for Alexander Dubcek and Oldrich Cerník by Commanders of the Czechoslovak People's Army, July 1, 1968, with Follow-up Talks between Dubcek and Marshal Yakubovskii', in Navrátil *et al.* (eds), *Prague Spring*, 191–92.
74 'Report on the Šumava Exercises by Generals I. Oláh and F. Szücs of the Hungarian People's Army tot the HSWP Politburo', 5 July 1968, in Navrátil *et al.* (eds), *Prague Spring*, 199–201.
75 'General Semyon Zolotov's Retrospective Account of the Šumava Military Exercises', in Navrátil *et al.* (eds), *Prague Spring*, 203.
76 See 'Letter from Leonid Brezhnev to Alexander Dubcek Inviting a CPCz Delegation to the Warsaw Meeting', 6 July 1968, in Navrátil *et al.* (eds), *Prague Spring*, 206.
77 Dubcek and Sugar, *Dubcek Speaks*, 50.
78 'Top-Secret Telegram from Ambassador Stepan Chervonenko to Moscow Regarding the CPCz CC Presidium's Decision Not to Attend the Warsaw Meeting', 9 July 1968, in Navrátil *et al.* (eds), *Prague Spring*, 207.
79 Ibid.
80 Information from the CPSU CC, transmitted by Soviet ambassador Basov in a meeting with Ceausescu, 12 July 1968, ANIC, RCP CC, IR, 100/1968, 6, 9.
81 Ibid.
82 Cf. Dubcek and Sugar, *Dubcek Speaks*, 57: 'Ceausescu held very strongly to one thing, not just in the talks, but in political practice, too.'
83 Békés, 'Hungary and the Prague Spring', 388.
84 Ibid., 389.
85 'Transcript of the Warsaw Meeting', 14–15 July 1968, in Navrátil *et al.* (eds), *Prague Spring*, 212–33.
86 Ibid.
87 Ibid.
88 Ibid.
89 Ibid., 229.
90 'The Warsaw Letter', 14–15 July 1968, in Navrátil *et al.* (eds), *Prague Spring*, 234–38.
91 'Transcript of the Warsaw Meeting', 230.
92 Navrátil *et al.* (eds), *Prague Spring*, 186–87.
93 See 'Message from Alexander Dubcek and Oldrich Cerník to Leonid Brezhnev', 14 July 1968, in Navrátil *et al.* (eds), *Prague Spring*, 210–11.
94 'Response by the CPCz CC Presidium to the Warsaw Letter', 16–17 July 1968, in Navrátil *et al.* (eds), *Prague Spring*, 243–49.
95 Ibid.; cf. 'Declaration by the Government of the USSR on the Principles of Development and Further Strengthening of Friendship and Cooperation between the Soviet Union and Other Socialist States', 30 October 1956, in C. Békés, M. Byrne and J.M. Rainer (eds), *The 1956 Hungarian Revolution: A History in Documents* (Budapest and New York, 2002), 301.
96 Dubcek and Sugar, *Dubcek Speaks*, 50.

97 Meeting between Bodnaras and Chinese diplomat Ma Siu-sen, 24 July 1968, ANIC, RCP CC, IR, 103/1968, 4.
98 Ibid., 6–14.
99 Ibid., 6.
100 Retegan, *In the Shadow of the Prague Spring*, 110.
101 'Press Conference with Lt. General Václav Prchlík', 15 July 1968, in Navrátil *et al.* (eds), *Prague Spring*, 240. For more information on General Prchlík, see Chapter 7 of this book.
102 'Soviet Government Diplomatic Note to the Czechoslovak Government', 20 July 1968, in Navrátil *et al.* (eds), *Prague Spring*, 265–67.
103 Navrátil *et al.* (eds), *Prague Spring*, 187.
104 Navrátil *et al.* (eds), *Prague Spring*, 277.
105 'Meeting Notes Taken by Chief of the Hungarian People's Army General Staff Károly Csémi on Talks with Soviet Generals in Budapest to Discuss Preparations for "Operation Danube"', 24 July 1968, in Navrátil *et al.* (eds), *Prague Spring*, 277.
106 'Speeches by Leonid Brezhnev, Alexander Dubcek, and Aleksei Kosygin at the Cierna nad Tisou Negotiations', 29 July 1968, in Navrátil *et al.* (eds), *Prague Spring*, 284–97, emphasis in original.
107 Ibid.
108 Dubcek and Sugar, *Dubcek Speaks*, 57–58.
109 'Vasil Bil'ak's Recollections of the Bratislava Conference', in Navrátil *et al.* (eds), *Prague Spring*, 323.
110 See 'Polish Views of the Situation in Czechoslovakia on the Eve of the Bratislava Conference', 2 August 1968, in Navrátil *et al.* (eds), *Prague Spring*, 319.
111 'Report by Soviet Ambassador to the GDR Pyotr Abrasimov on East Germany's Position vis-à-vis Czechoslovakia', 28 July and 1 August 1968, in Navrátil *et al.* (eds), *Prague Spring*, 316.
112 'Report by Soviet Ambassador to Bulgaria A.M. Puzanov on Bulgaria's Position vis-à-vis Czechoslovakia', 1 August 1968, in Navrátil *et al.* (eds), *Prague Spring*, 317.
113 Ibid., 318.
114 See 'The Bratislava Declaration', 3 August 1968, in Navrátil *et al.* (eds), *Prague Spring*, 326–29.
115 'Vasil Bil'ak's Recollections', 321.
116 Cf. for the East German reaction 'Alexander Dubcek's Recollections of the Crisis: Events Surrounding the Xierna and Tisou Negotiations', in Navrátil *et al.* (eds), *Prague Spring*, 303.
117 'The "Letter of Invitation" from the Anti-Reformist Faction of the CPCz Leadership', August 1968, in Navrátil *et al.* (eds), *Prague Spring*, 324–25.
118 'Statement by the CPCz CC Presidium after the Talks at Cierna and Bratislava', 6 August 1968, in Navrátil *et al.* (eds), *Prague Spring*, 330.
119 See Kádár's speech, ANIC, RWP CC, IR, 15/1965, 331–32.
120 'Report by Soviet Ambassador Stepan Chervonenko to the Kremlin on his Meeting with Alexander Dubcek', 7 August 1968, in Navrátil *et al.* (eds), *Prague Spring*, 335.
121 'CPSU CC Politburo Message to Alexander Dubcek', 13 August 1968, in Navrátil *et al.* (eds), *Prague Spring*, 344.
122 'Transcript of Leonid Brezhnev's Telephone Conversation with Alexander Dubcek', 13 August 1968, in Navrátil *et al.* (eds), *Prague Spring*, 345–56.
123 See 'The CPSU Politburo's Instructions to Ambassador Chervonenko for Meetings with Czechoslovak Leaders', 13 August 1968, and 'Dubcek's Notes, Regarding the CPCz's Purported Failure to Carry Out Pledges Made at Cierna

and Bratislava', 16 August 1968, in Navrátil *et al.* (eds), *Prague Spring*, 357–59, and 366–69.
124 Shawcross, *Dubcek*, 137.
125 'János Kádár's Report on Soviet-Hungarian Talks at Yalta', 12–15 August 1968, in Navrátil *et al.* (eds), *Prague Spring*, 360–62.
126 Conversation between Nicolae Eacubescu and the Czechoslovak ambassador in the UN, Geneva, 13 September 1968, ANIC, RCP CC, IR, 131/1968, 2–3.
127 Meeting between the Romanian and the Czechoslovak leadership, Prague, 15 August 1968, ANIC, RCP CC, IR, 107/1968, 44–45.
128 Ibid., 24, 37.
129 Toasts offered by the Czechoslovak party, 16 August 1968, ANIC, RCP CC, IR, 107/1968, 76; cf. Dubcek and Sugar, *Dubcek Speaks*, 57, on the Czechoslovak 'understanding with Ceausescu', who practised what he preached.
130 'Summary of Alexander Dubcek's Meeting with János Kádár at Komárno', 17 August 1968, in Navrátil *et al.* (eds), *Prague Spring*, 372.
131 'The Soviet Politburo's Resolution on the Final Decision to Intervene in Czechoslovakia', 17 August 1968, in Navrátil *et al.* (eds), *Prague Spring*, 377.
132 'Draft "Letter of Warning" from the CPSU CC Politburo to the CPCz Presidium', 17 August 1968, in Navrátil *et al.* (eds), *Prague Spring*, 387.
133 Ibid.
134 'Ambassador Stepan Chervonenko's Report on his Meeting with Czechoslovak President Ludvík Svoboda', 17 August 1968, in Navrátil *et al.* (eds), *Prague Spring*, 391.
135 Ibid., 392–94.
136 See 'The Invasion in Retrospect: The Recollections of General Ivan Pavlovskii', in Navrátil *et al.* (eds), *Prague Spring*, 431–32.
137 'Leonid Brezhnev's Speech at a Meeting of the "Warsaw Five" in Moscow', 18 August 1968, in Navrátil *et al.* (eds), *Prague Spring*, 399.
138 'Message from the CPSU CC Politburo to Members of the CPSU CC and Other Top Party Officials Regarding the Decision to Intervene in Czechoslovakia', 19 August 1968, in Navrátil *et al.* (eds), *Prague Spring*, 402.
139 'General Semyon Zolotov's Account of the Final Military Preparations for the Invasion', in Navrátil *et al.* (eds), *Prague Spring*, 375.
140 'Cable to Ambassador Stepan Chervonenko from Moscow with a Message for President Svoboda, August 19, 1968, and Chervonenko's Response, August 21, 1968', in Navrátil *et al.* (eds), *Prague Spring*, 406, 408.
141 'Report by Defense Minister Dzúr, June 9, 1970, Regarding his Activities on the Night of August 20–21, 1968', in Navrátil *et al.* (eds), *Prague Spring*, 412.
142 M. Kramer, 'The Prague Spring and the Soviet Invasion of Czechoslovakia: New Interpretations', in J.G. Hershberg (ed.), *From the Russian Archives*, CWIHP Bulletin No. 3 (Washington, 1993), 48. Brezhnev had thwarted Ulbricht's desire to also offer combat troops: the appearance of German troops on Czechoslovak territory was considered too painful after the German invasion in Czechoslovakia in 1939.
143 'Statement by the CPCz CC Presidium Condemning the Warsaw Pact Invasion', 21 August 1968, in Navrátil *et al.* (eds), *Prague Spring*, 415.
144 Letter from the five socialist countries to RCP CC, 21 August 1968, ANIC, RCP CC, IR, 133/1968, 34.
145 Ibid., 35–36.
146 'Protocol Nr. 32 of the session of the RCP CC politburo', 21 August, ANIC, RCP CC, IR, 133/1968, 2–3.
147 Minutes of the session of the RCP CC politburo, 21 August, ANIC, RCP CC, IR, 133/1968, 18.

148 Meeting of the leadership on 23 August 1968 (16), FIG APC, Leadership, 1968, mf 020, 0911.
149 Discussion between Bodnaras and Aristov, the Soviet ambassador in Poland, Southern Mongolia, 21 August 1968, ANIC, RCP CC, IR, 122/1968, 1, 3.
150 Cf. C.L. Petrescu, 'Performing Disapproval toward the Soviets: Nicolae Ceausescu's Speech on 21 August 1968 in the Romanian Media', in M. Klimke, J. Pekelder and J. Scharloth (eds), *Between Prague Spring and French May. Opposition and Revolt in Europe, 1960–1980* (New York and Oxford, 2011), 199–210.
151 'Information report, 29.8–11.9.1968', Bucharest, 11 September, 1968, SAPMO-BArch, DY 30/IVA2/20/375, 147.
152 Cf. Discussion between Bodnaras and Aristov, the Soviet ambassador in Poland, Southern Mongolia, 21 August 1968, ANIC, RCP CC, IR, 122/1968, 10.
153 Cf. the analysis of the Italian Communist Party: 'Meeting of the leadership on 23 August 1968 (16)', FIG APC, Leadership, 1968, mf 020, 0921.
154 'Initial On-Site Report by Kirill Mazurov to the CPSU CC Politburo', 21 August, in Navrátil *et al.* (eds), *Prague Spring*, 452.
155 Conversation between Nicolae Eacubescu and the Czechoslovak ambassador in the UN, Geneva, 13 September 1968, ANIC, RCP CC, IR, 131/1968, 6.
156 See 'Discussions Involving Certain Members of the CPCz CC Presidium and Secretariat, at the Soviet Embassy in Prague and the CSSR President's Office', 22 August 1968, in Navrátil *et al.* (eds), *Prague Spring*, 460–64.
157 'Stenographic Account of Alexander Dubcek's Talks with Leonid Brezhnev and Other Members of the CPSU CC Politburo', 23 August 1968, in Navrátil *et al.* (eds), *Prague Spring*, 465–68.
158 Ibid.
159 'Minutes of Soviet-Czechoslovak Talks in the Kremlin', 23 and 26 August 1968, in Navrátil *et al.* (eds), *Prague Spring*, 469–73.
160 'The Moscow Protocol', 26 August 1968, in Navrátil *et al.* (eds), *Prague Spring*, 477.
161 Ibid., 478–80.
162 'Minutes of the First Post-Invasion Meeting of the "Warsaw Five" in Moscow', 24 August 1968, in Navrátil *et al.* (eds), *Prague Spring*, 474–76.
163 Minutes of the discussions between Soviet ambassador Basov and Ceausescu, 25 August 1968, ANIC, RCP CC, IR, 111/1968, 4–5.
164 Minutes of the politburo of the RCP CC, 25 August 1968, ANIC, RCP CC, C, 135/1968, 25–28.
165 Communication from CPSU CC to RCP CC, 4 September 1968, ANIC, RCP CC, IR, 49/1959–70, 50.
166 Soviet Deputy Foreign Minister Ilichev to the Romanian ambassador in Moscow, 21 August 1968, ibid., 46.
167 'Situation Report by the US State Department', 29 August 1968, in Navrátil *et al.* (eds), *Prague Spring*, 491.
168 'Information Report, 29/8–11/9/1968', 11 September 1968, GDR embassy in Bucharest, SAPMO-BArch, DY 30/IVA2/20/375, 145.
169 'Moscow's strategy and Albanian withdrawal', *Il Tempo*, 15 October 1968, FIG APC, Czechoslovakia, mf 0552, 1001.
170 'Information Report', 12 Nov. 1968, GDR embassy in Moscow, SAPMO-BArch, DY 30/IVA2/20/163, 139.
171 'Summary Notes of the 590th Meeting of the National Security Council', 4 September 1968, in Navrátil *et al.* (eds), *Prague Spring*, 494.
172 Ibid., 496.
173 'Unofficial Enunciation of the "Brezhnev Doctrine"', 26 September 1968, in Navrátil *et al.* (eds), *Prague Spring*, 502–3.
174 Ibid., 502.

175 'Stenographic Account of the Meeting of the "Warsaw Five"', 27 September 1968, in Navrátil et al. (eds), *Prague Spring*, 505.
176 'Stenographic Account of Soviet-Czechoslovak Negotiations in Moscow', 2–4 October, in Navrátil et al. (eds), *Prague Spring*, 526–29.
177 'The CPCz Leadership's Assessment of the Treaty on Soviet Troop Deployments', October 1968, in Navrátil et al. (eds), *Prague Spring*, 544, emphasis added.
178 See 'Bilateral Treaty on the "Temporary Presence of Soviet Forces on Czechoslovak Territory"', 16 October 1968, in Navrátil et al. (eds), *Prague Spring*, 533–36.
179 Meeting with Karel Kurka, the Czechoslovak ambassador in Bucharest, 8 November 1968, ANIC, RCP CC, IR, 185/1968, 49–53. See for the rapid normalisation of relations between Czechoslovakia and Hungary, because the 'HSWP [...] had correctly judged the situation in Czechoslovakia', letter from Dr Plaschke to Oskar Fischer, Budapest, 3 January 1969, PA AA, MfAA, C 1106/72, 2–3. The Hungarians were also the first to argue for troop withdrawals.
180 'Minutes of the Soviet-Czechoslovak Negotiations in Kiev', 7–8 December 1968, in Navrátil et al. (eds), *Prague Spring*, 555.
181 'Vasil Bil'ak's Recollections of Preparations for the April 1969 CPCz CC Plenum, and the Removal of Alexander Dubcek', in Navrátil et al. (eds), *Prague Spring*, 562.
182 See Chapter 7.
183 Cf. Navrátil et al. (eds), *Prague Spring*, 441.
184 'Talks between CSSR Defense Minister Dzúr and Soviet Defense Minister Grechko', 1 April 1969, in Navrátil et al. (eds), *Prague Spring*, 565.
185 Navrátil et al. (eds), *Prague Spring*, 441.
186 'Talks between Dzúr and Grechko', 569.

7 Closing ranks, while clashing with China

> When people are confronted with a firmly sustained position, they yield.[1]
> (Ion Gheorghe Maurer, Romanian Prime Minister)

The Prague Spring and the invasion of the Eastern European 'coalition of the willing' in Czechoslovakia on 21 August 1968 have put such a stamp on the year 1968 in Eastern Europe that it is easy to forget that there were still several unresolved issues within the Warsaw Pact that initially demanded more attention than the situation in Czechoslovakia. Although the Romanian dissent on a non-proliferation treaty had been neutralised by issuing a separate declaration of the 'six' during the PCC meeting in Sofia on 6–7 March 1968, further proposals on military reforms had been postponed to the next PCC meeting, as it was impossible to bypass Romania on the reforms of an alliance of which it was itself a member. The WP's only official organ remained the PCC, and no consensus had been reached on intra-allied coordination on military and foreign policy issues. The question of the intergovernmental versus supranational nature of the alliance's institutions had not yet been resolved, nor had the Bucharest Declaration on European Security of July 1966 been complemented by a more concrete proposal. The WP had even been sidelined through the multilateral decision making during the Prague Spring. The WP, accordingly, found itself in limbo until the next PCC meeting in March 1969.

This chapter thus deals with the same period as the previous one, but from a totally different angle. Instead of assessing the role of the WP during the Prague Spring, it aims to examine the functioning of the alliance by focusing on the issues that have been central to the rest of this book. Even though the WP played no role in resolving the crisis in Czechoslovakia, the customary issues, such as WP military reforms and European security, did not grind to a halt during the Prague Spring. On the contrary, business continued (almost) as usual, and during the first PCC meeting after the Prague Spring, in March 1969, several issues were resolved that had been dominating WP discussions throughout the 1960s. According to Mastny, this meeting even represented the PCC's 'landmark event'.[2] Against the backdrop of the German question and the Sino–Soviet split the issues of reforms and European security will be analysed during the period that also witnessed Dubcek's rise and fall: starting with the PCC meeting in Sofia in March 1968, and finishing with the one in Budapest in March 1969, this chapter will trace a decisive period in the evolution of the WP, in which the alliance was confronted with a simple question: to consolidate or to disintegrate.

The Warsaw Pact under pressure

The consolidation of the WP became particularly urgent since its Western counterpart, NATO, had overcome the crisis that the dissent of French President Charles de Gaulle had caused, by the end of 1967. Although the French government had decided to withdraw from NATO's military structures in March 1966, it ultimately agreed to sign the Harmel Report, which enshrined NATO's reforms, in December 1967.[3] In this report it was decided to restructure NATO according to the slogan 'defence cum détente', which indicated that NATO would strive for a relaxation of tensions with Eastern Europe and the Soviet Union, while deterring a further escalation of such tensions by an increased defence capability.[4] Thus NATO had resolved its internal crisis through the Harmel Report, which also 'stressed the importance of having military capabilities that covered the full spectrum of potential conflict' in order to 'deter aggression and counter the political influence of Soviet military power, paving the way for détente'.[5] In December 1967 NATO had adopted the military strategy of 'Flexible Response', which proclaimed an incremental escalation of the fighting in case of a war with the WP.[6] Through the Harmel Report the Western alliance had not only solved its political crisis by neutralising the French *Alleingang*, but it had also found a new purpose by redefining itself as a military alliance in order to further détente. The Warsaw Pact had, however, not found a solution to dealing with Ceausescu's 'Gaullist challenge'.

At the same time, the Eastern European alliance had not yet overcome its internal crisis. The German question had become all the more sensitive, as a new direction in West German foreign policy threatened to sow even more disunity in the alliance. The so-called new *Ostpolitik* of the social democratic West German Foreign Minister Willy Brandt to seek an improvement of relations with Eastern Europe, while still refusing to recognise the GDR, created a delicate divide between Eastern Germany and the other WP countries. When Willy Brandt became chancellor in October 1969, the reaction to his *Ostpolitik* became an even more urgent issue. Meanwhile, the Sino–Soviet split was about to turn from an ideological battle into a military one, which would even culminate in the Soviet Union and China being on the brink of war during Sino–Soviet border clashes in March 1969.

While the WP was under pressure from two fronts, the Prague Spring further exacerbated the situation within the Eastern bloc. The alliance had been split into a 'club' of five, leaving Romania and Czechoslovakia isolated, while Albania had officially withdrawn from the alliance in protest at the invasion in Czechoslovakia in September 1968. The restructuring of the alliance thus became all the more imperative, and the WP members urgently had to find an appropriate response to NATO's Harmel Report. Since the WP's Sumava Exercise in June 1968 caused a lot of tensions, whereas the invasion in Czechoslovakia on 21 August 1968 was *not* a WP venture at all, the functioning of the alliance's military aspects remained questionable. After the invasion in Czechoslovakia, the WP members now had to show to the world that they could make a positive contribution to the relaxation of European tensions, as well as underlining their unity after several members had sailed a different course during the Prague Spring. Meanwhile, the WP leaders also needed to finalise the alliance's military consolidation in reaction to the increased emphasis on military strategy within NATO. At the same time the beginning of 1969 heralded the reign of Richard Nixon as US president, who immediately proclaimed his intention to strengthen NATO.[7]

Military reforms

The military restructuring of the WP, proposed by Brezhnev in January 1966, was intended to strengthen the alliance's military capability vis-à-vis NATO. Up to 1966 the military dimension of the WP had been even less institutionalised than the political one: apart from a (Soviet) supreme commander with a general staff there were no military organs at all within the alliance. Soviet military thinking was not shared in detail with the other members of the alliance, and 'even the leading GDR general officers had not been privy to the real-time planning of Moscow's strategists'.[8] The same applied, presumably, to other WP officers, who were merely supposed to cooperate in an all-out nuclear strike in Europe, if NATO were to attack. None of these plans were, however, discussed within any WP organs, even though the 'plans envisaged greater sacrifices for the Soviet allies than for the Soviet Union itself'.[9] Although the WP members would be likely to close ranks in the event of an actual war with NATO, Soviet unilateralism on a *military* front seemed to have grown so much out of sync with the *political* multilateralisation of the WP that the military reforms within the WP became all the more urgent.

The WP defence ministers had agreed to establish a staff of the Unified Armed Forces and a Committee on Technology during a meeting in May 1966, but the reforms had stagnated ever since due to Romanian dissent.[10] In the first half of the 1960s Romania had already 'adopted an independent military doctrine of "Total People's War for the Defence of the Homeland", as well as a national military structure entirely separate from that of the Warsaw Pact', and Ceausescu had prohibited joint WP manoeuvres on Romanian territory.[11] The Romanian leadership was accordingly determined to use the process of reforms to safeguard Romanian sovereignty in military matters too. The Romanians were particularly concerned about a potential transfer of jurisdiction over their national army to the Warsaw Pact's supreme commander, and they had proposed the creation of a Military Council in order to control the power of the supreme commander.[12] After Ceausescu had succeeded in removing the discussion of any kind of reforms from the agenda during the PCC meeting in Bucharest in July 1966, the Kremlin finally tried to breathe new life into the military reforms in preparation for the PCC meeting, which Ceausescu had convened in Sofia on 6–7 March 1968 in order to discuss the non-proliferation treaty.

The meeting of the chiefs of the General Staff from each WP country, which took place from 29 February until 1 March 1968 in Prague, nevertheless sealed the Romanian *Alleingang* on military reforms. To the great delight of the Romanian delegation, the other delegations accepted the Romanian proposal to create a Military Council, after the Romanians had supposedly abandoned their insistence on the principle of unanimity. Although the other delegates were prepared to agree on a draft statute for the Council in question, the Romanians objected to the pressure on 'deciding in a great hurry', and Romanian Chief of Staff General Ion Gheorghe insisted on discussing matters of principle first, while including these in a new statute of the Unified Command, before creating any more organs.[13] The Romanian delegation was particularly interested in specifying the relations between the Unified Command and the respective governments, as well as the Unified Command and the PCC, in order to determine where the power to decide over the individual armies would reside.

Moreover, the Romanian delegates wanted to prevent their allies from being misled by the name 'Unified Command'. Referring to the provisions of the Warsaw Treaty, the Romanians claimed that a Unified *Command* does not imply unified *armed forces*, while emphasising that the armed forces of the WP countries would *not* unite, but remain under national command. The Romanians thus attempted to ensure that the Unified Command would not turn into a supranational organ either, which would entail the Romanian loss of control over its own armed forces. In order to enshrine the intergovernmental nature of the Unified Command, the Romanian participants had even brought their own draft statute of a Unified Command with them. In an ironic reversal of roles, the other participants claimed that they had no mandate to discuss the Romanian draft.[14]

Meanwhile, the Kremlin feared that the Romanian instrumental use of the Warsaw Treaty served to undermine the existence of the Unified Armed Forces altogether, and decided to leave the approval of 'the establishment of principal institutions of the Unified Armed Forces' open to 'the sides interested in a positive resolution to this matter'.[15] Allowing Romania 'an open opportunity to join and participate in the established institutions whenever it recognises this to be appropriate', the Soviet leaders were accordingly prepared to tolerate a Romanian version of the French withdrawal from NATO's military structures in March 1966.[16] The Romanian Gaullism was once more underscored by the protocol of the meeting, which stated that all delegations apart from the Romanian one had agreed.[17] A Romanian appendix underlined in turn the necessity of resolving problems of principle first.[18]

The military reforms were, accordingly, at this stage still much more pressing than the WP stance towards the Prague Spring. The Romanian delegates were pleasantly surprised by the cordial atmosphere during the meeting, and by Dubcek's personal greetings to Ceausescu.[19] Although the disagreement during the meeting pre-empted any resolution on military issues during the ensuing PCC meeting in Sofia, it was, however, decided at the PCC meeting that the ministers of defence would analyse the documents and put forward their own proposals within six months.[20] Meanwhile, Soviet Supreme Commander Marshall Yakubovskii travelled across Eastern Europe in an attempt to lobby the respective WP leaders for the Soviet proposals. The initiative on military reforms was still clearly a Soviet prerogative that needed to be prepared bilaterally.

Yakubovskii on tour

Yakubovskii started his journey with one of Moscow's most ardent allies: the Polish leader Gomulka. On 19 April 1968, four weeks after the Dresden meeting of 'the six', Yakubovskii further increased Romanian isolation by underlining that drafts of the statutes had been sent to all governments except the Romanian one, although he did 'not exclude the possibility of visiting Romania' at a later stage.[21] Gomulka was not at all averse to bypassing Romania altogether, and 'emphasised the urgency of quickly implementing the documents even without Romania's participation'. Underlining that the PCC should be 'a full decision-making institution', which is exactly what the Romanians wanted to avoid, Gomulka clearly attempted to use the bilateral meeting to undermine the Romanian stance. Gomulka also drew the situation in Czechoslovakia into the conversation by adding that '[t]he disorganisation of their army leaves the border with the FRG practically open', which he considered a valid 'reason to keep Soviet forces in Czechoslovakia, within the framework of the Warsaw Pact'.[22] The link between the Czechoslovak situation and the WP was a Polish, not a Soviet one.

The Hungarian leader Janos Kadar was, however, not at all keen on using the military reforms as a pretext for sending Soviet troops to Czechoslovakia. When Yakubovskii visited Hungary, the Soviet reform proposals met with caution instead. Kadar wanted to *prevent* the reforms from enabling troop deployment on the territories of WP member states without their approval, thus also forestalling a possible invasion in Czechoslovakia. He also differed from Gomulka in his attitude to Romania, and advised Yakubovskii that 'preventing a break with Romania, which could mean the end of the alliance, was more urgent than the situation in Czechoslovakia'.[23] As in the Prague Spring in general, Kadar also occupied the position of a mediator in Soviet-Romanian relations, urging Brezhnev to tread his ground carefully to prevent alienating Romania from the WP.

Soviet-Romanian relations had, in fact, deteriorated to such an extent that Romanian and Soviet delegates had spent almost 100 days negotiating on a treaty of friendship and cooperation in the heat of the Prague Spring.²⁴ This stood in sharp contrast with the speedy conclusion of a friendship treaty between Romania and Czechoslovakia, as we have seen in the last chapter. The Soviet-Romanian treaty was subject to severe rows as to whether the WP would be mentioned or not, and to Ceausescu's insistence that 'provisions be added to ensure that Romanian troops would be used only in Europe and only against "imperialist" countries, not against other Communist states'.²⁵ The Romanian leadership thus wanted to ensure that its troops could not be used against China, but the provisions ironically ruled out any interference in Czechoslovak affairs, too. The Kremlin ultimately yielded to the Romanian demands, although with a delay of more than two years: the new treaty was concluded in July 1970.²⁶

Yakubovskii nevertheless decided to send the documents to the Romanian government in May. In direct contradiction with the Polish view, Romanian Defence Minister Ion Ionita stressed the consultative nature of the PCC again and argued that the Supreme Command should not be turned 'into a supranational command and control organ', since the armed forces of the WP states should 'remain subordinate to the national commands'. The Military Council should therefore have 'functions of consultation and recommendation', in which proposals cannot be adopted 'by a simple majority of votes', as that is 'a principle applicable within the internal framework of the parties and states, and I think it cannot be extended to relationships between parties and states'.²⁷ The Romanians thus prevented the principle of democratic centralism from being transferred to international relations, as they had argued in January 1965.²⁸ Distinguishing yet again between domestic politics and international relations, the Romanians prevented the WP from functioning like a politburo writ large.

The Romanian leadership also unprecedentedly reserved the French option for itself: 'As a follow-up to this position, the Socialist Republic of Romania, without declaring that it is leaving the Treaty, places itself outside of the integrated military organs of the Warsaw Treaty Organisation'. This would also have direct military consequences, as it would imply 'the right to review the number of tactical and operational units [...] in the structure of the Unified Armed Forces with a view toward reducing them'.²⁹ The Romanians thus had an instrument to undermine the alliance's tendency towards supranationalism, and defended their scope for manoeuvre in military terms as ardently as in political terms. Potentially copying the behaviour of the most recalcitrant NATO member, the Romanian side almost turned the WP's evolution into an alliance more akin to NATO into a self-fulfilling prophecy: the Romanian *Alleingang* could not be resolved within the tradition of democratic centralism.

When Yakubovskii travelled to Prague as part of his tour to improve 'the combat readiness of the Warsaw Pact', the meeting with Czechoslovak Defence Minister Martin Dzur 'took place in a spirit of full understanding'. Despite the Prague Spring, the Romanian leaders were at this stage still much more radical on military reforms than their Czechoslovak comrades. Discussing ways 'to strengthen the Warsaw Pact's military institutions', the Czechoslovak delegation 'proposed adjustments' according to which the supreme commander 'must base his activity not only on the decisions of the Political Consultative Committee, but also at all times on the consent of the governments or defence ministers of the member countries concerned'. Apart from echoing the Romanian emphasis on intergovernmental decision making, the Czechoslovak proposal also resembled the Romanian proposal that the chief deputies of the supreme commander 'may be chosen from among the armed forces of any member country'. All Czechoslovak proposals were 'taken into consideration [...] with an open mind', and the Czechoslovak defence minister sincerely believed that the discussions had contributed 'to the strengthening of mutual relations'.[30]

At the beginning of July, before the fateful meeting of the five socialist leaders in Warsaw on 14 July, the Czechoslovak side responded much more constructively to the Soviet proposals, and stressed its 'strong resolution to strengthen the allied ties within the Warsaw Treaty', while backing Yakubovskii's proposals 'to make the Warsaw Pact more flexible and operational'. It also referred to the resolve within the CPCz action programme 'to contribute to joint activities of [...] the Warsaw Treaty in a more active way', as well as 'seeking to increase our active share in the joint defence of the Warsaw Treaty states, as we do not want to be a mere passive member'.[31] Instead of considering opting out of the WP's military structures in the Romanian way, the Czechoslovak leaders seemed ready to embark on a self-consciously constructive course.

General Prchlik's challenge

There were, however, several leading officials whose views on military matters were more extreme than those of the Czechoslovak leadership. The most prominent of those was Lt General Vaclav Prchlik, who had been in charge of the CPCz CC department for state organs since February 1968,[32] and who had developed a report on 'the Internal and External Security of the State', which would serve as 'the starting point for formulating decisions of the Extraordinary 14th Party Congress'. This report argued for a 'Czechoslovak defence system', which would be based on a 'Czechoslovak military doctrine' instead of 'operational tasks set forth by the Warsaw Pact command'.[33] The report underscored that 'the doctrine will also take as its starting point the alliance obligations to the Soviet Union and other Warsaw Pact partners', but it mirrored the Romanian emphasis on intergovernmentalism, and it was clear that it paved the way for the kind of emancipation that Romania had already achieved.[34] If this were to be implemented at the Congress in September 1968, it might well become the Czechoslovak 'declaration of independence'. Although Romania already had its own military doctrine, a Czechoslovak one carried still more risks, as the country was increasingly straying from the path of communism, and geopolitically was more important to the WP.

Prchlik also gave a press conference on the last day of the meeting of the five socialist countries in Warsaw, which he strongly condemned. Increasingly frustrated by the fact that Soviet troops had still not withdrawn after the Sumava Exercise, he had attempted to find out whether the Warsaw Treaty legitimised 'the right to deploy [...] units arbitrarily on the territory of other member states', but had discovered instead that the treaty emphasised 'the need to respect the sovereignty of states as well as the principle of non-interference in their internal affairs'. Prchlik accordingly argued 'that necessary qualitative changes should also be carried out in the Warsaw Pact's concept of its function and in the establishment of relations within the Warsaw Pact'. Arguing for 'genuine equality of all members of the coalition', he proposed to 'reinforce the role of the Political Consultative Committee', while also criticising the fact that the WP's Unified Command 'consists solely of marshals, generals, and other senior officers of the Soviet army'.[35]

Most of Prchlik's proposals were not new, but they acquired a dynamics of their own within the heat of the Prague Spring. Prchlik ominously concluded his press conference with 'the fact that views within the Warsaw Pact itself are now divergent. As I see it, we must do what we can to exploit this divergence, and we must also take advantage of the different views expressed by fraternal parties outside the Warsaw Pact'.[36] Whereas the CPCz leaders had been eager to profess their unflinching loyalty to the alliance, Prchlik's press conference was an explicit exhortation to undermine the unity of the WP still further. Thus Dubcek's pledges of allegiance lost their credibility.

The Soviet reaction to Prchlik's remarks was, accordingly, very violent, and Prchlik was accused of 'distort[ing] the essence of this structure and its organisation [...], divulg[ing] some top-secret information',[37] and 'undermining the Warsaw Pact'. Reminding Czechoslovakia of its 'responsibility to the Warsaw Pact' instead, the Soviet government expressed its expectation that 'effective measures will be taken to establish the necessary border control system on the frontiers with the FRG and Austria', where the borders were still open, thus echoing Gomulka.[38] Dubcek ultimately decided to close altogether the CPCz CC State Administration Department, which was headed by Prchlik, but this did little to salvage the situation. The fact that Prchlik was the only one to be replaced during the Prague Spring nevertheless clearly illustrates that Prchlik's depiction of the WP also exceeded Dubcek's intentions. Prchlik's removal was, however, too late to reassure the Kremlin of Czechoslovak loyalty to the WP.

Reforms in the post-invasion period

The invasion in Czechoslovakia on 21 August 1968 toned down Soviet military ambitions. Even though the invading armed forces faced no Czechoslovak resistance, the Soviet army 'ran into bottlenecks and its supply lines became strained in ways that could be fatal in combat conditions'.[39] Meanwhile, Soviet troops were ordered not to engage in battle during a hypothetical encounter with NATO troops, whereas NATO decided not to interfere and struggled with a dysfunctional communication system. Not only were both sides 'caught unprepared', as Mastny convincingly argues, but the invasion in Czechoslovakia also suggested that 'Europe was not so much safe *for* war as safe *from* war'.[40] Mastny accordingly regards the invasion in Czechoslovakia as a 'strategic watershed' in the Cold War, as the restraint from both sides 'highlighted the growing divergence between the pointless U.S.-Soviet nuclear rivalry and the more important confrontation of the two military groupings in Europe', and accordingly 'fostered the budding détente'.[41] At the same time, the invasion also exposed the military shortcomings within the Soviet bloc, and made the conclusion of the WP's military reforms all the more pressing.

Meanwhile, the Romanian leadership used the invasion in Czechoslovakia to demarcate its sovereignty all the more clearly. The Grand National Assembly immediately adopted a law that prohibited the presence of foreign troops on Romanian territory, and subordinated the Romanian Army exclusively to the Romanian parliament.[42] It is therefore no coincidence that Marshall Yakubovskii decided to visit Ceausescu and Maurer a month after the invasion, on 28 September 1968. Ignoring Ceausescu's severe condemnation of the intervention, Yakubovskii returned to business as usual, and discussed a new version of the drafts with the Romanian leadership, after he had already coordinated them with the Romanian Defence Minister General Ion Gheorghe.[43] Concurrently with the normalisation in Czechoslovakia, relations with Romania needed to be normalised too, and Yakubovskii had gone to great lengths to incorporate Romanian suggestions in the revised drafts, while also stressing that the observations from *all* defence ministers were included.

Yakubovskii accordingly proposed that decisions within the Military Council should be made by a majority of two thirds instead of a simple majority, as a compromise for the Romanian preference for unanimity. In order to avoid subordinating the WP defence ministers to the supreme commander, he suggested that the deputy defence ministers should participate in the Military Council, while creating a military committee also to provide the defence ministers with an instrument for consultations within a WP framework. This would significantly increase the intergovernmental dimension of military consultations within the WP, while preventing the supreme command from becoming supranational. Ceausescu was, therefore, not averse to the Soviet suggestions, but emphasised that the supreme commander could only 'make recommendations' about the deployment of troops of the United Armed Forces on the territory of a WP country, with 'the agreement of *all countries*'.[44] This was, interestingly, an issue on which the Czechoslovak side had also presented an alternative proposal, which Yakubovskii praised.

Ironically, Yakubovskii had more difficulty with understanding the Romanian objections, since he failed to grasp why the agreement of those WP members who did not participate in the deployment was also needed. Ceausescu explained that when troops were deployed 'in the name of the Treaty' it is necessary 'that we all take responsibility'. Emphasising that acting 'outside the Treaty' was an altogether different matter, Ceausescu clearly alluded to the invasion in Czechoslovakia while striving to prevent the WP from being used as an instrument to legitimise such a deployment of troops. Yakubovskii now understood, and Ceausescu therefore declared himself 'ready to participate in the meeting of the Political Consultative Committee'.[45] Despite the crisis in Czechoslovakia the targets at the March 1968 PCC meeting had accordingly been met: all governments had reviewed the proposals within half a year after the meeting in Sofia.

The impending PCC meeting was this time prepared by the ministers of defence, on 30 October 1968 in Moscow. The consensus was greater than usual. All delegations agreed to ask the PCC and the respective governments to approve the creation of a Committee of Defence Ministers, a statute of the Unified Command, a technical committee, a statute of the Military Council, and an anti-aerial defence system, and recommended that a general staff and a technical committee should be formed in the first half of 1969.[46] The Romanian delegation nevertheless appended a separate opinion to the protocol, 'reserving itself the right to review' article 12a of the statute of the Unified Command, according to which the 'governments in common agreement' would decide about the dislocation of troops, but insisted on 'the agreement of *all* countries', as they had done in their conversation with Yakubovskii a month earlier.[47] Since the meeting took place while the Soviet leaders were negotiating the deployment of their troops on Czechoslovak soil, this was a particularly sensitive issue. The meeting accordingly ended with agreement on everything apart from article 12a, which once again sealed the customary difference between Romania and the rest. This seemed to herald the return of 'the six', despite the fact that 'five' of those had invaded the other one.

Two months later, when Dubcek was still struggling to 'normalise' Czechoslovakia, the Czechoslovak General Staff even contrasted Czechoslovakia 'as a pillar of the coalition' to the 'detrimental endeavours' of Romania in an official 'Study on the Warsaw Treaty'. Considering the WP 'too loose' an alliance, which could not 'compare to the organisational refinement of NATO', the study emphasised the need to strengthen the military bodies, and criticised Romania for its 'narrow perception of state sovereignty'. The report nevertheless credited the Romanians with revealing 'a statutory lack in the military organisation of the coalition, i.e. a vagueness concerning the rights and duties of both the Supreme Commander and the General Staff, as well as concerning the influence of coalition members on their activities'. The Romanian insistence on procedural matters had thus inspired its allies with a more critical look at the proposals for reforms, which, according to the study, had 'reached a qualitative turning point'.[48]

Concluding that 'the events of 1968 in Czechoslovakia have [not] had a substantial impact on the development of these problems', the study had identified a very peculiar fact of the year 1968: the Prague Spring and its suppression did not really seem to have changed the dynamics within the Warsaw Pact at all.[49] Although the proposals for military reforms were more strongly coordinated by the Kremlin than other issues within the WP, this is logical concerning the fact that the military dimension of the alliance had solely been a Soviet prerogative up to the reforms. The NSWP members had, however, considerable room for manoeuvre, as is illustrated by the Romanian *Alleingang*, which continued unhampered after the Prague Spring, and even seemed to approximate the French stance within and outside NATO. The invasion in Czechoslovakia nevertheless added a very delicate perspective to the reforms, by clearly illustrating the military repercussions of a lack of input from *all* WP members in the decision making, albeit *outside* the official WP framework.

The 'qualitative turning point'

The discussion on military reforms had, indeed, reached such a 'qualitative turning point' that the Soviet leaders deemed the time ripe to convene the PCC in March 1969 in order to finalise the documents. Although this was the first PCC meeting since July 1963 whose convention was actively initiated by the Kremlin, the Romanian leadership managed to assert its authority yet again by postponing the meeting until 17 March.[50] Moreover, the Hungarian leader Janos Kadar suggested adding an appeal on European security to the agenda.[51] On 7 March Brezhnev and Kosygin duly sent a letter to all WP leaders, in which they proposed to convene the PCC in Budapest on 17 March in order to reach an agreement on the military reforms, 'adopt a short appeal' on European security with the renewed proposal to convene a European security conference, and to conduct 'an exchange of opinions' on such international issues as the situation in Vietnam, and 'the intensification of NATO's aggressive activity'. Brezhnev explicitly suggested 'that it would be useful to ask the Hungarian comrades, as organisers of the conference, to assume the task of preparing [...] the drafts of the appeal and the communiqué'.[52]

Brezhnev's letter represented the first time that he had explicitly asked another WP member to prepare the meeting. The choreography that seemed to have been lacking throughout the 1960s was thus entrusted to the Hungarian leadership. Although Budapest was a logical venue for a PCC meeting, as it was the only WP capital where it had not yet been convened apart from Berlin, the fact that the Hungarian leadership was asked to prepare the meeting testified to the Hungarian emancipation during the Prague Spring. Brezhnev's trust in the Hungarian leadership was particularly striking as the Hungarian press had frequently underlined Hungary's different stance on the invasion in Czechoslovakia.[53] After Kadar's mediating role between the WP five and Dubcek throughout the crisis in Czechoslovakia, he nevertheless seemed the only leader who might be able to unify all participants. This was, after all, the first PCC meeting after the invasion in Czechoslovakia, in which the Romanian leadership re-joined the multilateral fold, six months after its severe condemnation of its allies' decision to invade Czechoslovakia.

The Hungarian leaders were particularly sensitive to the delicate situation, and advised their Soviet comrades on how to proceed. In a preliminary discussion on 9 March Kadar even advised the Soviet leaders against any discussion on political reforms, and he 'stressed that given recent events, the very fact that the Political Consultative Committee is convening has political significance. The main focus should be on signing the military documents'.[54] Kadar attempted to establish common ground between all participants, while emphasising that 'intelligent compromises should be made. It should not happen that there are seven of us there, but only six sign'. Although the Kremlin was therefore greatly interested in close coordination with the Hungarian leaders, Kadar 'agreed with the Soviet comrades that though we were the hosts, they should take the task of political agitation, for they were the only people here that could have an impact on the sides present'.[55] In stark contrast to the Romanian leaders' tendency unilaterally to coordinate the PCC meeting in Bucharest in 1966 to achieve *their* aims, Kadar intended to use his position as host to transcend his domestic interests and unite the participants.

The PCC's convention in Budapest also proved a strategic move from the Romanian point of view, as Kadar's moderation on the Prague Spring, but also before, had prevented severe antagonism between the two leaderships. The Romanian reaction to the convention of the meeting and its agenda was unprecedentedly positive. The Romanian leadership did, however, suggest preparing the PCC by convening the WP's deputy foreign ministers or foreign ministers before the meeting started, which was also suggested by the Hungarian and Polish leaderships.[56] The request was granted, and the deputy foreign ministers arranged to meet in Budapest on 16 March 1969.

Meanwhile, Brezhnev's request for Hungarian preparation of the appeal on European security and the communiqué illustrated both Moscow's increased willingness to treat its WP allies as equals, and Brezhnev's attempt to regain some control over the process. The fact that the Soviets had prepared the definitive drafts of all the military documents, whereas the preparation of the documents on European security was delegated to an NSWP member, also shows that the Kremlin was much more likely to share the responsibility on foreign policy issues than on military issues. As Brezhnev had underlined in his letter, the European security conference would be a truly multilateral occasion, in the preparation of which *all* members of the WP would participate.[57] The military reforms would, on the contrary, be elucidated by Marshall Yakubovskii at the beginning of the PCC meeting. They were, however, reviewed by *all* WP defence ministers, who had accordingly become involved within the alliance, too. The agenda for the PCC meeting thus testified to the alliance's multilateralisation in both a political and a military dimension.

The Hungarians, meanwhile, rose to the occasion, and proactively organised the meeting. They decided that all delegations apart from the Soviet one would be housed in the same hotel, which meant that the Hungarians could coordinate matters with the Soviet comrades unhampered.[58] Much to Brezhnev's delight, the Hungarian leaders insisted that the meeting could be concluded in one day,[59] which would be a record, and in order to speed up the process Brezhnev asked his allies not to prepare any speeches.[60] The absence of speeches illustrated that this meeting was not a mere rhetorical ploy, but that, on the contrary, it was a means to a far more important end. The purpose of this meeting was not only to consolidate the alliance through military reforms, but also to underscore the Warsaw Pact's unity to the world, after it was severely questioned in the light of the events in Czechoslovakia. A constructive appeal for a European security conference would underline the alliance's quest for peace. A WP response to NATO's strategy of 'defence cum détente' had become all the more urgent, and the pursuit of European détente became particularly pressing in the wake of the invasion in Czechoslovakia. The PCC meeting would thus serve to conclude a number of issues that had remained unresolved since the severely contested PCC meeting in Warsaw in January 1965.

The Sino–Soviet split

The purpose of the meeting was overshadowed by a severe escalation in Sino–Soviet tensions, as it took place two weeks after severe Sino–Soviet border clashes on the island of Zhenbao at the Ussuri river had begun on 2 March, which had led to a number of casualties on both sides. As a consequence of the Sino–Soviet split, the mutual border had become increasingly militarised on both sides during the 1960s.[61] According to the latest evidence, the Chinese leadership had provoked the attack either as a 'reaction to the Soviet intervention in Czechoslovakia', or to create a kind of war hysteria in the heat of the Cultural Revolution 'to forge national unity'.[62] The Kremlin was bewildered by the Chinese offensive. Since Sino-Soviet communication had ground to a halt during the Cultural Revolution, the border clashes caused huge misperceptions on both sides. Failing to fathom their limited scope, the Soviet leaders allegedly started to ponder the possibilities of an invasion or a pre-emptive strike against China's nuclear facilities.[63]

The border clashes escalated on 15 March with a disproportionately large Soviet counter-attack, causing still more casualties, and coinciding with the Warsaw Pact's deputy foreign ministers meeting on 15–16 March.[64] The Soviet reaction confirmed Chinese fears of a repetition of the invasion in Czechoslovakia, with the result that both sides thought that the other side was about to embark on a full-scale war.[65] As the Polish ambassador to Beijing recounts, this was a 'more than frightening prospect' for the WP leaders, as 'they had only minimal influence – or rather none at all – in the course of events on the Sino-Soviet border'.[66] The intention to restore unity to the WP had, accordingly, become all the more urgent, as there was much more at stake than the WP's fragmentation after the invasion in Czechoslovakia. The fact that Brezhnev had ordered the counter offence on 15 March during his train journey to the PCC meeting in Budapest could imply that he hoped to force his WP allies to close ranks on the Sino–Soviet split.[67] The dynamics of the Cold War had changed to such an extent that the WP did not need to unite in the face of an imperialist enemy, but in the face of a communist one.

The Kremlin nevertheless aimed to use the meeting of deputy foreign ministers to formulate a united stance against Chinese aggression, and Soviet Deputy Foreign Minister Firyubin proposed to include Chinese condemnations in the communiqué. The Romanian delegates nevertheless persisted in their refusal to turn the WP against China. Thus the customary dichotomy between the Poles and East Germans on the one hand, and the Romanians on the other threatened to undermine the unity for which the Hungarians and Soviets were striving. Firyubin described the Romanian attitude as 'a deliberate attempt to bury the organization of the Warsaw Pact', but the Romanian leadership was more interested in limiting the scope of the WP than destroying it altogether.[68] Arguing that the Romanian delegates had no mandate to discuss any issues that were not on the agenda, the Romanian representative Malita added that a WP stance on the Sino–Soviet border clashes contradicted article 4 of the Warsaw Treaty, which confined the WP members' mutual assistance to an 'armed attack in Europe'.[69] The WP was, after all, 'conceived as an instrument of defence against aggression of the imperialist countries of Europe', and not against aggression from a communist neighbour.[70] Thus the Romanians succeeded again in using the Warsaw Treaty as an instrument to support their own arguments.

The Romanians were consistent in their insistence that the alliance should not be directed against China, which they had also successfully avoided by arguing against the Mongolian accession to the WP in July 1963.[71] The invasion of the five socialist countries of Czechoslovakia had provided the Romanians with an extra reason to avoid any extension of the WP, as politburo member Gheorghe Stoica argued in a simultaneous politburo meeting in Bucharest. Referring to the doctrine 'of limited sovereignty' (a.k.a. the Brezhnev doctrine), which the Romanians and the Yugoslavs had severely denounced, Stoica emphasised the importance of the 'European character' of the treaty, which should simply remain 'an instrument of defence against imperialist aggression […], and cannot be used in another situation of intervening in any socialist country'. The Romanians had to ensure that the WP was not retrospectively employed to justify the invasion in Czechoslovakia under the guise of the Sino–Soviet split. If the WP was no longer a primarily 'anti-imperialist' alliance, it could serve to legitimise the Brezhnev doctrine, and turn against any other socialist country in future, including Romania. Stoica therefore suggested using the PCC meeting to condemn the invasion in Czechoslovakia instead, as it was 'a severe transgression of the treaty'. As the Romanians also wanted to avoid any further isolation, it was, however, agreed only to mention 'the problem with Czechoslovakia' if the situation required it.⁷²

Meanwhile, the Romanian politburo members feared that the Kremlin intended to do exactly the opposite by concentrating on the Sino–Soviet border clashes. They believed that 'the Soviets would use it to exercise pressure on the communist parties' to condemn the Chinese actions.⁷³ A severe condemnation of China would considerably strengthen Brezhnev's hand now that the Sino–Soviet split had become irreversible. Stoica even argued that the border clashes were so widely publicised, *because* they coincided with the PCC meeting, since previous Sino–Soviet border clashes had hardly gained any attention. This did not seem a farfetched suggestion, as the Hungarian report of the meeting shows that Firyubin had already drafted a communiqué on 9 March, six days before the escalation of the border clashes, which 'even condemned the Chinese for border violations without citing them by name'.⁷⁴ The Romanians therefore continued to emphasise that any Sino–Soviet disputes should be resolved bilaterally. It was decided to oppose firmly the added paragraph on China in the communiqué, which had 'a tone as though we are on the threshold of a world war'.⁷⁵ The 'anti-imperialist' nature of the alliance was thus, ironically, consolidated by the Romanians.

The other delegations were nevertheless adamant that the Chinese actions should be condemned within the WP framework, as Brezhnev stressed in one of his preliminary conversations with Ceausescu. Ceausescu and Maurer insisted that the Chinese issue went beyond the confines of the Warsaw Treaty and could not be discussed within the framework of the PCC. The situation threatened to turn into the usual division of 'six' against 'one', as Brezhnev asked '[h]ow can one ask six parties and states to renounce their positions [...] in favour of one country? Why should Gomulka or Zhivkov concede to do what pleases Ceausescu?' These rhetorical questions enabled Ceausescu once again to criticise the principle of democratic centralism, which drove Brezhnev to such despair that he began to shout about the 'situation of war' in the Far East, but he nevertheless conceded only to discuss the Chinese question unofficially after the PCC meeting, outside the WP framework, and without committing the discussion to paper.⁷⁶ Just as the Prague Spring had been kept out of the WP framework, so the Romanians had kept the Sino–Soviet split out of the PCC. The alliance's multilateralisation clearly implied that Soviet concerns could no longer occupy centre stage.

Brezhnev's concession to the Romanian opposition was all the more timely, as Ceausescu had gained an ally during the PCC meeting in 1969: several hours before the PCC meeting the Czechoslovak leader Dubcek had a private conversation with Ceausescu in the lobby of the hotel, in which Dubcek warmly thanked Ceausescu for his 'support and solidarity' during the Prague Spring and the period afterwards. Confessing that his assessment of the invasion in Czechoslovakia would never change, Dubcek underscored his defiance of the Soviet Union, and emphasised that he fully agreed with the

Romanian opposition to raising the Chinese issue at the PCC. Nervously looking around him to see that no one overheard them, Dubcek even related that he had to chair the meeting 'according to the principle of rotation', but that he had refused to accept an agenda that contained 'other items than those previously agreed'. While other delegates in the hotel tried to work out what they said, Dubcek told Ceausescu that he nevertheless wanted to restore unity to the meeting, so that he would not be held responsible for disagreements.[77] After the invasion in Czechoslovakia the 'six' had, however, turned into the 'five', and Romania was no longer isolated.

The Romanian insistence to prevent the WP from being used against China was no mean success. As the American historian Bernd Schäfer argues, the Romanian insistence saved 'all Eastern European alliance members [...] from being drawn into a potential conflict'.[78] The Romanian leadership had reigned in the military ambitions of the WP, while also preventing further legitimation of the Brezhnev doctrine. By ensuring that the WP could only be targeted against 'imperialism', the alliance could by no means justify an invasion of a socialist country. The WP could not be used to turn China into another Czechoslovakia, and the Kremlin could not count on military backing from its allies as it had done during the Cuban Missile Crisis and the second Berlin Crisis. The Romanians had successfully limited the scope of the WP as well as Soviet ambitions, instead of limiting anyone's sovereignty.

European security

The Romanian leadership had ensured that the central concern of the WP remained European security, which was officially on the agenda for the meeting of deputy foreign ministers. In the wake of the invasion in Czechoslovakia, which lay at the heart of Europe, a European settlement was particularly desirable. Some WP members, such as the GDR, considered 'the safeguarding of European Security' an essential response to NATO's military build-up, whereas others, such as Hungary, again began to emphasise the need for a European security conference in an attempt to salvage European détente after the invasion in Czechoslovakia.[79] Moreover, the East German and Polish members fully agreed in putting both the German question and 'European Security in the foreground of [their] foreign policy', with as 'starting-point [...] the recognition of the *status quo* in Europe'.[80] Against the backdrop of the Sino–Soviet border clashes, détente within Europe had become still more important. The Kremlin even argued that 'because the Soviet Union was making preparations for the European Security Conference, China intended to show its existence and assert influence through fighting the battle'.[81]

The meeting was in fact supposed to deal with the preparation of a communiqué and an appeal on European security. The Kremlin had drafted both documents, but the Hungarian leaders had agreed to present it as their own proposals, presumably to forestall Romanian defiance of Soviet proposals, even though the Hungarians considered the draft of the communiqué 'so bad' that it was 'out of the question that it would be accepted and signed by the Romanians'. According to the Hungarians, 'the German Question was outlined in the usual way', with the FRG being represented as 'an aggressor, a revanchist, a provocateur'. The Hungarian side therefore 'asked the Soviet comrades to consider what exactly we wanted and what could be a realistic goal', and suggested only issuing a short and factual communiqué. The Soviets were so eager to bring the meeting to a good conclusion that they 'agreed with [the Hungarians] in everything by the letter'.[82] The Soviet-Hungarian willingness to compromise was, however, not shared by all participants. Brezhnev had already confided to Kadar that he 'considered the main problem to be convincing Comrades Gomulka and Ulbricht'. After the Polish delegation had unsuccessfully put forward its own draft of an appeal for European security, 'whose tone was sharper than the original', the Polish and East German participants engaged in 'an unfruitful debate' with the Romanian delegation, with the former recommending 'lengthening the drafts and strengthening the wording', and the latter desiring 'to cut the content and dilute the text'.[83]

Romanian Deputy Foreign Minister Malita thought that his Polish colleague wanted to go into far too much depth about the condemnation of the FRG, by *inter alia* denouncing the West German claim to West Berlin, and concentrating on the West German nuclear ambitions. Although Malita agreed to emphasise the inviolability of the European borders and the existence of two German states in the communiqué, he refused to mention explicitly the Oder–Neisse border and to condemn West German imperialism.[84] The Polish delegation clearly intended to use the communiqué to secure the 'Warsaw Package', according to which it had conditioned potential diplomatic relations with the FRG on a number of demands that served to consolidate Polish and East German sovereignty.[85] Whereas the Polish delegation wanted to reintroduce the Warsaw Package into the WP via the back door, the Romanian delegates wanted to prevent this at all costs.

In vain, Brezhnev attempted to resolve the issue by visiting all delegations separately, but 'no matter what room he visited, he found a different position'. Declaring that '[i]t would not matter [...] if only six delegations signed the political documents', as had happened during the meeting of deputy foreign ministers in February 1967, the East German and Polish delegates totally undermined the Soviet-Hungarian attempts to restore unity within the alliance. They were particularly disgruntled that the criteria for a normalisation of relations with the FRG, which constituted the Warsaw Package, were not included in the appeal. Instead of referring to the *recognition* of the GDR and the Oder–Neisse border as a prerequisite for a European security conference, the appeal mentioned 'the *inviolability* of the existing borders and the recognition of the *existence* of the GDR' as a condition for European security itself.[86] Prioritising the normalisation of relations to the recognition of the status quo, the appeal hardly served Polish and East German interests.

Ulbricht and Gomulka deemed the price for WP unity too high, if it meant that the European Security Appeal would not secure *their* borders. It was, after all, this interest that had spurred the Polish campaign on European security. Gomulka and Ulbricht therefore stuck to the tested method of bypassing and isolating Romania where necessary, while underestimating the necessity of restoring unity to the alliance after the invasion of Czechoslovakia.

The conference revealed an interesting shift in Brezhnev's priorities: he considered Ulbricht and Gomulka 'the main problem', instead of Ceausescu, and Kadar's willingness to compromise the solution.[87] Brezhnev's attempt to avoid Romanian isolation also served Soviet interests, because Brezhnev particularly valued a normalisation of relations with West Germany in the wake of the Prague Spring, and had even embarked on a 'renewed dialogue with Bonn over renunciation of force'.[88] In his first meeting with Ceausescu, Brezhnev emphasised his willingness to conclude a short communiqué, but after visiting all other delegations, Brezhnev returned to Ceausescu late at night in a somewhat more pessimistic mood. He explained that the German question was still a major bone of contention: whereas the Romanians insisted on 'weakening' the appeal regarding the position on West Germany, the other delegations intended to 'strengthen' it. Ceausescu nevertheless argued for a realistic assessment of the situation, as the West German Foreign Minister Willy Brandt had been critical of NATO, and this West German tendency deserved support. Although Brezhnev had failed to reach an agreement with the other delegations on the communiqué, Ceausescu concluded the meeting with the uncharacteristically positive observation that 'the spirit of collaboration' was such that he trusted that there would be 'a realistic foundation for agreement'.[89]

Ceausescu accordingly accepted Gomulka's proposal to solve the issue bilaterally. The crux of the matter was an extremely delicate issue. The remaining disagreement was not so much about the German question, as an indirect condemnation of the invasion in Czechoslovakia. The Romanian delegation had ingenuously suggested introducing a paragraph 'to terminate with the demonstrations of force and manoeuvres […] in the interest of peace', which actually served to delegitimise the intervention in Czechoslovakia altogether. The Polish delegates were particularly vexed, as they had vigorously defended the 'fraternal assistance' to Czechoslovakia, and fully realised the ramifications of the Romanian amendment. They therefore agreed to remove their amendment on rejecting the West German claim to Berlin in exchange for a Romanian concession on *their* amendment. The Romanians accepted a new formula, which stated that no European state should 'undertake actions that could serve to poison the atmosphere in the relations between states'.[90] The Brezhnev doctrine was, accordingly, undermined in the European Security Appeal, too.

The fact that a bilateral meeting between the Polish and Romanian leaders had resolved the conference's most contested issue seemed to indicate that the Polish and Romanian positions yet again determined the dynamics within the alliance. The Polish delegation was, however, supported by Soviet Deputy Foreign Minister Firyubin, who 'conducted the greatest part of the discussion [...], while the Poles remained passive'.[91] It is illustrative of the weakened stance of the Polish delegation that it needed support from a Soviet comrade in a supposedly *bi*lateral meeting in order to explain its point of view to the Romanian delegation. The authority of the East German and Polish hawks thus seemed to have eroded after their pressure to invade Czechoslovakia.

Meanwhile, the Romanians successfully exploited the East German and Polish participation in the invasion to force their allies to modify their stance on the FRG in a 'significantly diluted' appeal for a European security conference.[92] At the same time, the Romanians had succeeded in phrasing the appeal in such a way that it could serve as a '[r]etrospective justification of the diplomatic recognition of West Germany by Romania', to the great chagrin of their East German colleagues.[93] With their insistence on the normalisation of relations with the FRG, the Romanians had inadvertently done their Soviet comrades a great service: for the latter, 'normalisation' within Czechoslovakia went hand in hand with a 'normalisation' of relations with the FRG.[94] The Romanian move had left the Polish and East German delegates largely empty handed by turning the Warsaw Package into an anachronism.

The appeal nevertheless contained aspects that served the interests of all participants. It stated the importance of sovereignty, equality and independence, and the need to overcome the division of Europe into two military blocs, while also emphasising the inviolability of borders and the need to recognise the GDR. Reiterating once again the proposal to convene a European security conference without any preconditions, the appeal stressed the necessity for security, cooperation and improving peace. The Romanian 'dilution' and the commitment of the WP allies to resolving European tensions had thus turned it into a very constructive document that emphasised the need for 'multilateral collaboration on a European level'.[95] The Warsaw Pact's multilateralisation had spilled over into its appeal for European security. A multilateral conference on a European level could now be envisaged, as its Eastern European proponents had grown accustomed to multilateralism within the framework of their own alliance.

Military reforms revisited

The Romanian emphasis on *un*limited sovereignty was also central to the Romanian stance on military reforms, which was governed by the refusal to allow any movement of troops on foreign territory, too. Although the military reforms had been largely approved by all members during the meeting of defence ministers on 30 October 1968, the Soviet leaders had to find a way to deal with the Romanian objection to paragraph 12a of the statute of the Unified Armed Forces, on the deployment of troops. The Kremlin seemed to have taken the Romanian reservations seriously, and had suggested a number of amendments, such as erasing paragraph 12a altogether, while emphasising in the statute that the armies would remain under the jurisdiction of the national governments in peacetime. This was a crucial concession to the Romanians, who wanted to avoid at all costs that the Soviet supreme commander could involve the Romanian Army in military manoeuvres without the government's consent. The intergovernmental aspect of the unified command, which the Romanians so much valued, was enshrined in paragraph 12b by emphasising that the governments, and not the PCC, decided about the dislocation of troops. Moreover, the Soviets had yielded to the Romanian request that the supreme commander did not in principle have to be a Soviet citizen, and they had limited his power by substituting the word 'recommendations' for 'orders', which provided his subordinates with the possibility 'to be or not to be in agreement'.[96]

The Romanian politburo convened the morning before the PCC meeting to discuss the Soviet proposals, which greatly pleased Ceausescu and his comrades. The statute of the Military Council had also been revised to take account of the Romanian objections, as it was explicitly stated that the council was 'consultative', and any measures required 'the approval of the government'.[97] The supranational nature of any of the reforms, which the Romanians had feared, had thus been completely undermined, and Ceausescu suggested approving the documents. The Romanian approval, before the PCC meeting actually took place, was unprecedented, and illustrated the Romanian political will to solve the issue on military reforms. Having successfully rallied every delegation behind the revised drafts in bilateral meetings preceding the PCC meeting, Brezhnev visited Ceausescu in his hotel room late at night and thanked him profusely for his constructive attitude on military reforms.[98] In this respect Ceausescu had obviously decided *not* to follow the Gaullist example.

In order to leave nothing to chance, Soviet Supreme Commander Yakubovskii stressed the intergovernmental nature of the reforms during the opening session of the PCC meeting on 17 March, as well as the consultative functions of the established organs – i.e. the Military Council and the Committee of Defence Ministers. The Soviets had clearly taken the Romanian fear of a supranational military alliance to heart. Emphasising the 'multilateral examination' of matters within the Military Council, Yakubovskii clearly stated that the military dimensions of the WP were no longer a Soviet prerogative.[99] The Warsaw Pact's multilateralisation had thus also affected its military organs, which became simultaneously institutionalised and multilateralised. To seal the intergovernmental nature of the reforms Ceausescu proposed 'that the decision be taken by the governments, not by the Political Consultative Committee', which the other delegates approved. To ensure that the documents were appropriately amended, Ceausescu tore out the page with the reference to the PCC from the official document, as Maurer had suggested, and signed the document in the name of 'the participating states' instead.[100] Supranationalism was thus literally ripped out of the WP, and the statute of the Committee of Defence Ministers, the statute of the Unified Command

and the statute of the Military Council were approved with genuine unanimity.[101] After more than three years of discussions on military reforms, all participants had gained a vested interest in consolidating the military dimensions of the alliance.

Whereas 'Gomulka considered the continued existence of the Warsaw Pact an immutable necessity and its consolidation the highest duty of the Polish People's Republic',[102] Ceausescu and his comrades had succeeded in using the military reforms to eliminate any elements of supranational decision making that could bind a WP member to certain measures against its will. Although Mastny argues that the Warsaw Pact remained 'a mere extended arm of the Soviet general staff' where it concerned the WP's 'operational significance', as the armed forces of the WP members only remained 'under their national command in peace time', the effect of the reforms on the NSWP members was still considerable.[103] They had introduced a number of unprecedented checks and balances, which had integrated the Soviet dominated supreme command in the political structures of the WP, thus multilateralising the military aspects of the alliance too, instead of leading a parallel existence as they had done throughout the 1960s. The intergovernmental aspect in the reforms gave the NSWP members a stake in the military structures of the alliance, which they had lacked previously. Apart from turning 'the alliance into a more effective military instrument', the reforms ensured that this instrument could no longer unilaterally be used by the Soviet Union.[104]

Moreover, the multilateralisation of *all* decision making in peacetime carried considerable advantages to all WP members, as it meant that the reforms actually prevented a repetition from the invasion in Czechoslovakia. Although the reforms were of 'diminished relevance [...] at the time of rising détente',[105] as Mastny argues, their relevance would only have diminished if they had catered for *war* instead of *peace*time. Since the likelihood of an all-out European war had considerably decreased in the wake of the invasion of Czechoslovakia, as Mastny himself argues, the reforms were all the more *relevant* at the time of détente: they did, after all, ensure that the Kremlin's power was considerably checked in peacetime. The way in which the reforms clarified the processes of decision making within the WP, while incorporating an intergovernmental aspect that was hitherto lacking, was of vital importance to the balance of power within Eastern Europe. Not only could the WP not be used to facilitate 'fraternal assistance', but it actually made such assistance illegitimate, as it enshrined the approval of each national government for a deployment of foreign troops on its territory. It is, accordingly, no coincidence that the Brezhnev doctrine was never enforced after the invasion in Czechoslovakia, not even during the Polish Crisis in 1980–81.[106]

The denouement

In a preliminary meeting of first secretaries and prime ministers, Brezhnev suggested adopting the military reforms, the European Security Appeal and the communiqué at the PCC meeting. At Ceausescu's request, the delegations received the ultimate draft of the communiqué, which was six pages shorter than the original proposal, and only stated that the military statutes and the appeal to all European countries had been accepted in a 'friendly spirit and comradely collaboration'.[107] The Sino–Soviet split was definitively removed from the alliance's confines, and the alliance was now directed to securing peace in Europe. Meanwhile, Ceausescu once again succeeded in enshrining the intergovernmental nature of the alliance by persuading his comrades to sign the communiqué in the name of 'the participating states' instead of the 'Political Consultative Committee'.[108]

Contrary to usual practice, everything had accordingly been agreed already before the actual PCC meeting started. Instead of being confronted with surprise proposals from various delegations during the PCC's convention, the participants merely had to listen to Yakubovskii's elucidation on the military reforms, and sign the documents. The PCC meeting itself did, however, contain a painful moment, as Dubcek 'got very nervous' about chairing the meeting, and arrived 'in an awful state'. According to Kadar, Yakubovskii 'gave his report in a very harsh, soldierly and frightening language, and nobody demanded the floor', apart from the Czechoslovak delegates, who 'went crazy, and since Dubcek did not know how to give himself the floor, eventually they did not speak'.[109] Dubcek's attitude illustrated that the relations between Czechoslovakia and its allies had far from normalised. The fact that he chaired the meeting a week before the Soviet-Czechoslovak ice-hockey crisis would force him to resign was a supreme instance of dramatic irony.

Both Brezhnev and Kadar were, however, enormously relieved that they had managed to reach agreement within the PCC, especially as it concerned issues that had been determining the debates within the alliance since 1965 or even earlier. Their conclusion had become increasingly urgent after the WP had become divided into a 'club' of five countries versus the rest, as Hungarian Prime Minister Jeno Fock confided to Ceausescu during the dinner after the meeting.[110] Evaluating the meeting in a Hungarian politburo meeting a week after the conference, Kadar accordingly stressed its 'great importance', as 'after painful months and years' all seven sides had finally reached an agreement.[111] The renewed unity did not only serve 'the relaxation of international tensions', but also the 'consolidation of relations among the member-states'. Although Kadar regretted that the military reforms were not complemented by political ones, he greatly looked forward to '[t]he preparation of a large international conference'.[112]

Meanwhile, the Romanian delegation also returned to Bucharest in an optimistic mood, and in the ensuing politburo meeting 'the extraordinary productive activity' of the Romanian delegation was praised profusely. Thus the power of the Romanian leadership was consolidated by its independent stance on foreign policy issues. However, the Romanian insistence on avoiding a warmongering stance also served a further purpose, as Bodnaras emphasised:

And when [the other delegations] go home many will breathe freely. The adventurous spirit has been stopped here. Both concerning the formulas about Europe, which were very bellicose, and concerning the spirit of European security, which was founded on the spirit of 21 August.[113]

The Romanian delegates accordingly claimed credit for turning the adventurous tide of the Warsaw Pact, and Maurer triumphantly concluded that 'when people are confronted with a firmly sustained position, they yield'.[114] Although the Romanians had forced some of their allies into submission, they too had learnt how to compromise for the sake of larger unity.

The consensus on the military restructuring of the alliance was, however, 'extraordinarily important' to the Romanian leadership, as Ceausescu underlined in a speech at the plenary session of the Council of State and the Council of Ministers on 10 April 1969. According to Ceausescu, the reforms had clarified '*that apart from our constitutional organs no one can engage our army*'. Emphasising that '*at Budapest we have not discussed the participation in other actions and we do not conceive that Romania can participate in other military actions than those enshrined in the Treaty and with the goal for which they are enshrined in the treaty*', Ceausescu made it clear that Romania would neither turn against a socialist country, nor allow a socialist country to turn against Romania.[115] The military reforms could thus serve to safeguard the sovereignty, which the Romanians had upheld so vigorously throughout the 1960s.

Conclusion: the Warsaw Pact multilateralised

The PCC meeting on 17 March 1969 in Budapest was, indeed, as Mastny argues, 'a landmark event'.[116] During the meeting the WP members had presented the world with *their* version of 'defence cum détente': a resolution on military reforms as well as another, more concrete, appeal for a European security conference. Although the WP's military reforms did not translate into a concrete military strategy, unlike NATO's strategy of flexible response, they prove that the WP members, too, considered a relaxation of international tensions and an improved military structure different sides of the same coin. Meanwhile, the conclusion of the PCC meeting in Budapest emulated the Harmel Report in terms of détente: by concluding both the military reforms and the European Security Appeal, the WP members had succeeded in complementing the slogan 'defence cum détente' with a concrete strategy for achieving a new, multilateralised version of détente. The campaign for European security thus gained precedence over the military reforms, which is why it was no bone of contention that the military reforms only applied to peacetime. In the shadow of the invasion in Czechoslovakia seven months earlier the allies had succeeded in restoring unity to the alliance, as well as imbuing it with a new purpose: peace in Europe.

The military reforms were surprisingly quickly agreed due to ample preparation. The military consolidation of the alliance had become all the more urgent because of the military measures taken to stem the internal reforms in Czechoslovakia. Although the military reforms enabled the Soviets to take control again over the evolution of the alliance, the Soviet leaders were prepared to make a lot of concessions in order to restore genuine unity to the alliance. During the period of 'normalisation' the Kremlin decided to 'normalise' relations with its Romanian comrades too, and in September 1968 Yakubovskii finally visited the Romanian leadership in order to gain its consent. Ultimately, the Romanian leaders deemed the military reforms also in Romanian interest, because they could serve to increase the scope for manoeuvre by preventing the Unified Armed Forces from turning to a supranational institution. The military reforms thus sealed the Warsaw Pact's intergovernmentalism, and prevented it from being a supranational institution that functioned like a mega-politburo. Meanwhile, the establishment of two organs in addition to the PCC – the Military Council and the Committee of Defence Ministers – testified to the alliance's multilateralisation. The Soviet leadership could no longer use the WP as a military transmission belt either, but had to consult its allies instead.

Another issue that had returned to the discussions with a vengeance was the Sino–Soviet split. The Soviet proposal to include the WP's stance towards China in a communiqué was all the more dramatic, because the meeting coincided with the escalation of the Sino–Soviet border clashes at the Ussuri river. The Romanian success in keeping the Chinese issue from the PCC's agenda enabled the Romanian leadership once more to define the limits of the alliance, and ensure that it would only be directed against potential 'imperialist' aggression. Thus a potential condemnation of the Romanian *Alleingang* through a WP framework was blocked once and for all, and the Brezhnev doctrine was fully undermined. The fact that the Chinese condemnation was so central in the discussion nevertheless underlines how far the alliance had drifted from its original purpose. The Cold War had developed in such a way that the bipolar antagonism between the USA and the Soviet Union no longer occupied centre stage, nor did the German question. The Romanian involvement in defining the limits of the WP also served to remind the other WP members of the original purpose of the alliance.

Meanwhile, the Romanian attempt covertly to condemn the invasion through the European Security Appeal testified to the way in which the Romanian leadership had gained the moral high ground by *not* participating in the intervention. This put the Romanian delegation in a position to force its allies to concede to a more lenient stance on the German question in the European Security Appeal, which therefore gained a remarkably constructive tone, even though European security had become a more controversial issue than military reforms in the wake of the invasion in Czechoslovakia. The Romanian delegation succeeded in limiting the Brezhnev doctrine of limited sovereignty on all fronts. It ensured that the WP could not interfere in China, which would *limit* the sovereignty of another socialist country, and firmly enshrined non-interference in the appeal on European security. Instead of limiting sovereignty, these moves safeguarded it.

The Hungarian leader Janos Kadar harvested the fruits of his moderation during the invasion. In the wake of the Prague Spring the Hungarian leadership had become a credible initiator on European security. This served to raise the Hungarian profile within the WP, and sealed Hungarian emancipation too. The Kremlin was particularly eager to coordinate the meeting with its Hungarian comrades, and Brezhnev unprecedentedly regarded the stance of Ulbricht and Gomulka – not Ceausescu – as the 'major problem'. The East German and Polish extremism during the Prague Spring seemed to have cost its leaders Soviet good will.

In addition, the normalisation of relations with the FRG had also become a Soviet priority in the wake of the Prague Spring. The Kremlin, meanwhile, seemed to have grown more comfortable with exercising a moderate amount of control over its allies in the wake of the Prague Spring. It prepared the PCC meeting in a much more proactive manner than usual, and showed a lot of initiative on military reforms. The multilateral decision making during the Prague Spring seemed to have forced the Kremlin to assume a more proactive and assertive role in dealing with its allies.

At the same time, the 1969 PCC meeting had been preceded by an unprecedented amount of preparation, which seemed to testify to the alliance's increased professionalisation. The fact that the meeting took place within the record time of one day and that all speeches were removed from the agenda illustrates that it was no longer a primarily rhetorical exercise, but really dealt with the actual issues at stake. The WP had thus turned into a mirror image of what it had been in the 1950s: it was no longer the Soviet leadership that pre-concocted the communiqués, but the NSWP members contributed to the meeting's choreography by discussing the declarations and communiqués in preliminary bilateral and multilateral sessions. The NSWP scope for manoeuvre had thus increased considerably, without the NSWP members undermining the interests of one another. After the 1969 PCC meeting *all* WP members could look back on a meeting that served their interests, even though the Polish and East German leaders were forced to reach a compromise on the German question. The genuine compromise that was reached on *all* issues was a far cry from the rhetorical unanimity that had characterised such meetings ten years earlier.

'Multilateral' had become the magic word, both in the European Security Appeal and in the documents on military reforms, and that too was not empty rhetoric. Since the Romanian leaders successfully insisted on signing the documents in the name of the governments, the WP had become more professional, more intergovernmental and more multilateral by March 1969. The Warsaw Pact was, accordingly, consolidated in a number of important ways. The internal crisis that threatened to paralyse the alliance halfway through the 1960s had, in fact, served to multilateralise the alliance, as it forced the NSWP members to identify their position clearly on a number of issues. The topics of European security and reforms had necessitated an increased number of consultations between all allies, which had in turn provided the NSWP members with a platform to participate in debates on both Soviet bloc foreign policy and the nature of the alliance. This turned the alliance into a more consultative and less hierarchical institution, and reinforced the interstate nature of the alliance. It also enhanced the political dimension of the alliance, as many of the contested topics concerned issues of foreign policy, such as non-proliferation, European security and the Vietnam War. The Romanians nevertheless clearly limited the WP to Europe at the PCC meeting in March 1969, by preventing their allies from using the alliance to condemn Chinese aggression. While beginning to look more like NATO, the WP's scope was also limited to meeting the challenge that NATO posed.

Notes

1 Minutes of the session of the RCP CC Politburo, 18 March 1969, ANIC, RCP CC, C, 40/1969, 11.
2 V. Mastny, 'Meeting of the PCC, Budapest, 17 March 1969, Editorial Note', PHP, www.php.isn.ethz.ch/collections/coll_pcc/ednote_69.cfm (accessed 12 September 2013).
3 Cf. A. Wenger, 'The Multilateralization of Détente: NATO and the Harmel Exercise, 1966–68', in A. Locher and C. Nünlist, *The Future Tasks of the Alliance. NATO's Harmel Report, 1966–1967* (2005), Parallel History Project on Cooperative Security (PHP), 10, www.isn.ethz.ch/Digital-Library/Publications/Detail/?id=108636&lng=en (accessed 21 September 2013).
4 North Atlantic Treaty Organization, 'The Future Tasks of the Alliance. The Harmel Report' (1967), www.nato.int/cps/en/natolive/official_texts_26700.htm (accessed 21 September 2013).
5 A. Wenger, 'Crisis and Opportunity. NATO's Transformation and the Multilateralization of Détente, 1966–68', *Journal of Cold War Studies* 6:1 (2004), 65.
6 V. Mastny, 'Was 1968 a Strategic Watershed of the Cold War?' *Diplomatic History* 29:1 (2005), 149.
7 Meeting between Ceausescu and Brezhnev, 16 March 1969, 10.30 pm, ANIC, RCP CC, IR, 7/1969, 21.
8 T. Diedrich, 'The German Democratic Republic', in J. Hoffenaar and D. Krüger (eds), *Blueprints for Battle. Planning for War in Central Europe, 1948–1968* (Lexington, 2012), 175.
9 Cf. V. Mastny, 'Imagining War in Europe. Soviet Strategic Planning', in V. Mastny, S.S. Holtsmark and A. Wenger (eds), *War Plans and Alliances in the Cold War. Threat Perceptions in the East and West* (London and New York, 2006), 29.
10 'Memorandum of Results of the Chiefs of General Staff Meeting Regarding Reorganization of the Warsaw Treaty', 1 March 1968, in V. Mastny and M. Byrne (eds), *A Cardboard Castle? An Inside History of the Warsaw Pact, 1955–1991* (Budapest and New York, 2005), 249–51.
11 M. Kramer, 'The Kremlin, the Prague Spring, and the Brezhnev Doctrine', in V. Tismaneanu, *Promises of 1968: Crisis, Illusion, and Utopia* (Budapest and New York, 2010), 286.

12 Protocol of the meeting of WP defence ministers, Moscow, 27–28 May 1966, ANIC, RCP CC, IR, 38/1968, 184.
13 Letter from General Ion Gheorghe to Ceausescu, 1 March 1968, ANIC, RCP CC, IR, 40/1968, 105–6. See for the draft statute of the Unified Command, ibid., 117–21.
14 Letter from General Ion Gheorghe to Ceausescu, 1 March 1968, ANIC, RCP CC, IR, 40/1968, 108.
15 'Memorandum of Results', 250.
16 Ibid., 251.
17 Protocol of the meeting of WP deputy defence ministers, Prague, 29 February and 1 March 1968, ANIC, RCP CC, IR, 40/1968, 113.
18 Appendix to the protocol of the meeting of WP deputy defence ministers, Prague, 1 March 1968, ANIC, RCP CC, IR, 40/1968, 116.
19 Letter from General Ion Gheorghe to Ceausescu, 1 March 1968, ANIC, RCP CC, IR, 40/1968, 110.
20 'Report to Nicolae Ceausescu on the Meeting of the Political Consultative Committee in Sofia', 3 June 1968, in Mastny and Byrne (eds), *Cardboard Castle*, 264–69.
21 'Record of Gomulka-Yakubovskii Conversation in Warsaw', 19 April 1968, in Mastny and Byrne (eds), *Cardboard Castle*, 261.
22 Ibid., 262.
23 Mastny, 'Watershed', 157.
24 'Message about the state of relations between the Soviet Union and the Socialist Republic of Romania', GDR embassy in Moscow, 10 June 1968, SAPMO-BArch, DY 30/IVA2/20/162, 413–14.
25 Kramer, 'The Kremlin', 286.
26 Ibid.
27 'Report to Nicolae Ceausescu', 267.
28 Cf. Chapter 4 of this book.
29 'Report to Nicolae Ceausescu', 269.
30 'Report by CSSR National Defense Minister Martin Dzúr on a Meeting with Marshal Yakubovskii, Commander-in-Chief of the Warsaw Pact Joint Armed Forces', 24–25 April 1968, in J. Navrátil (ed.), *The Prague Spring 1968* (Budapest and New York, 2006), 112–13.
31 'Czechoslovak and East German Views on the Warsaw Pact', July 1968, in Mastny and Byrne (eds), *Cardboard Castle*, 302–3.
32 Kramer, 'The Kremlin', 290.
33 '"Problems with the Policy of Safeguarding the Internal and External Security of the State, their Status at Present, the Basic Ways to Resolve Them," Czechoslovakia's Plans for Future Changes in Military and National Security Policies', July 1968, in Navrátil (ed.), *Prague Spring*, 268–76.
34 Ibid.
35 'Press Conference with Lt. General Vaclav Prchlik', 15 July 1968, Navrátil (ed.), *Prague Spring*, 239–42.
36 Ibid.
37 Letter from Marshal Yakubovskii to Alexander Dubcek on Gen. Prchlík's News Conference, 18 July 1968, in Navrátil (ed.), *Prague Spring*, 259–60.
38 'Soviet Government Diplomatic Note to the Czechoslovak Government', 20 July 1968, in Navrátil (ed.), *Prague Spring*, 265–67.
39 Mastny, 'Imagining War', 30.
40 Ibid.
41 Mastny, 'Watershed', 176.
42 See M. Munteanu, 'When the Levee Breaks: The Impact of the Sino-Soviet Split and the Invasion of Czechoslovakia on Romanian-Soviet Relations, 1967–70', *Journal of Cold War Studies* 12:1 (2010), 56.

43 Discussions between Ceausescu, Maurer and Yakubovskii, 28 September 1968, ANIC, RCP CC, IR, 140/1968, 1–8.
44 Ibid., 5.
45 Ibid., 7–8.
46 Protocol of the meeting of WP defence ministers, 30 October 1968, ANIC, RCP CC, IR, 40/1968, 17–18.
47 Separate opinion of the Romanian delegation about article 12a, 30 October 1968, ANIC, RCP CC, IR, 40/1968, 20.
48 'Czechoslovak General Staff Study on the Warsaw Treaty', 21 December 1968, in Mastny and Byrne (eds), *Cardboard Castle*, 317–19.
49 Ibid.
50 Conversation between Basov and Ceausescu, 5 March 1969, ANIC, RCP CC, IR, 8/1969, vol. I, 72.
51 C. Békés, 'Der Warschauer Pakt und der KSZE-Prozess 1965 bis 1970', in T. Diedrich, W. Heinemann and C.F. Ostermann (eds), *Der Warschauer Pakt. Von der Gründung bis zum Zusammenbruch 1955 bis 1991* (Berlin, 2009), 231.
52 Letter from Brezhnev and Kosygin to their WP comrades, 7 March 1969, ANIC, RCP CC, C, 37/1969, 6–8.
53 'Note concerning some aspects about the Hungarian frame of mind', ANIC, RCP CC, IR, 8/1969, vol. I, 98.
54 Mastny, 'Meeting of the PCC, Budapest, 17 March 1969, Editorial Note', 1.
55 Minutes of the Hungarian Party Politburo Session – Report on the PCC Meeting by the First Secretary of the MSzMP (János Kádár), 24 March 1969, PHP, www.php.isn.ethz.ch/collections/colltopic.cfm?lng=en&id=18017&navinfo=14465 (accessed 21 September 2013).
56 Letter from Ceausescu and Maurer to Brezhnev and Kosygin, 11 March 1969, ANIC, RCP CC, C, 37/1969, 5. For the Hungarian and Polish proposal see Mastny, 'Meeting of the PCC'.
57 Letter from Brezhnev and Kosygin to their WP comrades, 7 March 1969, ANIC, RCP CC, C, 37/1969, 8.
58 Diplomatic note, Budapest, 14 March 1969, ANIC, RCP CC, IR, 8/1969, vol. I, 94.
59 Diplomatic note, Budapest, 15 March 1969, ANIC, RCP CC, IR, 8/1969, vol. I, 91.
60 Minutes of the session of the RCP CC politburo, 18 March 1969, ANIC, RCP CC, C, 40/1969, 10.
61 L. Lüthi, 'Restoring Chaos to History: Sino-Soviet-American Relations, 1969', *The China Quarterly* 210 (2012), 382.
62 Ibid., 379.
63 Rowiaski, in X. Liu and V. Mastny (eds), *China and Eastern Europe, 1960s–1980s. Proceedings of the International Symposium: Reviewing the History of Chinese-East European Relations from the 1960s to the 1980s. Beijing, 24–26 March 2004*, Zürcher Beiträge zur Sicherheitspolitik und Konfliktforschung Nr. 72 (Zurich, 2004), 106.
64 Cf. L.M. Lüthi, 'Restoring Chaos to History', 383; and B. Schäfer, 'The Sino-Soviet Conflict and the Warsaw Pact, 1969–80', in M.A. Heiss and S.V. Papacosma (eds), *NATO and the Warsaw Pact: Intrabloc Conflicts* (Ohio, 2008), 208.
65 N. Bernkopf Tucker, 'China under Siege: Escaping the Dangers of 1968', in C. Fink, P. Gassert and D. Junker (eds), *1968: The World Transformed* (Cambridge, 1998), 193–216.
66 Rowiaski, in Liu and Mastny (eds), *China and Eastern Europe*, 107.
67 Schäfer, 'The Sino-Soviet Conflict', 208.
68 'Note on the Meeting of the Deputy Foreign Ministers', 15 March 1969, PHP, 2, www.php.isn.ethz.ch/collections/colltopic.cfm?lng=en&id=17250&navinfo=15700 (accessed 21 September 2013).

69 'The Warsaw Treaty', 14 May 1955, in Mastny and Byrne (eds), *Cardboard Castle*, 77–79.
70 Minutes of the session of the RCP CC politburo, 16 March 1969, ANIC, RCP CC, C, 39/1969, 7.
71 Cf. Chapter 2.
72 Minutes of the session of the RCP CC politburo, 16 March 1969, ibid., 10–12.
73 Ibid.
74 Mastny, 'Meeting of the PCC, Budapest, 17 March 1969, Editorial Note', 1.
75 Minutes of the session of the RCP CC politburo, 16 March 1969, ibid.
76 Meeting between Ceausescu and Brezhnev, Budapest, 16 March 1969, 10.30 pm, ANIC, RCP CC, IR, 7/1969, 20–30.
77 Note concerning discussions between Ceausescu and leaders of the delegations at the PCC meeting in Budapest, 16–17 March 1967, ANIC, RCP CC, IR, 7/1969, 31–33.
78 Schäfer, 'The Sino-Soviet Conflict', 209.
79 'Information report 38/1968', GDR embassy in Moscow, 10 December 1968, SAPMO-BArch, DY 30/IVA2/20/163, 235.
80 'Information about the politics of the PRP, Division neighbouring countries', Berlin, 19 April 1968, PA AA, MfAA, C 332/711, 39.
81 Li Xiangqian, in Liu and Mastny (eds), *China and Eastern Europe*, 124.
82 Mastny, 'Meeting of the PCC, Budapest, 17 March 1969, Editorial Note'.
83 Ibid.
84 Minutes of the meeting of deputy foreign ministers, 16 March 1969, SAPMO-BArch, DY 30/ JIV2/2A1362, 72.
85 See Chapter 4 of this book.
86 D. Selvage, 'The Warsaw Pact and the European Security Conference, 1964–69: Sovereignty, Hegemony, and the German Question', in A. Wenger, V. Mastny and C. Nuenlist (eds), *Origins of the European Security System. The Helsinki Process Revisited* (London and New York, 2008), 93.
87 Mastny, 'Meeting of the PCC, Budapest, 17 March 1969, Editorial Note', 1.
88 Selvage, 'The Warsaw Pact and the European Security Conference', 93.
89 Meeting between Ceausescu and Brezhnev, Budapest, 16 March 1969, 10.30 pm, ANIC, RCP CC, IR, 7/1969, 21, 27, 30.
90 Minutes of the RCP CC politburo session, 18 March 1969, ANIC, RCP CC, C, 40/1969, 9.
91 Note concerning discussions between Ceausescu and leaders of the delegations at the PCC meeting in Budapest, 16–17 March 1967, ANIC, RCP CC, IR, 7/1969, 34.
92 Mastny, 'Meeting of the PCC, Budapest, 17 March 1969, Editorial Note', 3.
93 'Information report, 11–24/3/69', GDR embassy Bucharest, 24 March 1969, SAPMO-BArch, DY 30/IVA2/20/375, 223.
94 T. Garton Ash, *In Europe's Name. Germany and the Divided Continent* (New York, 1993), 16 and 280.
95 'APPEAL from all states participating in the WP to all European states', ANIC, RCP CC, IR, 7/1969, 40.
96 Minutes of the session of the RCP CC politburo, 16 March 1969, ANIC, RCP CC, C, 39/1969, 18.
97 Ibid.
98 Meeting between Ceausescu and Brezhnev, 16 March 1969, 10.30 pm, ANIC, RCP CC, IR, 7/1969, 21.
99 Minutes of the PCC meeting, Budapest, 17 March 1969, ANIC, RCP CC, IR, 7/1969, 7.
100 Minutes of the RCP CC politburo session, 18 March 1969, ANIC, RCP CC, C, 40/1969, 10.
101 See for all these statutes ANIC, RCP CC, IR, 8/1969, vol. I, 117–49.

102 PUWP 5th Party Conference, Warsaw, 29 November 1968, SAPMO-BArch, DY 30/IVA2/20/1160, 85.
103 Mastny and Byrne (eds), *Cardboard Castle*, 39.
104 Ibid., cf. Brezhnev, in Minutes of the PCC meeting, 17 March 1969, SAPMO-BArch, DY 30/JIV2/2A 1362, 97.
105 Mastny, 'Watershed', 175.
106 Cf. M.J. Ouimet, *The Rise and Fall of the Brezhnev Doctrine in Soviet Foreign Policy* (Chapel Hill, 2003), 5, 131–70; and for primary sources, which corroborate this assertion: A. Paczkowski and M. Byrne (eds), *From Solidarity to Martial Law. The Polish Crisis of 1980–1981* (Budapest and New York, 2007), 446–55.
107 'Communiqué of the PCC of the states participating in the WP', 17 March 1969, ANIC, RCP CC, IR, 7/1969, 48. Cf. for the original Hungarian proposal, with Romanian amendments: ANIC, RCP CC, IR, 8/1969, vol. II, 223–34.
108 Note on the meeting of the WP first secretaries, 17 March 1969, ANIC, RCP CC, IR, 7/1969, 16.
109 Minutes of the Hungarian Party Politburo Session, 4.
110 Note on conversations with Kadar, Fock, Zhovkov and Svoboda during dinner, Budapest, 19 March 1969, ANIC, RCP CC, IR, 7/1969, 35, 39.
111 Minutes of the Hungarian Party Politburo Session, 4.
112 Mastny, 'Meeting of the PCC, Budapest, 17 March 1969, Editorial Note', 3.
113 Minutes of the RCP CC politburo session, 18 March 1969, ANIC, RCP CC, C, 40/1969, 13.
114 Ibid., 11.
115 Ceausescu's speech at the Council of State, 10 April 1969, ANIC, RCP CC, C, 174/1969, 2, emphasis in original.
116 Mastny, 'Meeting of the PCC'.

Conclusion
International relations in Eastern Europe reconsidered

> An international monolithic organisation with a directive international centre does not exist and cannot exist in the communist movement.[1]
> (Zenon Kliszko at the PUWP Third Party Plenum, 7 April 1965)

The PCC meeting, which took place in March 1969, sealed the WP's transformation from a 'cardboard castle' into a multilateral alliance. Various NSWP members left the meeting with the feeling that their input was taken seriously. The Hungarian leader Janos Kadar concluded that both the alliance and the relations between its members had 'consolidated', a Polish delegate 'returned home from Budapest with an impression that his country's room for manoeuvre had increased', and the Romanian leadership happily concluded that the Kremlin had 'yielded' to Romanian pressure.[2] The WP had turned from a primarily Soviet instrument in 1955 into one that the NSWP members could use to further their national interests. At the same time it had become more political, more professional and more multilateral. The WP had, in short, matured. The stigma of the WP as a cardboard castle had turned into an anachronism.

Straight after the PCC meeting several other issues drew to a close, which would further determine the course of the Cold War in the 1970s. The preparatory gathering for another international communist conference, organised by the Kremlin, took place the day after the PCC meeting. During this meeting in Moscow, in which 66 fraternal parties participated, Brezhnev also tried in vain to get support for a general condemnation of the Chinese Communist Party.[3] Brezhnev ultimately managed to contain the Sino–Soviet tensions instead by meeting Zhou Enlai at Beijing airport and showing that 'neither side had the strategic intent of launching a large-scale, direct military conflict'.[4] Although the international communist conference from 5–17 June 1969 was meant to 'overcome past divisions – divisions not only over Czechoslovakia but also over the PRC'[5] – Brezhnev attempted to use it to rally support for the creation of an Asian security system similar to the WP, presumably 'because he knew that some WAPA [Warsaw Pact] members previously had rejected the use of that alliance against China', as the Swiss historian Lorenz Lüthi argues.⁶ Brezhnev failed on this account, too, and was accordingly back to square one.

China drew different conclusions from the Soviet Union after the border clashes: where the Kremlin intended to isolate China further, China wanted to break through its isolation by orienting its foreign policy to the USA. In July 1969 both the US and Chinese administrations tentatively began to consider rapprochement.⁷ In August 1969 US President Richard Nixon even travelled to Bucharest, which was 'the culmination of Ceausescu's drive for international recognition',⁸ and at the end of his stay 'he asked his host to play "a mediating role between [the USA] and China"'.⁹ This heralded a process that would later come to be known as 'triangular diplomacy'.¹⁰ Meanwhile, the Romanian autonomy and its rapprochement with the West were sealed by the postponement until the autumn of Brezhnev's trip to Romania finally to sign the Romanian-Soviet friendship treaty, in order to receive US President Nixon first.¹¹

Both the Romanian and the Chinese turn to America proved another blow to Soviet hegemony, but also showed how much Cold War dynamics had changed since the early 1960s. The fact that Ceausescu prioritised meeting Nixon over meeting Brezhnev again testifies to the Romanian emancipation from the Soviet grip, but Ceausescu was not the only WP member to begin to move more unilaterally. Gomulka, too, decided to bypass Moscow in an attempt to salvage some of the remnants of the 'Warsaw Package', which had been sacrificed in the Budapest appeal of March 1969. In December 1970 he managed to move the German social democrat Willy Brandt, who had become chancellor in October 1969, into concluding the so-called 'Warsaw Treaty', which included West Germany's *de facto* recognition of the Oder–Neisse border. Brandt's *neue Ostpolitik* ironically granted Gomulka what the Budapest appeal had denied him. Although the treaty in question was concluded two months after Brezhnev had concluded the similar 'Moscow Treaty' with Brandt over Gomulka's head, Gomulka 'insisted on different language than the Soviet-West German treaty' in order to 'underline [Polish] sovereignty'.¹²

Paradoxical though it may seem, it was the multilateralisation of the WP that had facilitated *inter alia* Romanian and Polish unilateralism on foreign policy. The dynamics of dissent within the WP had, after all, increased the WP members' self-consciousness and had spurred their quest for sovereignty, as the alliance had provided them with a platform to further their state interests. It was through the assertion of the member states' individual interests that the WP turned from a monolith into a multilateral forum. This forum also served as a convenient platform for the launch of a proposal on a European security conference at the PCC meeting in Budapest in March 1969, which paved the way for a European, multilateral concept of détente.

The Budapest appeal of March 1969 proved the first concrete step in the preparation for a multilateral conference on European security, and already in May 1969 the Finnish President Urho Kekkonen offered Helsinki as the venue for a European security conference.[13] The Eastern European proposal was seriously discussed within NATO in the latter half of 1969 and the first half of 1970, and further developed at another WP meeting in Budapest, in July 1970. At this meeting the Western ideas on such a conference were taken into consideration, as well as the potential inclusion of the USA and Canada. The fact that this was decided upon in Budapest, too, was no coincidence: the Hungarian leadership had begun to use the WP to assume a 'mediating role' in the whole process.[14] Other WP members also gained considerable input in the process, and according to an American report, 'the post-1968 European Security campaign [...] became an instrument that individual Warsaw Pact member states used for the pursuit of autonomous policies', with Poland, Romania and East Germany playing the most active roles.[15] However, these countries had already developed their 'autonomous policies' through asserting their interests within the WP.

This move removed the last obstacles for convening a conference on the Western side, and in November 1972 the 'Conference on Security and Co-operation in Europe' (CSCE) was kick-started with Multilateral Preparatory Talks just outside Helsinki.[16] In the process of multilateral negotiations, representatives from 35 European countries (except Albania) convened in order to negotiate on such issues as the inviolability of borders, economic issues and human rights, which culminated in the signing of the Helsinki Final Act in August 1975.[17] This heralded the so-called 'Helsinki Process', which entailed a series of follow-up conferences to monitor the conduct of the participating states. The conference was a turning point in the Cold War, as it was the first time since World War II that 'all-European negotiations could take place' within a multilateral forum.[18] The WP had provided its members with the diplomatic platform that proved essential in the preparation for the negotiations within the Helsinki Process. It was, accordingly, not the Helsinki Process that served to emancipate the WP members from the Soviet grip, as is often assumed; instead, the multilateralisation of the WP had facilitated the WP members' autonomous stance within the Helsinki Process.

The Helsinki Process and the WP were so closely related that the WP members finally agreed on the establishment of a Committee of the Ministers of Foreign Affairs (CMFA) in 1976 in order to prepare or follow-up the CSCE meetings, which ensued from the conclusion of the Helsinki Final Act.[19] After the intra-European relations were normalised and the Eastern European borders declared inviolable through the Helsinki Final Act, the WP members agreed on further consultations on foreign policy within an official WP framework. At the height of European détente, WP foreign policy had become more important than its military structures. Moreover, the establishment of the CMFA served both as a way to recognise the 'increased political weight' of the NSWP members in the wake of the CSCE, as well as preventing WP disintegration through the allies' increased autonomy.[20] By this time the NSWP members had emancipated so much from the Soviet grip that

The transformation of a 'cardboard castle'

This book demonstrates that the Warsaw Pact evolved in the 1960s from an institution that resembled a cardboard castle, a Soviet transmission belt or an empty shell, into a multilateral alliance that provided the allies with considerable scope for manoeuvre. The mere framework of the WP taught its members a new kind of diplomacy, according to which they could negotiate with one another on equal terms, which was very different from the kind of bilateral negotiations with the Kremlin to which they had been accustomed. The WP actually compelled the Soviet leadership, *pace* John Lewis Gaddis, 'to deal with independent thinking' in *other* ways 'than to smother it', and there was a 'sense of mutual interest' within the alliance.[21] This 'mutual interest' paved the way for the successful conclusion of military reforms and the declaration on European security in March 1969. Contrary to conventional wisdom, *communist* states could cooperate, too.[22]

The tensions in the alliance did not even primarily arise in the relationship between the Kremlin and the smaller allies, as is often assumed,[23] but between the NSWP members themselves. They turned more severely against Albania than the Soviet Union during the PCC meeting in 1961, and the Romanian quest for autonomy was primarily frustrated by the East German transmission belt approach and the Polish attempt to get more coordination on foreign policy. Conversely, the East German quest for recognition frequently met with Romanian dissent, or was outwitted by a Polish move. Although the Romanians challenged the sense of mutual interest that was generally fostered by the other 'six' members, Soviet-Romanian relations were less bleak than is often suggested. The Romanian stance towards the West, such as on the normalisation of relations with the FRG, could be quite useful to the Kremlin at a time when it sought to foster détente, but posed a far greater threat to the East German and Polish allies.

The mere foundation of the alliance was, however, already the product of a paradigm shift in Soviet foreign policy under Nikita Khrushchev, who founded the WP in 1955 one day before declaring Austria neutral and several days before flying to Belgrade to mend fences with Tito. The abolition of the COMINFORM one year later testifies to Khrushchev's intention to cast intra-Eastern European relations in a new mould. The reforms in 1969 definitively undermined democratic centralism by ensuring a process of intergovernmental decision-making in the new organs. It was, as such, fundamentally different from the intra-party, coercive and primarily *communist* COMINFORM, and had become an interstate organisation with hardly any specific communist features instead.

Albania was the first NSWP member that unprecedentedly used the Warsaw Pact as an instrument to question Soviet hegemony in 1961, when it sided with China in the Sino–Soviet split. Apart from the impact of Albanian dissent on the Romanian course, the influence of Sino-Romanian relations was of paramount importance, too, especially since the Chinese leadership took the initiative in the spring of 1963 to improve its relations with the Romanian leadership, because it appreciated the Romanian attempts to withstand Soviet pressure within COMECON. The Sino-Romanian rapprochement accordingly coincided with the Romanian opposition to the accession of Mongolia in July 1963, and paved the way for Romania's critical stance within the WP.

The relations with China were instrumental in charting Romania's course within the WP. They enabled the Romanian attempt at 'mediation' between China and the Soviet Union in the spring of 1964, which facilitated the subsequent 'declaration of independence'. The weekly conversations between the Romanian leadership and the Chinese ambassador served both to assist the Romanians in developing their strategy vis-à-vis the other WP members, and to provide the Romanian leadership with ammunition to block certain processes in the alliance, such as the reforms or the non-proliferation treaty. As the Romanians confessed in a conversation with their Chinese comrades during the Prague Spring, the contacts with the Chinese had paved the way for Romanian emancipation. The Romanians even attempted to extend the WP to Asia through the active involvement of Asian observers, so as to counterbalance the increasing focus on the German question.

The fact that the Asian coalition within the WP never materialised reflects the extent to which the communist movement had crumbled in the wake of the Sino–Soviet split: the sense of a common purpose had weakened, and the Asian leaders had no inclination to intensify their contacts with their Eastern European comrades. The diversification of power and the breakdown of ideological unity in the communist bloc provided the NSWP members with more scope for using the WP to further their national interests. It also compelled the Kremlin to take the interests of its allies seriously, as WP unity had become more important than Soviet supremacy. The emphasis thus shifted from intra-party relations within the communist movement to interstate relations in the WP.[24] In order to avoid fighting a Cold War on two fronts, it stimulated the Kremlin to improve its relations with the American leadership, as well as seeking to normalise relations within Europe. The Sino–Soviet split drove the WP into the arms of Western Europe. The bipolar perspective thus proves inadequate for interpreting the Cold War, which fits with the findings in New Cold War History.

Moreover, the Cold War cannot be understood without paying sufficient attention to the German question, which has often been underestimated.[25] The East German drive for recognition and the Polish drive for the recognition of its borders determined the dynamics of the WP to a large extent. They played a crucial role in the East German stance on reforms and the Polish campaign for a European security conference, as well as the debates on MLF and non-proliferation, which gave an impulse to a greater frequency of consultation within the WP in order to prevent the nuclearisation of the FRG.

The quest for European security was not only a way to seek security Westwards in the shadow of the Sino–Soviet split, but it was also an attempt to resolve the German question by seeking to improve relations with Western Europe instead of exacerbating the differences between both Germanys. A united stance on European security could alleviate the adverse affects of the division of Germany. The drive for European security in the second half of the 1960s was part of a multilateral process in which all WP members together strove to find a way to alleviate tensions within Europe. The political decision making was, accordingly, determined by *security* concerns, such as the concern for the nuclearisation of West Germany, and not by *ideological* ones, as is often assumed within New Cold War History.

The German question constituted an impulse to European détente exactly because security reasons demanded an improvement in East-West relations. This is also why the WP played such an important role in proposing a conference on European security. In the second half of the 1960s the WP members were consciously developing a strategy that aimed to secure the Eastern European borders on the one hand – an ardent desire of Poland and the GDR – and to normalise relations within Europe on the other – something Romania strove to emphasise. Although the roots of the CSCE are often attributed solely to the charismatic West German Chancellor Willy Brandt and his *neue Ostpolitik*, Polish Foreign Minister Adam Rapacki had already proposed a conference on European security at the UN in December 1964, and the WP had served as a platform for the preparations for this process ever since.

Much of the WP's reputation is nevertheless linked to its alleged role in the invasion of Czechoslovakia. Any decision making on the impending invasion was, however, deliberately conducted *outside* the confines of the WP, and the military operation was not conducted under the aegis of the alliance. The Kremlin was not eager to call the shots, but sanctioned an invasion in Czechoslovakia under persistent pressure from its junior allies: East Germany, Poland and Bulgaria. The ensuing Brezhnev doctrine was not a product of the WP either, but its validity was discredited by the subsequent reforms and the Budapest appeal on European security in March 1969, both of which safeguarded national sovereignty and guaranteed non-interference within Europe.

The fact that the Budapest appeal was taken seriously by NATO testifies to the evolution of the WP itself. By 1969 it had become a mature counterpart of NATO. Although Wenger concludes that 'NATO, unlike the Warsaw Pact, resolved its internal crisis [...] by transforming itself into a more political and participatory alliance', this is exactly what the WP did too.[26] Both alliances seemed to have found a format that catered for the emancipation of the smaller allies, and which enabled them to overcome the rigid division of the world into two blocs and embark on a multilateral campaign for European security.

Multilateralisation on either side of the Iron Curtain

By 1969 both NATO and the Warsaw Pact had overcome their respective crises. Whereas NATO had faced the danger 'of developing into a sort of "shell with no real spirit left in it"', as German Chancellor Kiesinger had feared in 1967,[27] the WP was forced by the NSWP members to develop from an 'empty shell' into an alliance with substance.[28] The development of both alliances in this period is strikingly similar, and proves that the WP was less of an anomaly than it is generally considered to be. Confronted with similar challenges, both NATO and the WP had experienced a process of emancipation, dissent and multilateralisation in the 1960s.

The German question played a key role in both alliances. A successful integration of both Germanys in the respective alliance was crucial in securing stability in Europe and managing the division of Germany. Just as the West German Chancellor Konrad Adenauer developed a strategy of *Westbindung* by orienting the FRG firmly towards Western Europe and integrating in all its institutions, so did his East German colleague attempt to do exactly the same in Eastern Europe. Both German leaders were often more extreme than their respective alliance leaders, as their sovereignty could only be safeguarded through their alliances. Ulbricht and Adenauer accordingly pressed their respective alliance leaders to take a firmer stance in the second Berlin Crisis, which stimulated a great amount of discussion within both alliances.[29]

Unlike the WP, NATO was, however, not in crisis yet in the early 1960s, even though the parameters of US hegemony had begun to shift. NATO's crisis began in January 1963 with the so-called 'triple non' of the French President General Charles de Gaulle to the British accession to the European Economic Community (EEC), Polaris missiles and MLF. By expressing his 'triple non', de Gaulle wanted to indicate clearly the French opposition to the increasing American influence within NATO.[30] The French obstruction paralysed decision making within NATO in a way that greatly resembles the dynamics of Romanian dissent in the WP.[31] Although the Romanian impact on the WP was in 1963 still fairly limited, the Romanian objections to the Mongolian accession in the WP in July 1963 only succeeded the French 'triple non' by six months. It was, accordingly, no coincidence that Romania sought to improve its relations with France in the wake of its declaration of independence in April 1964, while becoming the first NSWP member to visit France in a top-level delegation in August 1964.

At the same time the nuclear issue and in particular the nuclearisation of West Germany caused the smaller allies in both alliances to ask for more consultations and a greater stake in the decision making in each alliance, respectively. Within NATO, too, the smaller allies had not been involved in the Limited Nuclear Test-Ban Treaty, which was concluded in July 1963 between the British, the Americans and the Soviets. Moreover, both the Americans and the Soviets had gone it alone in the Cuban Missile Crisis in October 1962, to the great frustration of their allies. The potential nuclearisation of West Germany and the proposals on MLF caused raised eyebrows in both alliances, as some NATO allies feared the nuclearisation of West Germany too.[32] Thus the debates on MLF sparked vehement discussions in both alliances, and contributed to the emancipation of the smaller allies.

The crisis within NATO was sealed by the French withdrawal from NATO's military structures in 1966.[33] As a nuclear power itself, France could afford such a move more easily than Romania, even though the Romanian development of a nuclear programme also enabled the Romanian leadership to avoid being ensnared in the WP's military structures. In the late 1960s Romania seriously considered following the example of France, and the Kremlin signalled that it would allow such a withdrawal. *De facto* Romania had already withdrawn from the WP's military structures by only sending token forces or none at all to military manoeuvres. The Kremlin increasingly began to deal with the Romanian dissent by isolating Romania, thus copying the US treatment of France.[34]

Moreover, the smaller countries on both sides of the Iron Curtain had begun to emancipate themselves from the control of the alliance leaders in order to prevent the two superpowers from taking more decisions over their heads, as had been the case in the second Berlin Crisis and the Cuban Missile Crisis. While Polish Foreign Minister Rapacki had become particularly proactive in the convocation of a European security conference within the WP from 1965 onwards, Belgian Foreign Minister Pierre Harmel had taken the initiative in the 'Harmel exercise' in 1966 'to study the future tasks which face the Alliance, and its procedures for fulfilling them in order to strengthen the Alliance as a factor for a durable peace'.[35] Just as Brezhnev had welcomed the Polish proposal on European security and had actively sought the Hungarian input in the preparation of the PCC meeting in March 1969, so US President Johnson was delighted that a smaller ally had taken the initiative on defining the future of NATO.[36] In both alliances the scope for manoeuvre had increased to such an extent that the smaller allies had the opportunity to use the alliance as an instrument to develop their initiatives.

The crises in the respective alliances compelled both alliance leaders to take the interests of the smaller allies more seriously. NATO, too, had been subject to 'the dynamics of dissent', since the French *Alleingang* also raised the self-consciousness of the smaller allies within NATO. The need for consultation grew on either side of the Iron Curtain, and both Washington and Moscow involved the allies in the negotiations on the non-proliferation treaty.[37] Thus the smaller allies gained a stake in defining détente even before it had multilateralised through the Helsinki Process.

The PCC meeting in March 1969 dealt with all the issues that the Harmel Report had already resolved within NATO in December 1967. The proposal on a European security conference resembled NATO's renewed purpose of détente, whereas the agreement on military reforms indicates that the WP members, too, regarded 'defence cum détente' – seemingly a contradiction in terms – as a natural combination. Both alliances had witnessed a huge increase in the number of consultations between the allies in the process of formulating the reforms, and both alliances had increasingly turned into a platform for discussions on foreign policy.[38] The new institutions that were created in the WP in March 1969, namely the Committee of Defence Ministers and the Military Council, facilitated NSWP participation in this area of the WP too, and the alliance greatly professionalised on procedural matters. While meetings had once been convened by the Kremlin at short notice, all of the allies had gained a stake in the convention, the agenda and the proceedings of the meetings in question, just as in NATO. The WP, too, had grown into a political alliance that could be used as an instrument for the preparation of the CSCE.

Certainly NATO was still far more institutionalised and better developed than the WP in 1969, as the WP still lacked a general secretary, a secretariat, weekly meetings and a body of civil servants exclusively devoted to running the alliance. Moreover, the Soviet Union held a nuclear monopoly within its alliance, unlike the USA. The Soviet nuclear umbrella was, however, generally welcomed by its allies as a safety-valve against Western aggression, and it did not prevent the WP from developing into a less hierarchical alliance. The achievements of the NSWP members in emancipating themselves from the Soviet grip and contributing to the alliance's multilateralisation are, accordingly, all the more impressive, while testifying to the fact that nuclear and military power alone are not sufficient to keep junior allies under control. Although the WP is still bound to fall short in comparison to NATO, it had become an institutionalised and professionalised multilateral alliance by 1969, and its transformation was at least as profound as that of NATO.

Both NATO and the WP had contributed to a process that paved the way for the 'multilateralisation of détente' and the ensuing process for the CSCE. It takes two to tango, and if the WP had still been a cardboard castle, détente could not have multilateralised beyond the Iron Curtain. Moreover, the crisis of both alliances led to a multilateralisation of decision making, which was a precondition for the multilateralisation of détente. European détente in the 1970s was possible precisely because both alliances had experienced a similar transformation that had emancipated the junior allies from the grip of the alliance leader.

Playing the alliance game

The fact that the Warsaw Pact began to share some of its features with NATO in the 1960s suggests that the WP members had begun to play the 'alliance game'. In defiance of alliance theory, there was no 'bargaining process' *before* the foundation of the Warsaw Pact,[39] but its existence actually facilitated a bargaining process *after* its foundation, precisely because it was such an empty shell to start with. The Warsaw Pact's *formative* process accordingly took place in the 1960s, when the NSWP members renegotiated the terms on which they committed themselves to the alliance, and emancipated themselves in the process. The WP members were also, therefore, confronted with the 'alliance security dilemma', as the American political scientist Glenn Snyder calls it, according to which the allies decide 'how firmly to commit themselves to the proto-partner and how much support to give that partner in specific conflict interactions with the adversary'.[40] The *'tension* between the risk of abandonment and the risk of entrapment',[41] which is central to this dilemma, also explains the dissent between the most active NSWP members, namely Albania and Romania on the one hand, and the GDR and Poland on the other hand, which largely determined the dynamics of the WP.

The Sino–Soviet split offered the WP members, who had little strategic interest in the alliance, a serious option of realignment. Albania's strategic interests in the WP had declined considerably in 1956, when Khrushchev reconciled himself with the Yugoslav leader Tito, because the Albanian leader Enver Hoxha had primarily valued the WP as a bulwark against Yugoslav irredentism. For Romania, the strategic interest in the WP had always been very low, as it was the only WP country that was solely encircled by communist countries, without bordering on a NATO country. Moreover, Romania had kept its commitment to the WP vague by maintaining good relations with China, the USA and the FRG throughout the 1960s. Although Albania ultimately decided to realign itself with China, the Romanians chose 'to keep their commitments tentative or vague as long as possible', in order 'to maximise bargaining leverage over the current partner by showing that they have alternatives'.[42]

The same did not apply to the GDR and Poland. Being respectively unrecognised or having unrecognised borders, both states needed the WP as a safeguard for their national security. Moreover, bordering on a potentially nuclearised West Germany, the unresolved German question prevented both Poland and the GDR from being ambiguous about their commitment. Their main aim was to ensure that the Soviet Union remained committed to their security interests, and to use the WP to commit the other allies to their security interests too. As Snyder predicts, 'asymmetrical dependence by itself will cause the more dependent ally to fear abandonment, but this anxiety will be reduced by a formal, explicit contract'.[43] It is, therefore, no coincidence that the East German leadership proposed reforms on foreign policy to increase the explicitness of the alliance, while concluding as many 'formal, explicit contract[s]' as possible in order to avoid abandonment. The same applied to the Polish leadership, which even presented the Warsaw Package in February 1967 to *entrap* its allies into agreeing to certain conditions before establishing diplomatic relations with the FRG, and also proposed various declarations on European security, which indirectly served to prevent abandonment by securing the intra-European borders.

The Romanian leadership, on the contrary, feared becoming entrapped in Ulbricht's approach, and therefore vehemently denounced the East German proposal on foreign policy reforms and on a non-proliferation treaty. Because the Polish proposals on European security did not constitute a mechanism of entrapment *within* the alliance, the Romanian leaders were more flexible on European security. Moreover, the Romanians were less averse to military reforms than to reforms on foreign policy, as the former would merely regulate the status quo, which was unlikely to change – Romania never seriously considered joining NATO – whereas the latter could entrap Romania in positions it did not want to occupy. The Romanian strategy was largely successful: its resistance against entrapment through foreign policy reforms enabled it to establish diplomatic relations with the FRG in 1967, as well as going it alone on the six-day Arab–Israeli war.

The formative process in the 1960s was, accordingly, largely determined by the Romanian fear of entrapment and the East German and Polish fear of abandonment. In terms of military reforms, the solution lay in a compromise that could allay both the fears of abandonment and of entrapment. The Romanian fear of supranationalism goes hand in hand with the fear of entrapment, whereas the eventual Romanian agreement to the military reforms stems from the fact that they actually served to decrease the risk of entrapment through their intergovernmental nature.

The resolution of a range of issues in 1969 thus testifies to the fact that the WP members had succeeded in finding a middle road between entrapment and abandonment. Both the military reforms and the declaration on European security provided the allies with aspects to reduce the fear of abandonment, such as an emphasis on the inviolability of the European borders, while also diminishing the risk of entrapment by leaving the ultimate decision on security issues with the respective governments instead of the organisation at large. The WP members had accordingly negotiated a bargain in which their disparity of interests was neutralised, whereas the negotiations on European security had increased the sense of mutual interest. The WP's formative process was only completed in March 1969, after a long bargaining process in which the individual allies sought to shape an alliance that served their level of commitment. The result was a compromise according to which the contract had become more explicit, although the commitment remained relatively vague.

In the 1960s the NSWP members began to play an active role in the 'alliance game'. Both the breakdown of the Sino-Soviet alliance and the crisis within NATO raised their awareness of the fact that there was a game to play. The most active players were those that had the most to lose. The WP turned from a cardboard castle into a multilateral alliance of sovereign states as soon as the NSWP members started playing 'the alliance game'. *Pace* Snyder, this game was *not* fundamentally different from the game being played simultaneously in NATO.

The alliance game within the WP was even played according to the central tenets of the Realist theory of international relations, which also forms the foundation for Snyder's theory. The quest for sovereignty, security and power to a large extent determined the contours of the game, which was further conditioned by each country's geographic position and material circumstances. Realism, however, usually has *not* been applied to Eastern Europe, presumably because the Realist starting point of *sovereign* states hardly seemed appropriate for an interpretation of the coercive and ideologically driven Soviet 'empire'. As we have seen, the NSWP members nevertheless used the WP throughout the 1960s as an instrument to safeguard their sovereignty and increase their security. As the Realist scholar Kenneth Waltz puts it, sovereignty means that '[s]tates develop their own strategies, chart their own courses, make their own decisions about how to meet whatever needs they experience and whatever desires they develop'.[44] It was exactly through the WP that the NSWP members could emancipate themselves into states that increasingly charted their own course, albeit as 'constrained and often tightly so' as any other sovereign state.[45]

In one important respect the WP leaders were even *less* constrained than their Western counterparts in their pursuit of their state's sovereignty and security, and their own power. Unhampered by electoral pressures or a civil society, the WP leaders had *carte blanche* in putting the interests of their state first. The WP in turn provided the NSWP leaders with an instrument to further these interests, while it emancipated its members from the major constraint of the Soviet hegemon. Not only did the WP itself evolve during the 1960s into a proper interstate organisation, but the participating states also developed into sovereign entities in the process. The NSWP members obtained a stake in negotiating the conditions according to which they would participate in the alliance, which marked a clear transition in international relations in Eastern Europe. International relations in the Soviet bloc could no longer be interpreted in imperialist terms, as it could be under Stalin, but in interstate terms. The concept of Eastern Europe as an 'empire by coercion' was seriously challenged by the end of the 1960s.[46] The Cold War had moved beyond a simple dichotomy between East and West.

Notes

1 Discussion at the 3rd plenum of the Polish United Workers' Party, 7 April 1965, FIG ACP, Poland, mf 0528, 51–52.
2 'Note on the March 1969 PCC Meeting for the HSWP (János Kádár)', 19 March 1969, PHP, 3, www.php.isn.ethz.ch/collections/colltopic.cfm?lng=en&id=18020&navinfo=14465; V. Mastny, 'Editorial note, PCC meeting 17 March 1969', PHP, www.php.isn.ethz.ch/collections/coll_pcc/ednote_69.cfm; and Minutes of the session of the RCP CC Politburo, 18 March 1969, ANIC, RCP CC, C, 40/1969, 11.
3 L.M. Lüthi, 'Restoring Chaos to History: Sino-Soviet-American Relations, 1969', *The China Quarterly* 210 (2012), 384.
4 Liu Qibao, in X. Liu and V. Mastny (eds), *China and Eastern Europe, 1960s–1980s. Proceedings of the International Symposium: Reviewing the History of Chinese-East European Relations from the 1960s to the 1980s. Beijing, 24–26 March 2004*, Zürcher Beiträge zur Sicherheitspolitik und Konfliktforschung Nr. 72 (Zurich, 2004), 127.

5 Lüthi, 'Restoring Chaos', 387.
6 Ibid.
7 Ibid., 388–89.
8 M. Munteanu, 'When the Levee Breaks: The Impact of the Sino-Soviet Split and the Invasion of Czechoslovakia on Romanian-Soviet Relations, 1967–70', *Journal of Cold War Studies* 12:1 (2010), 58.
9 Lüthi, 'Restoring Chaos', 389–90.
10 R.D. Schulzinger, 'Détente in the Nixon-Ford Years, 1969–76', in M. Leffler, and O.A. Westad (eds), *The Cambridge History of the Cold War. Volume II: Crisis and Détente* (Cambridge, 2010), 378.
11 Munteanu, 'When the Levee Breaks', 58.
12 D. Selvage, 'The Warsaw Pact and the German Question, 1955–70', in M.A. Heiss and S.V. Papacosma (eds), *NATO and the Warsaw Pact: Intrabloc Conflicts* (Ohio, 2008), 188.
13 J. Hanhimäki, 'Détente in Europe, 1962–75', in M. Leffler and O.A. Westad (eds), *The Cambridge History of the Cold War. Volume II: Crisis and Détente* (Cambridge, 2010), 213.
14 C. Békés, 'Der Warschauer Pakt und der KSZE-Prozess 1965 bis 1970', in T. Diedrich, W. Heinemann and C.F. Ostermann (eds), *Der Warschauer Pakt. Von der Gründung bis zum Zusammenbruch 1955 bis 1991* (Berlin, 2009), 238–39.
15 A.R. Johnson, *The Warsaw Pact's Campaign for 'European Security'. A Report Prepared for United States Air Force Project Rand* (Santa Monica, 1970), viii.
16 Hanhimäki, 'Détente in Europe', 213.
17 For an excellent account of the real nature of the Helsinki Final Act, see: R. Davy, 'Helsinki Myths. Setting the Record Straight on the Final Act of the CSCE, 1975', *Cold War History* 9:1 (2009), 1–22.
18 Hanhimäki, 'Détente in Europe', 215.
19 A. Locher, 'Shaping the Policies of the Alliance – The Committee of Ministers of Foreign Affairs of the WP, 1976–90', PHP, www.php.isn.ethz.ch/collections/coll_cmfa/cmfa_intro.cfm?navinfo=15699#Faltering (accessed 22 September 2013).
20 Cited in G. Holden, *The Warsaw Pact. Soviet Security and Bloc Politics* (Oxford and New York, 1989), 24.
21 J.L. Gaddis, *We Now Know. Rethinking Cold War History* (Oxford, 1997), 289.
22 See for this assumption: T. Risse-Kappen, *Cooperation among Democracies. The European Influence on U.S. Foreign Policy* (Princeton, 1995), 4.
23 Cf. A. Lalaj, 'Albanien und der Warschauer Pakt', in T. Diedrich *et al.* (eds), *Der Warschauer Pakt: Von der Gründung bis zum Zusammenbruch 1955 bis 1991*, 27–42; and D. Deletant, 'Taunting the Bear: Romania and the Warsaw Pact, 1963–89', *Cold War History* 7:4 (2007), 495–507; and H. Harrison, *Driving the Soviets up the Wall. Soviet-East German Relations, 1953–1961* (Princeton, 2005).
24 Cf. Z.K. Brzezinski, *The Soviet Bloc: Unity and Conflict. Revised and Enlarged Edition* (Harvard, 1967), 433.
25 Cf. M. Leffler, 'Bringing it Together: The Parts and the Whole', in O.A. Westad (ed.), *Reviewing the Cold War. Approaches, Interpretation, Theory* (London, 2000), 48.
26 A. Wenger, 'Crisis and Opportunity. NATO's Transformation and the Multilateralization of Détente, 1966–68', *Journal of Cold War Studies* 6:1 (2004), 71.
27 Ibid., 71.
28 A. Korbonski, 'The Warsaw Treaty After Twenty-five Years: An Entangling Alliance or an Empty Shell?' in R.W. Clawson and L.S. Kaplan (eds), *The Warsaw Pact. Political Purpose and Military Means* (Ohio, 1982), 3.
29 See for Adenauer's 'rigidity', M. Trachtenberg, *A Constructed Peace. The Making of the European Settlement, 1945–1963* (Princeton, 1999), 274–82.

30 A. Locher, 'A Crisis Foretold. NATO and France, 1963–66', in A. Wenger, C. Nuenlist and A. Locher (eds), *Transforming NATO in the Cold War. Challenges beyond Deterrence in the 1960s* (London and New York, 2007), 108.
31 See for the French obstruction: A. Locher, *Crisis? What Crisis? NATO, de Gaulle, and the Future of the Alliance, 1963–1966* (Berlin, 2010), 60–92.
32 H. Haftendorn, *NATO and the Nuclear Revolution. A Crisis of Credibility, 1966–1967* (Oxford, 1996), 134–39.
33 Locher, *Crisis? What Crisis?* 267.
34 Cf. France's isolation within NATO in December 1966: Wenger, 'Crisis and Opportunity', 39.
35 L.S. Kaplan, 'The 40th Anniversary of the Harmel Report', *Reviewing Riga* (Spring 2007), www.nato.int/docu/review/2007/issue1/english/history.html (accessed 22 September 2013); and Wenger, 'Crisis and Opportunity', 59.
36 Wenger, 'Crisis and Opportunity', 69.
37 H. Brands, 'Non-Proliferation and the Dynamics of the Middle Cold War', *Cold War History* 7:3 (2007), 389–423.
38 Cf. Wenger, 'Crisis and Opportunity', 68.
39 G.H. Snyder, 'The Security Dilemma in Alliance Politics', *World Politics* 36:4 (1984), 463.
40 Ibid., 466.
41 Ibid., 484, emphasis in original.
42 Ibid., 468.
43 Ibid., 474.
44 K.N. Waltz, *Theory of International Politics* (Boston, 1979), 96.
45 Ibid.
46 L. Bohri, 'Empire by Coercion. The Soviet Union and Hungary in the 1950s', *Cold War History* 1:2 (2001), 47–72.

Note on the sources

One of the reasons why the Warsaw Pact has not previously been examined from a multilateral angle might be that there are simply too many archives to consult. It is practically impossible to consult all the relevant archives of the eight former Warsaw Pact members for the purpose of writing one monograph. This problem has been partly remedied by the *Parallel History Project on Cooperative Security* (PHP), which has published online thousands of pages of archival evidence from all these countries, translated into English. Needless to say, all these documents have been avidly perused, particularly in the early stages of this research. The documents published by the PHP nevertheless only cover the meetings that took place within the framework of the WP, and not the preparations for those meetings or other transactions between WP members that took place behind the scenes. Despite the focus on the multilateral dynamics of the alliance, many of the issues arose bilaterally or trilaterally. The periods between meetings are particularly important for the scope of this research, since the WP members only convened every year or two years in the first half of the 1960s.

This book is therefore based on an archival strategy that has enabled a detailed examination of the evolution of the WP without consulting the archives in eight different countries, by concentrating on the archives in Berlin, Bucharest and Rome. The archives in the first two cities facilitated an analysis of the WP from two opposite ends of the spectrum, whereas the research into the archive of the Partito Comunista Italiano at the Fondazione Gramsci in Rome has provided an *intra*-communist, but *extra*-Warsaw Pact perspective. Research of the PHP documents already indicated that the GDR leadership was particularly proactive within the WP, offering *inter alia* proposals on ways to resolve the second Berlin Crisis, on reforms of the alliance, and on non-proliferation, while taking an exceptionally active stance on the discussions on European security. Since the German question defined the issues at stake in the WP to a large extent, Germany seemed a logical place to start the archival research. The East German leadership had a particular interest in the WP, as the only international organisation to recognise the GDR. The archival research in Berlin yielded a great deal of evidence, consisting of *inter alia* thousands of pages of minutes of meetings within the Warsaw Pact, diplomatic reports, letters and speeches.

Moreover, the evidence showed that there was one NSWP member in particular whose aims and strategies were opposed to those of the GDR – namely, Romania. Whereas the East German leaders wanted a rigidly structured Warsaw Pact in order to use it all the more efficiently to further *their* interests, the Romanian leaders strove to keep the alliance as flexible and loosely structured as possible so as to use it as an instrument to emphasise their autonomy vis-à-vis the Kremlin. Many of the crises that plagued the WP in the 1960s originated in disagreements between the East German and Romanian leaders, none of whom was prepared to budge. Because the dynamics within the WP seemed largely to be determined by the clash of interests between the East German and Romanian leaders, Bucharest seemed a logical place to continue the archival research.

The combination of archival research in Berlin and Bucharest has another advantage: the East German and Romanian leaders not only occupied opposite ends of the spectrum within the WP, but also in their diplomatic relations at large. The research in both archives was therefore largely complementary. Whereas the archives in Berlin abound in diplomatic reports and analyses relating to the Soviet Union, Czechoslovakia, Poland and Hungary, the archive in Bucharest contains numerous files on the diplomatic relations with and developments in Albania and China. The policies of countries with a particular stake in the German question are particularly well represented in Berlin, while the archive in Bucharest contains extremely useful and revealing information on the countries that were involved in the Sino–Soviet split. Since Romania was the only active WP country that maintained good relations with China throughout the 1960s, the Romanian archive also provides a particularly valuable insight into the way in which the Sino–Soviet split affected the dynamics within the WP. The fact that I was also allowed to peruse the documents on international relations under Ceausescu, which are still largely classified, made the archival research in Bucharest all the more worthwhile.

The archival research in Bucharest and in Berlin not only complemented, but also corroborated each other. Conflicting evidence was almost non-existent, different emphases at most. Moreover, the archival research in Romania confirmed the hypothesis that the tensions between the East German and Romanian leaders affected the WP's dynamics in an important way. Whereas the East German leaders were the most proactive WP members in terms of proposals on foreign policy and reforms, the Romanians were the most zealous members in terms of expressing the right of veto. The other NSWP member that put a particularly large stamp on the alliance's dynamics was Poland. Since Poland and East Germany were, however, on very good terms in the 1960s, it has been possible to reconstruct the Polish point of view by using the German archives. Moreover, the Polish scholar Wanda Jarzabek and the American historian Douglas Selvage have already examined the Polish stance within the 1960s so extensively that their articles and source collections have largely remedied any potential gaps in Polish evidence.

Note on the sources

The evidence from Rome has proven very valuable in corroborating and checking some of the evidence found in Berlin and Bucharest. Since the leadership of the Italian Communist Party operated relatively independently from Moscow and was closely involved in the developments within the communist world movement in the 1960s,[1] the Italian documents proved especially useful in gauging the increasingly independent stance of the NSWP countries in the communist movement, which seemed to mirror their development within the Warsaw Pact. It also confirmed that some WP countries, such as Albania, Romania, the GDR and Poland, emancipated themselves particularly quickly in the 1960s. The fact that these countries are examined at greater length than others in this book, therefore, does not reflect an archival bias, but rather a focus on the countries that took the most initiative within the WP, and whose stance affected the WP to the greatest extent.[2] This monograph is accordingly the product of research that is extensive, but by no means exhaustive. Although there may still be scope for more emphasis on each country's national perspective, all the issues that were at stake within the WP in the 1960s have been covered in depth. The multilateral approach towards the evolution of the alliance has been the guiding principle in the conduct of the archival research.

Notes

1 D. Sassoon, *The Strategy of the Italian Communist Party. From the Resistance to the Historic Compromise* (London, 1981), 91.
2 Although there is, for example, evidence on Czechoslovak ideas to reform the alliance, none of the Czechoslovak suggestions were put forward at a PCC meeting, so the proposals did not have an impact on the actual policies of the Warsaw Pact. Cf. V. Mastny, '"We are in a Bind": Polish and Czechoslovak Attempts at Reforming the Warsaw Pact, 1956–69', in C. F. Ostermann (ed.), *Cold War Flashpoints*, CWIHP Bulletin No. 11 (Washington, 1998), 230–50. The reason why *inter alia* the Czechoslovak reforms were not put forward are discussed in this book.

Bibliography

Archives

Berlin, Germany

Stiftung Archiv der Parteien und Massenorganisationen der DDR im Bundesarchiv (SAPMO-BArch)
Deutsche Demokratische Republik, Parteien: Sozialistische Einheitspartei Deutschlands
Höchste gewählte Gremien
    Politbüro des ZK der SED
Büros und Sekretariate
    Büro Walter Ulbricht (DY 30/3288–3754)
    Internationale Beziehungen der SED und Außenpolitik der DDR
    Zusammenarbeit der Warschauer Vertragsstaaten und Mitgliedsländer des RGW
    Internationale Konferenzen, Beratungen, Treffen, Initiativen
    Parteibeziehungen SED-KpdSU
    Internationale Beziehungen der SED zu Staaten und Parteien

Politisches Archiv des Auswärtigen Amtes (PA AA)
Ministerium für Auswärtige Angelegenheiten der DDR (MfAA)
Hauptgruppe 3: Internationale Organisationen
    Aktengruppe 34: zwischenstaatliche Organisationen der sozialistischen Länder
Ländergruppenkürzel LG 4.5: Warschauer Vertragsstaaten
    Albanien, L 2
    Bulgarien, L 25
    CSSR, L 179
    DDR, L 36
    Polen, L 138
    Rumänien, L 146
    Sowjetunion, L 159
    Ungarn, L 183

Bucharest, Romania

Arhivele Naţionale Istorice Centrale ale României (ANIC)

Comitetul Central al P.C.R., Secţia Relaţii Externe, perioada 1958–65
Comitetul Central al P.C.R., Secţia Relaţii Externe, perioada 1966–80
Comitetul Central al P.C.R., Secţia Cancelarie

Rome, Italy

Fondazione Istituto Gramsci
Archivio Partito Comunista Italiano (FIG APC)

Sezioni di lavoro, 1943–79
    Esteri
Organismi di direzione, 1943–90
    Comitato Centrale
    Direzione
    Segreteria
Esteri, 1943–90
    Paesi
    Incontri internazionali

Parallel History Project on Cooperative Security
Records of the Warsaw Pact Political Consultative Committee, 1955–90

www.php.isn.ethz.ch/collections/colltopic.cfm?lng=en&id=14465&nav1=1&nav2=1&nav3=2
Edited by Vojtech Mastny, Christian Nünlist, Anna Locher and Douglas Selvage, May 2001

PCC Meetings 1956–1969

I Prague, 27–28 January 1956
II Moscow, 24 May 1958
III Moscow, 4 February 1960
IV Moscow, 28–29 March 1961
V Moscow, 7 June 1962
VI Moscow, 26 July 1963
VII Warsaw, 19–20 January 1965
VIII Bucharest, 4–6 July 1966
IX Sofia, 6–7 March 1968
X Budapest, 17 March 1969

Records of the Warsaw Pact Committee of the Ministers of Foreign Affairs, 1976–90

www.php.isn.ethz.ch/collections/colltopic.cfm?lng=en&id=15699
Edited by Anna Locher, May 2002

Forerunners, 1959–75
I Warsaw, 27–28 April 1959
II Moscow, 6–17 June 1966
III Warsaw, 8–10 February 1967

Records of the Meetings of the Warsaw Pact Deputy Foreign Ministers
www.php.isn.ethz.ch/collections/colltopic.cfm?lng=en&id=15700&nav1=1&nav2=1&nav3=5
Edited by Csaba Békés, Anna Locher and Christian Nünlist, 5 September 2005

I Warsaw, 10 December 1964
II East Berlin, 10–12 February 1966
III East Berlin, 26–27 February 1968
IV Budapest, 15–17 March 1969
V East Berlin, 21–22 May 1969

Published primary sources

Békés, C., Byrne, M. and Rainer, J.M. (eds), *The 1956 Hungarian Revolution: A History in Documents* (Budapest and New York, 2002).
Betea, L. (ed.), *Partea lor de adevăr* (Bucharest, 2008a).
—— 'Convorbiri neterminate cu Corneliu Mănescu', in L. Betea (ed.), *Partea lor de adevăr* (Bucharest, 2008b), 558–71.
Dobrynin, A., *In Confidence. Moscow's Ambassador to America's Six Cold War Presidents (1962–1986)* (New York, 1995).
Dubcek, S. and Sugar, A., *Dubcek Speaks* (London, 1990).
Hershberg, J.G. (ed.), *Inside the Warsaw Pact*, CWIHP Bulletin No. 2 (Washington, 1992).
—— *From the Russian Archives*, CWIHP Bulletin No. 3 (Washington, 1993).
—— *Cold War Crises*, CWIHP Bulletin No. 5 (Washington, 1995).
—— *The Cold War in the Third World and the Collapse of Détente in the 1970s*, CWIHP Bulletin No. 8/9 (Washington, 1996).
Johnson, A.R., *The Warsaw Pact's Campaign for 'European Security'. A Report Prepared for United States Air Force Project Rand* (Santa Monica, 1970).
Mastny, V. and Byrne, M. (eds), *A Cardboard Castle? An Inside History of the Warsaw Pact 1955–1991* (Budapest and New York, 2005).
Navrátil, J. (ed.), *The Prague Spring 1968* (Budapest and New York, 2006).
North Atlantic Treaty Organization, 'The North Atlantic Treaty' (Washington, DC, 4 April 1949), www.nato.int/cps/en/natolive/official_texts_17120.htm.
—— 'The Future Tasks of the Alliance. The Harmel Report' (1967), www.nato.int/cps/en/natolive/official_texts_26700.htm.
Ostermann, C.F., *Cold War Flashpoints*, CWIHP Bulletin No. 11 (Washington, 1998).
—— (ed.), *Uprising in East Germany 1953. The Cold War, the German Question, and the First Major Upheaval behind the Iron Curtain* (Budapest and New York, 2001).
—— *Inside China's Cold War*, CWIHP Bulletin No. 16 (Washington, 2007/2008).
Preda, D. et al. (eds), *România – Republica Federală Germania. Începutul relațiilor diplomatice 1966–1967. Vol. I* (Bucharest, 2009).

Westad, O.A., Jian, C., Tonnesson, S., Tung, N.V. and Hershberg, J.G. (eds), *77 Conversations between Chinese and Foreign Leaders on the Wars in Indochina, 1964–77*, CWIHP Working Paper No. 22 (Washington, 1998).
Zedong, M., 'US Imperialism is a Paper Tiger', 14 July 1956, www.marxists.org/reference/archive/mao/selected-works/volume 5/mswv5_52.htm.

Secondary literature

Baev, J., 'The Warsaw Pact', in R. van Dijk (ed.), *Encyclopaedia of the Cold War*. Volume 2 (London and New York, 2008a), 960–62.
——'The Warsaw Pact and Southern Tier Conflicts, 1959–69', in M.A. Heiss and S.V. Papacosma (eds), *NATO and the Warsaw Pact: Intrabloc Conflicts* (Ohio, 2008b), 193–205.
Bange, O. and Niedhart, G. (eds), *Helsinki 1975 and the Transformation of Europe* (London and New York, 2008).
Barras, G.S., *The Great Cold War. A Journey through the Hall of Mirrors* (Stanford, 2009).
Békés, C., 'Cold War, Détente, and the 1956 Hungarian Revolution', in K. Larres and K. Osgood (eds), *The Cold War after Stalin's Death. A Missed Opportunity for Peace?* (Lanham, 2006), 213–31.
——'Der Warschauer Pakt und der KSZE-Prozess 1965 bis 1970', in T. Diedrich, W. Heinemann and C.F. Ostermann (eds), *Der Warschauer Pakt. Von der Gründung bis zum Zusammenbruch 1955 bis 1991* (Berlin, 2009), 225–44.
——'East Central Europe, 1953–56', in M. Leffler and O.A. Westad (eds), *The Cambridge History of the Cold War. Volume I: Origins* (Cambridge, 2010), 334–52.
——'Hungary and the Prague Spring', in G. Bischof, S. Karner and P. Ruggenthaler (eds), *The Prague Spring and the Warsaw Pact Invasion of Czechoslovakia in 1968* (New York and Plymouth, 2011), 371–95.
Bernkopf Tucker, N., 'China Under Siege: Escaping the Dangers of 1968', in C. Fink, P. Gassert and D. Junker (eds), *1968: The World Transformed* (Cambridge, 1998), 193–216.
Betea, L, 'Primăvara de la Praga, vara de la București', in L. Betea et al. (eds), *21 august 1968. Apoteoza lui Ceaușescu* (Bucharest, 2009), 40 ff.
Betea, L. et al. (eds), *21 august 1968. Apoteoza lui Ceaușescu* (Bucharest, 2009).
Biberaj, E., *Albania: A Socialist Maverick* (Boulder, 1990).
Bischof, G., Karner, S. and Ruggenthaler, P. (eds), *The Prague Spring and the Warsaw Pact Invasion of Czechoslovakia in 1968* (New York and Plymouth, 2010).
Bohri, L., 'Empire by Coercion. The Soviet Union and Hungary in the 1950s', *Cold War History* 1:2 (2001), 47–72.
Bozo, F., 'France, "Gaullism", and the Cold War', in M. Leffler and O.A. Westad (eds), *The Cambridge History of the Cold War. Volume II: Crisis and Détente* (Cambridge, 2010), 158–78.
Brands, H., 'Non-Proliferation and the Dynamics of the Middle Cold War', *Cold War History* 7:3 (2007), 389–423.
Brown, A., *The Rise and Fall of Communism* (London, 2009).
Brzezinski, Z.K., *The Soviet Bloc: Unity and Conflict. Revised and Enlarged Edition* (Harvard, 1967).

Clawson, R.W. and Kaplan, L.S. (eds), *The Warsaw Pact. Political Purpose and Military Means* (Ohio, 1982).
Crampton, R.J., *A Short History of Modern Bulgaria* (Cambridge, 1987).
——*A Concise History of Bulgaria* (Cambridge, 1997).
Davy, R., 'Helsinki Myths. Setting the Record Straight on the Final Act of the CSCE, 1975', *Cold War History* 9:1 (2009), 1–22.
Deletant, D., 'Taunting the Bear: Romania and the Warsaw Pact, 1963–89', *Cold War History* 7:4 (2007), 495–507.
Deletant, D. and Ionescu, M., *Romania and the Warsaw Pact: 1955–1989*, CWIHP Working Paper No. 43 (Washington, 2004).
Diedrich, T., 'The German Democratic Republic', in J. Hoffenaar and D. Krüger (eds), *Blueprints for Battle. Planning for War in Central Europe, 1948–1968* (Lexington, 2012), 175–201.
Diedrich, H. von T., Heinemann, W. and Ostermann, C.F. (eds), *Der Warschauer Pakt. Von der Gründung bis zum Zusammenbruch 1955 bis 1991* (Berlin, 2009).
Dijk, R. van (ed.), *Encyclopaedia of the Cold War. Volume 2* (London and New York, 2008).
Dikötter, F., *Mao's Great Famine. The History of China's Most Devastating Catastrophe, 1958–62* (New York, 2010).
Dragomir, E., 'The Perceived Threat of Hegemonism in Romania during the Second Détente', *Cold War History* 12:1 (2012), 116.
Fink, C., Gassert, P. and Junker, D. (eds), *1968: The World Transformed* (Cambridge, 1998).
Fink, C., Hadler, F. and Schramm, T., *1956: European and Global Perspectives* (Leipzig, 2006)
Fursenko, A. and Naftali, T., *'One Hell of a Gamble'. Khrushchev, Castro and Kennedy, 1958–1964* (London and New York, 1998).
Gaddis, J.L., *We Now Know. Rethinking Cold War History* (Oxford, 1997).
——'On Starting All Over Again: A Naïve Approach to the Study of the Cold War', in O.A. Westad (ed.), *Reviewing the Cold War. Approaches, Interpretation, Theory* (London, 2000), 27–42.
Gaiduk, I.V., *The Soviet Union and the Vietnam War* (Chicago, 1996).
——*Confronting Vietnam. Soviet Policy toward the Indochina Conflict, 1954–1963* (Washington, 2003).
Garthoff, R.L., 'When and Why Romania Distanced Itself from the Warsaw Pact', in J. Hershberg (ed.), *Cold War Crises*, CWIHP Bulletin No. 5 (Washington, 1998), 111.
Garton Ash, T., *In Europe's Name. Germany and the Divided Continent* (New York, 1993).
Gavin, F.J., 'Nuclear Proliferation and Non-proliferation during the Cold War', in M. Leffler and O.A. Westad (eds), *The Cambridge History of the Cold War. Volume II: Crisis and Détente* (Cambridge, 2010), 395–416.
Gheorghe, R.E., 'Romania's Nuclear Negotiations Postures in the 1960s. Client, Maverick and International Peace Mediator', *Romanian Nuclear History Project Working Paper* No.1 (2012), www.roec.ro/wp-content/uploads/2012/08/Gheorghe_Nuclear-Negotiations-Postures_EN.pdf.
——'Atomic Maverick. Romania's Negotiations for Nuclear Technology, 1964–70', *Cold War History* 13:3 (2013), 373–92.
Gildea, R., Mark, J. and Warring, A. (eds), *Europe's 1968. Voices of Revolt* (Oxford, 2013).

Granville, J., *The First Domino. International Decision-making During the Hungarian Crisis of 1956* (Texas, 2004).
Griffith, W.E., *Albania and the Sino-Soviet Rift* (Massachusetts, 1963).
——*The Sino-Soviet Rift* (London, 1964).
Guang Zhang, S., 'The Sino-Soviet Alliance and the Cold War in Asia, 1954–62', in M. Leffler and O.A. Westad (eds), *The Cambridge History of the Cold War. Volume I: Origins* (Cambridge, 2010), 353–75.
Haftendorn, H., *NATO and the Nuclear Revolution. A Crisis of Credibility, 1966–1967* (Oxford, 1996).
Hanhimäki, J., 'Détente in Europe, 1962–75', in M. Leffler and O.A. Westad (eds), *The Cambridge History of the Cold War. Volume II: Crisis and Détente* (Cambridge, 2010), 198–218.
Harper, J.L., *The Cold War* (Oxford, 2011).
Harrison, H., *Ulbricht and the Concrete 'Rose': New Archival Evidence on the Dynamics of Soviet East German Relations and the Berlin Crisis, 1958–1961*, CWIHP Working Paper No. 5 (Washington, 1993).
——*Driving the Soviets up the Wall. Soviet-East German Relations, 1953–1961* (Princeton, 2005).
——'The New Course: Soviet Policy toward Germany and the Uprising in the GDR', in K. Larres and K. Osgood (eds), *The Cold War after Stalin's Death. A Missed Opportunity for Peace?* (Lanham, 2006), 193–299.
Heinemann, W. and Wiggershaus, N. (eds), *Das internationale Krisenjahr 1956: Polen, Ungarn, Suez* (Munich, 1999).
Heiss, M.A. and Papacosma, S.V. (eds), *NATO and the Warsaw Pact. Intrabloc Conflicts* (Ohio, 2008).
Herring, G.C., *America's Longest War. The United States and Vietnam, 1950–1975* (New York, 1979).
——*The Secret Diplomacy of the Vietnam War. The Negotiating Volumes of the Pentagon Papers* (Austin, 1983).
Hershberg, J.G., *Who Murdered 'Marigold': New Evidence on the Mysterious Failure of Poland's Secret Initiative to Start US-North Vietnamese Peace Talks, 1966*, CWIHP Working Paper No. 72 (Washington, 2000a).
——'The Crisis Years, 1958–63', in O.A. Westad (ed.), *Reviewing the Cold War. Approaches, Interpretation, Theory* (London, 2000b), 303–25.
——*Marigold. The Lost Chance for Peace in Vietnam* (Stanford, 2012).
Hershberg, J.G., Wolff, D., Vámos, P. and Radchenko, S. (eds), *The Interkit Story: A Window into the Final Decades of the Sino-Soviet Relationship*, CWIHP Working Paper No. 63 (Washington, 2011).
Hoensch, J.K., 'The Warsaw Pact and the Northern Member States', in R.W. Clawson and L.S. Kaplan (eds), *The Warsaw Pact. Political Purpose and Military Means* (Delaware, 1982), 27–48.
Hoffenaar, J., 'East German Military Intelligence for the Warsaw Pact in the Central Sector', in J. Hoffenaar and D. Krüger (eds), *Blueprints for Battle. Planning for War in Central Europe, 1948–1968* (Lexington, 2012), 75–92.
Hoffenaar, J. and Krüger, J. (eds), *Blueprints for Battle. Planning for War in Central Europe, 1948–1968* (Lexington, 2012).
Holden, G., *The Warsaw Pact. Soviet Security and Bloc Politics* (Oxford and New York, 1989).

Jarzabek, W., '"Ulbricht Doktrin" oder "Gomulka Doktrin"? Das Bemühen der Volksrepublik Polen um eine geschlossene Politik des kommunistischen Blocks gegenüber der westdeutschen Ostpolitik 1966/1967', *Zeitschrift für Ostmitteleuropa Forschung* 1:55 (2006), 79 ff.
——'Preserving the Status Quo or Promoting Change. The Role of the CSCE in the Perception of Polish Authorities, 1964–89', in O. Bange and G. Niedhart (eds), *Helsinki 1975 and the Transformation of Europe* (London and New York, 2008a), 144–59.
——*Hope and Reality. Poland and the Conference on Security and Cooperation in Europe, 1964–1989*, CWIHP Working Paper No. 56 (Washington, 2008b).
——*PRL w politycznych strukturach Ukladu Warszawskiego w latach 1955–1980* [The Polish People's Republic in the Political Structures of the Warsaw Pact, 1955–1980] (Warsaw, 2008c).
——'Die Volksrepublik Polen in den politischen Strukturen des Warschauer Vertrags zu Zeiten der Entspannung und der "Ostpolitik"', in T. Diedrich, W. Heinemann and C.F. Ostermann (eds), *Der Warschauer Pakt. Von der Gründung bis zum Zusammenbruch 1955 bis 1991* (Berlin, 2009), 133–48.
——'Polish Reactions to the West German Ostpolitik and East-West Détente, 1966–78', in P. Villaume and O.A. Westad (eds), *Perforating the Iron Curtain. European Détente, Transatlantic Relations, and the Cold War, 1965–1985* (Copenhagen, 2010a), 35–56.
——'Poland in the Warsaw Pact 1955–91: An Appraisal of the Role of Poland in the Political Structures of the Warsaw Pact', PHP (2010b) www.php.isn.ethz.ch/collections/coll_poland/Introduction.cfm?navinfo=111216.
Jones, C.D., *Soviet Influence in Eastern Europe. Political Autonomy and the Warsaw Pact* (New York, 1981).
Kaiser, D.E., *American Tragedy. Kennedy, Johnson, and the Origins of the Vietnam War* (Massachusetts, 2000).
Kaplan, L.S., *NATO Divided, NATO United. The Evolution of an Alliance* (Westport, 2004).
——'The 40th Anniversary of the Harmel Report', *Reviewing Riga* (spring 2007), www.nato.int/docu/review/2007/issue1/english/history.html.
Kemp-Welch, A., *Poland under Communism. A Cold War History* (Cambridge, 2008).
——'Eastern Europe: Stalinism to Solidarity', in M. Leffler and O.A. Westad (eds), *The Cambridge History of the Cold War. Volume II: Crisis and Détente* (Cambridge, 2010), 219–37.
Kenez, P., *A History of the Soviet Union from the Beginning to the End* (Cambridge, 1999, 2006).
Klimke, M., Pekelder, J. and Scharloth, J. (eds), *Between Prague Spring and French May. Opposition and Revolt in Europe, 1960–1980* (New York and Oxford, 2011).
Knight, A., *Beria. Stalin's First Lieutenant* (Princeton, 1993).
Korbonski, A., 'The Warsaw Treaty After Twenty-five Years: An Entangling Alliance or an Empty Shell?' in R.W. Clawson and L.S. Kaplan (eds), *The Warsaw Pact. Political Purpose and Military Means* (Ohio, 1982), 3–25.
Kramer, M., 'New Sources on the 1968 Invasion in Czechoslovakia', in J.G. Hershberg (ed.), *Inside the Warsaw Pact, CWIHP Bulletin No. 2* (Washington, 1992), 1, 4–13.
——'The Prague Spring and the Soviet Invasion of Czechoslovakia: New Interpretations', in J.G. Hershberg (ed.), *From the Russian Archives*, CWIHP Bulletin No. 3 (Washington, 1993), 2–13, 54–55.

—'"Lessons" of the Cuban Missile Crisis for Warsaw Pact Nuclear Operations', in J.G. Hershberg (ed.), *The Cold War in the Third World and the Collapse of Détente in the 1970s*, CWIHP Bulletin No. 8/9 (Washington, 1996), 348–54.

—'Introduction: International Politics in the Early Post-Stalin Era: A Lost Opportunity, a Turning Point, or More of the Same?', in K. Larres and K. Osgood (eds), *The Cold War after Stalin's Death. A Missed Opportunity for Peace?* (Lanham, 2006), xiii–xxxiv.

—'Die Sowjetunion, der Warschauer Pakt und blockinterne Krisen während der Breznev-Ära', in T. Diedrich, W. Heinemann and C.F. Ostermann (eds), *Der Warschauer Pakt: Von der Gründung bis zum Zusammenbruch 1955 bis 1991* (Berlin, 2009), 274–336.

—'The Kremlin, the Prague Spring, and the Brezhnev Doctrine', in V. Tismaneanu, *Promises of 1968: Crisis, Illusion, and Utopia* (Budapest and New York, 2010), 276–362.

—'The Prague Spring and the Soviet Invasion in Historical Perspective', in G. Bischof, S. Karner and P. Ruggenthaler (eds), *The Prague Spring and the Warsaw Pact Invasion of Czechoslovakia in 1968* (New York and Plymouth, 2011), 35–58.

Kurlansky, M., *1968: The Year that Rocked the World* (New York, 2004).

Kyrow, A. and Zselicky, B., 'Ungarnkrise 1956. Lagebeurteilung und Vorgehen der sowjetischen Führung und Armee', in W. Heinemann and N. Wiggershaus (eds), *Das international Krisenjahr 1956: Polen, Ungarn, Suez* (Munich, 1999), 95–133.

Lalaj, A., '"Albania is not Cuba." Sino-Albanian Summits and the Sino-Soviet Split', in C.F. Ostermann (ed.), *Inside China's Cold War*, CWIHP Bulletin No. 16 (Washington, 2007/2008), 183–340.

—'Albanien und der Warschauer Pakt', in T. Diedrich, W. Heinemann and C.F. Ostermann (eds), *Der Warschauer Pakt. Von der Gründung bis zum Zusammenbruch 1955 bis 1991* (Berlin, 2009), 27–42.

Larres, K. and Osgood, K. (eds), *The Cold War after Stalin's Death. A Missed Opportunity for Peace?* (Lanham, 2006).

Leffler, M., 'Bringing it Together: The Parts and the Whole', in O.A. Westad (ed.), *Reviewing the Cold War. Approaches, Interpretation, Theory* (London, 2000), 43–63.

Leffler, M. and Westad, O.A. (eds), *The Cambridge History of the Cold War. Volume I: Origins* (Cambridge, 2010a).

—*The Cambridge History of the Cold War. Volume II: Crisis and Détente* (Cambridge, 2010b).

—*The Cambridge History of the Cold War. Volume III: Endings* (Cambridge, 2010c).

Lemke, M., *Die Berlinkrise 1958 bis 1963. Interesse und Handlungsspielräume der SED im Ost West Konflikt* (Berlin, 1995).

Liska, G., *Nations in Alliance. The Limits of Interdependence* (Baltimore, 1962).

Liu, X. and Mastny, V. (eds), *China and Eastern Europe, 1960s–1980s. Proceedings of the International Symposium: Reviewing the History of Chinese-East European Relations from the 1960s to the 1980s. Beijing, 24–26 March 2004*, Zürcher Beiträge zur Sicherheitspolitik und Konfliktforschung Nr. 72 (Zurich, 2004).

Locher, A., 'Shaping the Policies of the Alliance – The Committee of Ministers of Foreign Affairs of the Warsaw Pact, 1976–90', PHP (2002), www.php.isn.ethz.ch/collections/coll_cmfa/cmfa_intro.cfm?navinfo=5699.

—'A Crisis Foretold. NATO and France, 1963–66', in A. Wenger, C. Nuenlist and A. Locher (eds), *Transforming NATO in the Cold War. Challenges beyond Deterrence in the 1960s* (Oxford and New York, 2007), 107–27.

―――Crisis? What Crisis? NATO, de Gaulle, and the Future of the Alliance, 1963–1966 (Berlin, 2010).
Locher, A. and Nünlist, C., The Future Tasks of the Alliance. NATO's Harmel Report, 1966–1967, PHP (2005), www.isn.ethz.ch/DigitalLibrary/Publications/Detail/?id=10 8636&lng=en.
Logevall, F., 'The Indochina Wars and the Cold War, 1945–75', in M. Leffler and O. A. Westad (eds), The Cambridge History of the Cold War. Volume II: Crisis and Détente (Cambridge, 2010), 281–304
Loth, W., Stalin's Ungeliebtes Kind. Warum Moskau die DDR nicht Wollte (Berlin, 1994).
Ludlow, N.P., The European Community and the Crisis of the 1960s. Negotiating the Gaullist Challenge (London and New York, 2006).
Lundestad, G., 'Empire by Invitation? The United States and Western Europe, 1942–52', Journal of Peace Research 23 (1986), 263–77.
―――'How (Not) to Study the Origins of the Cold War', in O.A. Westad (ed.), Reviewing the Cold War. Approaches, Interpretation, Theory (London, 2000), 64–80.
Lüthi, L.M., 'The People's Republic of China and the Warsaw Pact Organization, 1955–63', Cold War History 7:4 (2007), 479–94.
―――The Sino-Soviet Split: Cold War in the Communist World (Princeton, 2008).
―――'Restoring Chaos to History: Sino-Soviet-American Relations, 1969', The China Quarterly 210 (2012), 378–97.
Mastny, V., The Cold War and Soviet Insecurity. The Stalin Years (Oxford, 1996).
―――The Soviet Non-invasion of Poland in 1980/81 and the End of the Cold War, CWIHP Working Paper No. 23 (Washington, 1998a).
―――'"We Are in a Bind": Polish and Czechoslovak Attempts at Reforming the Warsaw Pact, 1956–69', in C.F. Ostermann (ed.), Cold War Flashpoints, CWIHP Bulletin No. 11 (Washington, 1998b), 230–50.
―――'Learning from the Enemy. NATO as a Model of the Warsaw Pact', Zürcher Beiträge zur Sicherheitspolitik und Konfliktforschung No. 58 (Zurich, 2001).
―――'The New History of Cold War Alliances', Journal of Cold War Studies 4:2 (2002a), 55–84.
―――China, the Warsaw Pact, and Sino-Soviet Relations under Khrushchev, PHP (2002b), www.php.isn.ethz.ch/collections/coll_china_wapa/intro_ mastny.cfm.
―――The Soviet Union and the Origins of the Warsaw Pact in 1955, PHP (2003), www.php.isn.ethz.ch/collections/coll_pcc/into_VM.cfm.
―――'Was 1968 a Strategic Watershed of the Cold War?' Diplomatic History 29:1 (2005), 149–77.
―――'Imagining War in Europe. Soviet Strategic Planning', in V. Mastny, S.S. Holtsmark and A. Wenger (eds), War Plans and Alliances in the Cold War. Threat Perceptions in the East and West (London and New York, 2006), 15–45.
―――'The Warsaw Pact. An Alliance in Search of a Purpose', in M.A. Heiss and S.V. Papacosma (eds), NATO and the Warsaw Pact. Intrabloc Conflicts (Ohio, 2008), 141–60.
―――'Soviet Foreign Policy, 1953–62', in M. Leffler and O.A. Westad (eds), The Cambridge History of the Cold War. Volume I: Origins (Cambridge, 2010), 312–33.
Mastny, V., Holtsmark, S.S. and Wenger, A. (eds), War Plans and Alliances in the Cold War. Threat Perceptions in the East and West (London and New York, 2006).
Mearsheimer, J.J., The Tragedy of Great Power Politics (New York, 2001).
Moreton, E., East Germany and the Warsaw Alliance. The Politics of Détente (Boulder, 1978).

Morgenthau, H.J., *Politics among Nations. The Struggle for Power and Peace* (New York, 1948, 1963).
Munteanu, M., 'When the Levee Breaks: The Impact of the Sino-Soviet Split and the Invasion of Czechoslovakia on Romanian-Soviet Relations, 1967–70', *Journal of Cold War Studies* 12:1 (2010), 43–61.
——'Over the Hills and Far Away: Romania's Attempts to Mediate the Start of U.S.-North Vietnamese Negotiations, 1967–68', *Journal of Cold War Studies* 14:3 (2012), 64–96.
Opriş, P., *România în Organizaţia Tratatului de la Varsovia (1955–1991)* (Bucharest, 2008).
Ouimet, M.J., *The Rise and Fall of the Brezhnev Doctrine in Soviet Foreign Policy* (Chapel Hill, 2003).
Paczkowski, A., *The Spring Will be Ours. Poland and the Poles from Occupation to Freedom* (Pennsylvania, 2003).
Paczkowski, A. and Byrne, M. (eds), *From Solidarity to Martial Law. The Polish Crisis of 1980–1981* (Budapest and New York, 2007).
Petrescu, C.L., 'Performing Disapproval toward the Soviets: Nicolae Ceausescu's Speech on 21 August 1968 in the Romanian Media', in M. Klimke, J. Pekelder and J. Scharloth (eds), *Between Prague Spring and French May. Opposition and Revolt in Europe, 1960–1980* (New York and Oxford, 2011), 199–210.
Pons, S., 'The Rise and Fall of Eurocommunism', in M. Leffler, and O.A. Westad (eds), *The Cambridge History of the Cold War. Volume III: Endings* (Cambridge, 2010), 45–65.
Pravda, A., 'The Collapse of the Soviet Union, 1990–91', in M. Leffler and O.A. Westad (eds), *The Cambridge History of the Cold War. Volume III: Endings* (Cambridge, 2010), 356–77.
Priest, A., 'From Hardware to Software: The End of the MLF and the Rise of the Nuclear Planning Group', in A. Wenger, C. Nuenlist and A. Locher (eds), *Transforming NATO in the Cold War. Challenges beyond Deterrence in the 1960s* (Oxford and New York, 2007), 148–61.
Radchenko, S., *The Soviets' Best Friend in Asia: The Mongolian Dimension of the Sino-Soviet Split*, CWIHP Working Paper No. 42 (Washington, 2003).
——*Two Suns in the Heavens: The Sino-Soviet Struggle for Supremacy, 1962–1967* (Stanford, 2009).
——'The Sino-Soviet Split', in M. Leffler and O.A. Westad (eds), *The Cambridge History of the Cold War. Volume II: Crisis and Détente* (Cambridge, 2010), 349–72.
Rajak, S., *Yugoslavia and the Soviet Union in the Early Cold War. Reconciliation, Comradeship, Confrontation, 1953–1957* (London and New York, 2010).
——'The Cold War in the Balkans, 1945–56', in M. Leffler and O.A. Westad (eds), *The Cambridge History of the Cold War. Volume I: Origins* (Cambridge, 2010), 198–220.
Remington, R.A., *The Warsaw Pact. Case Studies in Communist Conflict Resolution* (Massachusetts, 1971).
Retegan, M., *In the Shadow of the Prague Spring: Romanian Foreign Policy and the Crisis of Czechoslovakia, 1968* (Oxford, 2000, 2008).
Rijnoveanu, C., 'Rumänien und die Militärreformen des Warschauer Paktes 1960 bis 1970', in T. Diedrich, W. Heinemann and C.F. Ostermann (eds), *Der Warschauer Pakt. Von der Gründung bis zum Zusammenbruch 1955 bis 1991* (Berlin, 2009a), 209–24.

———A *Perspective on Romania's Involvement in the Sino-Soviet Conflict (1960–1965)*, Cold War History Research Centre, Budapest (May 2009b), www.coldwar.hu/html/en/publications/Rom_Sino_Riv.pdf.
Risse-Kappen, T., *Cooperation among Democracies. The European Influence on U.S. Foreign Policy* (Princeton, 1995).
Romero, F., *Storia della guerra fredda. L'ultimo conflitto per l'Europa* (Turin, 2009).
Sassoon, D., *The Strategy of the Italian Communist Party. From the Resistance to the Historic Compromise* (London, 1981).
Savranskaya, S. and Taubman, W., 'Soviet Foreign Policy, 1962–75', in M. Leffler and O.A. Westad (eds), *The Cambridge History of the Cold War. Volume II: Crisis and Détente* (Cambridge, 2010), 134–57.
Schäfer, B., 'The Sino-Soviet Conflict and the Warsaw Pact, 1969–80', in M.A. Heiss and S.V. Papacosma (eds), *NATO and the Warsaw Pact. Intrabloc Conflicts* (Ohio, 2008), 206–18.
Schulzinger, R.D., 'Détente in the Nixon-Ford Years, 1969–76', in M. Leffler and O.A. Westad (eds), *The Cambridge History of the Cold War. Volume II: Crisis and Détente* (Cambridge, 2010), 373–94.
Selvage, D., 'Khrushchev's November 1958 Ultimatum: New Evidence from the Polish Archives', in C. Ostermann (ed.), *Cold War Flashpoints*, CWIHP Bulletin No. 11 (Washington, 1998a), 200–3.
———'The End of the Berlin Crisis. New Evidence from the Polish and East German Archives', in C. Ostermann (ed.), *Cold War Flashpoints*, CWIHP Bulletin No. 11 (Washington, 1998b), 218–29.
———*Poland and the Sino-Soviet Split, 1963–1965*, CWIHP E-Dossier No. 10, www.wilsoncenter.org/publication/poland-and-the-sino-soviet-rift-1963-1965 (1963–65).
———*The Warsaw Pact and Nuclear Nonproliferation, 1963–1965*, CWIHP Working Paper No. 32 (Washington, 2001).
———'The Warsaw Pact and the European Security Conference, 1964–69: Sovereignty, Hegemony, and the German Question', in A. Wenger, V. Mastny and C. Nuenlist (eds), *Origins of the European Security System. The Helsinki Process Revisited* (London and New York, 2008a), 85–106.
———'The Warsaw Pact and the German Question, 1955–70', in M.A. Heiss and S.V. Papacosma (eds), *NATO and the Warsaw Pact: Intrabloc Conflicts* (Ohio, 2008b), 178–92.
Shawcross, W., *Dubcek. Dubcek and Czechoslovakia, 1968–1990* (London, 1990).
Skilling, H.G., *Czechoslovakia's Interrupted Revolution* (Princeton, 1976).
Smyser, W.R., *From Yalta to Berlin. The Cold War Struggle over Germany* (London, 1999).
Snyder, G.H., 'The Security Dilemma in Alliance Politics', *World Politics* 36:4 (1984), 461–95.
———'Alliance Theory: A Neorealist First Cut', *Journal of International Affairs* 44:1 (1990), 103–23.
———*Alliance Politics* (Ithaca, 1997).
Soutou, G., *La guerre de Cinquante Ans. Les relations Est-Ouest 1943–1990* (Paris, 2001).
Stone, R.W., *Satellites and Commissars. Strategy and Conflict in the Politics of Soviet-Bloc Trade* (Princeton, 2002).
Suri, J., *Power and Protest. Global Revolution and the Rise of Détente* (Massachusetts, 2003).

Suri, J., 'The Promise and Failure of "Developed Socialism": The Soviet "Thaw" and the Crucible of the Prague Spring', *Contemporary European History* 15:2 (2006), 133–58.

Țăranu, L., *România în Consiliul de Ajutor Economic Reciproc, 1949–1965* (Bucharest, 2007).

Taubman, W., *Khrushchev. The Man and his Era* (London, 2003).

Tismaneanu, V., *Gheorghiu-Dej and the Romanian Workers' Party: From De-Sovietization to the Emergence of National Communism*, CWIHP Working Paper No. 37 (Washington, 2002).

——*Promises of 1968: Crisis, Illusion, and Utopia* (Budapest and New York, 2010).

Tompson, W.J., *Khrushchev. A Political Life* (New York, 1995, 1997).

Trachtenberg, M., *A Constructed Peace. The Making of the European Settlement, 1945–1963* (Princeton, 1999).

Uhl, M., 'Soviet and Warsaw Pact Military Strategy from Stalin to Brezhnev: The Transformation from "Strategic Defense" to "Unlimited Nuclear War", 1945–68', in J. Hoffenaar and D. Krüger (eds), *Blueprints for Battle. Planning for War in Central Europe, 1948–1968* (Lexington, 2012), 33–54.

Umbach, F., *Das rote Bündnis. Entwicklung und Zerfall des Warschauer Paktes 1955–1991* (Berlin, 2005).

Villaume, P. and Westad, O.A. (eds), *Perforating the Iron Curtain. European Détente, Transatlantic Relations, and the Cold War, 1965–1985* (Copenhagen, 2010).

Walt, S.M., *The Origins of Alliances* (Ithaca, 1987).

Waltz, K.N., *Theory of International Politics* (Boston, 1979).

Watts, L., *A Romanian INTERKIT? Soviet Active Measures and the Warsaw Pact 'Maverick', 1965–1989*, CWIHP Working Paper No. 65 (Washington, 2012).

——*Romanian Security Policy and the Cuban Missile Crisis*, CWIHP E-Dossier No. 38 (Washington, 2013), www.wilsoncenter.org/publication/e-dossier-no-38-romania-security-policy-and-the-cuban-missile-crisis.

Wenger, A., 'Crisis and Opportunity. NATO's Transformation and the Multilateralization of Détente, 1966–68', *Journal of Cold War Studies* 6:1 (2004), 22–74.

——'The Multilateralization of Détente: NATO and the Harmel Exercise, 1966–68', in A. Locher and C. Nünlist, *The Future Tasks of the Alliance. NATO's Harmel Report, 1966–1967*, PHP (2005), www.isn.ethz.ch/DigitalLibrary/Publications/Detail/?id=108636&lng=en, 2–18.

Wenger, A., Mastny, V. and Nuenlist, C. (eds), *Origins of the European Security System. The Helsinki Process Revisited* (London and New York, 2008).

Wenger, A., Nuenlist, C. and Locher, A. (eds), *Transforming NATO in the Cold War. Challenges beyond Deterrence in the 1960s* (London and New York, 2007).

Westad, O.A. (ed.), *Reviewing the Cold War. Approaches, Interpretation, Theory* (London, 2000a).

——'Introduction: Reviewing the Cold War', in O.A. Westad (ed.), *Reviewing the Cold War. Approaches, Interpretation, Theory* (London, 2000b), 1–26.

——*The Global Cold War. Third World Interventions and the Making of Our Times* (Cambridge, 2007).

Wettig, G., *Chruschtschows Berlin-Krise 1958 bis 1963. Drohpolitik und Mauerbau* (Berlin, 2006).

Wilke, M., 'Ulbricht, East Germany, and the Prague Spring', in G. Bischof, S. Karner and P. Ruggenthaler (eds), *The Prague Spring and the Warsaw Pact Invasion of Czechoslovakia in 1968* (New York and Plymouth, 2011), 341–70.

Williams, K., *The Prague Spring and its Aftermath. Czechoslovak Politics, 1968–1970* (Cambridge, 1997).

Windsor, P. and Roberts, A., *Czechoslovakia 1968. Reform, Repression and Resistance* (London, 1969).

Zagoria, D.S., *The Sino-Soviet Conflict 1956–1961* (Princeton, 1962).

Zhai, Q., *Beijing and the Vietnam Peace Talks, 1965–1968: New Evidence from Chinese Sources,* CWIHP Working Paper No. 18 (Washington, 1997).

——*China and the Vietnam Wars, 1950–1975* (Chapel Hill, 2000).

——'Coexistence and Confrontation: Sino-Soviet Relations after Stalin', in K. Larres and K. Osgood (eds), *The Cold War after Stalin's Death. A Missed Opportunity for Peace?* (Lanham, 2006), 177–92.

Zubok, V.M., *Khrushchev and the Berlin Crisis (1958–1962)*, CWIHP Working Paper No. 6 (Washington, 1993).

——*A Failed Empire. The Soviet Union in the Cold War from Stalin to Gorbachev* (Chapel Hill, 2007, 2009).

Zubok, V.M. and Pleshakov, C., *Inside the Kremlin's Cold War. From Stalin to Khrushchev* (Harvard, 1996).

Index

Adenauer, K. 26, 46, 110, 113
Adzhubei, A. 116
Albania 2, 6, 9, 21, 25, 28, 33, 36–37, 49, 57, 59–69, 76–77, 83–84, 87, 102, 113, 119, 170, 175–76, 203, 236, 245, 259: China, and 38, 59–68, 71, 218; Fourth Party Conference (1961) 62–64; Soviet Union: split with 63–73
Albanian Workers Party 61–63
Andropov, Y. 73–74, 80, 116
Antonov, A.I. 28
Aristov, A. 222
Austria 265: State Treaty 17, 22, 25–26

Bahr, E. 223
Basov, V. 229–30, 244
Beijing 3, 35, 48, 74, 100, 192–96, 270
Belgrade 62
Beria, L. 18, 20
Berlin 1, 198, 268, 275; border between sectors 106–8; second Crisis 2–4, 9, 43, 45, 47, 57, 98, 100, 108–9, 122–23; Wall (1961) 69–70, 98, 108–11, 123; West 44, 100
Berlinguer, E. 199
Bierut, B. 31
Bilak, V. 224–25, 236, 241, 247
Bodnaras, E. 41, 86, 175–76, 178, 180, 186, 192, 233–34
Bonn 275
Brandt, W. 259, 275
Bratislava conference (1968) 236, 238, 243
Brezhnev, L. 35, 117–18, 171, 177–78, 180, 182, 186, 188, 190, 197, 200, 202, 216, 219, 222, 224–25, 227, 231, 235, 237–40, 243–45, 248–49, 260, 268–74, 277; doctrine 218, 245–46, 249, 271, 273, 275, 281
Brzezinski, Z. 2, 7, 57, 122

Bucharest 1, 59, 65, 87, 186, 188, 192, 194, 226, 241, 246, 279; declaration 156; *see also* PCC
Budapest 34, 198, 259; *see also* PCC
Bulganin, N. 20, 30
Bulgaria 17, 19, 21, 31, 68, 114, 173, 219, 233, 246

Camp David 57
'cardboard castle' *see* Warsaw Pact
Castro, F. 224
CCP 30
Ceausescu, N. 10, 170–204, 217, 220, 224–25, 229, 233–34, 238–39, 241–42, 244, 248–49, 261–63, 266–67, 272, 275–80
Cernik, O. 221, 230, 232, 235, 238, 242
Checkpoint Charlie 109, 123
Chervenkov, V. 19, 30
Chervonenko, S.V. 229, 240, 242
China 6, 32, 46, 79, 87, 258–72, 281, 283; Communist Party *see* CCP; *see also* Interkit, People's Republic, PRC, Romania
Cierna nad Tisou 235, 237, 239, 243
COMECON 5, 30, 74–76, 82, 107, 111, 187, 220, 227
COMINFORM 24–25, 31, 36, 48, 72–73, 79
Communist Information Bureau *see* COMINFORM
Communist Party of Czechoslovakia *see* CPCz
Communist Party of the Soviet Union *see* CPSU
Conference on Security and Co-operation in Europe *see* CSCE
Council for Mutual Economic Assistance *see* COMECON

CPCz 216, 229–32, 236, 241, 247, 264–65; Action Programme 221, 227; fourteenth Congress (1968) 226, 264; 'open letter' 221; Plenum (May-June 1968)
CPSU 29, 33, 229, 240, 247; Moscow meeting (1968) 222–23; Twentieth Congress (1956) 27; Twenty-second Congress (1961) 70, 108, 110
CSCE 3, 8, 290
Cuba 236
Cuban Missile Crisis 4, 74–75, 79, 84, 114, 117
'cultural revolution' *see* PRC
Czechoslovakia 3, 10, 17, 19, 22, 30–31, 33, 40, 38, 78, 100, 105–6, 113, 119, 173, 215–50, 259, 262–64, 273, 276, 281; invasion (1968) 241–50, 259–60, 266–69, 275–76, 278; Soviet troop presence 246, 267; *see also* Prague Spring

Declaration on European Security (1966) 258
de Gaulle, C. 4, 112, 174, 203, 277; *see also* NATO
Deletant, D. 42
Democratic Republic of Vietnam *see* DRV
Deng Xiaoping 33, 68, 75, 182
'de-satellization' 7, 122
de-Stalinisation 18, 31–32, 34, 41, 44, 58, 67
'détente' 8, 9, 266, 270, 280
Dragomir, E. 83
Dresden: meeting (1968) 218–21
Dobrynin, A. 45, 117, 245
DRV 171; *see also* Geneva 'accords'
Dubcek, A. 201, 215–50, 259, 262, 265, 267–68, 272, 279; Hungary visit (June 1968) 226
Dulles, J.F. 26
Dzur, M. 240, 247, 263

East German National People's Army 43
Egypt 193
Eighteen Nations Disarmament Committee *see* ENDC
Eisenhower, D.D. 2, 18, 25, 46, 57, 99, 101, 112
'empty shell' *see* Warsaw Pact
ENDC 113–15, 173, 197–98
Erhard, L. 113, 116

European Community 5
European Security Appeal 275–76, 278, 280–82

Finland 17
'flexible response' 259, 280
Fock, J. 201, 279
France 83, 99, 216
FRG 21, 26, 28, 44, 77, 98–124, 199, 216, 223, 259, 262, 265, 274, 276

Gaddis, J.L. 6
Gagra 80, 98, 115
Gaza Strip 193
GDR 20–22, 25–26, 32–33, 37, 44, 46–48, 79–80, 98–124, 199, 218–19, 223, 246, 260, 273, 276; separate peace treaty 101, refugees 101, 105; uprising 20
General European Treaty on Collective Security in Europe 26
Geneva 26, 200; 'accords'(1954) 171; foreign ministers conference (1959) 45–46
Germany 9, 58; Democratic Republic *see* GDR; Eastern 17, 273; Federal Republic *see* FRG
Gheorghe, E. 174, 178
Gheorghe, I. 266
Gheorghiu-Dej, G. 22, 40–42, 59, 73–74, 76–80, 176–79, 181–82, 234: death 181–82
Gilpatric Committee *see* Nuclear Proliferation
Golan Heights 193
Gomulka, W. 31–33, 39–40, 62, 102, 105, 107, 110, 112–16, 122–24, 176–81, 184, 189–90, 200, 204, 217, 219, 222–24, 233, 238, 243, 245, 248, 262, 274–75, 278, 282; 'Doctrine' 40; 'Plan' 114–16
Gottwald, K. 19
Great Britain *see* UK
'Great Leap Forward' 46, 192
Grechko, A. 238
Greece 22, 25, 38, 63
Griffith, W.E. 73
Gromyko, A. 41, 104, 170, 186, 188, 190

Haftendorn, H. 4
'Hallstein Doctrine' 26, 116
Hanoi 173, 174, 185, 187, 192–96
Harmel, P.C.J.M. *see* Harmel Report
Harmel Report 259, 280

Harriman, W. Averell 184
Harrison, H. 6, 43, 100, 101, 107, 122
Hajek, J. 223
Helsinki: Final Act 3, 290; Process 9, 10, 290
Ho Chi Minh 71, 171
Hoxha, E. 2, 37–39, 60, 62–69, 73–77
HSWP 237
Hungarian Workers Party see HWP
Hungary 17, 21, 33–34, 39–41, 44, 48, 117, 217, 233, 244, 246, 262, 268, 273–74, 282; Revolution 9, 17, 31, 34–37, 43, 47, 60, 71; Soviet intervention (1956) 35, 248
Husak, G. 247
HWP 34

India 176
Interkit 195
Israel 192; 'six-day war' 192
Italy 216; Communist Party 62, 199

Jarzabek, W. 40, 123
Jegalin, I.K. 73, 182
Johnson, L.B. 171–72, 216

Kadar, J. 34–36, 107, 191, 201, 217, 219, 224–27, 230–31, 237–39, 248, 262, 268–69, 274–75, 279
Kang Sheng 58, 182
Kennedy, J.F. 102–3, 105, 108, 112
Khrushchev, N. 2, 3, 6, 9, 17–18, 20–22, 25–29, 31–37, 42–44, 47–49, 57–59, 66, 69, 75–87, 98–124; ouster 117–18, 171, 174; 'secret speech' 9, 29, 44, 58
Kiev 247
Kliszko, Z. 85, 120
Konev, I. 17, 27–28, 39, 72
Korea: North 59, 71, 84, 175; War 19
Kosygin, N. 135, 171, 181, 182, 202, 235, 268
Kramer, M. 216
Kremlin 1, 9, 23, 27–28, 32, 34–36, 39, 46, 60–62, 66–67, 69, 72, 75, 195–97, 200, 203–4, 223, 229, 239, 242–44, 249, 263, 265, 268–69, 273, 281–82
Kroll, H. 106, 110
Kuznetsov, V. 112, 198

Leffler, M. 6
'Lenin Polemics' 59
Li Fenglin 38, 173

Limited Test Ban Treaty (1963) see NTBT
Liu Fan 81, 86, 175–76, 178–83
Liu Shaoqi 33, 35
Locher, A. 4
Lundestad, G. 6
Lüthi, L. 6, 77

Malenkov, G. 18, 20, 44
Manescu, C. 186, 188, 190, 197, 225; President of UN General Assembly 195
Mao Zedong 9, 29, 32, 35, 39, 46, 49, 58, 172, 181–82, 192–93, 224, 234
Marxism-Leninism 47, 63, 66, 73, 195, 245
Mastny, V. 4, 24, 47, 87, 218, 258, 266, 278, 280
Maurer, I.G. 85, 176–81, 190, 192–97, 244, 258, 266, 280
Mikoyan, A. 38, 80
MLF 4, 9, 98, 112–13, 117–21, 175, 179, 199–200
Molotov, V. 18, 21, 37, 41, 44
Mongolia 41, 71, 75–76, 87, 195, 271
Moscow 26–28, 35–36, 39, 100, 195–96, 267: conference (1960) 62–63, 65; Declaration (1960) 62–63, 68, 71–75, 79–82; Protocol (1968) 243–44, 246; see also PCC
Multilateral Nuclear Forces see MLF
Murville, Couve de: Romania, visit 185

Nagy, I. 34–35
Naszkowski, M. 85, 120
National Security Council 196, 216
NATO 1, 4, 5, 6, 8–10, 17, 21–23, 38–39, 43, 48, 76, 82–83, 98, 105, 113, 118–19, 194, 216, 247, 260, 266, 268, 273, 275, 280, 283; French military withdrawal 185, 203, 259, 261
Nixon, R.M. 260
NLF see DRV
Non-Proliferation 197, 258, 283; Treaty 10, 174, 177, 179, 199–201, 203
Non-Soviet Warsaw Pact see NSWP
North Atlantic Treaty Organization see NATO
Novotny, A. 19, 31, 107, 111, 216–18, 247
NSWP 1–3, 6, 8–10, 25, 27, 37, 48, 64–70, 77, 79, 84, 86, 122, 185, 282
NTBT 75–76, 173, 196

Nuclear Test Ban Treaty *see* NTBT
Nuclear Proliferation: Gilpatric Committee 173, 180
Nuclear weapons *see* PRC; NTBT; Romania

Ochab, E. 31–32
Oder-Neisse line 33, 40, 274
'Operation Danube' 234–35
'Operation Marigold' 184
'Operation Rolling Thunder' 172
Ostpolitik 149, 152, 162, 223, 259, 293

Parallel History Project on Co-operative Security 4
Paris: 'agreements' 21; summit conference (1961) 99–100
PCC 2, 3, 10, 23, 27, 29, 42–43, 48, 58, 65, 68, 71, 76–77, 80, 82–83, 99–103, 114, 118–21, 176, 183, 188, 198, 201–2, 258, 265–69, 277, 279, 281: Bucharest meeting (1966) 154–56, 188–91; Budapest meeting (1969) 154–56, 188–91, 247, 264, 268–75, 280–83; Moscow meeting (1961) 64–67, 103; Sofia Meeting (1968) 199, 215, 220, 261–62, 267; Warsaw meeting (1965) 137–40, 177–80
Pavlovskii, I. 240, 249
Pervukhin 45, 104
Pilsen: workers' protest 19, 30
Plovdiv 19
Podgorny, N. 117
Poland 2, 10, 21, 31–35, 40, 44, 47–48, 76, 99–100, 105–6, 110, 112, 114, 117, 119, 173, 190–92, 218, 233, 246, 274–75; crisis (1981–82) 278; uprising (1956) 71; *see also* Vietnam War; Warsaw
Political Consultative Committee (of Warsaw Pact) *see* PCC
Polish United Workers Party *see* (PUWP): 3rd Congress (1959) 40
Poznan 32
Prague 27; Spring 10, 201, 203–4, 215–50, 258–59, 263, 268–69, 272, 275, 282
Pravda 117, 245
Prchlik, V. 234; report on 'External and Internal Security of the State' 264–65
PRC 29, 60, 75, 195: 'cultural revolution' 170, 172, 192–93, 202, 234, 270; nuclear weapons tests 117, 173; Soviet specialists withdrawn 61;

Warsaw Pact foreign ministers meeting (1959) 45, *see also* 'Great Leap Forward', Mongolia
PUWP 32, 85

Radchenko, S. 6
Rajak, S. 24
Rakosi, M. 34
Rapacki, A. 40, 42, 48, 76, 100, 112, 115–16, 184
Rapallo agreement (1922) 110, 116; policy 112, 123
Retegan, M. 78
Rijnoveanu, C. 84
Risse-Kappen, T. 7
Romania 2, 8, 9, 17, 21, 24, 33, 35, 40, 57, 63, 73, 76–79, 87, 102, 114, 170–204, 271–72, 275–77, 281; China, and 73–74, 170–84, 191–97, 202, 220, 244–45, 248, 259; Communist Party Conference (1960) 58; Declaration of Independence 81, 85, 263; nuclear programme 174, 225; Prague Spring, and 232, 236, 241–42; shuttle diplomacy 195; 'Total People's War for the Defence of the Homeland' 260; Workers' Party; *see also* RWP, Vietnam War
Rome 1
Rusk, D. 196, 245
RWP 74, 79–82, 181–82

Schäfer, B. 273
Schröder, G. 111
SED 20, 103, 108, 119–20
Selvage, D. 106
Shawcross, W. 217, 237
Shehu, M. 28, 38, 64–65, 68
Shelepin, A. 222, 238
Shelest, P. 236
shuttle diplomacy *see* Romania
Sino-Soviet: border clashes 3, 10, 259, 270–73, 281; split 3–4, 6, 9, 10, 17, 32, 57, 61–62, 66, 71, 75, 78, 82, 86–87, 102, 117, 124, 170, 174, 180, 195, 202, 204, 259, 270–72, 279, 281
'six-day war' *see* Israel
Sixth Fleet (American) 63–64
Slovakia 224, 235
Snyder, G.H. 7
Soldatov, A. 196–97
Sofia: Declaration (1968) 200, 258; *see also* PCC
Soviet-Romanian treaties 263

Soviet troop deployment in WP states 276–77; *see also* Czechoslovakia
Soviet Union 1, 21; foreign policy 2; navy 66; 'New Course' 19
Sozialistische Einheitspartei Deutschlands *see* SED
Spaak, P-H. 113
Stalin, J. 18, 29, 40, 48, 111; death 17–18, 33, 72
Statute of the Warsaw Treaty Unified Command 27
Stone, R. 5
Sumava Exercises 228, 235, 260
Suslov, M. 117
Svoboda, L. 240, 242, 247
Sweden *see* World Ice Hockey Championship (1969)
Syria 193, 199

'Tet offensive' 216
Tirana 38, 64, 71, 187
Tito, J. 18, 24–25, 35, 37–38, 48–49, 72
Tonkin, Gulf of 172
Trachtenberg, M. 4, 45
Transylvania 41
'Treaty on Friendship and Cooperation', GDR and Soviet Union 43
Tsedenbal, Y. 71, 75–77
Turkey 22
'Two Thousand Words' manifesto 227–29

U2 'spy plane' 59, 100
UK 99
Ulan Bator 41
Ulbricht, W. 2, 6, 20, 28, 31–33, 43–44, 47, 69, 72, 77, 81–82, 85, 98–124, 176–77, 180, 189, 204, 219, 222–24, 230, 233–35, 238, 243, 248, 274–75, 282; doctrine 113, 117

Umbach, F. 2
United States *see* USA
USA 8, 21, 25, 46, 99, 194, 200; *see also* National Security Council, Sixth Fleet
Ussuri (river) 3, 10, 270

Vakulic, L. *See* 'Two Thousand Words'
Vienna 25; conference (1961) 105; *see also* Austria
Vietnam: National Liberation Front (NLF) 171,183; North 59, 71, 84, 175; South 171; Soviet Declaration (1966) 188–91; USA, negotiation with 194; War 4, 170, 183–84, 188, 268, 283; *see also* Bodnaras, DRV, 'Operation Marigold', 'Operation Rolling Thunder', 'Tet Offensive'
Vlorë 37, 61, 63–64, 67, 72

Warsaw 25, 32, 39; letter of the 'five' 231–32; meeting of the 'five' 230, 265; 'package' 159, 223, 274; student protests (1968) 217; *see also* PCC
Warsaw Pact: as 'cardboard castle' 1, 27, 47, 291; as 'empty shell' 3, 291
Washington 174, 187, 193, 195–96
Wenger, A. 8
Winzer, O. 85, 116, 118–22
World Ice Hockey Championship (Sweden, 1969) 247, 279

Yakubovskii, I. 228, 249, 262–64, 266, 269, 277, 279, 281
Yugoslavia 18, 24, 37–38, 61, 236

Zhivkov, T. 19, 30, 66–67, 200–201, 224, 230, 233–34, 236, 238, 243, 248
Zhou Enlai 62, 171, 182; Romania, visit 186–87, 192–96